The Madison Avenue Lectures

The Madison Avenue Lectures
Historic Baptist Principles and Practice Defined and Defended

Henry G. Weston

Editor

Solid Ground Christian Books
Birmingham, Alabama USA

Solid Ground Christian Books
2090 Columbiana Rd, Suite 2000
Birmingham, AL 35216
205-443-0311
sgcb@charter.net
http://solid-ground-books.com

The Madison Avenue Lectures
Historic Baptist Principles and Practice Defined and Defended

Henry G. Weston (1820-1909)

From 1867 edition from American Baptist Publication Society, Philadelphia

Solid Ground Classic Reprints

First printing of new edition June 2005

Cover work by Borgo Design, Tuscaloosa, AL
Contact them at nelbrown@comcast.net

ISBN: 1-932474-97-8

INTRODUCTORY NOTE.

THE Lectures composing the Series embraced in this volume, were delivered in the Madison Avenue Baptist Church, New York, by special request of the pastor, Henry G. Weston, D. D.

The marked excellence of the Lectures, as expositions of the truths which are embodied and exhibited in the precious ordinances of the gospel, and of the views which are held by the members of the "Baptized Churches," as they were originally called; their broad and thorough survey of the topics brought under discussion; and the genial spirit of true Christian courtesy which breathes through them, give promise of a wide usefulness. Hence they are committed to the press, in the earnest hope that the Lord will use them as a means of advancing his own truth and of promoting that object so dear to the Lord, and to all who walk in fellowship with him,—the full, and joyous union of his people in that truth.

CONTENTS.

LECTURE I.
THE BIBLE THE ONLY STANDARD OF CHRISTIAN DOCTRINE AND DUTY.. 7
By ALVAH HOVEY, D.D., Professor of Christian Theology in the Newton Theological Institution.

LECTURE II.
THE OBLIGATION OF THE CHURCH RESPECTING THE HOLY SCRIPTURES 36
By HENRY C. FISH, D.D., Pastor of First Baptist Church, Newark, N. J.

LECTURE III.
THE SPIRITUAL CONSTITUTION OF THE CHRISTIAN CHURCH.. 61
By Rev. C. B. CRANE, Pastor of South Baptist Church, Hartford, Conn.

LECTURE IV.
BAPTISM.. 85
By Rev. G. D. B. PEPPER, Professor in the Newton Theological Institution.

LECTURE V.
BAPTISM A SYMBOL... 115
By GEORGE D. BOARDMAN, D. D., Pastor of the First Baptist Church, Philadelphia.

LECTURE VI.
THE QUALIFICATIONS FOR BAPTISM............................ 136
By Rev. HENRY E. ROBINS, Pastor of the Central Baptist Church, Newport, R. I.

LECTURE VII.
THE EVILS OF INFANT BAPTISM................................ 160
By A. N. ARNOLD, D.D., Professor of Biblical Interpretation in Hamilton Theological Seminary.

LECTURE VIII.
THE COMMUNION 183
By HENRY G. WESTON, D. D., Pastor of Madison Avenue Baptist Church, New York.

LECTURE IX.
THE SYMBOLISM OF THE COMMUNION........................... 196
By Rev. LEMUEL MOSS, Professor of Systematic Theology in University at Lewisburg, Pennsylvania.

Contents.

LECTURE X.
QUALIFICATIONS FOR THE COMMUNION.................... 217
    By JOHN W. SARLES, D.D., Pastor of Central Baptist Church, Brooklyn, N. Y.

LECTURE XI.
THE RELATION BETWEEN BAPTISM AND THE COMMUNION...... 243
    By THOMAS D. ANDERSON, D.D., Pastor of First Baptist Church, New York City.

LECTURE XII.
CHURCH POLITY.. 261
    By GEORGE W. SAMSON, D.D., President of Columbian College, D. C.

LECTURE XIII.
CHURCH WORSHIP....................................... 289
    By SAMUEL L. CALDWELL, D.D., Pastor of First Baptist Church, Providence, R. I.

LECTURE XIV.
BAPTIST CHURCH HISTORY............................... 309
    By Rev. R. J. W. BUCKLAND, Pastor of Calvary Baptist Church, New York.

LECTURE XV.
THE RISE AND DEVELOPMENT OF SECTARIANISM IN CHRISTENDOM... 337
    By WILLIAM HAGUE, D.D., Pastor of Shawmut Avenue Baptist Church, Boston, Massachusetts.

LECTURE XVI.
MISSSION OF BAPTISTS................................. 364
    By J. B. JETER, D.D., of Richmond, Virginia.

LECTURE XVII.
THE RELATION OF THE CHURCH AND THE BIBLE............. 387
    By E. G. ROBINSON, D.D., Professor in the Rochester Theological Seminary.

LECTURE XVIII.
THE CHURCH IN ITS RELATIONS TO THE STATE 420
    By WILLIAM R. WILLIAMS, D.D., late Pastor of Amity Street Baptist Church, New York City.

MADISON AVENUE LECTURES.

I.

THE BIBLE THE ONLY STANDARD OF CHRISTIAN DOCTRINE AND DUTY.

By ALVAH HOVEY, D. D.
Professor of Christian Theology in the Newton Theological Institution.

"HOWBEIT, WHEN HE, THE SPIRIT OF TRUTH, SHALL COME, HE WILL GUIDE YOU INTO ALL TRUTH."—*John* xvi. 13.

It is my hope that you will consent to go back with me to one of the first principles of our belief, and that we shall be able, within the limits of an hour, to verify anew its soundness and worth. The principle to which I refer was dear to our fathers, was asserted by them with intelligent zeal, was felt to be the source of whatever distinguished them from other Christians, and was reverenced as an Ithuriel's spear by which error could be detected, and its real nature made manifest, "for no falsehood can endure

> 'Touch of celestial temper, but returns
> Of force to its own likeness.'"

This cardinal principle is the truth, not yet unfamiliar to our ears, *that the Bible is the only standard of Christian Doctrine and Duty;* a principle which is repudiated by some, because they deny the divine authority of the Bible, and by others, because they deny the sufficiency of its teaching. Moreover, at different points between these extremes and the central position held by us, many are moving to and fro in doubt, either assigning to the Bible a merely indefinite superiority to other books, or charging it with more or less incompleteness in the exhibition of needed truth.

You will therefore, I am sure, regard as timely an argument for the soundness and sacredness of the principle, that the Bible is the only proper standard of Christian faith and practice;—a principle which may be easily drawn from the language of my text: "*Howbeit, when He, the Spirit of truth shall come, he will guide you into all the truth.*" Not—as the authorized version, which omits the article, may suggest—into all truth of whatever domain, scientific, historic, philosophic; but into all the truth which pertains to the religion of Christ as adapted to men in their present state, and which, by its office in making known the moral perfections of God and the way of eternal life for man, outshines all other truth, even as the sun at noonday outshines all other light.

Into this truth, the highest and the best, was the Holy Spirit to guide the eleven disciples addressed by our Saviour; and it will be my aim to show that the promise recorded in my text involves the divine authority and completeness of the Bible, as a source of Christian truth.

I. *It involves the divine authority of the Bible.* This will be evident, if it can be made to appear that Christ was an infallible teacher; that he uttered this great promise, and that the apostles were upright men. For if this promise was made by an infallible being, it was surely fulfilled, and the apostles were in due time guided into all the truth; and if the apostles were honest men, they taught by pen and tongue what they knew, namely, the truth; and if they taught the truth, it will be easy to establish by their words the divine authority of the Bible. So that what we need to show, without assuming

for this purpose the inspiration of the Scriptures, is—
1. That Jesus Christ was infallible. 2. That he uttered the promise of my text, and 3. That his apostles were upright men.

To establish the infallibility of Christ, I will first appeal to four great letters of Paul, namely, those to the Romans, to the Corinthians, and to the Galatians. These letters are instinct with reality. They are at the furthest possible remove from the realm of fancy. They are full of the pith and substance, the bone and muscle, the spring and force, the ardor and glow of actual life. They deal with specific evils. They refute particular errors. They check definite disorders. They repel given slanders. They prescribe for distinct offences. They assert special rights. Sharp logic, open rebuke, fervid appeal, follow one another in swift succession. What rapidity, variety, freedom, and fire do we perceive! Yea, what zeal, yea, what carefulness, yea, what clearing of himself, yea, what indignation, yea, what vehement desire. How intensely personal are these letters! How sensitive was their writer to the opinions and practices of those addressed! What love to them glows in his language! What readiness to be spent in their service! What downright honesty, fidelity, and greatness of soul breathe from every page! These sentences were called for by the wants of living men, or we may close up the volume of history. Whoever can deem them a work of fiction or of falsehood has lost the sense of reality, the power of discriminating between the actual and the ideal, and may well despair of finding any thing true in all the records of the past. Even the remorseless unbelief of Baur spared these four letters.

Let us, then, open these writings of Paul and study their language; for they take us back within the quarter of a century which followed the death of Christ, and give us the words of a self-denying, keen-sighted, trustworthy man.

Hence their testimony may be expected to shed no little light upon the character of Christ and his apostles. It sheds much. For they affirm that in his human nature Christ was made of a woman; made under the law, made in the likeness of sinful flesh, that he was the promised seed of Abraham and a descendant of David. They teach that in virtue of his higher nature he was the Son of God, who though rich, for our sakes became poor. They assert that he knew no sin, yet died for men as a propitiatory sacrifice, to exhibit the righteousness of God. They declare that believers are justified by his blood and saved from wrath through him, and that God was in Christ reconciling the world to himself. They assure us of his resurrection, and infer from it the resurrection of all his saints. They say that he "died for our sins according to the Scriptures; that he was buried, and that he rose again the third day; that he appeared to Cephas, then to the twelve; after that, he appeared to above five hundred brethren at once; of whom the greater part remain until now, but some are fallen asleep. After that he appeared to James, then to all the apostles. And last of all he appeared to me also, as the one born out of due time."

According to these letters, Paul himself had seen the Lord, had received from him the great truths of the gospel with a charge to bear them to the Gentiles, and had preached them with marked success. He had been recognized by the other apostles as their peer, and had gone forth to his work in their fellowship. He knew Peter, James, and John, and his view of Christ was approved by them. Hence their estimate of the Lord's character may be learned from his. If Paul gloried in being a servant of Christ, so did the other apostles.

The Bible the only Standard.

And I do not quite see how any intelligent man can make these letters of Paul a study without being at length assured that, in his judgment, Christ was not only an infallible teacher, holy and true, the source of light and peace to men, but also in his higher nature, "God over all blessed forever."

And when we look again into these letters to ascertain what sort of a man the apostle was made by Christian faith; when we note his love and zeal, his purity and wisdom; when we read his powerful words, and compare his spirit, gushing out in streams of generous emotion, with that of Cicero as revealed by his familiar letters—we have reason enough to say that by faith in Christ he came to be a new creature, old things passed away, and all things became new.

And when we learn from his words the influence of Christianity over those who had been converted under his preaching, there will be no less reason to believe that the glad news respecting Christ had indeed proved itself to be the power of God, and the wisdom of God unto salvation. In a word, these four letters of Paul establish the chief events of our Lord's earthly mission and the general truth of his teaching; they do more than this, they establish the great fact of his resurrection from the dead, and thereby the absolute authority and truth of his word. A patient study of these letters will carry the mind from point to point, until it is seen that the whole Bible is true. The remaining letters of Paul, and all the writings of the New Testament, will be found in vital unity with these; and especially will the life and character of Christ, as set before us in the gospels, be seen to underlie all the teaching of Paul. If this be true, these four letters go far toward proving that Christ was a teacher of truth, without any mixture of error.

Again, to establish the infallibility of Christ I will

appeal to the four gospels. For so unique and original, so pure and perfect, so truly human and yet manifestly divine, is the character of Christ as portrayed by the evangelists, that we cannot suppose it to be an ideal creation. The story of this deep and marvelous life, moving on, calm, clear, free, intense, earnest, full of light and love, of strength and beauty, can be traced to no earthly imagination. It was a real life; the most real and genuine in all the ages. To feel this, it may be necessary to look more closely at the gospels; for our familiarity with them often prevents us from doing justice to their superlative excellence. Here, then, are four distinct records, diverse yet harmonious. So marked are the differences, even in relating the same events, that some have rashly inferred contradiction; yet so deep and pervading is the harmony, that others have inferred transcription.

Let it now be supposed that the gospel of Mark, which is the shortest of the four, beginning with the public ministry of Jesus, was the first written. This record gives us action chiefly and not discourse. It represents Christ as going from place to place, over the hills and through the villages of Palestine, and doing mighty works. It is objective, minute, graphic, picturesque. It abounds in notices of such particulars as would fix themselves in the memory of a keen observer. In several instances it mentions the bearing of Christ, the dialect which he used, and the expression of his countenance. It makes brief record of parables, discourses, and pregnant sayings. And every where, from first to last, this rapid narrative sets before us a being of transcendent power, love and grace—a being divine as well as human, walking upon the earth but having commerce with the skies. But the picture, though faultless in execution, so far as it goes, is unfinished; for to

The Bible the only Standard. 13

say nothing of other defects, there is no reference in it to the birth or lineage or early days of Jesus. It is an incomplete picture, but the work of a master; reminding us of the great painting of Washington Allston, which still waits for an artist to finish it. If this gospel were a product of imagination and art, ages might be expected to pass before a man of genius and daring, equal to the task of completing it, would appear.

But no; it has scarcely seen the light, before the gospel of Matthew is written; a record of discourse as well as of action, giving a far ampler rehearsal of parables, sermons, predictions; pointing out the fulfillment of prophecy in the person of Christ, showing him to be the promised Messiah of Israel, thus binding together the old dispensation and the new, and supplying a brief account of his birth and early history. Here are large additions and considerable omissions; yet the character is not changed, the total impression is the same. The birth of Christ is in harmony with his life; the quiet of his boyhood with the simple dignity and speech of his manhood. If, then, the life of Jesus as delineated by Mark is grand and holy beyond the power of any writer to originate by an effort of imagination, so that we are sure it was taken from nature, how much surer may we be, that no second writer of that age could give us another and a fuller delineation of the same life, without changing its character or marring its beauty, unless he too were sketching from nature and were familiar with the original.

But the difficulty grows. Not only have we a second gospel, but also a third, quite unlike the first and second —a gospel which recounts with greater minuteness the events attending Christ's birth and childhood; which adds parables of thrilling interest and beauty; which describes the incidents of an extended journey, scarcely noticed by the others; which shows that Jesus looked beyond the people of Israel and took pity on the gentiles; which traces his lineage back to Adam, and represents him as Saviour of the world. But the character is still the same. The stream of life has become a little fuller, and it seems to flow into regions not mentioned before; but it is just as pure and deep, powerful and refreshing as ever. To pronounce it an imaginary life is to charge the record with falsehood, and yet believe it a miracle of skill: it is to charge the author of a marvelous work with repudiating the same, and proving himself to be at once a liar and a fool.

This, however, is not the end: there is a fourth gospel, diverse exceedingly from all the rest. It illustrates the life of Christ by new scenes, miracles, discourses. It omits all the parables and a large part of the events recorded by the first three. It dwells on the ministry of Christ in Jerusalem, and passes lightly over his labors in Galilee. It takes back our thoughts into eternity, and reminds us of the glory which he had with the Father before the world was. It repeats the clearest words of the great Teacher respecting his own mysterious nature. It leads us up by a spiral ascent higher and higher, bringing us round to the same view again and again, but always from a loftier position, until we seem almost in heaven itself. Yet, I need but remind you, the character delineated is still the same. We hear no discordant word; we detect no incompatible element; we see no unfamiliar feature. The halo round his brow may be more intense; but that is all; the veil which covers his face may be raised a little higher, but nothing more.

I will not pursue this examination. "It has been often and truly said that the character of our Lord, as drawn by the evangelists, is in itself the one sufficient proof of their veracity. No character could have been further removed from the popular ideal of the time; none more entirely beyond the conception of men reared amidst dreams of national hope, and checked at every step by the signs of foreign power." The harmony in diversity which pervades the gospels is so remarkable as in itself to prove their veracity. The fourfold portrait of this "greater man," must have been taken from life; and if so, the limners of it were simply faithful, while the subject of it was the true Word of God manifested in flesh. The life which they describe was real. The person whom they place before our minds once walked in Galilee and suffered death at Jerusalem. The story is so simple and sublime, so artless and consistent, so human and withal so divine, that no man could have invented it; much less could four men, each in his own way, have delineated so peerless an ideal. And more; I must even deny that four men, though personally witnesses of what they relate, could, if left to themselves, have given us these wondrous pictures of that wondrous life. They would have been sure at some point to mar their work. They would have been tempted here and there, to explain, apologize, speculate, or eulogize. But no, all is direct, simple, open, fair. The historians do not speculate. "In its grand, childlike, and holy simplicity, the narrative passes by questions of the mere intellect, just as a child moves among the riddles of nature and of life, as if they existed not." And if the gospels are truthful records, the being whose ministry they describe was infallible. I say infallible; for consider his claims, how high they were:—to know heavenly things directly: "I speak that which I have seen with my Father;"—to know the Father exclusively: "Neither knoweth any one the Father, save the Son;" to speak the Father's words only: "The word which ye hear is not mine, but the Father's;" to teach immutable truth: "Heaven and earth shall pass away, but my words shall not pass away;" and to utter sayings the rejection of which is fatal: "Every one that heareth these sayings of mine, and doeth them not, shall be likened to a man which built his house upon the sand; and the rain descended, and the floods came, and the winds blew and beat upon that house, and it fell;" "The word that I have spoken, the same shall judge him at the last day." With what certainty and authority did Jesus speak! not groping darkly after truth, and uttering it doubtfully with reason; but seeing it with perfect vision and declaring it positively, as a king. "We speak that we do know, and testify that we have seen." Plato taught like a man, with subtle reason and sore toil, worming his way through darkness up to partial light, watching the shadows of the cave, and conjecturing what might be the life above; but Jesus taught like a God, standing in the face of the sun, and holding in his eye all the infinite verities of being, forever! He was king of the realm of truth.

Hence, too, the impression which he made on his disciples. They believed him to be cognizant of their very thoughts. One of them testifies that he could not be taken at unawares; that he needed not that any should testify of man, for he knew what was in man. He read the secrets of the heart as easily as we read the pages of a book. His eye pierced the veil which hides the future, and he foretold such events as the betrayal, the desertion, the denial, the crucifixion, the resurrection. He was full of grace and truth. He was the light of men. His teaching was not merely true, it was by way of eminence the truth; as such his disciples preached it to the Roman world in the first century, and such, I may add, it has proved itself to be by its influence on the

The Bible the only Standard.   17

souls of men from that day until now. This is the first point in my argument.

But was the promise of my text uttered by Christ to his disciples? May not the gospels be true for the most part, with here and there an error? This is certainly conceivable, and indeed probable, unless the evangelists were divinely assisted in their work. But we have already seen that the perfection of this work, the harmony in diversity which distinguishes the four-fold gospel, is a reason for believing them to have been thus assisted. Apart, however, from this presumption, it is scarcely possible to doubt the accuracy of John's record in the present case. For when we think of the nature of the promise before us; of the hour when it is said to have fallen from the lips of Christ; of the profound interest which an assurance of this kind would kindle in the hearts of the disciples; and of the effort which they would surely make to recall the last words of their now glorified Master; it seems very improbable that a mistake would occur in this matter. And when, still further, we bear in mind that this passage does not stand alone, but is buttressed on every side by kindred promises; when we read the words: "It is expedient for you that I go away; for if I go not away, the Comforter will not come unto you; but if I depart, I will send him unto you;" and a little further on: "I have yet many things to say unto you, but ye cannot bear them now. Howbeit, when he, the Spirit of truth, is come, he will guide you into all the truth: for he shall not speak of himself; but whatsoever he shall hear, that shall he speak: and he will show you things to come. He shall glorify me; for he shall receive of mine, and shall show it unto you." Or, going back a little in the same discourse: "When the Comforter is come, whom I will send unto you from the Father, even the Spirit of truth, which proceedeth from the Father, he shall testify of me;" and again: "But the Comforter, the Holy Ghost, whom the Father will send in my name, he shall teach you all things, and bring all things to your remembrance, whatsoever I have said unto you." When we read these various promises, all referring to the same Divine Helper, and describing the different aspects of his work for the disciples, there is no longer any room for doubt. The assurance of my text was given to the Eleven by their Lord in the evening before he was betrayed. But long ere this, he had uttered words of encouragement to them, not very unlike those contained in his last discourse. For by the triple testimony of Matthew, Mark, and Luke, we are certified of his saying: "When they bring you unto the synagogues and magistrates and powers, take no thought how or what thing ye shall answer, or what ye shall say; for the Holy Ghost shall teach you in the same hour what ye ought to say." There is, then, every reason to believe that the promise of my text was addressed by Christ to his disciples.

And there is no less reason to believe that this language was a promise of inspiration, properly so called. For observe once more that the coming Helper is described as the Spirit of truth; that he was to take the place of Christ, and teach them many things which they were not now able to bear; that he was to bring to their remembrance all that Christ had said; to testify of Christ; to take the things of Christ and show to them; to reveal to them things to come and teach them all things. In a word, Jesus promised to continue and complete the revelation of his truth to his disciples by the agency of the Holy Spirit.

But wherefore? Because they were to bear witness of him, making known his will, even as he had made known his Father's will: "As the Father hath sent me, even so send I you."

And if the Spirit of truth was pledged to the Eleven for the purpose of qualifying them to teach with divine authority the things of Christ, he was virtually pledged to every one intrusted by Christ with the same office and mission. Hence Paul, when called to be an apostle, was entitled to expect the presence of the Spirit to guide him into all the truth. And that he was put in trust with the apostleship must be certain to every man who admits his veracity or understands his character; for he distinctly avers that he was recognized by the other apostles as their equal, that the signs of an apostle were wrought by him; and that he had received immediately from Christ his gospel and commission. Moreover, Peter ranks his letters with the other Scriptures, while the narrative of Luke, in the Acts, proves him to have been not a whit behind the very chiefest of the apostles in knowledge and zeal.

My second point has, therefore, been established, and its bearing upon the divine authority of the New Testament is obvious.

But were the apostles upright men? Though furnished themselves with the whole truth, may they not have been unfaithful to their trust, withholding a part of their message or adding to it cunningly devised fables? How to answer this question I know not. God forbid, that we should distrust the integrity of men chosen by Christ to make known his will! God forbid, that we should imagine the truth-revealing Spirit unable to move such men to utter their message, or to restrain them from adding to it earth-born fancies! God forbid, that we should read the pages of the New Testament and doubt the transparent integrity of their writers! The very soul of manliness and truth animates their language. In life, they were still imperfect; but when they spoke for Christ, the Spirit gave them utterance. As men, they were sometimes weak; but in doing the work of their apostleship, the Comforter made them strong and wise. I cannot persuade myself that any one of you needs to be convinced that the apostles were, through and through, upright, delivering to men with all fidelity the glad news which had been revealed to them by Christ and his Spirit. They could not but speak the things which they had seen and heard. We are, therefore, in possession of three facts; namely, that Jesus Christ was infallible, that he uttered the promise of my text to his disciples, and that they were upright men, teaching the truth which they knew.

These facts, if there were no others equally in point, (as there are many,) evince the divine authority of the New Testament. For, with a few exceptions, the New Testament Scriptures were written by apostles, that is, by men whom the Holy Spirit was to guide into all Christian truth. And the exceptional books were written by associates of apostles, long before the death of John, and, according to the testimony of the early church, were received as apostolic teaching. The penmen were probably inspired, and their writings were certainly welcomed as sacred. Indeed, these three facts are firm granitic pillars, on which the whole doctrine of inspiration rests unshaken, and will rest to the end of time. For if the writings of the New Covenant are clothed with divine authority, so likewise are those of the Old. The later Scriptures have set their seal to the earlier. By their testimony, we know that in the progress of revelation, "coming events cast their shadows before." The reality is preceded by the type, the spiritual by the natural, the fulfillment by the promise; just as the most holy place of the tabernacle was entered through the holy

The Bible the only Standard.

Our Saviour taught that not one jot or tittle of the law should pass till all be fulfilled; he declared that the Scripture (meaning the Old Testament) cannot be broken; and on a certain occasion, "beginning with Moses and all the prophets, he expounded unto them in all the Scriptures the things concerning himself." Peter pronounces the wonders of Pentecost to be that which was spoken by the prophet Joel, and the suffering of Christ to be that which God had showed before by the mouth of all his prophets, asserting also that holy men of old spoke as they were moved by the Holy Ghost. And Paul identifies the promise to Abraham with the gospel, represents the law as a schoolmaster bringing us to Christ, and teaches that every Scripture (that is, of the Old Testament) is given by inspiration of God, and is profitable for doctrine, for reproof, for correction, for instruction in righteousness, that the man of God may be perfect, thoroughly furnished unto all good works.

Besides, the pages of the New Testament are studded with passages from the Old. Sentences are quoted with reverence from the first chapter of Genesis to the last chapter of Malachi, few books of the earlier record failing to contribute somewhat to the later; and nothing can well be more evident than the fact that Christ and his apostles admitted the divine authority of the Old Testament. The whole Bible is, therefore, to be accepted as emanating from God. It was delivered to men by messengers accredited by him, and is to be honored with the same respect which it would challenge if written by the finger of Jehovah. It is the word of God addressed to mankind.

This language, I know, has been charged with extravagance. The Bible, it has been said, is not the word of God, but it contains the word of God. The contents of it must, therefore, be sifted, winnowed, weighed: the dross separated from the fine gold, the human from the divine, the letter from the spirit. Reason and moral sense must be the ultimate standard. By a proper use of these faculties we may be able to find in the Scriptures the word of God.

If this language were meant simply to affirm that we ought, when interpreting the words of Scripture, to distinguish between those which profess to make known to us directly the will of God, as uttered by Christ, by apostles, or by prophets, and those which make known to us the sayings and doings of evil spirits, of wicked or uninspired men, it would be quite true, but also quite irrelevant. For much of the Bible professes to report the speech and action of uninspired men, and no thoughtful Christian imagines the words of such men to be truthful simply because they are preserved in a true record. All admit that a sentiment may be wrong when the report of it is correct, and an act evil when the account of it is useful.

But this is not the whole meaning of those who insist that the Bible merely *contains* the word of God. They suppose it possible for human reason to winnow chaff from the wheat, even where the volume purports to have nothing but wheat. In this opinion they are utterly mistaken, as the light of another day will help them to see.

Having shown that the promise of the Saviour, in my text, involves the divine authority of the Bible as a source of Christian truth, I now proceed to say—

II. *It involves the completeness of the Bible*, as a source of Christian truth. This is evident—

1. From the words of the promise itself: "he will guide you into *all* the truth." According to the obvious sense of this promise, the apostles were to be guided into all the truth which belongs to the religion of Christ as

adapted to men in their present state. The language cannot fairly be made to signify less than this. For when Christ and his apostles speak of *the truth* by way of distinction, they mean the doctrine of salvation through Christ, the great facts and principles which underlie, determine, and pervade all right forms of Christian life. It need not be supposed that they were to become familiar with all the applications of Christian truth to the ever changing conditions of human society, but they were to be made acquainted with all the principles of this truth; not, however, at once, as may be concluded from the verb chosen by our Lord—"He will *guide* you into all the truth,"—and as may be learned from the history of the apostles; but gradually, though rapidly, as events called for the use of those principles. The Holy Spirit was to teach them what to say *when* standing before kings and governors, and not in anticipation of such an hour; and so, likewise, he was to teach them the way of God more perfectly as they had occasion to make it known. Peter did not have his vision of the sheet let down from heaven until Cornelius was ready for the gospel, and the fullness of the time had come for giving it to the Gentiles. It is not, therefore, possible for us to fix precisely the date *prior* to which the apostles had been guided into all the truth of the Christian system; nor can we certainly know from our text that every apostle was furnished by inspiration with the same amount of truth. This principle may have been communicated to one, and that to another, until as a body they were in possession of the whole truth. We only know that Paul had his gospel in its completeness directly from Christ. The remaining apostles may have learned particular truths from one another, some of them receiving the light earlier than their associates; but all received it as rapidly as the calls of duty required them to use it.

And this circumstance, that their knowledge came so often at the beck of Providence, not being a regular growth from within, but a gift from without when most needed, justifies us in believing that it was fully declared to others, and committed to writing for ages to come. While, then, the promise of my text proves the apostles to have been made acquainted with all the truth of the Christian system adapted to men in their present life, the manner in which this promise was fulfilled, by enlarging and clearing their views from time to time, as the exigencies of their mission demanded—bringing to their remembrance the words of Christ, unfolding the true import of those words, lifting the vail which hides the future and permitting some of its scenes to pass before them, or directing them in the application of principles to the shifting affairs of church, of state, of family—all this tends to prove that they had knowledge given them, not to hoard but to use, the Spirit ever whispering in their ears, "freely ye have received, freely give."

A confirmation of this view, viz., that my text involves the completeness of the Bible as a source of Christian truth, may be drawn—

2. From the position and work given to the apostles in the church. In his response to the noble confession of Peter, "Thou art the Christ, the Son of the living God," Jesus said: "Blessed art thou, Simon Barjona; for flesh and blood hath not revealed it unto thee, but my Father who is in heaven. And I say unto thee also, Thou art Peter, and on this rock will I build my church; and the gates of Hades shall not prevail against it. And I will give to thee the keys of the kingdom of heaven; and whatsoever thou shalt bind on earth shall be bound in heaven; and whatsoever thou shalt loose on earth shall be loosed in heaven." Here, as you will be careful to observe, Christ first traces the knowledge of Peter to a

The Bible the only Standard.

divine source, first recognizes him as speaking with the voice of inspiration: "flesh and blood hath not revealed it unto thee, but my Father who is in heaven;" and then, in view of his clear confession of the fundamental truth, thus revealed to him, pronounces him a rock on which the church was to be built. It was not Peter as a man distinguished for firmness and faith, but Peter as an inspired confessor and teacher of truth, who was to be the rock on which the spiritual body of Christ should rest securely. In just this character, is he addressed by our Saviour; and in just the opposite character, viz., as a denier of his Master's word, is he shortly after denominated Satan. Whether he speaks in our passage for the twelve, to all of whom the same great truth had been revealed, or simply for himself, cannot be certainly known; but we do know from other parts of the New Testament that his relation to the church was not peculiar. For Paul writes to the Ephesians: "Now, therefore, ye are no more strangers and foreigners, but fellow-citizens with the saints and of the household of God; and are built upon the foundation of the apostles and prophets, Jesus Christ himself being the chief corner-stone;" and John declares in the Revelation, that "the wall of the city had twelve foundations, and in them the name of the twelve apostles of the Lamb." Hence the church was built upon the rock Peter, in the same sense as it was built upon the rock Paul, or the rock John. As inspired teachers, all the apostles spoke with the authority of their Master; and there is not a particle of evidence for the opinion that, after Christ's ascension, Peter was in any special sense his vicar, exercising authority over the other apostles and the church universal; nor is there a particle of evidence for the opinion, that he either did or could transfer his supposed authority to other hands.

The scriptural argument for the papacy is a rope of sand.

Returning to the words of Jesus in his response to Peter, we observe that he exchanges one figure of speech for another, proceeding thus: "And I will give unto thee the keys of the kingdom of heaven, and whatsoever thou shalt bind on earth shall be bound in heaven, and whatsoever thou shalt loose on earth shall be loosed in heaven." With this language, it is natural to compare the words which Christ addressed to all the apostles, after prescribing the method of discipline for private offences: "Verily I say unto you, whatsoever ye shall bind on earth shall be bound in heaven, and whatsoever ye shall loose on earth shall be loosed in heaven." Hence the apostles were to be the foundation stones of the Lord's house, and yet stewards over the same; they were to settle with divine authority the fundamental principles of our religion, and were also to carry into effect proper rules of admission to the church, and exclusion from it; in a word, to look after order and discipline; and their action in this respect was to be ratified on high. Of similar import, were the Saviour's words when he first met the collected disciples in a closed room after his resurrection: "Peace be unto you. As my Father hath sent me, even so send I you. Receive ye the Holy Ghost. Whose soever sins ye remit, they are remitted unto them; and whose soever you retain, they are retained." Thus apostolic teaching, whether of Christian doctrine or duty, was to be sanctioned by the Master as his own. In their official action they were representatives of Christ. Tarrying in Jerusalem, and continuing with one accord in prayer until they were endued with power from on high, they then entered at once upon their great work of bearing witness for Christ, both in Jerusalem and in all Judea and in

Samaria, and unto the uttermost part of the earth; and no fact in the past is more certain than this, that their teaching was delivered, and was accepted as ultimate authority on all matters of Christian faith and practice. Their testimony was the truth. Their doctrine was the word of God. Their directions, even as to order and decorum in social worship, were the commandments of the Lord, and those who could speak with tongues and prophecy were to obey them. They testified of Christ, expounded the meaning of his work, promulgated the laws of his kingdom, and completed the revelation which he began. Their office and relation to the church were peculiar, based upon supernatural endowments. They were witnesses to the fact of Christ's resurrection; and the Holy Spirit ratified their testimony, with signs following. They were inspired teachers, having a plenitude of spiritual gifts. They could recall the past, speak with tongues, prophecy, interpret. They were related to all future believers, as foundation-stones to the structure which is built upon them, or as stewards of a house, charged with deciding who may enter and who must leave it, to the household itself, to its order, discipline, life, and character. By the laying on of their hands, other Christians obtained special gifts. They had no peers. Their knowledge of all the truth makes it very probable, and their relation to all the church makes it almost certain, that they put this truth on record for the benefit of Christians to the end of time.

Having inferred, from the knowledge and office promised to the apostles, that the record of Christian truth as left by them was complete, I may likewise infer the same:—

3. From the actual contents of the Bible. Let us look at these by way of contrast. The most self-reliant philosophy of to-day has only the following to offer as reli-

gious truth, viz. : That God is simply an idea, or that he is the universe, or that he is the unknown antecedent of an original fire-mist, out of which all things have been evolved; that man, emerging from darkness and sinking again into darkness, is the crowning effort of nature hitherto; and that the future is big with possibilities of higher life for other orders of being. This is the sum. Of sin, of providence, of pardon, of eternal life for you and me, it has nothing to say. Nor should it have; for an attempt to evoke the verities of religion from an irreligious mind by process of logic, is like "sinking broken buckets into empty wells, and growing old in drawing nothing up." Yet a philosopher of this school is commonly satisfied with himself, thinking that he possesses at least "the rudiments of omniscience." Alas! in the realm of spiritual, supernatural truth, he is, indeed, blind and ignorant, knowing nothing; as the poet has said,

> "One to whose smooth-rubbed soul can cling
> Nor form, nor feeling, great or small,
> A reasoning, self-sufficing thing,
> An intellectual all-in-all."

But the Scriptures, written by men who spake as they were moved by the Holy Ghost, have enough to teach. They are filled with religious truth, drawn from the wells of salvation. They speak to us of God, affirming that he is a spirit, self-existent, eternal, omnipresent; that he is living, active, personal; that he is all-wise, all-holy, all-good. They testify of his creative power and exact providence, of his fatherly care and spontaneous grace. They set before us Jesus Christ, the image of the invisible God, to the end that by contemplating his character —his power, purity, love, and purpose—we may know the character of God. What more can be done? How can the Most High be brought nearer to human thought and feeling?

They speak to us of man, affirming that he was made in the image of God and under law to right; that he fell into sin, and drew upon his soul the wrath of Jehovah, with floods of darkness and woe; that he communicated to his offspring a depraved nature, so that they go astray from birth; and that, left to itself, the whole race would rush with stubborn will away from the Father of lights into the outer darkness. Is not this enough? Does it not explain the history of mankind and evince the need of divine grace?

They speak to us of redemption, affirming that God was in Christ reconciling the world unto himself; for God so loved the world that he gave his only begotten Son, that whosoever believeth in him should not perish but have everlasting life. They testify that Christ is the way, the truth, and the life; and that no man cometh unto the Father but by him. Their language is clear, direct, positive. It exhausts the subject; declaring, on the one hand, that Christ is able and willing to save to the uttermost all that come unto God by him, and on the other hand, that there is salvation in no other, for by one offering he has perfected forever all them that are sanctified.

They speak to us of the new birth; of repentance, faith, and love; of their nature, origin, fruits, and value. They tell us what we may be and do, what we may suffer and enjoy, in fellowship with Christ. They describe to us the work of faith and labor of love and patience of hope, by which the grace of God makes us meet for an inheritance with the saints in light. The ethics of the Bible are perfect. "What we call the moral progress of the ages is simply their retrogression toward the evangelic standard." And so it will be to the end. The stream will never reach a higher point than its source; the last generation of believers on earth will gladly sit at the feet of Paul and John, receiving by the aid of divine grace perennial supplies from the fullness of truth which was revealed to them.

They speak to us of the church, prescribing qualifications for membership, deaconship, and eldership, with rules of discipline for offenses, both public and private. They set before us the rites and worship, the lofty aims and sad mistakes, of churches under apostolic guidance. They cast a jet of light upon every important question; and what they have left in darkness may well remain so, until we see as we are seen and know as we are known.

They speak to us of the future, sketching in bold outline the onward flow of events until time shall be no longer—the conflict between good and evil, truth and error, light and darkness, waxing fiercer and fiercer, until the Son of man shall come in his glory and separate the wicked from the just.

And more, they give us glimpses of the "undiscovered country;" they permit us to hear faint echoes of the eternal song; they take us up, on ladders of imagery, to the gate of heaven and suffer us to look upon its outer glory.

This is enough for the present life; and the voice of Jesus declares: "If any man shall add unto these things, God shall add unto him the plagues that are written in this book. And if any man shall take away from the words of the book of this prophecy, God shall take away his part out of the book of life and out of the holy city."

Meagre, indeed, and most unsatisfactory is the sketch which I have given of what the Scriptures teach. But time will not permit me to dwell upon the inexhaustible theme. The Sacred Record is a vast temple, which cannot be explored in a life, with places holy and most holy, with pillars and arches, with galleries and domes, reaching further and rising higher than human thought has yet been able to follow; while every stone and pillar, every wall and ceiling, every door and arch, every altar and window, every statue and fresco, is conceived by infinite wisdom and executed with matchless skill. Every part of it is precious and significant to him who has entered its holy courts. "Standing without, you may see no glory, but standing within, every ray of light reveals a harmony of unspeakable splendors." I envy not the man who dares to remove one stone, or add one fresco to this grand cathedral. I honor not the church which enlarges it by wooden courts and painted statues. Let it stand as the inspired workmen built it! Mar not its proportions, murmur not at its height, despise not its age; but enter and worship—not the temple, but the God of the temple—and you will find it radiant with spiritual light and vocal with the music of Paradise.

Again, the completeness of the Bible as a source of Christian truth may be inferred—

4. From the failure, thus far, of all attempts to make any worthy additions to its teaching. There has been no lack of enterprise in this direction. Many of the Jews imagined the written law to be incomplete, and desired to supplement it with further rites and ceremonies: hence the Mishna, or Second Law, handed down by tradition, and placed by them on a level with the Pentateuch. Hence, too, the Scribes and Pharisees took it upon themselves to reprove Jesus for doing miracles on the Sabbath, and for permitting his disciples to eat with unwashen hands. "It is not lawful for thee to heal on the Sabbath." "Why do thy disciples transgress the tradition of the elders?" But Christ replied: "Why do ye also transgress the commandment of God by your tradition?" "Full well do ye frustrate the commandment of God, that ye may keep your tradition." "Well hath Esaias prophesied of you hypocrites: This people honor

eth me with their lips, but their heart is far from me. Howbeit, in vain do they worship me teaching for doctrines the commandments of men." Such was the view which our Saviour took of the oral law as compared with the written, of tradition as compared with Scripture. The one was human, the other was divine.

But the additions made to the written law by Jewish teachers, on the basis of alleged tradition, were not very unlike those which have been made, by ecclesiastical authority, on the basis of alleged tradition, to the doctrines and duties taught by the New Testament. In neither case, do their tendency and spirit agree with the word of God. They lack its simplicity and spirituality. They exalt the efficacy of rites and forms, of priestly mediation and sanctimonious endeavor. They interpose many things besides the blood of Christ between the soul and God. The church, the sacraments, the Virgin Mary, the saints, are too much extolled, while Christ and his word are too much neglected.

Passing through an open way in the city of Rome, I read this inscription under a picture of the mother of Jesus: *"Lodata sempre sia col divin figlio, la Virgine Maria del buon consiglio:"* "Ever lauded with her divine Son be the Virgin Mary of good counsel!" And this motto feebly expresses a sentiment which has become almost universal in the papal communion. During a residence of three months in Italy, I was in the habit of visiting the churches on the Lord's day, at the hours of public worship. There were masses and genuflexions and crossings and chantings enough; but only once, in all that time, did I hear a Roman Catholic attempt to preach; and in that instance, the sermon was devoted to the Virgin Mary, affirming that she was born as free from the stains of moral evil as Christ himself, and urging the people to pay her devout homage. The Roman Catechism

The Bible the only Standard.

teaches that "we should resort to the most holy Virgin with pious supplication, that by her intercession she may secure to us sinners the favor of God and the blessings necessary for this, and for eternal, life. Hence we exiled sons of Eve *ought* to invoke assiduously the mother of mercy and advocate of believing people, and it is impious, execrable for any one to doubt that she has pre-eminent merits with God and the highest desire to assist mankind." This doctrine of the immaculate conception and this duty of praying to the so-called mother of God, are specimens of what man can do by way of completing the standard of Christian truth.

With them, may be naturally associated the invocation of saints and of angels; a practice which betokens distrust of the infinite compassion of Christ, which overlooks the finite nature of created beings, and which rests upon extra-biblical authority alone. With them, may also be associated the reverence paid to images, relics, and sacred places; a reverence which the Scriptures nowhere enjoin, and which the voice of history pronounces superstitious or productive of superstition.

Time would fail me to speak of the celibacy of the clergy, of the monastic orders and life, of auricular confession and penance and purgatory, and of the many sacraments and ceremonies which have been added by church authority to the simple worship described in the New Testament. "A Catechism of the Christian Religion, published with the approbation of the Right Rev. John B. Fitzpatrick, Bishop of Boston," does not go far enough when it says that "the church, to facilitate the conversion of Jews and Gentiles, retained some of the ceremonies of the Jews, and others that had been copied by the Gentiles from the Jews." It would have been more correct to say, that the Papal Church has dedicated not only temples and statues, but also ceremonies of heathen origin to her use.

I should not do justice to my own sense of truth and propriety, were I to close this part of my discourse without saying, that the doctrine of official grace derived by Episcopal succession from the apostles, the doctrine of baptismal regeneration as taught by the Liturgy, the use of sprinkling or pouring for baptism, and the application of this rite to infants, are further examples of what man can do by way of completing the standard of Christian truth and duty. None of them owe their existence to the plain sense of Scripture, and some of them lie at the root of the worst papal errors. And so, I hesitate not to say, that all attempts to make worthy additions to biblical teaching have to this hour been failures.

Such, then, in brief, are our reasons for believing the Bible to be a complete as well as a divine standard of faith and practice. As Baptists, we claim no monopoly in this doctrine, but rejoice that many who walk not with us accept it heartily. Many there are who have maintained this principle with unrivaled eloquence and noblest reason, assigning to the Bible a position solitary and supreme above all other writings, be it creed or liturgy, whether for establishing doctrine or impressing it on the hearts of men. By an unconscious reception of extra-scriptural views, have they deviated, if at all, from the straight line of duty to the Master. We give them honor. Yet in the application of the truth before us, in the uniform consistency with which we have rejected every opinion and practice not founded on the plain sense of Scripture, in the persistent care with which we have separated the human from the divine, and striven to build our churches after the apostolic model, we do, and must, claim a special relation to the principle set forth to-night; we do, and must, believe our position to be in advance of that held by any other body of Christians; we do, and must, think that God is on our side, and that the views which distinguish us will surely in the end commend themselves to the whole family of God on earth. Is this too much to expect? Not if our principles are drawn from the living word. Assured of their divine origin, it would be culpable unbelief not to anticipate their final success. Truth will be laurel-crowned at last. We may have reason to charge ourselves with inertness, we may illustrate the saying of Christ, that the children of this world are wiser in their generation than the children of light; but the cause will not fail, the principles we teach will go forth conquering and to conquer, and gladly, after our best efforts, will we take up for ourselves the sacred words, "Not unto us, not unto us, but unto thy name give glory."

We have no fear for the cause. The word of God will stand; and those who are built upon the foundation of the apostles and prophets, Jesus Christ himself being the chief-corner, as they are fitly framed together in him, will grow unto an holy temple in the Lord. Of this number, my brethren, we all hope to be found, lively stones, meet for the Master's use!

II.

THE OBLIGATION OF THE CHURCH RESPECTING THE HOLY SCRIPTURES.

By HENRY C. FISH, D.D.,
Pastor of First Baptist Church, Newark, N. J.

"I HAVE SET BEFORE THEE AN OPEN DOOR, AND NO MAN CAN SHUT IT: FOR THOU HAST A LITTLE STRENGTH AND HAST KEPT MY WORD, AND HAST NOT DENIED MY NAME. BECAUSE THOU HAST KEPT THE WORD OF MY PATIENCE, I ALSO WILL KEEP THEE FROM THE HOUR OF TEMPTATION, WHICH SHALL COME UPON ALL THE WORLD."—*Rev.* iii. 8, 10.

It is of the church at Philadelphia, one of the "Seven Churches" of Asia Minor, that this was said. And history records a striking verification of the assurance here given. An "open door" was set before this church which no one was able to shut. It was a door of deliverance, ("and consequently one of utterance," such as Paul speaks of,) and looks to the trials here referred to, "the hour of temptation which was to come upon all the world"—all the Roman world. The ten years of fierce persecution under Trajan is commonly held to be this period of temptation. And it is an historic fact, that while all the other churches were laid waste, this one at Philadelphia was wonderfully kept. Its ministers were not martyred; its members were not scattered. It stood like a solitary column amid surrounding ruins.

But what is especially noticeable, is the reason assigned for this preservation of the church at Philadelphia: namely, its fidelity to the revealed will of Christ. "I have set before thee an open door, for thou hast a little strength, (thou feelest thy weakness,) and hast kept my word, and hast not denied my name." And "Because thou hast kept the word of my patience, (my word enjoining and succouring patience,) I will also keep thee." And this thought indicates the subject of the present discourse, which is *Loyalty to Christ*, or the *Obligation of the Church to maintain revealed truth.*

1. It must be maintained against the SPECIOUS LIBERALISM OF THE TIMES.

Walking one day in New York, I saw in a shop-window a sign reading thus: "Liberal books for independent thinkers." It was a symbol of the age. Changing, as he does, his methods of attack, the great enemy of truth and righteousness does not appear, in our day, in the form of the unbeliefs so common in the centuries gone by. The cold, critical atheism of the English deists and French philosophers of the eighteenth century, which denied, outright, a revelation, and deified human Reason, and treated Christianity with scorn and sarcasm, is not now widely prevalent. Nor have we much to fear from that form of infidelity which, in later years, has sought its support in the alleged discrepancies between the Bible and the natural sciences. The skepticism of to-day takes the garb of religion. It is respectful toward Christianity. It affects reverence for sacred things. It would not do to scout devotion: man needs a religion; and so Satan would give him one that is better than that of the Bible. The Bible is not to be discarded: that were impolitic; but, then, it must be received with certain allowances. Some of its parts are to be rejected as mythical, and others must be interpreted according to an "*enlightened understanding!*" Scripture terms are to be retained, but, then, they are to have their *particular meaning.* And by affecting to be religious, this species of infidelity is spreading like a malaria. It is infecting multitudes who are surrounded by seemingly Christian influences.

Our young men especially, and among them, numbers of the most prominent and influential, are imbibing, to a fearful extent, this delicious poison. It is seen in the frequent assertion that man is his own saviour; that he must win heaven for himself; and that (to quote from the papers of a popular Review) "to believe that a trust in a blood of atonement can cleanse a corrupt nature, and redeem a lost soul, is to believe sorcery." It is seen in the rapidly increasing tendency to smooth down the sterner attributes of Deity; to say but little, and that softly, about future punishment; and to form an ideal Christ, possessed of grace, but not of justice and holiness. It is seen in the swift advance of one wing of Unitarianism into downright infidelity, and the institution of a "Broad Church," where Swedenborgians, Unitarians, Universalists, Friends, and Independents—all sorts of beliefs and unbeliefs, may thrive in amicable neighborhood in one inclosure. It is seen in the general loosening up of the common mind from the moorings of great Scripture truths, and its readiness to adopt the vagaries of spiritism, and mesmerism, and whatever *isms* and *ologies* may chance to present themselves. It is seen in the war against a sound divinity, that is urged on under the outcry against "merciless dogmas," and "straight-laced creeds," and "dead formularies," and "shams," and "priestcraft," and "intolerance" in religion; and in the disposition among the churches to think lightly of the great doctrines of the Bible, and of carefully defined systems, if not to cast away entirely all articles of faith; and also, in the readiness of some to disregard the divinely established relation between the ordinances.

What is styled the *liberty of the church*, comes from the same spirit. Says a distinguished Congregational divine,[*] in a sermon recently published, "I concede and

---

[*] Rev. Henry Ward Beecher.

I assert, first, that infant baptism is nowhere commanded in the New Testament. Secondly, I affirm that the cases where it is implied, as in the baptism of whole households, are by no means conclusive and without doubt, and that, if there is no other basis for it than that, it is not safe to found it on the practice of the apostles in the baptism of Christian families. Therefore, I give up that which has been injudiciously used as an argument for infant baptism. And thirdly, I assert that the doctrine, that as a Christian ordinance it is a substitute for the circumcision of the Jews, is a doctrine that is utterly untenable, to say nothing more. If any body ask me, 'Where is your text for baptizing children?' I reply that there is none. And if I am asked, 'Then why do you baptize them?' I say, '*Because it is found to be beneficial.*'"

The same liberty is claimed, of course, in respect to the Lord's supper. Those who are held to be unbaptized, and even unconverted, (if only seeking the truth,) are invited to partake. The number of ministers, and churches, in different denominations, who assert views substantially like these, is not small, and is constantly increasing. Nor is it to be thought strange. Though less emphatically proclaimed, this "liberty" with the Scriptures has been generally assumed as allowable. Professor Stuart, in his work on Baptism, quoted approvingly Calvin's remark: "It is of no consequence at all whether the person baptized is wholly immersed or merely sprinkled, although the word baptized signifies immerse, and the rite of immersion was practiced by the ancient church." And in the matter of Infant Baptism, he (Professor Stuart) frankly said: "Commands, or plain and certain examples, in the New Testament relative to it, I do not find;" adding, "Nor, with my views of it, do I need them."

All this chimes in admirably with the taking catchwords,—"Liberal books for independent thinkers." But how does it suit the standard by which all opinions are to be tried? How does all this tally with God's orderings, and God's word? It is written: "There is one Lord, one faith, one baptism." *One;* not two, or three, or any number, and all equally correct. And particularly, there is one *faith;* that is, one system of belief; one precise set of truths and principles, ordained and established by God. It must be so. Had God made two diverse revelations, one must have been wrong. In accepting the one we must have rejected the other. Both could not be right. Hence it is a peculiarity of truth, that it is simple, absolute, certain; while error is manifold and uncertain. Truth is simply the revelation of God's will; and as such, it must be definite and fixed. It cannot change or be modified, any more than can his nature. It must stand perfect and entire forever.

Truth is the most exclusive of all things. It is a tower of adamant. It yields not an inch. It concedes nothing. "Truth, sir," said Henry Clay, "makes no compromises?" Hence any alleged doctrine of Scripture, which is not exclusive, is no doctrine; it knows nothing, affirms nothing. It is a weak device of Satan. God did not put it in the Bible. What he put there is flint. It is diamond, with sharp angles, cutting every thing, cut by nothing. It shuts out every thing else, and says, "I am from God! I am right, and all besides is wrong!" From its very nature it must be so.

And, then, let it be remembered that God has a right to say what shall be. He sits supreme. Man, his workmanship, and his care, is subject to his dictation and control. He is to have no will and no way of his own. One thing is demanded, that he bow to his sovereign behest. God's government is not a republican government. And for that very reason earthly governments ought to be republican. If he be Head Supreme, there ought to be no other pretended head supreme. God's government is an absolute monarchy, and for that reason no man can be an absolute monarch. Both in the world and in the church, "there is one law-giver." God is over all. Every necessary foundation truth he has established, either as respects the world or the church. Men have but to execute what he has ordained. Law-making, then, so far as it infringes upon great cardinal principles, on the part of man, is a wicked presumption. The revelation of man or angel is no revelation. If God has instituted certain relations between me and my fellow, and laid on us certain obligations, who shall change them? If, in things spiritual, he has said, upon such conditions man shall die, and upon such he shall live; and if, in his churches, he has established his laws and ordinances, what have men to do in modifying or annulling them? That is not their business; if they make any new laws, then they are to be regarded as no laws. Setting up their appointments in opposition to God's is disloyalty. Liberalism is therefore atheism. It is casting off God's yoke. "Liberal" books and teachings, untying what God has bound together, and divulging new principles, are insurrective, mutinous, seditious. They are the highest insult to God, especially when they come into the domain of religion. There is one faith— one system of truths. Any other faith is no faith. It is God's prerogative to make a creed for man. And all his "independent thinking" will not change one of the great facts and principles which he has established.

Was not this so regarded at the first? Standing at the early times, one is struck with the fact that the revealed religion was altogether positive and uncompromising. It was forbidden to Judaism, under the most fearful penalties, to affiliate with the false theologies of the surrounding nations. And when, in the new era, Christianity went forth on its sublime career, how did it refuse to symbolize with paganism! How high and exclusive its demands!—not willing to give and to take, for the sake of adjustment, but claiming and demanding unlimited control. Paganism would have gladly voted for Christ a seat with the other gods on Olympus, and for his religion a place in the Pantheon among the other religions of the day; but Christianity said, "No!" It spurned the proffer, and gave battle to every opposing system, and demanded exclusive headship for Christ—his complete enthronement as God over all.

And then, looking into the Scriptures, how positively and sharply defined is the truth, as laid down by Christ and his apostles. As to the way of salvation, we read, "I am the way, the truth, and the life: no man cometh to the Father but by me." "He that believeth not shall be damned." "If any man love not the Lord Jesus Christ, let him be anathema." And as regards taking liberties with the divine ordinances, and virtually or formally modifying the exact written record, we read, "Teaching them to observe all things whatsoever I have commanded you;" and "if any man shall add unto these things, God shall add unto him the plagues that are written in this book. And if any man shall take away from the words of the book of this prophecy, God shall take away his part out of the book of life, and out of the holy city, and from the things which are written in this book."

Even the amiable and beloved John speaks in language the most polemic and intolerant, as men would term it, for he says, we are not even to countenance the bearer of strange doctrines: "If there come any unto you, and bring not this doctrine, receive him not into your houses, neither bid him God speed." And the bold denunciation of Paul was: "Though we, or an angel from heaven, preach any other gospel unto you than that we have preached unto you, let him be accursed." And, as if to render it more emphatic, he repeats it: "As we said before, so say I now again: If any man preach any other gospel unto you, let him be accursed"! How world-wide all this from that spurious charitableness which would condemn nobody as wrong; which is so careful about other's feelings as never to say they are in an error; which makes one hesitate to say, "I know I am right," and which covers his own timid, cautious, half-formed notions with the plea, "There are good people holding all kinds of religious opinions!" In particular, how far removed all this from that vaunted "liberality" which makes one religion as good as another, only so its possessor be sincere! which honors Jesus Christ, and just as much honors Confucius, and Zoroaster, and Socrates, and Mohammed! which respects Paul, and Peter, and James, but would by no means condemn Arius, and Socinus, and Emerson, and Brownson, and Theodore Parker, and Hosea Ballou! which believes in the Bible, but would not say that the teachings of the Hindoo Vedas, and the Rabbinical writers, and of Emanuel Swedenborg are wrong; and which believes that the followers of Christ will be saved, but will not dare to affirm that those who reject him and follow strange guides, will be lost! Or which, in respect to the sacraments, asserts that "an ox yoke is as strictly an ordinance as is baptism," as a popular divine, before referred to, declares.

We have not so learned Christ. If such liberties are to be taken with the Scriptures; if such laxity of interpretation is to prevail—such tampering with plain truths —then nothing can be settled, much less remain settled. We are all adrift, without compass, rudder, or chart, and may well despair of either ascertaining or enforcing scriptural obligations. This tendency must be counteracted. Every lover of truth should especially consider himself "set for the defence of the gospel," when it is thus in danger of depreciation. It was once a trick of rogues to gouge out portions of gold coin, by plowing into the edge, and then so filling up and galvanizing over the groove as to make detection almost impossible. The coins were still current, but sadly depreciated. Let it not be so of doctrines. A high duty is that, especially reposed in ministers, of keeping every scriptural verity up to its original standard; of preserving the integrity of the gospel as it is understood by the people; of having an eye upon those who, Joab like, profess friendship for sacred truth, but slyly thrust it through under the fifth rib. Let us "earnestly contend for the faith once delivered to the saints." Let us love the truth with such ardor as to be compelled to say with the excellent Dr. Nevins, "I bear to error a degree of the same hatred which I feel toward sin, and am determined to persecute the one as I do the other."

2. The truth is to be maintained against FALLACIOUS SCHEMES OF CHRISTIAN UNION.

It is unmistakable that a deeper and more fervent desire for intimate and visible union among Christians of different denominations exists now than in former years. All good men rejoice in this yearning of kindred hearts for closer fellowship. It is one of the favorable signs of the times. Let it be cultivated and cherished in every becoming way. But, in the meantime, it should not be forgotten that there may be unity in variety; that unity does not of necessity suppose sameness. There is not identity in the works of creation; and yet there is wonderful unity. There is not sameness in any of the works of God; but there is harmony—harmony in diversity. So may there be among Christians much diversity and yet a real unity. A true union, therefore, already exists among the people of God. If Rome asks where is the unity of Protestantism? we say, behold it in heart, in aim, and, to a happy extent, in opinion. We are all, of whatever name, renewed by the same Spirit; we have the same hopes and fears; we look up to the same God and Father; we trust in the same almighty Saviour; we are in sympathy with the same object—the saving of souls, and the building up of Christ's kingdom, and cheerfully co-operate in promoting this object; and upon many points, and those the most vital, we hold the same views. So that there is, after all, in Protestantism, a real and true unity. The great thing to be aimed at is, for religious denominations to live in peace, and love one another, despite their differences. Let them teach and preach fully what they believe to be truth, but let it be the speaking of truth in love. "Whereunto they have attained, let them walk by the same rule; let them mind the same thing." If half the time and energy spent by some in efforts to break down ecclesiastical enclosures which they do not like, were wisely employed in efforts to awaken more real love in the several denominations one toward another, there would be a great gain to the cause of truth.

One thing is clear: there should be no unity at the expense of truth. However ardently outward unity in the truth is to be desired, any agreement, except *in the truth*, would be precarious in its nature, and at the same time traitorous to Christ. In such a unity, somebody must have betrayed him; somebody has got rid of his conscience; somebody has sacrificed truth; for here opposites meet, and two beliefs, in some respects essentially hostile, are dwelling in loving embrace. Calvin, in the preface to one of his polemical tracts, insists that disagreement may proceed without any violation of charity;

and to the outcry that the unity of the church is rent in pieces, he makes a noble reply, which is especially worthy of note just now, when so much is said about ecclesiastical union, and when some people seem to think that if all denominations would only shake hands together, and sit down once in a while and commune with each other, the millennium would have already come! "We acknowledge," says Calvin, "no unity except in Christ, and no charity of which he is not the bond; and, therefore, the chief point in preserving charity is to maintain faith sacred and entire." Let this be remembered: "*The chief point in preserving charity is to maintain faith sacred and entire.*"

Such an outward unity, whose basis is the cordial adoption of all the teachings of Christ, every one should pray for; but any other unity falsifies itself, and should be looked upon with distrust. I agree on this point most heartily with a clergyman of the Church of England: "From the peace which is bought at the expense of truth, may the good Lord deliver us!" One particle of truth in God's sight is of infinite moment; and were we to relinquish it for some seeming advantage, we might almost expect to hear a voice from heaven, crying out, "First loyal, then liberal!" "Behold to obey is better than sacrifice!" The command is, "First pure, then peaceable." And I protest against calling any man who inflexibly holds to what he in conscience believes to be a truth of God's word, "a bigot," "a sectarian," an "uncharitable man." Perchance he is tenacious of a great principle, now calumniated and assailed, but yet of vital moment; and perchance, because he loves those from whom he differs, *therefore* he persists in telling them the truth; for that is a sound maxim, "The greatest charity consists in telling the greatest amount of truth." He must be a very shallow thinker, or a very dishonest reasoner, who advocates conciliation by compromise, in the realm of moral truth. It looks well, but it is a specious deception. Its voice is the voice of Jacob, but its hands are the hands of Esau.

Herein is justified our denominational position in respect to the order of God's house. While extending *Christian* fellowship to all who love our common Lord, *church* fellowship is restricted to baptized believers. We are blamed for this; and never was there such a pressure upon us to break down this "hated enclosure" as now; and the plea is that there may be Christian unity. It is even urged that we have accomplished our mission as Baptists, and should merge into other denominations. And it is gravely asked, "What difference is there between us? and what separates us except a little water?" To all which and every thing like it, we answer, *It is for the sake of the truth that we stand where we do.* It is not that we love our respected brethren of other names less, but that we love the Master and the truth more. Freely acknowledging that they hold the cardinal points of the "one faith," we yet maintain that they reject the "one baptism," and receive instead an ordinance of man. And we maintain, moreover, that from their theory of infant church-membership, the truths which they do hold are held insecurely.

Three times has the very citadel of the "one faith" been seized by the enemy, from his having carried, beforehand, the outworks which the Baptists would sacredly guard—from his having demolished the instituted safeguard around the church—"believer's baptism." This was first effected in the great apostasy of the middle ages, which is undeniably attributable to the introduction of unconverted material into the church, by means of infant baptism, as it is called. Most truly is it said of Antichrist, in a Waldensian writing dating back at least to the year 1100: "He (Antichrist) arrived at maturity when men whose hearts were set upon the world multiplied in the church, and by the union of church and state, got the power of both into their hands." And then it is added (which explains the fact): "He teaches us to baptize children into the faith," etc. Thus was the "one faith" well nigh swept from the earth. It was effected a second time, subsequent to the Reformation. Luther and his coadjutors did not carry the reform far enough. They retained the error of birth-right church-membership, and it shortly brought into the Reformed churches a flood of corruption, which almost obliterated, on the fields of their grandest triumphs, the work of those noble men. And to-day, what are Oncken and Wiberg and their brethren in Germany and Sweden doing, but *reforming the Reformation;* but recovering the citadel of truth—justification by faith alone—and building up around it, for defence, the walls of a converted church? The third success of the enemy, in the way described, was in our own New England, previous to the times of President Edwards and Whitefield, when evangelical piety had almost died out. Dr. Joel Hawes, of Hartford, in his work entitled "A Tribute to the Pilgrims," attempts to account for this deplorable circumstance; and mentions, as a chief cause, the introduction of the half-way covenant, by which "the children of unconverted persons (but yet of sober lives and owning the covenant) might be baptized." By this means, multitudes of unsanctified persons (yet desiring to bring their children to the sealing ordinances) came to be church members. And it soon transpired that these unconverted parents and their unconverted offspring, all in the church together, were having things their own way. The preaching conformed to this state of things, and religion sunk into a routine of cold formalities. Says the late Dr. Archibald Alexander, of Prince-

Obligation of the Church. 49

ton, in his Lectures, as to the times of which I speak: "It was very much a matter of course for all who had been baptized in infancy to be received into communion at the proper age, without exhibiting or possessing any satisfactory evidence of a change of heart. The habit of the preachers was to address their people as though they were all pious, and only needed instruction and confirmation." As you see, the egg from which this destructive viper was hatched, was the dogma of infant church-membership.

Now this dogma the Baptists strenuously oppose, and always have opposed, since its existence. And their healthful opposition is still needful. The error in question is still maintained. Dr. William A. Stearns, now President of Amherst College, in his work on infant church-membership, says: "Baptized children are in the same inclosure with the parents, and are equally members of the church, long before they make any profession of their faith. Properly speaking, the question can never come up, whether they shall join the church. They belong already, and a profession of religion with them is simply their own most hearty acknowledgment of this fact, and of the obligations it implies." Dr. Charles Hodge, in the Princeton Review of 1858, says: "The status of baptized children is not a vague or uncertain one, according to the doctrine of the Reformed churches. They are members of the church; they are professing Christians; they belong presumptively to the number of the elect." To these high authorities, representing the New and the Old School Presbyterians, none others need be added. Now with this old and fearful error of infant church-membership still retained (and there is not a denomination in Christendom free from it, except the Baptist), who will say that among our Pedobaptist brethren the soul and essence of the "one faith" is held securely?

Who will undertake to guarantee that a growth of fearfully corrupt opinions and practices shall not again crop out from this mischievous germ?

From this point of observation, it is plain that we yet have, as Baptists, a mission. It is ours to neutralize this leaven, and prevent its permeating the whole lump. Strong, intelligent, respectable, the churches of other names around us nevertheless feel our influence, and are largely indebted to it for their existing purity and efficiency. When, therefore, we are asked, "What special mission have you as distinct from ourselves?" we answer, "To prevent your errors from again going to seed." It was when Unitarianism, subsequent to the days of Edwards, had almost wholly subverted the "Orthodox" church in New England, that from the then existing and strictly evangelical Baptist churches in Boston, there went out a redeeming influence—a revival of pure religion. To that influence, every denomination and church is to-day indebted. And if a similar service to the cause of the truth shall not again be required, it will be owing largely to the steady working of the strong conservative power of our churches. Here, then, is sufficient reason for maintaining our present denominational position. It will be seen that something more than "a little water" divides us from those whom we yet love as Christians. It is a difference upon the radical question as to who shall be received to baptism, and acknowledged as members in Christ's church. We say believers—they, believers and their unbelieving children. We cannot walk in church fellowship with those who thus persist in modeling the Christian church after the Hebrew commonwealth, instead of the pattern given in the New Testament. We must, for the truth's sake, continue to protest against so grave an error.

Besides, this "little water," as it is called, carries with

it more than is sometimes supposed. In objecting to our course as to communion, Dr. H. A. Boardman of Philadelphia, in his sermon on Christian union, says: "You" (Baptists) "believe that our Saviour has prescribed one form of baptism. We believe that he has prescribed another form." In this he falls into the mistake (common to his brethren on this subject) that it is a "form of baptism" for which we contend. This we deny. It is not mode, not form, but *the thing itself*. In our view, there cannot be scriptural baptism without immersion. No immersion, no baptism. And, surely, we could not be asked to commune at the table with those whom we consider unbaptized—a thing which no denomination of which I speak does, or has a right to do. They all alike ask for what they believe to be baptism, before communion. This is all we do. We only ask for what we believe to be baptism—valid baptism. And we insist on this, not out of a sectarian spirit, but simply because it is demanded by Christ. It is one of his positive laws, and is not to be treated with indifference. We hold that we have no more right to dispense with baptism as preceding the communion, or to change the relative place of the ordinance, than to dispense with or change the most important point of faith. In this sense, there are no non-essentials. We have no right to say, "This command of Christ's is important; that is not important." We are to conform to "all righteousness," *i. e.*, all God's righteous requirements.

And we are tenacious as to this matter of baptism on other grounds. When John Hooper, more than three hundred years ago, was answering before young King Edward for refusing to wear the vestments of a bishop, to which office he had just been appointed, he insisted that these vestments were the inventions of men, and introduced into the church in its corruptest ages; moreover, that they were badges of a priesthood, and that as the priesthood of Aaron was done away by Christ's sacrifice of himself, once for all, priestly array was now sanctioning a lie and a blasphemy. And he also insisted that the people did still think these vestments to have some magical effect, so that without them divine service was vain. For these reasons, he said, they ought not to be worn. And when Cranmer, the archbishop, replied, "The vestments are respected by the clergy, and have descended through many generations," he insisted that this respect was not a sufficient warrant in religious matters, and that usage and tradition were not authority. And when it was said, "This is a small matter; what harm can there be in a cape, a surplice, a cap, a tippet?" he retorted: "Albeit they be only dumb rags, yet they be written all over with mass! mass! They be the symbols of Antichrist! They be the scarlet woman's livery!" And he cried, "Avaunt with her badges!" And sooner than put them on, he took imprisonment—first, in his own house, then with the stern archbishop, and finally, in the Fleet Prison, where he lay two months in a cell "with a little grated window in it, and a lone deal table with a bit of bread and a mug of water upon it."

Might we not, on the same grounds, refuse to accept of or sanction sprinkling, and its application to children? We believe and affirm that it is of Romish origin. And we have the authorities of the world with us. A remarkable testimony has recently been given by that eminent and learned scholar of the English Church, and Professor of Church History at Oxford, Dr. Stanley. It occurs in his History of the Eastern Church. Speaking of baptism, as practised in the Eastern Church, Dr. Stanley says: "There can be no question that the original form of baptism—the very meaning of the word—was complete immersion in deep baptismal waters; and that, for at least four centuries, any other form was either unknown, or regarded, unless in the case of dangerous illness, as an exceptional, almost a monstrous case. To this form, the Eastern Church still rigidly adheres, and the most illustrious and venerable portion of it, that of the Byzantine Empire, absolutely repudiates and ignores any other mode of administration as essentially invalid." After making the above statement, Dr. Stanley proceeds to say that the Latin Church *changed* the mode of baptism on its own authority, without even attempting to plead the teachings of Scripture, or primitive usage; and that now the only witness for the scriptural mode of baptism among the Romanists is the church at Milan; and among Protestants, the Baptists.

With authorities like this to sustain us, are we not justified in affirming that sprinkling is from Rome, and in taking up against it the very argument of Hooper as to the surplice? "This practice is one of the inventions of men, and introduced into the church in its corrupt ages. Moreover, it is in imitation of the priesthood—of a dispensation that has passed away." And we surely might add, that "the people, multitudes of them, do still believe that it has some magical effect in it, without which all their services (as to the salvation of their children) are vain." And when it is said to us, "But this practice is respected by the clergy, and has descended through many generations," we might answer, "This is not a sufficient warrant in religious matters; and tradition is not authority." And when it is said, "This is a small matter, only a little water, dropped in a moment from the fingers upon a child's face," we might reply, "Albeit it is only a dumb ceremony, yet it is written all over with Rome! Rome! It is a symbol of Antichrist! It belongs to the scarlet woman's livery! Avaunt with her badges!"

And it is worth mentioning just here, that any branch of Protestantism, marshaling an array of battle against

Rome, can scarce expect success while wearing a conspicuous part of the uniform of that hated power: proofs of which we have seen in the controversy of some champions of Protestantism with Romish ecclesiastics, and which the Romanists themselves have often admitted. Bishop Bailey, of Newark, New Jersey, recently said to a minister of a Pedobaptist denomination: " We Romanists have little to fear from you: the controversy is not between us and you: it is with the Baptists. There are but two parties in the contest, *ourselves and the Baptists.*" This was a frank confession, and we commend it to the consideration of those who speak evil of us. In assailing us, they are committing a greater mistake than when the Union soldiers in the late war several times ignorantly fired upon their own comrades. The Baptists are the very vanguard, the advance line, the assaulting column, in the fight against Rome. Viewed in this light, there is no injustice like that done to the Baptists. When Protestants assail us, they are injuring their best friends and defenders. Could Rome destroy the Baptists, she would hold jubilee, and fix another carnival week in her calendar. What double injustice, then, to us and to themselves, when Protestants would do us harm.

But, treat us as they may, we cannot accept as scriptural a rite of man's appointment. We cannot be parties to an act whereby a divine ordinance is displaced. Nations have their escutcheons, their crests, their monuments, and ensigns. Armies and navies have their shields and banners; and families their badges and coats of arms. Their object is to express and cluster into a close compass some certain qualities or events, giving them resemblance in these devices. And we know what associations gather around these devices, and how sacredly they are regarded, and how proudly they are displayed. Now, baptism is a device, a badge, a coat of arms, so to speak, in Christ's kingdom. It was chosen and appointed by Christ, to express and to cluster into a close compass certain truths and certain events, by means of resemblances—as when the washing in the pure water shows our inward cleansing; or, our being buried in it, and rising from it, our death to sin and rising to a new life; as also (and particularly) the burial and resurrection of our Redeemer. And it is against the expunging of this sacred device that we protest. For this, deem us not "illiberal!" Call it not "narrow-mindedness" when we avow our attachment to the genuine old family badge! Ask the Italians to give up their tri-colored flag, the long-forbidden, green, red, and white! Urge that it is only a few square yards of coarse bunting, and of no value. You know the answer! Then pardon *our* attachment to *this* ancient symbol, invested with associations which touch whatever is deep and tender in the heart. Demand of the Queen of Britain, or of one of her loyal subjects, if you may not pluck away the unicorn or the lion from her national escutcheon, or expunge one of the mottos written there. You know the answer! Then chide us not, if we will restrain the hand that would mar this device of our Sovereign's kingdom! Ask the people of Massachusetts if you may not cast down her monument on Bunker's Hill, or go up and efface some of its inscriptions. You know the answer! Then marvel not if we cry, "Hold! hold!" to those who would demolish this memorial column, or wipe out its record of the conflicts and triumphs of our King. You would honor the American soldier who would sooner receive the sword of the invader in his bosom than exchange uniforms, or see the flag of his country insulted. Honor *our* loyalty, then, who, at some sacrifices now (and more in the ages gone by), would save from affront this old significant symbol of Christian baptism, borne aloft on so many a hard fought field, by men of iron nerve and adamantine faith!

These are our reasons why we can neither give up our identity, nor coalesce with others in church fellowship; which, it may be added, would be found to be, in the end, equivalent to giving up our identity, as observation and a sound logic would show.

Here, then, amid whatever of opposition or misconstruction or reproach, we are called upon patiently to stand as a testimony to the truth. As we understand it, there is no alternative. Nor can the charge of exclusiveness be brought against us. We are the excluded, not the excluding party. If a business firm, or an organization of any kind, be rent by the introduction of new rules and regulations, the innovators, not those who stood by the old rules, are responsible for the division. So here. It cannot be charged that unity is broken by those who stand to the rule, but rather by those who depart from it, or come not up to it. And coming up to the rule, and this alone, will restore it. Unity on the basis of dispensing with the rule, instead of being a unity of subjection to Christ, were a combination against him; an agreement to treat with contempt his laws. The Lord keep us from such unity! Better a thousand times our existing Christian sects, than disloyalty to the truth! And if there are consequences for a time seemingly calamitous, let us remember that God does not ask us to share with him the responsibilities of his government. Our duty is to obey. He will take care of the consequences. If it is his will that there ever shall exist an outward unity in all particulars among his people on earth, he will, in his own good time, indicate the methods of its accomplishment.

Moreover, for our encouragement, let us remember that the church of Christ has always been strongest when most uncompromising. The "Broad Church" project, realizing the idea of a liberal, roomy comprehensiveness, endeavoring to conciliate opposition by making concessions, has always, and in every form, proved a miserable failure. Strength, impregnability, aggressive power—these features of the church have been seen in her, not when her creed has been, like the hatter's conformatory, shaping and fitting itself to everybody's head; not when her pulpit has been ready to produce truth "to order," as the clothier does his garments; not when she has abated her claims and concealed her objectionable features, but when bold, authoritative, absolute, unyielding. It is a proposition capable of being sustained, that just in proportion as the church of Christ, desiring to enlarge her door, to increase her members, and to show herself generous and liberal, has endeavored to put off her exclusiveness, just in that proportion she has put off her power and lost her energy, and, in the end, her influence. Not to go further, what an illustration of this is found in our own denominational history! When young Eugenio Kincaid, now our veteran missionary, went to an old Baptist itinerant preacher to get some book to settle his mind upon the subject of baptism, and the aged man gave him one from his saddlebags, Eugenio thought he had made a mistake, and ventured to say, "Did you not give me the wrong book, sir? I see this is the New Testament." Stretching himself up at full length, and looking Kincaid fairly in the face, the white-haired patriarch sternly said: "Young man! if you want any better book on baptism than the Bible, don't come to me!" It was a representative act. We have been built up by the New Testament. We have grown because we have held it uncompromisingly. How striking the words of the text, as a statement of our denominational experience! Is it too much to believe that the Master had his eye upon us when he uttered them? "I know thy works: behold, I have set before thee an open door, and no man can shut it; for thou hast a little strength, and hast kept my word, and hast not denied my name. Behold, I will make them of the synagogue of Satan, which say they are Jews, and are not, but do lie; behold, I will make them to come and worship before thy feet, and to know that I have loved thee. Because thou hast kept the word of my patience, I also will keep thee from the hour of temptation, which shall come upon all the world, to try them that dwell upon the earth." How has he kept us, amid sharp and long temptations! How has he set before us an open door, which no one has been able to shut! How has he multiplied us, until we have the largest number of communicants of any one Evangelical body in the world! Surely, it has been for this reason (it could have been for none other), that, feeling ourselves possessed of but a little strength, we have yet resolutely clung to and kept the Divine word.

So must it continue, if our future be worthy of the past. We are essentially a reforming body, and hence cannot be popular. Ceasing to be challengers and champions of the truth, it would find other representatives, and leave us behind, as mummies of a buried life, fossilized relics of a heroic race, that was, and is not. Believe me—if true to our mission, we shall yet be hated even of our brethren.* It is better to expect it; and those who are faint-hearted, let them fall out of the ranks. Indeed, it is a sorrowful and humiliating thought that any Baptist can turn his back upon his own churches, and cast himself into the arms of a Pedobaptist church, where his influence is against what he holds to be the truth, and in support of what he believes to be error. But a multitude, praised be God, instead of faltering, will bind reproach to their brow as a shining diadem, and exultingly declare with Paul, "I glory in mine infirmities; for when I am weak, then I am strong!" They will persist in the old habit of demanding a "Thus saith the Lord," and say with Cyprian, the eminent Latin Father of the third century: "God hath testified that we are to do those things that are *written :* whence have you that tradition? If it be in the Gospels or the Epistles, then let us observe it." And with Cyril, of the fourth century: "It behoveth us not to believe the very least thing of the sacred mysteries of faith without the Holy Scriptures. This is the security of our faith, not what is delivered of our own inventions, but what is demonstrated from the Holy Scriptures." And with Jerome, who survived twenty years of the fifth century: "Those things which, without the authorities and testimonies of the Scriptures, men invent of their own heads, as from Apostolic traditions, are smitten of the sword of God." The hearts of growing numbers will thrill with responsive feeling to Luther's brave words, when, upon the Pope's bull of excommunication, they began to burn his books—"Let them destroy my works; I desire nothing better; for all I wanted was to lead Christians to the Bible, that they might afterward throw away my writings. Great God! if we had but a right understanding of the Holy Scriptures, what need would there be of my books?" And to the equally grand utterance of that noble reformer and martyr, Bishop Hooper, before referred to, who did not much care what company he kept, only so he was on the side of truth, declaring, "I had rather follow the *shadow* of Christ, than the *body* of all the general councils or doctors since the death of Christ." "It is mine opinion," he adds, "unto all the world, that the Scriptures solely, and the apostles' church, is to be followed, and no man's authority, be he Tertullian, or even cherubim or seraphim." Men of this high-souled loyalty to revealed truth we welcome to our ranks. Come, and let us be fellow-helpers to the truth. Come, and let us bear the reproach of Jesus. Come, and let us accept and verify what Ronge uttered as a slur, "If Roman Catholics have a Pope at Rome, Protestants have made a Pope of a Book!" Come, and let us gird ourselves for a religious contest, both sure and soon to come, unparalleled since the days of the great reformation, between Inspiration only, and Inspiration with "church liberty" and tradition. Come, and let us make yet more formidable Rome's acknowledged foe. Come, and let us combine, with higher aims and a holier and deeper enthusiasm, to justify the Baptist position, and to pioneer the way of all the churches up to that point where shall be solved what Schenkel terms "The Protestant church problem, namely, to incorporate the particular churches into the one true church—and so to *identify the church of the believing with the church of the baptized.*" Nor can the issue be doubtful: for, in the language of Hubmeyer, that learned and eloquent Baptist reformer and martyr, whose voice comes sounding down to us through almost four centuries—" Divine truth is immortal; it may, perhaps, for long, be bound, scourged, crucified, and, for a season, be entombed in the grave; but, on the third day, it will rise again victorious, and rule triumphant forever."

III.
THE SPIRITUAL CONSTITUTION OF THE CHRISTIAN CHURCH.

By REV. C. B. CRANE,
Pastor of South Baptist Church, Hartford, Conn.

"IN WHOM ALL THE BUILDING, FITLY FRAMED TOGETHER, GROWETH UNTO A HOLY TEMPLE IN THE LORD: IN WHOM YE ALSO ARE BUILDED TOGETHER FOR A HABITATION OF GOD THROUGH THE SPIRIT."—*Ephesians* ii. 21, 22.

I HAVE selected the text as the point of departure for the discussion of the *Scriptural* idea of the *Spiritual Constitution of the Christian Church.*

For the development of this idea, I shall pursue two distinct lines of argument: *first*, concentrating upon it the light of divine and verbal inspiration; and *secondly*, showing the natural and necessary gravitation of the idea toward certain fundamental and cardinal doctrines of Scripture, which, in turn, verify the correctness of it.

I. *First*, then, the *Scriptural* argument for the *Constitution of the Church.*

It may help us in the prosecution of this argument, to bear in mind that the church as an organization, in the Bible use of the term, refers both to the local church as the elementary unit, and, in a more indirect and inferential way, to the universal church as the complex unit. There is also a wider use of the term, which, leaving out the idea of organization, contemplates the entire community of Christian believers, perpetuated through all the centuries of time into the illimitable range of eternity, as the church of Christ.

This last meaning of the term, as being incompatible with the idea of formal constitution and organization, does not enter within the scope of our investigation. We have to do solely with the local church as an elementary unit, and the universal church as an organic and complex unit.

It is a very fixed habit of Baptists, offended at the mechanical and artificial ecclesiastical unity which has been constructed by other Christian denominations, and much in love with the mutual independency of their own separate societies, to repudiate the name of church as applied to their entire body, and to affix it to their local communities alone. They do not seem to consider that a unit which abideth alone, and is incapable of entering organically into a larger unit, is a dead unit, like fruitless and non-working faith; that life always tends toward wider organization. They forget that Nature, on every hand, furnishes specimens of broad unities, which are in no respect incompatible with the completeness and independence of the lesser constituent units. And we may discover, before we have finished our discussion, that, without contemplating mechanical and artificial organization, it is equally correct to style the entire body of spiritual commonwealths, and the local community, the church; that with equal propriety we may speak of the Baptist churches and the Baptist church as being synonymous terms.

Meantime, so homogeneous are the lesser and greater units, so identical except in magnitude, that they will stand to each other in the relation of the microcosm to the macrocosm; so that whatever Scriptures apply to the one, will apply with equal pertinency to the other.

Thus much being premised in the way of preparation for the intelligent and easy handling of our argument, let us proceed to the examination of the more salient and expressive passages of inspired Scripture, which look toward the true idea of the constitution of the Christian church.

The text teaches distinctly, that the structural unity of the family of God, the organized body of Christians, the spiritual temple, is in Jesus Christ,—"in whom all the building is fitly framed together." By virtue of this fact, we call our ecclesiastical superstructure the "church of Christ," or the "Christian church," repudiating all such pseudo-philanthropic and *ad captandum* designations as "liberal church," and "broad church;" and even using with reluctance the cognomen, "Baptist church," as forced upon us by the necessities of a polemic theology, and not voluntarily assumed by ourselves.

Immediately, upon this declaration of a structural ecclesiastical unity in Christ, we are confronted by the question, rising out from a prevalent theory and polity, which are widely different from our own: Is this unity merely in the outward and objective work of atonement which Christ has accomplished in the midst of humanity, and in behalf of it? or does it consist in the actual communion, as between the entire church and Christ, of the spirit and life of Christ? In other words: May inwardly unregenerate, merely sacramentally regenerate, persons be mortised into the structural church, by virtue of the general and formal redemptive work of Christ, with hope that they shall subsequently be brought, through inward regeneration, into the fellowship of the mind and will of Christ? or must each member of the church be entered into it, because he is actually and essentially born of God, and spiritually in him who by the Holy Spirit is every where present in the ecclesiastical organism?

This question is not merely a speculative one, a bar or ring for the gymnastic exercise of the limber theologian; but is of the utmost practical importance. For, whatever may be the mutual contradictions of other religious denominations than our own, they are all united, though differing in intrepidity of statement and in methods of argument, in the defence of the thesis that, by reason of what Christ has done in the respect of a formal and objective atonement, unregenerate persons may be more or less closely organized into the Christian church. We cannot, therefore, avoid the consideration and answering of this question. It lies at our threshold, and must be disposed of in the initiative of all our polemic sorties.

Meantime, in our reply from a Scriptural standing-point to the interrogation, Whether the structural unity of the church in Christ allows the introduction into it of the unregenerate, or only of the regenerate:. we shall arrive at once at the announcement and the evidence of our theory of the constitution of the church.

Observe, then, I pray you, that other Scriptural statements and figures than are found in the text, teach distinctly and exclusively the actual regeneracy of all who compose the Christian church.

Take, for instance, the similitude of the vine and its branches, a first-hand announcement from Christ himself of the doctrine which we are discussing. If this symbol indicates any thing, it is the actual participation, by the entire membership of the church, of the Christly life. As every branch is developed out from the vine, not beginning to be till it begins in the life of the vine, so every true member of Christ's mystical organism is developed out from that organism, and has the beginning of its condition of membership in his essential and communicated life. There is no provision here for grafting, for insertion of something that is dead into that which is alive, in hope that it may be made alive; but the whole course of thought implies the germination and development from the life of Christ, of the entire membership of the church. True, Paul, in the Epistle to the Romans, while commenting upon the rejection of Christ by the Jews and his acceptance by the Gentiles, makes allusion to the horticultural symbol of grafting; but his entire argument implies that he intends merely the temporary substitution of one race for another in the gracious purpose of God, and that he does not even remotely intend the constitution of the church.

Indeed, in the similitude of the vine and the branches, Christ distinctly teaches that when a man, upon any theory whatever, claims to belong to the mystical vine, and does not, meanwhile, share the life of the vine, he is to be thrust out even from his nominal claim, and cut off. Unregeneracy is a bar of church membership.

Notice, again, that the structural and regenerate unity of the church in Christ is set forth with equal distinctness in the symbol of the body, which is used so frequently by the apostle Paul, and which gave rise to the doctrine of the "mystical body" of the elder theologians. Looking from an objective point of view at the operation of the joining of an individual to the body of Christ, the apostle declares: "For by one Spirit are we all baptized into one body, . . . and have been all made to drink into one Spirit." And since the baptism by water is the emblem of inward regeneration by the Spirit, this passage teaches, when divested of its emblematic imagery, that every member of the church, which is the body of Christ, is regenerated into it.

Yet it is plain that all the analogies which this symbol of the body suggests, indicate that regeneration is not into the body, but out from it; that all the members of it have their original life from the organic life of it; that they are not mechanically added to it like legs of wood and hands of steel, in the hope that they may afterward receive the life of it; but Christ, the living Head, creates and develops them out from his own essential life. They do not exist at all, in the respect of their new relations and condition, till they are thus formed by him, and developed. Thus, every true member of the church is at once the product and the receptacle of the life of the church; and he is not by the sacraments of baptism and the Lord's Supper joined to the church, but receives them rather as signs of his being already a sharer of the life which the members all receive from their living head, and hence, as being already interiorly and organically members of his body.

Notice, again, that every true member of the church is declared by the word of inspiration to be himself a "temple of the Holy Ghost," indwelt of that detergent personality, whose office it is successively to regenerate and sanctify, and glorify the nature of the believer.

The same thought, with a different form and color of imagery, is expressed in the figure of living or "lively stones," by which the exclusively regenerate character of the membership of the church is not merely indicated, but is also positively taught. Every member is a living stone; through which, courses and pulses the divine vitality, dilating it, working the disintegrating power of sin out of it, toning up and conserving its organization, bringing it forward to divineness.

Now, by virtue of this *fellowship* in the Christly life of all the parts of the temple, the whole temple groweth toward symmetry and largeness of perfection. It groweth, and is not builded, by reason of the constitution of the entire membership in a living organism.

But if there are mere mechanically, or, what is the same thing, sacramentally, added parts to it, which cannot, in the very nature of things, share the common life of it, the temple will increase unsymmetrically, and become in its ugly disproportionateness the scandal of both reason and faith. Either the living members, to revert to the symbol of the body, will grow into an undue preponderance over the legs of wood and hands of steel; or these added members will be artificially magnified, and be brought into the condition of overmuchness. Indeed, since these latter do not grow at all —cannot grow in fact—there will be such anxious contriving to enlarge them, that they will be exaggerated into a grotesque outline and contour, and thus give a false and unlovely seeming to the entire body, bringing it into disrepute, doing for it what is done by dead flies for the potted ointment of the apothecary.

Thus the apparently innocuous operation of joining infants by the sacrament of holy baptism to the church—even though, by reason of an evangelicity of sentiment which could not be wholly abandoned at once, they were so remotely joined as not to be esteemed in the ecclesiastical membership at all—led forward in one direction, by virtue of the exigent force of logic and philosophy, to the heresies of infant church membership and baptismal regeneration, and thence to all the stupendous falsehoods which germinally abide in those dogmas; and in another direction, as in the case of the New England Pedobaptistic polity, to the notorious "half-way covenant," which plunged scores of churches into the turbulent current of the Unitarian apostasy.

The symmetrical growth of the "holy temple" of the church requires as its invariable condition the regeneracy and spirituality of all its members, the exclusive entrance into its superstructure of living stones; and when this condition is violated, in theory or in practice, there is lack of proportion and a departure of comeliness.

Emerging now from our Scriptural argument, we find ourselves possessed of the result of it, to wit: that the *true idea of the constitution of the church requires*, *and consists in, an organic union of Christian believers, an exclusively regenerate membership.* This is the *Baptistic idea*, basilar and central in our creed, emblazoned upon our banners, organized into our life.

Meantime, fairness requires that I admit that other than Baptist churches verbally announce the same doctrine. Dr. Hodge, the eminent exponent of the Presbyterian theology, expressly declares that the Sacraments (which are the signs of the structural unity of the church) belong only to believers. Yet the Presbyterian church, in its practice of infant baptism, organizes unregenerate persons more or less closely into its superstructure.

Dr. Lyman Beecher, one of the most eminent representatives of New England Congregationalism, in his discourse on "the Design, Rights, and Duties of Local Churches," lays down the following propositions, which I give in his own words: "The requisite qualifications for membership in a church of Christ, *are personal holiness in the sight of God, and a credible profession of holiness before men.* * * * The commission given by our Saviour to his apostles at his ascension directs them, first to make disciples, and then to baptize them, inculcating universal obedience. * * * A regularly ordained ministry, an orthodox creed, and devout forms of worship, cannot constitute a church of Christ, *without personal holiness in the members.*"

The Rev. Charles Beecher, the compiler of the so-called autobiography of his father, writes and prints as follows: "According to the primitive Puritan faith, a local church is not a voluntary association on purely human principles, but a divine family, a household of children spiritually born of God, heirs of God, and joint heirs with Christ. * * * God creates the church by creating the spiritual children who are *ipso facto* its members. True sonship to God constitutes membership in the visible church, as really as natural birth in the natural family. All that the local church can do, according to this view, is to recognize as members, on suitable evidence, those who are such by birth divine." Yet the Congregational church organizes into itself, by the administration of what it is pleased to name Christian baptism, unregenerate infants. Says Dr. Bushnell, "All those classes of Christian disciples who practice infant baptism conceive it, of course, to have a certain common character with adult baptism, and so to create a supposed, or somehow supposable, membership in the church."

Meantime, advanced and logical thinkers, like the eminent preacher and author whose words I have just quoted, proceeding from the fact of infant baptism, and in some instances, implying a sacramental, or earlier congenital, regeneration of those who are the subjects of it, demand that they be acknowledged as entered into the membership of the church.

Said a scholarly and distinguished minister in a council of Congregational churches, at which I chanced to be present: "If you deny the church membership of baptized infants, your Baptist brethren have you on the hip." The baptism of infants, even in accordance with the most evangelical Congregational theory, conducts to the doctrine of a membership in the church of those who are thus baptized.

In the articles of faith of the Methodist Episcopal Church, I read that "the visible church of Christ, is a congregation of faithful (in the Scriptural sense, regenerate) men." Yet, while affirming baptism to be the sign, either of a profession of Christian faith, or of regeneration, the creed of this church declares that "the baptism of young children is to be retained in the church." And since the infant subjects of baptism have no faith to profess, the ordinance must signify as concerning them

—if it signifies any thing—either a regeneration by it accomplished, or a congenital holiness which is equivalent to regeneration. Indeed, Dr. Whedon, one of the most accomplished thinkers of the church, declares, if I correctly understand him, that infants are to be baptized, because by virtue of the general atoning work of Christ, they are born into a condition of holiness. Logically consequent upon this, of course, is the church membership of baptized infants.

The Protestant Episcopal Church in its articles of faith declares the "visible church to be a congregation of faithful (Scripturally, regenerate) men." Yet, by the baptism of infants, and even of manifestly unconverted adults, it admits them into the membership of the church, according to the formula in the office of baptism: "Seeing now, dearly beloved brethren, that this child, or this person, is regenerate, and grafted into the body of Christ's church." Meantime, though affirming the doctrine of baptismal regeneration, yet, when pressed by the Baptistic polemics, it is often forced to admit, that such regeneration does not mean a real and spiritual renewal, but only a change of the outward relations of the one baptized, with the hope and expectation that it will lead forward to a correspondent inward change.

The fact is that the application of the initial ordinance of the church to any person whatever, logically contemplates the church membership of that person. And when Dr. Bushnell demands this on the ground of the propagated character of the believing parent to the child; and Dr. Whedon demands it on the ground of the inborn holiness of all infants; and the Episcopal divines demand it on the ground of the regenerative efficacy of baptism; they do all pass forward in logical procedure from the Pedo-baptistic premises to the inevitable conclusion.

And I confess to you, that when I reflect how irresponsible and unconsenting the infant subjects of baptism are, I am conscious that, if I accepted such a procedure of logic, a necessity would be laid upon me to advance to a conclusion more nearly ultimate, enlarging the boundaries of the church till they included the whole humanity. I would go forward till I stood with the eloquent and fascinating Charles Kingsley, according to whom, the church is the world in a certain aspect. Says Rev. J. H. Rigg, in his "Modern Anglican Theology," giving Kingsley's theory of the church: "the world is called the church, when it recognizes its relation to God in Christ, and acts accordingly. The church is the world, lifting itself up into the sunshine; the world is the church, falling into shadow and darkness. When and where the light and life that are in the world break out into bright, or noble, or holy word or deed, then and there the world shows that the nature and glory of the church live within it. Every man of the world is not only potentially, but virtually, a member of Christ's church, whatever may, for the present, be his character or seeming. Like the colors in shot silk, or in a dove's neck, the difference of hue and denomination depends merely upon the degree of light, and the angle of vision. In conformity with this principle, Mr. Kingsley's theology altogether secularizes the kingdom of Christ." That is to say, Kingsley speaks the last word of the syllogism, whose first word falls upon our ears from ten thousand lips all around.

I am bold, therefore, to declare, since I deny inborn and hereditary holiness and baptismal regeneration, that all other churches than our own, according to their own confused and often contradictory declarations, comprise in their membership mixed regenerate and unregenerate elements.

It follows, that the Baptist church, if its practice correspond with its theory, is a fabric with a selvaged edge of regeneracy, separate from the world, the well-defined body of divine truth and life: while the Pedo-baptistic church is a fabric with a ravelled edge, organically united by its unregenerate membership with the unregenerate world, not the well-defined body of divine truth and life.

The true idea of the constitution of the church of Christ, then, being that of an organized society of Christian believers, I pass to say,

II. Secondly, that this idea gravitates naturally and necessarily toward the recognition and practice of important and cardinal doctrines of Scripture, which in turn verify the divine truthfulness of it; while the idea, which is the more or less pronounced contradiction of this, gravitates toward dogmas which are the polar opposites of those doctrines.

(*a.*) *First*, then, this idea gravitates toward such a conception of the doctrine of *regeneration* as makes it exclusively a radical and interior change of the nature, solely in consequence of which, it is proper for the regenerate to enter into a sacramental relation with the church. It requires that a man be born of God, be set loose from the dominance of sin, be made a partaker of the divine nature, be in purpose and character a true disciple of Christ, as the precedent condition of entering into the organized Christian membership. It withholds from him the sacraments of baptism, and the Lord's Supper, till he be interiorly a new creature. The administration of these ordinances does not contemplate him as a sinner, but only as a saint. Spiritual fitness in him is the sole ground of his reception of them. And when this fitness is produced by the operation of the Holy Ghost, then the ordinances of the church are administered to him as the signs and tokens of it.

Thus does the Baptistic idea of the constitution of the

church, by a necessity of its own nature, contemplate regeneration as an inward and radical thing, as a thing essential to an entrance into ecclesiastical relations, as a primal and all-important thing; and thus does it guard and conserve it in its true import and purity. It sets aside the fact of incorporation into the visible body of Christ, by the sacraments of baptism and the Lord's Supper, as being no sufficient evidence of discipleship; and resting the evidence solely upon a condition of spiritual regeneration, as revealed in character and life, at once exalts regeneration into due pre-eminence, and tends toward the development and culture of inward piety.

The ecclesiastical system, on the other hand, which admits unregenerate persons into relations which imply regeneracy, even though it be with the hope that they may thereby be brought forward into the regenerate condition, is not merely unphilosophical as well as unscriptural, but it also tends to the making dangerously overmuch of the merely outward change of relations. If it be the all-important thing to be entered into the body of Christ's church by the dripping of baptismal waters— falsely so called—from priestly fingers, then, not to have been thus entered into the church, is to remain in a most unpromising and forlorn condition. Hence, it is no strange thing that the rigid logicians of the establishment of the apostolic succession can offer no assured promise of salvation to unbaptized infants and dissenting Christians, leaving them all with generous sadness to the uncovenanted mercies of God. The sacramental, and not the ante- or post-sacramental regeneration, is the thing most eminent in thought and faith. Indeed, since to those who are thus, consciously or unconsciously, made the subjects of baptism and outwardly regenerated, all the best names which can belong to the ripest saint are accorded, such as "regenerate children," "sons of God," "disciples of Christ," "dearly beloved and holy brethren;" and since there are no new names to be accorded after the contemplated inward change is effected, there is possible, and even realized danger that such inward change will be deemed an unimportant, if not a visionary thing.

Hence, the tendency of this false idea of the constitution of the church is toward the corrupting and denial of the doctrine of spiritual regeneration, and toward merely formal religion instead of inward and genuine piety.

(b.) *Secondly*, the theory of an exclusively regenerate membership of the church, whereby all who compose it are on terms of spiritual equality, looks toward a *democratic ecclesiastical polity*, in the operating of which, and by its reflex influence, there is attainment to manliness and womanliness in the religious, as well as in the social and political spheres. Monarchy and aristocracy, according to Neander, do not harmonize with the spirit of Christianity. The in-dwelling in all, of the divine Spirit, is the enfranchisement of all; for "where the Spirit of the Lord is, there is liberty;" "the truth shall make you free;" "if the Son, therefore, shall make you free, ye shall be free indeed." And the condition of enfranchisement is, under God, the condition of self-government. Hence, since the entire membership of the church is lifted into the plane of a divine freedom, and is subject only to Christ, it is endowed with autocracy; in its totality it elects and deposes its officers, determines all its methods of procedure, augments or diminishes its numbers by the exercise of its discipline. It projects no select guild or order of men above itself for its sovereign control, nor does it accept the imposition upon itself, from any source whatever, of such a sovereign guild.

We are learning, in these last days, that if we would

make a *man* of a human being, we must lay responsibility upon him; endow him with the right of self-control; admit him to the handling of august and sacred things; thrust him into the fellowship of legislative and administrative work. And in the kingdom of Christ, where is neither Greek nor Jew, bond nor free, male nor female, we are to respect, in the matter of liberty and co-ordinate authority, no distinctions of caste, or age, or sex.

Accepting, as Baptists have done, this divinely appointed constitution of the church, there has been produced among them so much freedom and personal independence, and common responsibility in ecclesiastical administration, that you find nowhere else such dignity and intelligence in the conduct of religious enterprises.

And it is a matter of history, that such men as Jefferson and Bancroft have discovered in the Baptistic polity the principles which should be organized into a free and democratic political superstructure.

True, this autocracy, under Christ, of the entire Christian membership, will sometimes lead to excesses. Majorities will not always be wise; liberty will, not unfrequently, develop into anarchy; men of iron will and capacity of control will develop from their fronts the unlovely garniture of horns. But better the extravagances of liberty than the unmanliness of servility; better the overmuch assumption of responsibility than the tame repudiation of it; better the occasional wild curvettings of freedom than the heavy clanking of chains; better the too high leap than the crushing of an iron heel. The force of gravitation is untiring. It is easier to curb a swift horse than to quicken a slow one. It is easier to tone down than to tone up, to repress than to elevate. And so liberty and self-government, shared by all, are good; and the Baptistic idea of church constitution gravitates toward them irresistibly.

But in the theory of the mixture of regenerate and unregenerate elements in the Christain membership, the latter dragging the former below the plane of spiritual freedom and a legitimate autocracy, a sovereign guild must, in some way, be introduced, naturally priestly or episcopal in its character, which shall govern the heterogeneous masses who are incompetent for self-government. And thus is developed among them, as arising from the withholding from them of just responsibility, an indifference toward ecclesiastical matters, an ignorance of them, sometimes an offensive bigotry concerning them, and a habit of progress by leading-strings, which is inconsistent with manly and intelligent independence with respect to the supreme concerns of religion.

(*c.*) *Thirdly*, the theory of an exclusively regenerate membership of the church makes the church, *in its totality, the witness, and embodiment, and representative of the truth.* In scriptural language, "*the pillar and ground of the truth.*" It is this, not because its creed is true, not because its sacraments are such as were appointed by Christ, not because it has the proper order of ministries —for the grossest heresies and the most pronounced worldliness are historically compatible with these—but because of its entire regeneracy; because, in its character and life, truth is displayed; because it is exclusively composed of those who are, by virtue of the indwelling of Christ, his epistles, known and read of all men.

Meantime, it should be considered, the witnessing of Christ and truth by the church is not to be confined to the temples where doctrine is preached and the ordinances are administered, nor yet to the fortunate few who may happen to hold its creed in their hands; but it is to be a universal testimony, on every street, in every family, in

Spiritual Constitution of the Church.

every shop, on every river and sea, in every place where a member and representative of the church may go or tarry. And this testimony, demanded, without exception, of all, consists, not in a verbal declaration of truth, but in the shining forth of it from a regenerate character and life.

The Baptistic idea of the constitution of the church provides for this, and by virtue of such providence the church becomes the "pillar and ground of the truth."

But the opposite idea, allowing the mixture of regenerate and unregenerate elements in the church, precludes the possibility of this universal witnessing; since they who are not shaped to truth cannot reveal its fair proportions, since they who are not made alive by it cannot manifest the life which abides in it.

(*d.*) *Fourthly*, the theory of an exclusively regenerate membership makes the *whole church a priesthood*. Thus are all Christians to "present their bodies a living sacrifice unto God;" thus are they all of the "royal priesthood;" thus are they all "kings and priests unto God." And the whole course of the Epistle to the Hebrews is determined by this grand idea of the priesthood of the entire Christian commonwealth. They are to consecrate themselves; they are to consecrate their children; they are to consecrate their possessions; they are to consecrate time and talents—all to God. They are to lift their lives thank-offerings to heaven; they are to get close to the ear and heart of God, all of them in their own proper persons; they are to offer fervent, effectual, intercessory prayer to the living God, on behalf of a dead humanity; they are to bear the names of those for whom they plead, graven, not upon onyx-stones, which rest in ouches of gold upon priestly shoulders, but upon their hearts, which pulsate with a divine solicitude. The vail which separated the Holy of Holies from the outer court is forever rent; and every member of the church, by virtue of his priestly character, is summoned to the altar and the mercy-seat. Thus does the Baptistic idea of the constitution of the church gravitate with singular energy toward the doctrine of the essential priesthood of the entire church.

By virtue of this priesthood, the entire church is ordained and consecrated to missionary and evangelical work. The advancing of the divine kingdom, the diffusion of the gospel among the heathen, the bearing of the glad tidings to neglected communities and neighborhoods in Christendom, is to be the duty, not of a "select class of Christians alone, but the most immediate concern of every individual." Since men are to be subdued to Christ by being inwardly changed, and not by being merely brought into sacramental relations with the church, the redemption is to be accomplished by the power of God, bestowed in answer to prayer, and in connection with earnest labor, and the power of a divinely inspired human influence. Hence in all Baptistic efforts for church extension, minister and laymen go forth together, share the prayers and exhortations, assume the common office of leading sinners to Christ, become a blazing fire to communicate their own flame.

But the Pedo-Baptistic idea, sometimes unconsciously, as often consciously, on the part of those who accept it, blindly gropes after a special holy guild, holier than the totality of the mixed regenerate and unregenerate Christian membership, which shall get into the more immediate presence of God, mediate between God, on the one hand, and church and world on the other, and become the channel for the conducting of the influences of heaven to the earth. Indeed, the natural consequence of such an outward projection of the divine kingdom as is accomplished by a merely sacramental construction of it, is a select

Spiritual Constitution of the Church.   79

and priestly order, in some real sense separate from the church, and above it.

This tendency is illustrated, even in the most evangelical Pedo-Baptistic churches, by the fact of the non-membership of the pastor in the church which he serves, of his peculiar relations with the Presbytery, of his amenableness solely to the jurisdiction of his clerical peers and their associate ruling elders.

The tendency is more marked and pronounced in the establishment of the apostolic succession, partly by virtue of which succession, partly by virtue of the incompetency of a mixed ecclesiastical membership to approach in its totality close to God, an order of ministry is created, to which the title of priesthood is intrepidly applied. The exclusive assumption of priestly offices by this select guild is the explicit denial of them to the entire laic membership. And so all the fine passages of Scripture which concede an essential priesthood to the whole church are virtually blotted out from the canon of inspiration. Yet this clerical order is not slow to arrogate to itself the priestly functions. It styles itself a priesthood; it kneels at altars; it secludes itself within chancels; it symbolizes its intercessory office by the fashion of its vestments; it communicates regenerative power by the touch of its dripping fingers; it pronounces absolution to the penitent; and, in the persons of those who have followed a pernicious logic to its conclusion, it awaits auricular confession from those whom it shall declare absolved from sin.

Yet the rectoral priesthood, august though it be, comes not immediately into vicarious and intercessory relations with Christ, the great head of the church; but derives the plentitude of its authority and communicable grace from a more exalted priestly order, perpetuated through an apostolic succession which was not broken nor vitiated in the protracted debauchery of Papal idolatry.

Why should there be a pause at the episcopate? "The aristocratic constitution," according to Neander, "will ever find it easy, by various gradual changes, to pass over to the monarchical." Why shall not bishoprics find their unity in archbishoprics, as is the fact in England, and the pronounced tendency in America? And why shall not archbishoprics find their unity in the Papacy, with a successor of Peter, a vicar of Christ, linking the entire church to God? Logic is logic; and let it be no occasion of wonder that Protestant priests and bishops, by the stress of it, find a home at last, and their instinct of completeness gratified, in the bosom of the Church of Rome —a temporary home, alas! since against the hoary and tottering structure the artillery of heaven is being trained for its stupendous overthrow.

A little while ago, I said that the Baptistic idea of the constitution of the church, making the whole church a priesthood, ordains and consecrates the entire Christian membership to evangelical and missionary work.

The Pedo-Baptistic idea, on the other hand, when logically developed, by its appointment of a special priesthood, limits the evangelical and missionary work to that priesthood. Since the church is to lengthen its cords and strengthen its stakes by the sacramental joining to it of those who are without, it needs but the priest with his font, and the bishop with his holy hands of confirmation, to institute the requisite relations between the consenting men and the holy body of Christ. Forth from the bosom of the laic membership no zealous saints are summoned, that they may plead in gentle entreaties with sinners, and lift them in the grasp of their strong prayers to God. The church, in the totality of its membership, is thus virtually excluded from personal effort for the advancement of the divine kingdom in the world.

Thus must we say, that to the Baptistic idea of the

constitution of the church, the conception of any thing else than a universal priesthood is totally alien. From the Pedo-Baptistic idea, the conception of a select priesthood proceeds in the way of natural generation.

(*e.*) *Fifthly*, and finally, the theory of an exclusively regenerate membership points toward a natural organization of all the local churches into a larger unit, which may properly be denominated "the church." This organization is not outward; it is not artificial and mechanical; it does not require presbyteries, and synods, and assemblies, and conferences; it does not require bishops, and archbishops, and popes;—but it is subjective; it rests upon an identity of spiritual consciousness; it is produced by the regenerate perception, in the entire brotherhood, of the will and authority of Christ, in whom the grand superstructure is organized, and by whom it is controlled. The unity is like that of beech trees in the beech, of men in man—a unity of fellowship of faith, and sentiment, and life; implying reciprocity between all the elementary units; providing a denominational investiture of ministerial functions for the teacher whom the local church would call to ordination; providing a denominational literature; providing facilities for denominational work; providing methods of interchange of membership between local churches.

And yet the unity has no smack of artifice or mechanics; it is a unity of faith and love—a unity in Christ. And it is all the firmer and closer, because it is so divinely voluntary and free. Each local church is united with all the others in strong bonds of obligation, yielding allegiance, and demanding allegiance; supervising them, and accepting their supervision; making claims, and acknowledging claims; judging, and being judged; counseling, and being counseled; but the strength of the bond is love.

And it is a singular and impressive fact, that local Baptist churches—revolving independently about their own centres; acknowledging no synodical, or conferential, or episcopal control; and taught of Christ by the spiritual insight of a regenerate membership—have attained to a wonderful unanimity of doctrine and polity; have become organized into a true and natural unit. If there is any denomination of Christians in the world that can claim to be, according to all the analogies of nature, a *church*, it is the Baptist denomination.

But an ecclesiastical society which admits an unregenerate element into its membership, cannot, in the nature of things, obtain or retain a unity of inward and spiritual consciousness, such as is produced by a regenerate perception of the will and authority of Christ; and if it strives after organization with sister societies, the organization must be, according to principles already suggested, more or less, hierarchichal, and artificial, and mechanical.

But it is more than time that I arrest the discussion to which you have listened with so kindly patience.

I have proposed the thesis that the true idea of the spiritual constitution of the church requires, and consists in, an organic union of Christian believers, an exclusively regenerate membership.

I have developed and vindicated this idea, *first*, by concentrating upon it the light of divine and verbal inspiration; and *secondly*, by showing the natural and necessary gravitation of it toward certain fundamental and cardinal doctrines of Scripture, which, in turn, verify its correctness. Did your patience permit, I might show you that, since all the doctrines of our holy religion are correlative, this central idea of our church creed and life gravitates toward them all—toward the doctrines of an inspired and infallible Scripture, the fall of man, the

Spiritual Constitution of the Church. 83

power of Christ upon character, justification by faith, sanctification by the Spirit, the divine purpose of grace, the perseverance of the saints.

But it is enough that I have shown you the tendency, without tarrying to elaborate its manifest developments.

This idea of the spiritual constitution of the church is central in all just theology and ecclesiastical polity. Deny it, corrupt it, thrust it from the centre, and all symmetry of system and organism depart.

How grand and august must be our conception of a church whose character is determined, and whose prosperity is augmented, by this divine and beautiful idea! How must such a church fulfill all the conditions which are requisite, in order that it may be, in the broad, blind, groaning, wicked world, the "pillar and ground of the truth!" How should you and I stand for that matchless idea, and labor to bring it forward toward realization, even though it be at the expense of sacrifice which impoverishes us, and of toil which saps our strength and abridges the term of our lives! How supremely proud we should be, how highly honored we should esteem ourselves, that we are permitted to be, through heavenly enlightenment, the champions of that idea!

We alone have conceived, and are striving for the realization of this lofty and incomparable idea of the Lord's church in the world. We alone demand that only they shall be admitted into its fellowship who have been born again by the regenerating power of the Holy Ghost.

With us, no witless babes are brought in the sweet arms of motherhood, no prattling children trip wonderingly to the marble font, that, by the falling dews of an unreal baptism, they may be introduced into an unreal household of faith.

With us, the Christian church is no merely organized means of grace, into which carnal men may be received by the drippings of priestly fingers, and by the confirmation of prelatic hands, in order that they may perchance be brought forward into the inheritance and practice of holiness.

At our gates stand more exacting wardens, who look for the sign-manual of Jesus upon the foreheads of those who would be admitted into the fellowship of the saints.

So would we, by all loving, and laborious, and patient fidelity to our idea, build up the holy church, the spiritual temple, of those whom love and salvation of God have blessed.

We would demand its acceptance by the ecclesiastical societies which reject it. We would make our characters and lives eloquent with it. And we would so extend our divine commonwealth, that when it embraced the whole humanity, the whole humanity should be holy—no unrepentant rebel, no unassoiled traitor, reconstructed into the sublime realization of the ideal celestial republic.

IV.

BAPTISM.

By REV. G. D. B. PEPPER,
Professor in Newton Theological Institution.

* * * "ONE BAPTISM."—*Ephesians* iv. 5.

"GOD is a spirit, and they that worship him must worship him in spirit and in truth."

These words express the pre-eminent spirituality of the Christian religion. It does not consist in forms and ceremonies, and the soul that has experienced its divine power can never submit to the bondage of mere ritualism. To speak in defence of such bondage is to war against the Holy Spirit.

But to me it has fallen to address you concerning the rite known as baptism. And is not baptism an externality? It is, and is not. It is; but it is also more. It is an externality, as human language is. The words which we utter—what are they but vibrations in the air, caused by certain movements of the vocal organs? These words written—what are they but forms traced in ink upon paper for the eye? The highest attainment of language in discourse—is it any thing more than combinations of these words? Is not language, then, an externality? What is it in our galleries of art which draws to them the sons of genius and the daughters of taste, and there holds them charmed and enchained? Do you say it is the pictures and statues, creations of immortal mind? But what are pictures but paint upon canvas? And what are statues but marble quarried and chiseled? And surely paint and marble are external and material things. Many a strong man in our army during the last four years, in hours of crisis and encounter, has been thrilled with intensest enthusiasm as his eyes have seen, waving above the embattled host and moving toward the rebel array, a certain old, familiar, starred and striped flag—and in that inspiration has been a courage which mocked at fear and courted death. There is no American heart which has not shared this noble enthusiasm, within which the sight and even thought of our flag has not kindled a glow of patriotic emotion, and wakened all its latent poetry. But that flag, lauded, loved, and sung—what is it but a piece of bunting, red, white, and blue? Far enough that, surely, from the spiritual. Language an externality! Yes, save when charged and vitalized with human thought and human emotion. Then it is life and spirit. The statue and the painting, when embodying grand ideals, have ceased to be material. Our flag, as symbol of national character, national history, national all, is no longer a piece of bunting, but a glory, almost a protecting divinity. Baptism, which, viewed in one way, is baldly outward, a mere rite and ceremony, viewed otherwise, and truly, is at once a language intensely charged with God's richest thought and sweetest affection; an incarnation of our Redeemer's fondest, brightest ideal; and the symbol of all that makes existence glorious. We are not, therefore, led away from the central, moving realities of our holy religion by a discussion of baptism. We rather stand for an hour in the presence of that form which best reveals to the eye those realities, and most naturally and effectually leads to them our spirits. Most unbecoming, therefore, would be an apology for speaking to you upon baptism. Most unjust to you would be the suspicion that you would not listen with closest attention to whatever would place the subject in its true light.

I have already indicated, that we may use the term baptism in a broader sense, and in a more limited sense. The latter includes only that which goes to constitute the external rite. But this purely external rite, whatever it may or may not be, has its design, and there is a spirit befitting its observance. This design and this spirit may not be absent from the rite, for without these it is null. Our government has prescribed an oath of allegiance, to be taken by certain persons. It is plainly essential to the complete idea of the oath, both that the prescribed form be used, and that it be used for the one express purpose of avowing loyalty, in all good faith and honesty. The form, or external act, required by the government, may, in a restricted sense, be called the oath. It is, indeed, a part, and an essential part. But as merely external, it is the body. There is needed, also, the inspiring soul—the indwelling life. So baptism has its body and its soul. Baptism, in its fullness, is not body only—is not soul only; but it *is body and soul, soul in body, body informed by soul.* Now, both in thought and in fact, these two can be separated. We can conceive of the outward by itself, and it is the outward which we are now to discuss. In this discussion it must be assumed, that Christ's appointments are of divine authority. To this principle we hold fast throughout.

1. My first proposition is, that Christ instituted for his disciples an external rite called baptism.

The first meaning of the word institute, as given by Webster, is "to establish, to appoint, to enact, to form and prescribe: as to institute laws; to institute rules and regulations." The idea is two-fold. It is that of both appointment and requirement. It is to designate some act, and command its performance, as in legislation. An enactment of Congress is not simply description, but also law. In this sense Christ instituted for his disciples an outward rite, which was called baptism. He both prescribed, or designated, the rite, and commanded its observance. He determined the outward act, and made it law.

Plainly, this is not to say, that he originated the act, devising something new, and unlike any thing in existence before. This conception is by no means necessary. Our Congress may enact a law, which, in every essential feature, was upon the statute book of the old Hebrews, or of the Roman republic, or of the empire of China. It matters not where it was first framed. If it is seen to meet the wants of our own nation, as a wise and just measure, it is taken, adopted, and made the law of this land. If no law is found upon the statute books of other nations which exactly meets our exigencies, our legislators are expected to originate a measure. This difference in the origin of laws in no respect affects them after enactment. By enactment measures are made laws, and the whole question of obedience settled. So of a rite instituted by our Lord; we raise no question as to its origin. The only question is upon enactment, by which the thing prescribed, whether borrowed or unborrowed, becomes law. It is, therefore, wholly unnecessary in this connection to ask ourselves, whether there existed among the Jews, before the Christian era, what is known as Proselyte Baptism. It has been affirmed, that such baptism did exist for those who entered the Jewish congregation as proselytes from Paganism, and that from this the Christian rite was derived. It may be well enough to know that a critical and exhaustive examination of this subject has recently been made by an eminent German scholar, Schneckenburger; that he pronounces decidedly against that earlier origin of the custom; and that he has carried with him the consent of the best scholarship of the age. But in this controversy we are not now to involve ourselves. For the same reason it is needless to decide whether John's baptism was or was not Christian. If he belonged to the Old Dispensation, and not to the New; if his baptism was introductory and preliminary, and not in very truth Christian,—let it be granted. It does not matter. Our only point is this, that a rite known as baptism, new or derived, was prescribed by our Saviour, and its observance required of his followers. Let it also be borne in mind, that we here ask no question concerning the permanence of the instituted rite. This subject is postponed for separate notice. Whether baptism was to remain only for a time, or perpetually, shall receive its answer in due time. Now, the single, simple question is, whether such a rite was instituted for the disciples.

If my aim were only to state and establish that which is in dispute among Christians, and not to exhibit the subject in its completeness and proportions; if it were to treat it with reference to the state of opinion and not to its own inherent merits,—I might tacitly assume the institution of the rite, and pass on to points in litigation; for upon this point there is in Christendom no controversy deserving mention. And is not this very unanimity among sects, so much at variance upon almost every other point, one obvious and striking evidence in proof, that Christ did prescribe to the first Christians some outward rite called baptism, and require its observance? It is, certainly, an indication of the conclusiveness of the more direct testimony. And how, save through such origin, could we explain the practice of a rite under that name by all branches of the church, from the first times of which we have record, not as a mere custom but as an imposed law? This is an effect for which there must have been an adequate cause. What cause so naturally suggests itself, as the legislation of the Founder of the Church?

We consult the records, and find the inference confirmed. One part of this confirmation is our Lord's attitude toward the rite of baptism during his ministry. Such a rite—whether identical with the Christian rite, we need not determine—we find administered by John the Baptist. And here we notice, that it is administered by him in his official character as precursor and herald of Messiah, and to such as gave evidence of repentance and inward fitness to receive and welcome that Messiah. As he was a prophet, and more than a prophet, the use of this ordinance in these relations betokens more than the exercise of his private judgment. There is a significance in it which suggests to us, at once a divine origin and a divinely determined connection with the dawning religion. This significance is emphasized by our Lord's submission to the ordinance at his entrance upon his public ministry. Whatever may have been the precise import of the baptism of Jesus, who was sinless, this much is clear, that his act at that time, his requirement of John to baptize him because thus it became him to fulfill all righteousness, with the descent of the Spirit upon him at the waters in dove-like form,—forbid the belief, that the rite thus honored had not a special connection with Christianity. We can hardly refrain from interpreting these facts as the adoption of the rite as a Christian ordinance to be observed by believers. Surely Christ's observance of it at that time, and the revelation there made, at once of his spiritual endowment and the Father's recognition of him as his beloved Son, or the Messiah, when added to John's authority as precursor, must have conspired to produce such conviction in the minds of the disciples. And besides, we find ever after, that Christ speaks of the baptism of John with peculiar reverence, and implies its heavenly origin. There is evidence, also, that his disciples were baptized. It is also expressly affirmed, that Jesus baptized, not in his own person, but by his disciples. He is thus made to sanction their action. Their deed is his, and it has the same significance as though wrought by himself. The entire attitude of our Saviour toward the rite tends strongly to the conclusion, that he adopted it as a law of his church.

But even if all thus far produced were to be set aside as having no value, there yet remain three undeniable facts, any one of which, by itself alone, clearly and completely proves that Christ did institute the rite. The first of these facts is, that when Christ commissioned his disciples to preach the gospel, he also commissioned and commanded them to baptize. "Go ye," he says, "disciple all nations baptizing them." "He that believeth, and is baptized, shall be saved." Here, directly from our Lord's lips, is not merely a recognition of the rite and its approval as a proper custom, but the most explicit and unequivocal command enforcing its observance. This is nothing less than its institution as a law of the church. Nor is there any thing in the insertion of this command into the last great commission that ought to strike one as unnatural. The whole attitude of the Saviour toward the rite previously, as we have already seen, was in perfect accord. Now, as from the beginning, his kingdom is purely spiritual; but now, as from the beginning, he does not forget that the profoundest verities of spirit must have fit embodiment. The second fact, which also by itself settles this question, is the language of the apostles in their teaching after the ascension. When the convicted sinner, alarmed and trembling, asked them, "What shall I do to be saved?" their reply was, "Believe and be baptized, and thou shalt be saved." Those who believe that Christ spake not his own words, but the words of his Father, need only recall his promises made to these apostles, that the Holy Spirit should bring to their remembrance all his words, guide them into all truth, give to them the keys of the heavenly kingdom, and make them, under him, founders of the everlasting church. Their words, therefore, must be taken as equivalent to Christ's words. They enforced what he committed to them. Their enforcement of baptism has, therefore, but one ground. This was committed to them as a prescribed observance—a law of the church. The third fact, having the same force with each of the preceding, is the apostolic practice. Let us still keep in mind their position as related to the head of the church and to the church itself. They teach by deeds as well as by words. Their practice expounds doctrine. Their unvarying practice, as we well know, was to baptize converts. This is not only repeatedly mentioned in the Acts, but in the Epistles it is several times implied, that all the saints addressed were baptized believers. This practice proves that Christ instituted the rite. But if this is established by each of these three facts singly, their combined force, added to all that was before adduced in evidence, makes assurance more than trebly sure. We can safely advance to a new position.

2. Christ instituted the rite as a permanent, perpetual ordinance. It is not now asserted, that it could never be modified. That question shall be reserved for separate discussion. This only is intended, that the external rite of baptism which our Saviour instituted, was, in some form, to be perpetual. This proposition it is easy to prove. It would be fair here, as in the preceding case, to use in evidence the common consent of all Christendom as manifested with the slightest exceptions in practice. But we need no such testimony, for there is enough that is stronger. First, there is nowhere given any limitation. The world may be successfully challenged to find in our

Christian Baptism.

New Testament a sentence which teaches, or a word which implies, that this ordinance, in its external character, was to pass away before the end of time. There is the history of its origin. There is the description of our Lord's attitude toward it during his ministry. There is his command to administer it. There are the often-repeated injunctions of his inspired representatives. There, also, is the record of their unvarying practice to the last. But you look in vain for a word or hint of limitation. Has not this fact a meaning? And is not that meaning clear? When a law is enacted and placed on the statute-book, making some prescribed act the duty of citizenship, and is there left, with no shadow of restriction either expressed or implied, must it not be understood to hold perpetually, unless subsequently repealed by the enacting power? What else is it possible to understand? What else then, I ask, unless we would stultify ourselves, can we understand of the divine law concerning baptism, when that is enacted, recorded, and left thus unrestricted? This law is surely permanent, unless repealed. And here now comes in as further evidence, and to complete the preceding, the fact that there exists in the world no repealing authority. But is not God in the world? And has he no power to repeal his own laws? God is, indeed, everywhere, and therefore here. He can repeal his own laws, provided only he has not pledged himself not to repeal them. He cannot lie. He cannot, therefore, break his pledge. If it were expressly stated by our Saviour that this law was to remain in force to the end of the world, this would be a pledge that it should not be repealed. Again, if he had given us good reason to believe the New Testament to be his last revelation to man, a perfect standard of faith and practice, to hold and abide while the world should stand, this also would be virtually a pledge to the same effect. I may here assume that this last pledge is given, for the first sermon of this series established the doctrine which involves it. I shall soon proceed to show that the other pledge is also given. It is not too much then to say, that the repeal of this law has been placed by the divine Legislator out of his own power. Has, then, the authority to repeal been delegated? It is clear that it could not have been delegated without involving self-contradiction on God's part, if it can be shown that he has expressly proclaimed its perpetuity. But, though this will be soon shown, we may now treat the matter without reference to that, and as though no such thing could be established. We have already seen that the apostles were placed on a peculiar elevation as the inspired representatives of Christ. But even they had not authority to repeal, or annul, Christ's law. Theirs was only the power of declaration, confirmation and enforcement. The promise to them was, "When he the Spirit of truth shall come, he shall guide you into all truth. * * * He shall glorify me; for he shall receive of mine, and shall show it unto you." Exalted as they were, they were only exalted in Christ as their head and the head of the church—exalted to declare and execute his will, as obedient servants, not as coequals, to legislate independently, or to annul his enactments. If apostolic authority were still resident in the church, or in the officers of the church, as Papists maintain, even this would not involve the existence of a power to repeal any law of Christ. But apostolic authority passed away with apostles. It resides not in churches nor in individuals. There have never since their day been, nor ever shall be, prerogatives so near the divine intrusted to men. But the authority which does not equal theirs, cannot, surely, transcend it. If they might not repeal, how clear that to none has the repealing power been delegated. I shall now go further, and make good my promise to show that God has given the pledge, that the law shall not be repealed, in that he has expressly declared its perpetuity. The commission, as recorded by Matthew, runs as follows: "Go ye, therefore, and disciple all nations, baptizing them into the name of the Father, and of the Son, and of the Holy Spirit; teaching them to observe all things whatsoever I have commanded you: and, lo! I am with you alway, even unto the end of the world." Here our Lord contemplates the process of evangelization as continuing through time, and expressly promises his presence, to the world's end. But he contemplates the administration of baptism as coextensive, in both space and time, with evangelization. He commands that it be made thus coextensive. And what is here expressly taught, is fully implied in Mark's narrative, where the Lord, in connection with the commission, says: "He that believeth and is baptized shall be saved." These passages are our Lord's declaration of the perpetuity of Christian baptism, and God's pledge, that its law shall not be repealed. This pledge is involved in Paul's charge to Timothy: "The things which thou hast heard of me among many witnesses, the same commit thou to faithful men, who shall be able to teach others also." The letters of this apostle show that one of these things which Timothy had heard from his spiritual father, was the law of baptism. This he was to keep and commit to others, able and faithful to teach still others, and thus to make perpetual the ordinance. And in yet other places there is involved in like manner its permanence. A distinct and emphatic testimony to its perpetuity is furnished by its relation to the Lord's Supper. These two rites were the two halves of one whole. Vitally and indissolubly connected, they together constitute a solid, complete unity. Our natural birth begins our natural life. Our new birth, our new life. Sanctification but carries forward toward completion, regeneration. We have no natural life without natural birth. We have no sanctification without regeneration. Now, as will doubtless be shown by another in this course, and as we have here a right to assume without pausing to give proof, baptism is the symbol of our spiritual birth. The Lord's Supper is the symbol of our spiritual life. We may change this statement, and say, that baptism is the new birth in symbol; the Lord's Supper, the new life in symbol. Clearly, as the realities are related, so are the symbols. Baptism must precede the Supper, since birth precedes life. And so long as the Supper has place, its correlate must continue. Any other conception does violence to nature. Now, the perpetuity of the Supper as an ordinance of God, is established by the arguments that have just been used to establish the perpetuity of its antecedent. There is, also, a more express and pointed affirmation of that perpetuity. "As oft as ye eat this bread and drink this cup, ye do show the Lord's death, till he come." This coming of the Lord, or end of time, is the exact point when the observance of this rite is to cease. But, as baptism stands or falls with the Supper, that also is the limit of its observance. If, now, any thing more were needed to make good our position, I would ask, is not the need that gave rise to the ordinance, permanent? The fact symbolized remains unaltered. The reasons that in the beginning required its symbolic declaration, hold to the end. Must not, then, the wisdom which instituted, preserve? Can it be made to appear consistent, that what was originated should, under the circumstances, be abandoned? But we will not pass from testimony to inference, from the certain to the probable. It is safe to leave this point where it now is, for I think no thoughtful man can fail to feel that the unanimity of the church, touching the permanence of baptism as an external rite, is justified, nay, is even compelled, by force of evidence.

3. I shall next show, that this rite—already proved to have been divinely instituted, and that as a perpetual ordinance—as originally given, was the person's immersion in water. I say, as originally given it was this. I mean that as instituted by Jesus Christ, declared, commanded and practiced by all the Apostles, it was this, and this only. My only aim now is to make good this assertion. It is not to decide whether a change was not made at a very early day, or to determine what was the day of the change. And as we are now speaking purely of the external rite, the simple outward act called baptism, it is not here the place to determine who are fit subjects, or who must administer the ordinance, or with what form of words, and in what manner, or what purpose and spirit should animate, on the one hand the candidate, on the other the administrator. Each of these questions deserves attention, and each has its proper answer. But they must not come in to mix themselves with the present question and create a mental confusion. Our sole, single inquiry is, What originally was that external rite called baptism? What constituted it? The answer given, and to be justified, is, the person's immersion in water. I am aware that this statement will not command the same general assent as do those which have preceded it. Yet there is one part of the answer, respecting which there will be no less perfect agreement. In defining the external rite, the two words, water and immersion, were used. By these words are designated, respectively, the two essential constituents of the rite. That water was essential to the rite is the common belief, and it is my welcome duty, first, to disclose the ground of that conviction. There are two or three thoughts that could not fail to

suggest themselves to the mind of one about to open and examine the record touching this point, and which, once suggested, could not be wholly without influence. The first is, that since the fittest emblem of sin is pollution, the most suitable thing to be used as an emblem of its removal, or of that change which involves its final, complete removal, would be a cleansing element. Fire is the most thorough refiner. But this is used upon metals, not upon men. To cleanse men, water is used. This, then, would occur to the mind as the most appropriate and significant element to be employed in token of an inward spiritual cleansing. Besides this, we could not but bear in mind the well-known fact, that in the East generally, and especially among the Jews, where baptism had its origin, water was constantly and universally used in token of moral cleansing. This also would prepare us, on the one hand to anticipate its use by our Lord in his symbol of the new birth, and on the other hand to regard it as essential to the symbol if we found him using it. With such considerations in mind we open our New Testament, and are not surprised to find water so constantly, and in such ways, mentioned in connection with the rite, as at once to convince us that it was never administered without water. Not only is the mention of water frequent, but there seems to be given to it a certain emphatic prominence, often, which harmonizes best with the altogether natural theory, that this element is indispensable to the rite, essential to its symbolic nature. How often is the Jordan mentioned! Once it is said that a certain place was chosen for baptism because of its abundance of water. The administrator and candidate go down into the water. The eunuch exclaims: "See, here is water! what doth hinder me to be baptized?" Peter asks, "Can any man forbid water, that these should not be baptized which have received the

Holy Ghost as well as we?" It is true, that if water had been used simply from convenience, and not because of its symbolic significance, we could understand all such language; but I think that few will feel that it would then be quite so natural. This interpretation is made more sure by a set of passages which seem to ascribe to water a regenerating efficacy. Christ told Nicodemus, that a man could not enter the kingdom of God unless he was begotten of water and the Spirit. (John iii. 5.) Paul wrote that Christ cleansed the church "by the washing of water in the word." (Eph. v. 26.) At another time he used these words: "According to his mercy he saved us, by the washing (laver or bath) of regeneration, and renewing of the Holy Ghost." To understand such language to imply that water, a material agent, has any virtue to cleanse from sin the soul, a spiritual agent, would be an offence not only against reason, but equally against the whole drift of Scripture. The spiritual energy is seen, and named in its symbol by a kind of picture-language, so common and natural. If, now, these passages, which I have cited, refer directly to baptism, as many first-class interpreters believe, and as to me seems most obvious, they give to the element, water, a significance which at once makes it vital and essential to the rite. And even if, with other interpreters equally skilled, they were not made to refer directly to baptism, but only to water as a recognized element of purity, they are almost equally decisive; for they show how the teachers of Christianity, including both Christ and the inspired apostles, viewed and spoke of the element which they also used in the rite which symbolized the new birth. It is impossible that they and the disciples at large could have had this view of the symbolic import of water, and yet not have attached to it significance in the great initiatory ordinance. But we come now to passages which at once, and by themselves, set the matter at rest. They are those which specify baptism, and ascribe to it, as do the others to water, a spiritually cleansing power. Ananias, by Divine direction, went to the converted Saul soon after his arrival at Damascus, and delivered to him this message: "Arise, and be baptized, and wash away thy sins, calling upon the name of the Lord." (Acts xxii. 16.) The cleansing power here ascribed to baptism, could, obviously, have been only by virtue of the element in which it was administered. There was nothing in the rite, but the water, which could have contained or suggested the notion of cleansing. In Peter's first Epistle is another passage still more explicit. After stating that Noah and his family were saved in the ark by water, he adds, in effect; "which element in its antitype, baptism, saves you also." (1 Pet. iii. 21.) Here water is expressly designated as that in baptism which saves us. It could not be more strongly declared to be an essential constituent of the rite. Of like import and clearness is the exhortation in Heb. x. 22, 23: "Having our bodies washed with pure water, let us hold fast the profession of our faith without wavering." With good reason, therefore, has the church, from the earliest times, in all its divisions, held fast the idea, that purity of heart was expressed to the eye in baptism by the use of water. Thus far they remain true to the doctrine of Christ.

It remains now to prove, that immersion was also originally essential to the rite. This is not to say, that it was or is essential to salvation, but only, as the use of water was one constituent of the rite, so also its use by immersion was the second constituent, like the first, essential, inseparable, and indispensable. And here it will at once occur to every mind, that immersion is only a mode of using water. I do not say a mode of applying it, for it can hardly be said to be applied, except when taken and either sprinkled or poured upon the person. The phrase, "mode of application," has arisen from another practice than that of the original Christian baptism. Still, though this phraseology, which has sometimes been made to play no unimportant part in so-called argument upon this theme, be disallowed as inaccurate, it is yet true, and must be conceded, that immersion is only a mode of using or employing water. But, as soon as this is conceded, there arises the question, how can mere mode, or manner, be essential to a thing, and one of its constituents? Does not this involve an absurdity and self-contradiction? With great energy and frequency this question has been answered in the affirmative; and this answer has been made the basis, sometimes of pity for Baptist blindness, and sometimes of indignation at Baptist bigotry. If there really is absurdity and self-contradiction necessarily involved in making mode constitute in part the essence of a thing, the proposition which I have promised to prove is self-destructive, admitting neither confirmation nor refutation. But it does not involve a self-contradiction. It is therefore not self-destructive. And it does admit of confirmation. It does not involve any absurdity, for mode or form is not necessarily without character, and may be itself the thing prescribed. But, if the thing prescribed is in whole or in part a form, then surely of that thing form belongs to the essence. Take, for example, the signal-service, by which the movements of a fleet are determined and the issues of battle decided. If the code prescribes that a flag of a given form shall have a given meaning, is the form nothing? Is the form non-essential? Let the signal officer disregard the form, and display a flag of different pattern! It was only form that he disregarded, but he has caused disaster. Or, let the law prescribe that a given motion of the flag shall be understood to mean a given thing. That is but a mode of using the flag. Does it, therefore, not belong to the essence of the signal? It is the signal. The mode is the thing. So a nod of the head, and a shake of the head, are each only a way, or mode of its use, but the child is not long in learning that they are by no means interchangeable. It is, therefore, not random talk to call immersion essential to the external rite known as baptism; nor is it a bewilderment of the logical faculty to undertake to prove the same.

There are two separate points to be established. The first is, that in administering the rite, immersion was originally practiced; and the second, that this immersion was itself of the essence of the rite. And here, also, before hearing the more direct evidence, one or two thoughts will suggest themselves, which ought not to be wholly without influence. One of these is, that in the person's immersion, and immediate consequent emersion, there is an obvious natural fitness to body forth forcibly to the eye vital truth connected with the spiritual birth. If this change were only an inward cleansing, without reference to Jesus Christ, and quite independent of any known facts in his history, the mere symbol of purification might be thought to cover the whole ground. But there are these two grand facts—the Saviour's sacrificial death; the Saviour's triumphal resurrection. The genuine Christian consciousness can never suffer these to fall into the back ground in his remembrance of the new birth. He becomes a new creature, not in his solitary separate self, but in Christ Jesus, the crucified and risen. To these external facts correspond the two chief phases of his inward experience. He dies to self, to the world, to sin; he rises in newness of life, to holiness and to God, in Jesus Christ. Now, both these outward facts in our divine Lord's life, and both these corresponding facts in the soul's own inward experience, are beautifully and forcifully expressed by immersion and emersion. Neither of them are even hinted at by the simple symbol of purity. Is it not as easy for the Christian heart to conceive, that a rite which Divine wisdom should institute to express the new birth, would leave unnoticed the idea of purity, as that it would wholly pass by these other sublime verities? Another thought is, that in a rite whose design it was to express silently to the eye invisible realities, the mode of using the element was a feature of too much prominence to be without significance. It would be quite as natural to believe the element destitute of meaning. How striking this circumstance of mode! How diverse and unlike the different possible modes! What scope for the introduction of confusion, and the loss of original unity, if the mode had been declared valueless! Such thoughts as these ought not to be without force in our examination of testimony. In confirmation of our first point, namely, that immersion, and that only, was originally practiced, stands at the beginning the undeniable fact, that the word baptism in all its other uses means immersion. Sane and intelligent men, when soberly discoursing in a language with which they are perfectly familiar, are accustomed to use words in their proper and established meanings. An English writer, attempting in good faith to describe to his readers the act of crying, would not invariably use the word laugh. At least the presumption would be, that he meant what he said. He who denied would have to make good his denial, or stultify himself. Still stronger is the case when several persons, equally intelligent, agree in describing the same familiar act by the same familiar word. If ten witnesses, independent and trustworthy, were to relate the destruction of a certain city by a great fire, could any thing be more preposterous than the assertion, that, in fact, it was a flood which they intended. And how would the case be still strengthened, if different witnesses were speaking under Divine inspiration, describing some act of great religious import, and enjoining it upon others as a duty for them solemnly to perform. Can language describe the boldness which, without convincing proof, would deny to a term, uniformly used under such circumstances, its fixed meaning, and affix to it an opposite signification? Now, the Greek language has a word which means to immerse. The most exhaustive and critical examination of its use in all other known connections has repeatedly been made, but not an instance has been found where it could be made to appear, that it did not involve the idea of immersion. It holds in the Greek exactly the same place that the word immersion holds in the English. Even the primary word from which it is derived, is proved to have with equal uniformity the conception of dipping, or submerging, in all its uses. I shall not weary you with an array of authorities, nor conduct you through a tedious examination. I state only that which is well established, and, by intelligent scholars, well understood. Now, in this same Greek language there is a word equally explicit to denote the act of sprinkling, another to designate pouring, another which means to wash, and another signifying to cleanse. These are all common words, as well known to one who can speak Greek, as even the English terms to any one of us. The word which means to immerse is $\beta\alpha\pi\tau\iota\zeta\epsilon\iota\nu$ (baptizein), the noun meaning immersion $\beta\alpha\pi\tau\iota\sigma\mu\alpha$ (baptisma). We find in our English Bible these terms, not translated, but transferred. Now, are we to be told, that as often as the different inspired writers use the word baptism, or immersion, they mean sprinkling, or pouring, or cleansing? Why will a man, how can a man, venture to deny that the writers of the New Testament meant immerse when they said immerse? It is not because there is any evidence compelling the perversion, for every candid scholar, who knows any thing of the controversy upon this point, is aware, that not even a plausible objection has as yet been urged against the literal and established sense of the word. I have no heart to touch upon those puerilities, the pretence of a scarcity of water, in a city abounding in baths; the pretence of lack of time to accomplish what is reported to have been done, when the notion of such lack has often been shown to be utterly groundless, and when the objection is also equally valid against sprinkling or pouring—for immersion, as a sacred rite, can be decently performed as rapidly as can either of the others; or that other pretence, which never had even a shadow of support, that the term baptize had become entirely emptied of all significance except to denote a sacred rite; or those other half dozen pretences, yet more absurd, which misguided ingenuity in the interest of party has succeeded during some centuries of effort in inventing and raking together.

This testimony, from the meaning of the word baptism, is corroborated by the descriptions of the administration of the ordinance. Mark writes, that Jesus was baptized by John "*into* the Jordan." True, our English version has it "in Jordan," but the Greek is "into." Now, it is quite natural to speak of immersing a man "into" the river, but how would you sprinkle or pour him into the stream? This, however, is the only passage where the preposition *into* stands in such connection; and, if there were any necessity, it might be understood as a condensed mode of saying, that Christ went into the Jordan, and was then baptized. But there is no reason for giving it another than its obvious interpretation. The preposition *in* is the one which commonly connects the word baptism with the element. No other is used, except in the single instance already adduced. Dr. Hovey, in some unpublished notes, says, that, besides the instance just noticed, "the element of baptism is mentioned sixteen times in the New Testament. In ten of these it is water, and in six it is the Holy Spirit. The Holy Spirit is always in the dative, and preceded by ἐν; water is likewise always in the dative, and preceded by ἐν in seven cases out of ten." (Cf. also 1 Cor. x. 2.) Accepting these results of his careful investigation, their bearing can easily be seen. The dative case, which is three times used without the preposition ἐν, expresses the sphere in which a thing is done, as well as the instrument by which. The preposition ἐν (in), with the dative, must be understood to express "the sphere in which," unless there is some decisive reason for giving it another meaning. Its first, natural, and common meaning is this. It is clear that the idea of immersion is decidedly favored by these passages, especially when it is remembered that never is the Greek words for *with* or *by*, employed in such connections. It is more natural to speak of immersing in water than of sprinkling or pouring in water. We sprinkle, but not pour, a person with water; or yet more accurately, we sprinkle or pour water upon a person. But the Greek writers never speak of baptizing one with or by water, much less of baptizing water upon one. With this exactly agrees the circumstance, that candidates are said to have gone down into the water. No good reason was ever yet assigned for such an act, unless they were to be immersed after they had gone down. But the case is made yet clearer by passages which speak of the selection of certain places for baptism because of the abundance of water. John selected Enon for this reason, and frequent mention is made of the Jordan. There is no one feature of any of the recorded descriptions which does not harmonize entirely with the theory of immersion, nor is there one feature which favors the notion of sprinkling or affusion. Further corroborating evidence is contained in references to the symbolic import of baptism. I have already noticed those passages which show that purity was symbolized. There are others, entirely different, which show that purity was not the only fact expressed. In Rom. vi. 3-5, Paul writes: "Know ye not, that so many of us as were baptized into Jesus Christ, were baptized into his death? Therefore we are buried with him by baptism into death; that like as Christ was raised up from the dead by the glory of the Father, even so we also should walk in newness of life; for if we have been planted together in the likeness of his death, we shall be also in the likeness of his resurrection." Again, in Col. ii. 12, he speaks of being "buried with Christ in baptism," and also "raised with him" in it. These passages teach, with all possible plainness, that baptism was understood by the apostle to represent to the eye a burial and a resurrection. This is here declared to be a part of its symbolic design, with no less clearness and force than elsewhere purity is declared to be expressed. But by no use of water is a burial and resurrection exhibited, except by an immersion and an immediate consequent emersion. No man needs any comment upon this plain language of the apostle; but, if comment were desired, it is at hand; for the scholarship of the church, past and present, with only the feeblest controversial dissent, has affirmed that in these cases immersion must be presupposed as Christian baptism. If further evidence were needed, it is furnished in the fact that the early church, after the apostles, knew no baptism but immersion, and that, as is well known, the Greek church still retains immersion. Dr. Conant, in his invaluable "Critical and Philological Notes," at the end of his revised version of the Gospel by Matthew, has collected in the original Greek of the church Fathers, their language, as it was that of the New Testament writers, and has translated into English a multitude of passages which show the position of the early church upon this matter. To these, he says, many others of the same tenor might have been added. What their tenor is, will sufficiently appear from a single example, which is a fair representative. Cyril, bishop of Jerusalem, in the last half of the fourth century, writes: "For as Jesus assuming the sins of the world died, that having slain sin he might raise thee up in righteousness; so also thou, going down into the water, and in a manner buried in the waters, as he in the rock, art raised again, walking in newness of life." Very many eminent scholars, in churches which practice sprinkling or affusion, have borne strong testimony to the fact, that originally only immersion was known. The language of Calvin, in his comment upon Jn. iii. 23, is as follows: "From these words it may be inferred that baptism was administered by John and Christ by plunging the whole body under water. * * * Here we perceive how baptism was administered among the ancients, for they immersed the whole body in water." This fairly represents the admission of a multitude of this class. Would such and so many men have borne witness against themselves, except compelled to it by the weight of evidence? All these facts which have been adduced must forever stand a full and sufficient justification of the assertion, that baptism, as originally practiced, was immersion. They constitute a defence never to be shaken by the petty objections which, in Liliputian mimicry of war, are marshaled and arrayed against them. There are some who try to ignore this solid granite mountain of truth. Like certain animals which burrow in the ground, they dig a little way into the looser covering which is over the rock, and when they have thus buried themselves, cry out, that they see no such mountain.

We have next to show, that the immersion originally practiced was of the essence of this rite, and not a mere accident. Here recall the two preliminary considerations already noticed: the first, that of the natural fitness of immersion to constitute such part; the second, the antecedent improbability that a feature so important should be merely accidental. Add to these the significant fact, that the very name of the rite is immersion. How unreasonable that intelligent men, and especially if inspired, should name the initiatory and perpetual rite of the church from a mere accident of that rite, and not from that which pertained to its essence. Every one would expect that its name would have been a word containing the idea of water, or at least of cleansing, if *water* had been the only essential thing. Still further, if water alone were essential, and the mode of its use quite indifferent, why was the most difficult, and, as some allege, indelicate mode adopted and employed? Is it of the genius of Christianity to impose upon its professors needless and senseless burdens? And yet, once more, why, when the apostle gave an interpretation of the spiritual import of the rite, did he once and again in his epistles, and, without doubt, habitually in oral instruction, seize upon the mode, to the entire omission of the element? Did he coldly purpose to mislead? or was he ignorant? There can be no other reason for his course than that immersion was then essential to the rite—a constituent and inseparable part of it. I trust that the assertion has been made good, that the divinely instituted and perpetual rite of baptism, as originally given, was the immersion of the candidate in water; that the element water, and the immersion with the consequent emersion, were both and equally essential to that rite.

4. Let us now advance together one step further. The divine, perpetual rite as instituted was never to be altered. There are three conceivable grounds, any one of which might justify, or be supposed to justify, an alteration. The first is an express command or permission; the second, the lodgement in the church, or some part of it, of a power to change the rite at will; the third, its little importance. No command or permission to change the ordinance has ever been found, unless such permission or command exist in the impossibility or impropriety of its administration in its original character. Those who are pleased to stigmatize immersion as indelicate, unbecoming, and improper, unfitted to the refinements of our modern civilization, and therefore to be set aside for something more genteel and elegant, are, perhaps, honest, are surely silly. To set their taste above Christ's law, would be monstrous, if it were not ridiculous. As to the impossibility of immersing, it does sometimes exist. Persons who are proper subjects are sometimes too feeble or otherwise unfitted to observe the ordinance. But what is the rational view to take of these cases? Is it, that for such persons another and different rite shall be substituted, or, rather, that these persons are, by divine providence, for the time excused from performing the outward act, and, instead of that, the inward disposition is accepted? The question carries its own answer. But how much more emphatic would be this answer, if it were claimed, that the inability of a few exceptional persons to be immersed justified such substitution, not for these only, but for the whole body of believers, sick and well, lame and sound. This would be a leap of logic astounding, bewildering. But it is said, that there are countries too cold to allow immersion; and, as Christ's religion

was for the race, he must have intended that the rite should be modified to make it tolerable. In this, then, is the divine permission. Permission for what? Not merely to excuse those of the cold clime from the outward act, which *impossibility* of performance would certainly justify. Is it then in these special cases to substitute another act in its place for them? No; it is even worse; it is a permission to give another rite to the whole church, in frigid, temperate, and torrid zones. But where are those regions whose cold makes immersion impracticable? The practice of the Greek church shows that they form no habitable part of this earth. Are they, then, on the dark side of the moon? I suspect they lie somewhere in the drear imagination of partisan objectors. This ground of divine permission or command to change Christ's ordinance is supported by no argument which can fairly be called respectable, even if courtesy shall concede the name of argument.

How, next, is it with that second ground, the lodgement in the church or its officers of an authority to change the ordinance at discretion? Does it not require precisely the same authority to change a law that it does to repeal? and the same to either change or repeal that it does to enact? Has Christ delegated this authority? We have already found the answer. We saw that not even to apostles was such authority delegated. How much less to their successors or the church of subsequent time!

And now can I speak soberly and temperately of that other supposed ground for changing God's law, to wit: its little importance. "Only a form;" "Merely external;" "Not essential;" "A mere question of the amount of water." Is it possible that men, who call Christ Lord, can use such a plea to justify a known change of his sacred ordinance? Are they really in earnest? Why do they not say of the Bible, "It is made up only of words and sentences? Words are but trifles. Why be so scrupulous to retain them, just as they came from the pen of inspiration? "Phariseeism! Bondage! Judaism! Let us, in the free Catholic spirit, which is the very genius of Christianity, drop a letter here, a word there, and a sentence elsewhere. Let us at will add and change, for elegance, convenience, or utility. The letter killeth, but the spirit giveth life. The letter killeth! Then kill the letter." No! Christian men dare not thus reason of the written word. They well know that to kill the letter, is to kill the indwelling spirit. How, then, dare they reason thus of that grand symbolic, pictorial language, in which our Lord incarnated, and visibly bodied forth to the view of the race, the central sublime verities of his holy religion? If possible, the sin is greater in the case of the rite than in that of the written word. The rite is alone, solitary. In the word, a multitude of passages contain the same ground truth. The rite is a summary, gathering into itself many truths. Often the word holds but one feature of one truth. The rite embodies verities which are at the very centre. Much of the Bible treats of exterior truth. But worse though the sin be, in some of its features, yet in principle it is just the same. It is vicious in the extreme. It degrades the authority of Christ. Suppose the rite worthless. You bid your child take from the floor a pin; may he disobey you because it is a pin, and not a diamond? It degrades the wisdom of Christ. Is he to be charged with the institution, and the perpetual requirement, of a trivial or worthless rite? It degrades the judgment, and outrages the Christian consciousness of the whole family of Christ; for the church deems the rite invaluable—her heart cherishes it as a sacred legacy. But, if it is so unimportant that one of its constituents may be cast aside, then, either or both may be rejected, and the whole ordinance discarded. There is, there can

Christian Baptism. 113

be, no ground which justifies any, the least change of that which belonged to the essence of the rite; hence no ground which will justify the substitution either of another element in place of water, or of another use of water in place of immersion. Every argument which we saw binding the church to retain the ordinance of baptism, and all these arguments combined which the church so unanimously and heartily, in word and practice, pronounce invincible, equally bind it to retain the rite as it was instituted. Indeed, not otherwise does she retain Christ's ordinance, but substitutes another and different. The command to observe it, given without any kind of limitation, expressed or implied; the non-existence of even the shadow of authority to repeal; the express declaration of its perpetuity to the end of time; its relation to the Lord's Supper, which by independent evidence is shown to be perpetual; and the continuance to the last of the same need which originated—all these, severally and conjointly, lift up the clear, articulate, solemn voice of authority, and command the church and the world to lay no desecrating hand upon God's ordinance, or change in the least his abiding decree. These all warn the erring to return to the right way, and those in that way to turn not one hair's breadth to right or left.

But too long already have I detained you with this discussion. Here let us pause, and by rapid glance mark the stages which we have traveled together, wearily perhaps, yet I trust with profit. The Christian religion is spiritual, yet it admits of expression by the language of symbol. The symbol may be external rite. The rite known as baptism, viewed in its purely external character, was taken as our theme. In the treatment of this theme we came to our present position by the following successive steps. Christ's appointments are of Divine authority. He instituted an external rite, known as bap-

10*

tism, to be observed by his disciples. This rite was designed by him to be permanent. There were originally two essential constituents in the outward rite—the one water, used as the symbol of purity; the other immersion, with the consequent emersion, as the symbol of burial and resurrection. The rite was absolutely unalterable in each and both of its constituents. These positions, severally and collectively, I believe must commend themselves to the candid and thoughtful, as true and scriptural. While held, they bind us to our good old Baptist faith and practice. If they are wrong, let it be proved. We will then gladly abandon them, though each is now dear to our hearts, because we believe each to be true. Discussion—fair, candid, earnest, Christian—we should never fear, should ever court. If the positions are right, we must maintain them, defend them, proclaim them, not indeed as Baptists, but as Christians. Far be it from the disciple of him who styled himself "the Truth," to cherish a partisan spirit in matters of Christian faith. In so far as we have attained, we have "One Lord, one Faith, one Baptism, one God and Father of all, who is above all, and through all, and in all." Wherein we have not attained, whether in spirit or in forms, be it ours to "reach forth toward the things that are before, and press forward toward the mark for the prize of the high calling of God in Christ Jesus our Lord." Thus shall "we all come into the unity of the faith and of the knowledge of the Son of God." Then, sometime in the fair future, the sun shall look down from the pure heavens, not upon a church ruptured, dissevered with jealous, jarring, warring members, but upon a church bound together, not by the external bands of ecclesiastical or State legislation, but by those softer yet stronger cords of a pure Christian faith and an imperishable Christian love

IV.
BAPTISM A SYMBOL.

By GEO. D. BOARDMAN, D.D.,
Pastor of First Baptist Church, Philadelphia.

"And now, why tarriest thou? Arise, and be baptized, and wash away thy sins, calling on the name of the Lord."—*Acts* xxii. 16.

"Know ye not, that so many of us as were baptized into Jesus Christ were baptized into his death? Therefore, we are buried with him by baptism into death; that like as Christ was raised up from the dead by the glory of the Father, even so we also should walk in newness of life. For if we have been planted together in the likeness of his death, we shall be also in the likeness of his resurrection."—*Romans* vi. 3-5.

"Buried with him in baptism, wherein also ye are risen with him."—*Colossians* ii. 12.

"All these things spake Jesus unto the multitude in parables; and without a parable spake he not unto them."—*Matthew* xiii. 34.

I. In this world of ours, where spirit and matter are joined in mysterious wedlock, truth unexpressed is but half a truth. She does not become whole and triumphant till she issues forth in symbol. It is an epoch, then, for Truth when she finds complete expression; for thus alone is her latent omnipotence liberated.

We loiter not to account for this fact; we only ask you to note the fact itself. "It is difficult," says the Guest in the Statesman of Plato, "fully to exhibit greater things without the use of patterns;" and Lord Bacon declares that "as hieroglyphics came before letters, so parables came before arguments. And even now, if any one wish to let new light on any subject into men's minds, and that without offence or harshness, he must still go the same way, and call in the aid of similitudes."* Truth

---
* Bacon's Works, vol. xiii., p. 80.

unexpressed is to human beings as though she were not. Truth expressed is the crowned conqueror of the eternities, and symbols are her coronation robes.

That God in communicating with the race proceeds on this principle, that truth in order to be seen and realized as truth must be expressed, is evident on every hand. Glance at some illustrations.

1. Look, first, at nature herself. That man has studied nature to but little purpose who has not learned that one of her chief ministries to her Divine Lord is to furnish forms, vehicles, symbols, for his truth. The question which Milton puts into the mouth of Raphael is not altogether puerile:

> "What if earth
> Be but the shadow of heaven, and things therein
> Each to other like, more than on earth is thought?"

The universe is one grand school, teaching man's soul by countless and pregnant analogies, patterns, symbols, parables. What though man perceives not its lessons? Is it any the less a school because he is dull, or perverse, and will not learn? Oh! it needs no poet's eye—only the thoughtful man's—to perceive that the universe is one vast temple of divine hieroglyphs, teaching the observant scholar gravest lessons of duty and obedience, love and sacrifice. The things on earth are patterns of the things in heaven. On all God's works are written God's truths, discoursing, in emblem and type, of divine power and wisdom, goodness and righteousness, greatness and patience; of man's responsibility, and sin, and duty, and destiny; of death, resurrection, judgment, immortality, heaven, hell. Nature, from atom to star, is one mighty parable of God to man, illustrating for him, by her manifold laws, and forces, and activities, and shows the sacred words which the Spirit has given to holy chroniclers and poets, prophets and evangelists, and preaching in a universal tongue through her countless phenomena of birth and death, growth and decay, sleeping and waking, sowing and reaping, light and darkness, mountain and ocean, numbers and spaces, universal gravitation and chemical affinity. Herein, in fact, is the significance of the soul's earthly life; herein, a final cause of her insertion among the manifold parables of nature, among its emblematic forces, and movements, and phenomena, that she may be educated unto God's glory, and her own perfectness in eternity.

2. Ascending, now, into the higher range of supernatural revelation, we are not surprised to find the same symbolic element thoroughly permeating all Holy Scripture, from the account of the arrangement of the first chaos into order beneath the brooding wind of God, emblematic of the arrangement of the soul's chaos into order beneath the brooding of the same Divine wind, or Spiritus, down to the types and figures of the world to come, beheld in Apocalyptic vision. Look at the Old Testament economy. See how densely packed it is with type and symbol; with typical localities, as Eden, Egypt, Sinai, Jerusalem; with typical personages, as Adam, Cain, Abel, Melchisedek, Abraham, Isaac, Ishmael, Moses, Joshua, David, Zerubbabel; with typical events, as the Deluge, the Call of Abraham, the Offering of Isaac, the Wrestling of Jacob, the Bondage in Egypt, the Passover by the Destroying Angel, the Exodus, the Wilderness Wandering, the Passage of the Jordan, the Settlement in Canaan, the Babylonian Captivity, the Restoration; with typical objects, as Jacob's Ladder, the Burning Bush, the Pillar of Cloud and of Fire, the Manna, the Smitten Rock, the Brazen Serpent, the Tabernacle, the Outer Court, the Laver, the Altar of Incense, the Candlestick, the Vail, the Holy of Holies, the Ark of the Covenant, the Mercy-Seat, the Cherubim;

with typical rites, as Circumcision, Lustration, Day of Atonement, Sacrifice, Sprinkling of Blood, Imposition of Hands, Scapegoat, and the like, almost endlessly. What, in fact, is this entire Old Testament economy but a magnificent scheme of symbol; or, as the writer of the Epistle to the Hebrews, in one all-comprehending word, describes it, parable?*

3. Nor, when we ascend into the still higher range of the New Testament, do we escape, as is sometimes imagined, the dominion of symbol. Look, for instance, at the characteristic method of Jesus as a teacher; and surely, if ever man taught with authority, it was he. See how commonly and naturally his doctrines take on a parable or symbol form. Erase from the gospels all that he has said in form of parable, and figure, and metaphor, leaving, as the record of his teaching, only what he taught in direct statements, and you will be amazed at the comparative meagreness of the residue; and you will feel that his biographers speak the truth when they say that without a parable spake he not unto the people.

4. And, finally, Jesus himself, the Son of God incarnated in the Son of Man, is himself the symbol of symbols, being himself the manifestation of the divine in the human, or the Word of God—that is, God's thought, and feeling, and character, expressed to men, the image of the invisible God.†

We state, then, as the result of our survey of nature and of Holy Scripture, that God's well-nigh universal method of declaring truth is by means of symbol, this being its form, vehicle, and interpreter. Perhaps I should say, without qualification, his *universal* method; for all expression, whether in form of speech, or writing, or act, or phenomenon, is really symbol. Truth, in order to be

---

* Heb. ix. 9. † Col. i. 15.

recognized and felt as truth, must take on some kind of form, and come out into aspect or expression.

II. Accordingly, when a human being, having been morally subdued by the most stupendous events which have occurred in this world's history, and made conscious in his own experience of a personal change so radical that he cannot call it less than a new birth, or second creation, wishes to declare these mighty truths, the strong presumption is raised in advance, that God, who has a symbol for his truth everywhere else, will also have a symbol for his truth here. So transcendent are the facts and truths involved in the act of regenerating a man's moral nature; so stupendous are the consequences, in space and time, flowing from it; so express are God's commands, that he who experiences these great truths should make them known to others, that we should unhesitatingly predict, in advance, that God would provide for these truths a special symbol, which should be as impressive as it is expressive; for, in fact, no truth can make impression till it has expression.

Let us now suppose that some one is standing before us as a candidate for membership in a church. He has just passed through this transcendent process of regeneration, and now wishes to make public confession of his faith. What are the leading truths, as connected with this great event of regeneration, which he would naturally wish to express?

1. The first is *confession of sinfulness*.

There are two figures or types under which Holy Scripture chiefly sets forth its conception of sin.

(*a.*) The first is that of *death*. We stay not to point out the frightful accuracy of the figure; we simply direct your attention to it. Whatever there is painful and repulsive in the spectacle of a corpse; its unnatural disfigurement; its insensibility to sight, and sound, and touch, and love; its utter, unending helplessness; its corruption and loathsomeness—all this is taken in Scripture as the portraiture of the sinner. He is "dead in trespasses and sins." "The soul that sinneth, it shall die." "In the day thou eatest thereof, thou shalt surely die." "The wages of sin is death."* Throughout Scripture, death and sin, as type and anti-type, evermore walk together in ghastly, inseparable wedlock. In making public confession of his sinfulness, then, this candidate, standing before us, would naturally, first of all, wish to set forth in symbol his belief in the Scriptural teaching, that sin is death. How, then, shall he symbolize to others his confession that he has been spiritually dead—buried in the sepulchre of sin?

(*b.*) The other most frequent Scriptural designation of sin is that it is *uncleanness*. How thoroughly this conception of sin, as being a state of impurity, defilement, pollution, pervades the Scripture, is evident from the immense stress laid by the Mosaic ritual on the necessity of guarding against all manner of ceremonial defilement. Particularly were all dead bodies, and those diseases which might be described as a living death, marked off as unclean, to be regarded as special types of the filth of sin. So contaminating was sin conceived to be, that whatever came in slightest contact with a dead body was defiled, and needed, whether it were animal, or man, or garment, or article of furniture, rites of purgation. Nor does this idea of uncleanness fall out in the New Testament conception of sin. Rather is it intensified. Under the old covenant, sin, regarded as a defiled and defiling principle, was surveyed chiefly in its outward, ceremonial, phenomenal aspects. Under the new covenant sin is set forth, as an inward defilement, being filthi-

---

* Ephes. ii. 1; Ezek. xviii. 4; Gen. ii. 17; Rom. vi. 23.

The Symbolism of Baptism. 121

ness of soul. Not that which goeth into a man defileth him, but that which cometh out of him—this defileth a man. For from within, out of the heart, proceed evil thoughts, adulteries, thefts, blasphemy, deceit, pride, foolishness. These are the evil things which, coming from within, defile a man.* The state of sin, therefore, is a state of uncleanness as well as of death. And precisely this it is which this candidate for the church, brought under the illuminating, regenerating influences of the Spirit, most keenly feels. With him sin is something more than a gloomy idea: it is a positive defilement. It is something more than an accidental flesh injury: it is a hereditary taint. It is something more than a superficial spot or stain, or local tumor of the skin: it is a total, radical defilement of the hidden man of the heart. And this it is which fills our new-born disciple with such intense self-loathing. "Unclean! unclean!" are the words of his heart as well as of his lips. It is this sense of defilement, this consciousness of total pollution, which has driven him to the purging blood of the Cross for cleansing. Impurity of soul is, therefore, a cardinal truth necessarily implicit in the gospel scheme. Had there been no uncleanness among the people, there had been no Fountain opened in the house of Judah. How, then, shall this convert to Jesus set forth this prime fact, doctrine, and consciousness of soul-uncleanness alongside with his acknowledgment of spiritual death? Surely both facts are cardinal enough to demand full, fit expression. Suppose he has invented some emblem for symbolizing his spiritual death—what shall he invent as the symbol of his total spiritual defilement?

2. The second great truth which this new convert to Jesus would naturally wish to express when making his public confession, is his *entrance upon a holy career*.

---

* Matt. xv. 17-20.

(*a*) Many are the figures which Holy Scripture uses to set forth its conception of the new state into which the regenerated sinner enters. Of these none is more frequent or expressive than the term *life*. As death is the standing type of sin, so life is the standing type of righteousness. "He that heareth my word, and believeth on him that sent me, hath everlasting life, and shall not come into condemnation: but is passed from death unto life." "The wages of sin is death; but the gift of God is eternal life, through Jesus Christ our Lord." "To be carnally minded is death; but to be spiritually minded is life and peace." "The law of the spirit of life in Christ Jesus hath made me free from the law of sin and death." The regenerate "walk in newness of life." "He that hath the Son hath life." "I am the bread of life." "I am come that they might have life, and that they might have it more abundantly." "He that believeth in me hath eternal life." "I give unto them eternal life."* This, in fact, is the chief aspect of redemption on its human side. Life, eternal life, is the key-note of the gospel.

Upon this new life our new-born disciple believes he has entered. He has passed from death unto life. Dead in sin, he has been raised unto God. Conversion is a resurrection. How vital, then, that in publicly avowing his belief that he has passed from death unto life, he should symbolize his resurrection! Having, as we will suppose, discovered or invented some symbol to set forth his spiritual death, how shall he find or devise some symbol to set forth his spiritual resurrection?

(*b*) But this resurrection is to a life of *righteousness or purity*. As in his unregenerate state he had not merely been dead, but also polluted, so now, in his re-

---

* John v. 24; vi. 35, 47; x. 10, 28. Rom. vi. 4, 23; viii. 2, 6. 1 John v. 12.

The Symbolism of Baptism. 123

generate state, he has not only been quickened, but also purged. Need you be reminded that total purification is the grand cardinal blessing of the gospel, so far as its simply *restorative* power is concerned? Even under the old covenant, a chief part of the Mosaic scheme and liturgy consisted in lustrating rites. And the superiority of the new covenant over the old is declared to consist in this very thing, that while the old could serve only to the purifying of the flesh, the cleansing from outward defilement, the new can purge the conscience itself, and inmost recesses of the soul from their inward defilement.* The grand distinguishing blessing of the gospel, considered as a remedial, restorative economy, is this, that it cleanses from all sin, purifying even as God is pure. And this man, standing before us, has, by our supposition, passed under the quickening power of the gospel, and, as a new-born soul, is undergoing its purifying processes. If, then, in making public confession of his faith, it be an appropriate and even vital thing that he express his sense of total defilement, it is equally appropriate, even vital, that he express his desire for total purification, and his belief in its possibility. How, then, shall he do it? The first problem is to symbolize his death in sin; the second, his resurrection to life; the third, his total defilement; the fourth, his total purification. What shall the symbol or symbols be?

3. The third great truth which this new convert to Jesus would naturally wish to express, is *the instrument and power by which he has been quickened and purged.*

This, of course, cannot be any act or volition of his own. Uncleanness cannot cleanse itself, death cannot resuscitate itself, any more than Beelzebub can cast out Beelzebub. What, then, is the energy by which the sinner, dead in filth, is made alive again and purged?

---

* Heb. ix. 13, 14.

(*a*) Need any Christian be told that the *death* of the Son of God is the source of his people's life? "I am the life-giving bread which came down from heaven. If any man eat of this bread he shall live forever: and the bread that I will give is my flesh, which I will give for the life of the world." "Whoso eateth my flesh, and drinketh my blood, hath eternal life." Since "without shedding of blood there is no remission," God hath sent forth his Son to be the "propitiation for our sins, through faith in his blood." "Christ, our passover, is sacrificed for us," "his own self bearing our sins in his own body on the tree, that we, being dead to sins, should live unto righteousness." "The church of God he hath purchased with his own precious blood." "We have redemption through his blood." "The blood of Jesus Christ, his Son, cleanseth us from all sin." "Being justified by his blood, we shall be saved from wrath through him."* Thus cardinal in the gospel scheme is the fact of Christ's death.

> "The gates of Paradise
> Open stand on Calvary."

(*b*) Observe now, that in that death the believer in Jesus, through God's grace and his own faith, is an actual *participant*. It is a clear and frequent teaching of Holy Scripture, expressed by a great variety of metaphors and idioms, that the church, that is, the true spiritual ecclesia, is organically united to Jesus Christ. Christ's people are one in and with him. He is the Vine: they are the branches. He is the Head: the church is his body. He is the Bridegroom: the church is his bride. He is the second Adam: the church is his spiritual posterity.† This is the profound meaning of that charac-

---

* John vi. 51, 54. Acts xx. 28. Rom. iii. 25; v. 9. 1 Cor. v. 7. Eph. i. 7. Col. i. 14. Heb. ix. 22. 1 Pet. i. 19; ii. 24. 1 John i. 7.

† John xv. 5; xvii. 11, 21-23. Rom. v. 12-19. Eph. v. 22-23. Col. i. 24.

The Symbolism of Baptism.

teristic, distinguishing formula of the Epistles which declares the believer to be IN CHRIST.

Now this fundamental doctrine of the believer's organic union with and in-being in Christ, involves in it the doctrine that the believer fulfilled the law of God in the person of Christ. The law said: "The soul that sinneth it shall die."* The believer has sinned—and still he shall live. And yet not one jot or tittle of God's law has failed or shall fail. The believer, in virtue of his being in Christ, died when Christ died. In virtue of his being in Christ, his sin *was* punished and the law vindicated when Christ endured the cross; and so the believer, in the sphere of Christ, fulfilled all righteousness. And with this doctrine all the Scriptural declarations concerning the believer exquisitely harmonize. For instance, St. Paul, writing to Christian believers, says: "We thus judge, that if one died for all, then all died." The believer is said to have "fellowship with Christ's sufferings;" to be a "partaker of his sufferings;" to be "filling up that which is behind of the afflictions of Christ for his body's sake, which is the church." He is said to have "suffered with Christ;" to have been "crucified with Christ;" "buried with Christ."† And as the propitiatory death of Christ is the source of his own life, so is his participation in Christ's death the instrumental means of his own resurrection.

(*c.*) But this resurrection is, as we have seen, a resurrection to a life of *purity*. How is it, then, that Jesus the crucified is not only the source and means of our resurrection to life, but also our purger from all unrighteousness? Who does not feel that Christ's mission to the world, surveyed simply in its *human* aspect, *i. e.*, in

---

* Ezek. xviii. 4.
† Rom. vi. 8; viii. 17. 2 Cor. v. 14. Gal. ii. 20. Phil. iii. 10. Col. i. 24; ii. 12. 1 Pet. iv. 13.

its relation to man himself, was a mission of cleansing—of restoration to the Edenic purity? It was for this very purpose that he was manifested, that he might take away sin, and so destroy the works of the devil.* Observe, the question under this head of discourse is not concerning God's nature and wrath, or man's penalty; but concerning the washing away of man's uncleanness. Behold, then, the Lamb of God, which taketh away the sins of the world.† But how does he take away the sins of the world? I content myself here, in this article of statement, with a single, direct, matter-of-fact answer. Christ *practically, i. e.*, in the sphere of our own human experience and consciousness, takes away the sin of the world by coming down into the world's plane, enduring sympathetically its burdens and woes, sharing with it its natural evil and curse, and so overcoming it with the evidences of a love and *co*-passion, that is divinely real and divinely great. What these evidences are may be seen in the manger, in the wilderness, in the garden, in the judgment-hall, on the cross, in the tomb. Ah! *here*, in the gloom, and damp, and noisomeness of the sepulchre, the proof of a love divinely real and divinely great culminates. Suffering love can soar no higher than when it sinks, a murdered, dungeoned corpse, in Joseph's grave. Love practically ceased to suffer, it is true, when Jesus, hanging on the cross, bowed his head and yielded up the ghost. But typically it reached the lowest deep of abasement when it lay shrouded and still in the grave. Jesus laid away in the tomb seems more dead to us than Jesus suspended on the cross. Oh! if this, the buried Jesus, does not break and melt my stony heart, then nothing can; and Mercy, incapable of mightier exploit, shall rightly join with Wrath in stamping it down to neth-

---

* 1 John iii. 8. † John i. 29.

The Symbolism of Baptism. 127

ermost hell. But as divine love culminates in Joseph's tomb, so does divine power. Love, descending out of heaven by the cross into the grave near by, passes under the guiltiest, lowest soul, and may lift it by its own celestial buoyancy. And this is the Power which is overcoming, cleansing, transfiguring humanity. Celestial love stands and knocks unweariedly at the door till the stolid, filthy occupant, subdued at last by her patience and all-conquering beauty, opens the door and lets her in; and then, having won her entrance, she sweeps, laves, and cleanses, and garnishes it, till at length, transfigured by her indwelling, she makes it clean and shining, like one of the justified spirits made perfect.* Thus does the blood of Jesus Christ, the Son of God, cleanse from all unrighteousness.† And as the most transcendent event in the world's history is the burial of the Son of God, pressed down into his grave by the weight of an infinite righteousness, which could save only as infinite love bore that weight; so the most transcendent event which ever occurs in the history of any human being is when this same infinite love subdues him, and purifies him, even as God is pure.

And this, by the supposition, is the belief of our new convert to Jesus. He is waiting to confess his faith in Jesus the crucified. If then it is appropriate, and even necessary, that he should symbolize both his death and defilement in sin, and his resurrection and cleansing, how much more appropriate and necessary that he should symbolize the most transcendent events in the world's history and his own, even the burial of that Jesus whose love to him, in order to raise and cleanse him from all unrighteousness, propitiated infinite justice by infinite self-oblation! The buried Jesus, being the sign and

---

* Heb. xii. 23. † 1 John i. 7, 9.

proof of a love that poured itself out to the death, what shall he invent and use as the symbol of his buried Friend, Vicar, Cleanser, and Saviour? The first problem is to symbolize his spiritual death; the second, his spiritual resurrection; the third, his total defilement; the fourth, his total purification; the fifth, the power and instrument by which he is resuscitated and purged. What shall the symbol, or symbols, be?

4. The fourth great truth which this new-born disciple would naturally wish to express in this his formal confession is that *this buried Jesus is indeed the Son of God, and so a resuscitating and cleansing Power divinely efficacious.*

It is a sad, unspeakably sad thing, to see the Son of man lying ghastly and mute in his grave. Was it after all nothing more than man's love that bore the fasting and temptation, the poverty and shame, the agony and bloody sweat, the cross and sepulchre? But look again! See the stone rolled away! Behold the shining angels standing at either end of the sepulchre! Listen! "Why seek ye him who liveth among the dead? He is not here, but is risen, as he said!" Ah, now! I know that Jesus is more than man. That dying love, bursting the bonds of death, has proved itself by that act to be divine. Now I am certified, beyond all manner of doubt, that Jesus, in undertaking to be both the Propitiator of Jehovah and Regenerator of character and Restorer of paradise, has undertaken a work to which he is adequate. I have the demonstration, that the gospel is indeed a gospel—a good tidings worthy of all acceptation; for the Father, in raising his Son from the grave, has set his seal to his Son's work that it is true.

Thus cardinal in the gospel-scheme is the fact of Christ's resurrection. How far Holy Scripture thus regards it will appear from a single citation: "If Christ be not risen, then is our preaching vain, and your faith is also vain: ye are yet in your sins."* See how much this apostolic statement involves. Christ rested the validity of his claims as the Messiah of God, and the attestation of his work as a Saviour, on the fact of his own resurrection. But if Christ did not rise, then his decaying corpse demonstrates that he was not what he claims to be, but instead thereof, a crazy enthusiast, or arrant impostor. If Christ did not rise, all that he had said was false—all that he had done and endured was in vain —all that his people had hoped for was blank and worthless. If Christ did not rise, the one thing alone which could have given to the atonement its worth as an accomplished and certified fact was wanting, and on the stone which had been rolled up against Joseph's sepulchre, might be inscribed: "No glad tidings! No pitying God! No vindicated law! No laver of regeneration! No Saviour! No heaven!" If Christ be not risen, then is our preaching vain, and your faith is also vain: ye are yet in your sins. But, on the other hand, if Christ *be* risen, then the gospel is certified as true; all becomes substantial and harmonious and complete. Nothing is wanting to prove the absolute perfection and divineness of the gospel fabric. For when Jesus rose from the dead, the keystone was inserted into the gospel arch, binding it together in immortal strength and symmetry. And nothing is left for us to do but to join with cherubim and seraphim in shouting: Grace, Grace unto it!

Observe now that as Holy Scripture represents the believer as having participated in Christ's death, so it represents him as having participated in Christ's resurrection. It asserts that believers are risen, not only like Christ, but also *with* him. They are said to be not only heirs of God, but joint heirs with Christ; if so be that we suffer

---

* 1 Cor. xv. 14–17.

with him, that we also may be glorified together. For if we be dead with him, we shall also live with him, and reign with him. God, who is rich in mercy, for the great love wherewith he loved us, even when we were dead in sins, hath quickened us together with Christ, and hath raised us up together, and made us sit together in heavenly places in Christ Jesus.* In virtue of the believer's mystical union with Christ, Christ's death was his death, and Christ's resurrection his resurrection.

To symbolize Christ's resurrection, then, is manifestly as essential as to symbolize his burial. How then shall our friend, who by the supposition has not only had fellowship with Christ's sufferings and been made conformable unto his death, but also with the power of his resurrection,† how shall he, about to make public confession of his Lord and Saviour, shadow forth to others the risen Jesus? What symbol shall he invent that will set forth before others his belief, that him whom wicked hands had crucified and slain, God has exalted to be a prince and a saviour? The first problem is to symbolize his spiritual death; the second, his spiritual resurrection; the third, his total defilement; the fourth, his total purification; the fifth, the sacrificial death in which he has participated; the sixth, the vindicatory resurrection in which he has shared. What shall the symbol, or symbols, be?

5. The fifth great truth which this new convert to Jesus would naturally wish to express, is his belief in *the coming resurrection of the body and the heavenly immortality.*

"If, in this life, only we have hope in Christ," exclaims an apostle, hunted down every day of his life like a partridge among the mountains, "we are of all men most miserable." ‡. And this is the grand, all-inspiring thing of the gospel, that it has the promise not only of the life which now is, but also of that which is to come.§

---

* Rom. vi. 8; viii. 17. Eph. ii. 4–6. Cor. iii. 1–4.
† Phil. iii. 10. ‡ 1 Cor. xv. 19. § 1 Tim. iv. 8.

The Symbolism of Baptism.

The religion of the Nazarene is, characteristically and intensely, a religion of hope. Other religions are bounded by visible horizons, and are expected to culminate in the sphere of the tangible. But the religion of Jesus Christ bursts through all such bars, and is at liberty only as it fills out the expanse of the eternities. Life, life; eternal life, is the keynote of Christ and his gospel. So, too, if there be any thing that was characteristically apostolic, it was the intense gaze which the apostles were wont to fasten on the future world. Their citizenship was in heaven. They walked by faith, not by sight. They endured as seeing him who is invisible. They felt that they were in very deed saved by hope. They looked for and hasted unto the coming of the day of God, when he, who was their life, should appear, and they should appear with him in glory. They watched, as if on tip toe, for that glorious re-appearing, when their absent King should come the second time without sin unto salvation.* They were pre-eminently men of expectation, drawing their daily and hourly inspiration from the powers of the world to come. They never preached Jesus without preaching also the resurrection. Oh, that resurrection, pre-supposing, as it did, the atoning death, sealing its worth and glorifying it—that blessed resurrection was their theme, their ecstasy, their conquering pæan.

This, then, is one of the grand, fundamental, characterizing truths of the gospel, that Jesus Christ hath abolished death, and brought life and immortality to light, being himself the resurrection and the life.† How, then, shall this friend of ours, who, by the supposition, has felt in his own breast the power of that resurrection,‡ as the earnest of his own, symbolize to others his blessed

---

* Rom. viii. 24. 2 Cor. v. 7. Phil. iii. 20. Col. iii. 4. Tit. xi. 13. Heb. xi. 28. 2 Peter iii. 12.
† John xi. 25. 2 Tim. i. 10. ‡ Phil. iii. 10.

assurance that death has lost its sting, being swallowed up in victory? What symbol shall he invent which shall shadow forth to others his confident expectation that the day is coming when this corruption shall put on incorruption, and this mortal immortality; and he himself shall walk with Christ in everlasting chastity and peace and glory? The first problem is to symbolize his own spiritual death; the second, his own spiritual resurrection; the third, his own total defilement; the fourth, his own total purification; the fifth, the atoning death by which he has been made alive and cleansed; the sixth, the accrediting and joy-giving resurrection; the seventh, the resurrection of his own body, and so the heaven to come. What shall the symbol, or symbols, be?

Such are the leading truths which any one about to make a public confession of his Lord and Saviour Jesus Christ would naturally wish to express. They are the cardinal points of a Christian's creed, *bearing him from this polluted earth to the saintly heaven through the redeeming work of a divine Mediator, first abased and then exalted.* I have asked you, at the close of each successive point, to select or devise some symbol which should shadow forth that point. I now ask you to invent a symbol which shall comprehend *all* these points in a single emblem. It will be a difficult task; for these truths contemplate the believer and his Saviour at the extremes of their conditions—the believer in his death and filth, and also in his quickening and spotlessness; the Saviour at the nadir of his humiliation and also at the zenith of his glorification. Nothing is so wide apart as the uncleanness of sin and the chastity of holiness, except Jesus the buried and Jesus the risen. And now I ask you to express, in one single emblem, these antipodal truths. It is a colossal task. Put, then, your inventive powers to utmost tension. Search the heavens above: search the

The Symbolism of Baptism. 133

depths below: what do you find above, below, that will help you?

III. But I will spare you the fruitless trouble. I will give you the pattern shown me in the mount. Wouldst thou symbolize thy death in sin and thy resurrection to holiness? Then be buried by BAPTISM into death; that like as Christ was raised up from the dead by the glory of the Father, even so thou also mayst walk in newness of life.* Wouldst thou symbolize thy total defilement and thy desire for total purification? Then arise and be baptized, and wash away thy sins.† Wouldst thou symbolize thy belief in a buried and risen Mediator, and thy participation in his death and resurrection? Then be buried with him in baptism, wherein also arise with him.‡ Wouldst thou symbolize thy confident expectation that thou shalt share in his blissful immortality? Then submit thyself to baptism—descending into the liquid tomb and emerging: for if thou art planted together with him in the likeness of his death, thou shalt be also in the likeness of his resurrection.§ Oh, glorious symbol this of the Christian's creed! He may tell me in words all that he believes about himself and about his Lord. He may tell me of his sins and his hopes—his tears for the past and his resolves for the future. He may tell me all that Jesus has done for him, and all that he intends to do for Jesus. But when I see him silently submitting himself to holy baptism, I read a more eloquent story, told in a language which all peoples of the earth can understand; which changes not with the flight of years; which no oratory can rival; which carries the head, because it has first carried the heart; which is the truth of God expressed in the act of man. Not that there is any thing in the ordinance which savours of re-

---

* Rom. vi. 4.   † Acts xxii. 16.
‡ Col. ii. 12.   § Rom. vi. 5.

generating or sanctifying tendency. For baptism is a *symbol*, not a power; a shadow, not the substance. And it shadows forth, at the same instant, the most momentous events in the history of Christ and in the history of the Christian; all that Christ has suffered and done for us; all that we mean to suffer and do for Christ; all that we are by nature; all that we hope to be by grace. Verily, none but a God infinite in counsel could have devised a rite so simple and yet so dense with meaning and glory! To him be all the praise!

IV. Brethren, my task is done. I have shown you that the principle of symbolism pervades all nature—all Scripture; that Jesus himself is the symbol of symbols —God's mighty parable to man. In asserting, then, that baptism is a symbol, I have asserted nothing which is an exception to God's method of communicating with the race, but something which is in exquisite harmony with it. In setting forth baptism as a symbol, I have shown you that it expresses the distinctive, cardinal, vital truths of the gospel; truths without which there is nothing but hell; with which the kingdom of heaven is opened unto all believers. I have shown you that baptism, as being a symbol, is also a creed; being as truly a doctrinal formula enunciated in act, as is the Apostles' creed or the Nicene enunciated in words. In carrying out this train of thought, you will bear me witness that I have assailed no man or sect or heresy, feeling assured that if there be error in the world, it can be best overcome, not by fighting it, but by quietly putting the truth alongside of it; for truth, although of slower growth than falsehood, is longer lived. It only remains for me to show that baptism, taken as a symbol, is, and was designed of the Master to be, a power, to be wielded as such by the church of the living God.

What power there is in a symbol, we need not go to the books or across the ocean to learn. Visit with me one of the battle-fields of the Civil War. All around us—right, left, before, behind—the red sea of battle heaves and roars. But look! By yonder turn in the valley the billow swells highest and reddest. Here seems the maelstrom of the fury—the crucible spot of the fight. Here platoon blends with platoon, bayonet crosses bayonet, breast hurtles against breast. And now another awful shock, fiercest of all; and then, above the groan of dying and boom of gun, swells a shout, long, clear, ecstatic: "*It is ours!*" What is "ours"? A smoke-blackened, shot-riddled, bayonet-rent bit of bunting—as a piece of cloth, nothing; as the star spangled banner, *every thing*. Into that banner are gathered country and constitution and government and liberty and glory and fireside and altar. As a piece of cloth it is nothing; as a symbol, it is the concentrated essence of the United States. And this is its power. So long as the flag floats over his ranks, the soldier feels that he has every thing to fight for—every thing to make him fight. Wrest his flag from him, and he feels that all is lost.

Even so is it with baptism, the heavenly devised banner of Immanuel's gospel and church. As a mere act, it is nothing but a ceremony; as a mere ordinance, nothing but a command; as a symbol, it is the gospel of the Nazarene crystallized into formula, or rather, vitalized into a conscious, joyous incarnation. Substitute any other banner for it, and you substitute a human device for a divine—a heresy for a gospel—secessionism for loyalty. Use it as a rite, but not as a symbol, and you surrender the flag, the day, the cause. Accept it as a symbol, preach it as a symbol, administer it as a symbol, and it will sweep forth conquering and to conquer, until throughout the whole world there shall be but one fold as already there is but one Shepherd. By this sign—not Constantine's, but Constantine's Master's, we shall conquer.

VI.

THE QUALIFICATIONS FOR BAPTISM.

By REV. HENRY E. ROBINS,
Pastor of Central Baptist Church, Newport, R. I.

"AND JESUS CAME, AND SPAKE UNTO THEM, SAYING, ALL POWER IS GIVEN UNTO ME IN HEAVEN AND IN EARTH. GO YE THEREFORE AND TEACH ALL NATIONS, BAPTIZING THEM IN THE NAME OF THE FATHER, AND OF THE SON, AND OF THE HOLY GHOST: TEACHING THEM TO OBSERVE ALL THINGS WHATSOEVER I HAVE COMMANDED YOU: AND LO, I AM WITH YOU ALWAYS EVEN UNTO THE END OF THE WORLD." AMEN.—*Matthew* xxviii. 18–20.

GOD, who, at sundry times and in divers manners, spake in time past unto the fathers by the prophets, hath, in these last days, spoken unto us by his Son. The Son of God has established churches on the earth, of which, as constituting his visible spiritual kingdom among men, he is King. As King, he has fixed the conditions of entrance into that kingdom, and ordained laws for the government of his subjects. These are unalterable by any human authority. They rest solely in his will. It is his to command: it is ours to obey.

In seeking, therefore, for the qualifications for Baptism, we turn to the New Testament. We are there, we think, unequivocally taught that *Baptism should be administered to those, and those only, who give credible evidence that they have been born again of the Holy Spirit.*

Regeneration is the great qualification which includes all others. So, when it is required, *repent, believe,* regeneration is necessarily presupposed. For repentance and faith, as well as all other Christian graces, are fruits of the Spirit; the work in the soul of the holy Author of the new birth. Of repentance, Peter expressly teaches that it is the gift of Christ.* And our Lord himself declares that the first great office of the Spirit is to convince of sin.† As to faith, Paul, in his Epistle to the Galatians, classifies faith with love, joy, peace, etc., as a fruit of the Spirit;‡ and in his first Epistle to the Corinthians, traces it directly to its Divine Author, when he says: no man can say that Jesus is Lord but by the Holy Ghost.§ When we insist, then, on regeneration as the qualification for Baptism, we do it as including and insuring *repentance* and *faith*.

To pass, now, to the proof of our position, we appeal:

I. *To the Great Commission:* which has been the device on the banners of the sacramental host of God's elect as it has gone forward, in all the centuries and through all lands, to the conquest of the world. However widely any division of the vast army may have departed from the instructions of our Great Captain, every one of them, without an exception, points to these august words as the authoritative command, in obedience to which it seeks to extend the Empire of the Cross. What, then, is the meaning of this sublime warrant of the Christian teacher's authority? According to the most obvious import of its terms, the disciples were sent forth to secure, first, converts to Christ, *i. e.*, the regeneration of men; secondly, to baptize them, in token of this fact; thirdly, to instruct them in all the duties resulting from their profession. But we do not argue that the *order* of the commission in itself proves what its Divine Author intended should be the method in the building of his spiritual temple: we would not rest in a mere array of words: but we do insist that the order is as authoritative as the command itself, unless proof to the contrary can be adduced from the Holy Scriptures. Nay, it be-

---

* Acts v. 31. † John xvi. 8. ‡ Gal. v. 22. § 1 Cor. xii. 3.

comes of the essence of the commission, if all the lines of evidence converge to corroborate it. What, then, is the order, not so much of the words, as of the ideas? To answer this question intelligently, we must not overlook the fact, that the commission was a growth, a development. It has its roots in a past. Wise interpreters of our national organic law are guided by the debates of the convention by which it was adopted, and the legislation of Congresses immediately succeeding. Let us imitate that wisdom, and so examine the great charter of Christian authority for the evangelization of the world. Our special inquiry now is, whence came Christian baptism, and to whom was it administered. About three years and a half before the ascension of Christ, John appeared in the wilderness of Judea, announcing that the kingdom of heaven was at hand. This, in the language of inspiration, was the beginning of the Gospel of Jesus Christ.* The baptism which he administered was so special a feature of his work, that it gave him his title: the Baptist. Whence came it? This baptism, the Saviour himself instructs us, derived its authority from heaven, not of men.† Hence, as an Ecclesiastical usage, we are not permitted to trace it to any other origin. Here our investigation is authoritatively terminated by the solemn declaration of the Head of the church. We may as well seek for the doctrines of this heaven-sent prophet of the wilderness, in the absurd and contradictory traditions of an effete hierarchy, as to find the origin of that rite which the Saviour consecrated in the waters of Jordan, in their unauthorized and corrupt ceremonies. The conditions, too, of the rite are plainly discoverable from the preaching of the forerunner:—these were, repentance and faith, which, as we have seen, presupposed regeneration.

---

* Mark i. 1. † Matt. xxi. 24–27.

The Qualifications for Baptism. 139

As to repentance, what saith the record? "In those days came John the Baptist, preaching in the wilderness of Judea, and saying, *repent* ye: then went out to him all Jerusalem and Judea and all the region about Jordan, *confessing their sins.*"* As to faith in Christ, Paul teaches, summing up the scope of the Baptist's preaching, "John verily baptized with the baptism of *repentance,* saying unto the people, that they should *believe on him that should come after him, that is, on Christ Jesus.*"† And, as if to put beyond question the fact that John required evidence of a change of heart in the subjects of the ordinance, it is recorded that he repelled the Pharisees and Sadducees who sought it at his hands, with an indignant emphasis of language, which implies that the serpent nature of evil was still theirs, rendering them unfit for it." O generation of vipers! who hath warned you to flee from the wrath to come? Bring forth, therefore, fruits meet for repentance."‡ During the period in which John was thus instructing the people and baptizing, our Lord appeared, was baptized, called disciples, and through them administered the same rite, and, as we infer from subsequent facts, upon the same conditions. We have no account of any formal command on the subject, given by him to his immediate attendants while they labored under his personal supervision. He seems to have taken it up as appropriately belonging to his work. Thus the two streams of teaching and practice, issuing from the same fountain, after flowing side by side with unruffled current for a season, were finally mingled, became one, and John's mission ceased. Soon the Saviour solemnly commissioned his disciples for the great conquest. In doing this he simply epitomized John's preaching and practice; assumed them formally as his own, and

---

* Matt. iii. 1, 2, 5, 6.   † Acts xix. 4.   ‡ Matt. iii. 7, 8.

sent them forth with higher sanctions, as the gospel of his grace to all kindreds and generations of men.

The beams of the morning star joined their light with the first gleam of the dawn, but were quenched at last by the peerless rays of the ascending Sun of Righteousness, destined to fill the earth with their healing power and illuminating glory. Such, in brief, is the anterior history in which the Great Commission has its root. Interpreting it by this certain light, we discover that baptism presupposes regeneration. Moreover, the commission has a history subsequent to its promulgation. Does this confirm the result we have now reached? How did the Apostles to whom it was primarily addressed understand the command? How did they act under it? Here, certainly, we may discover conclusive evidence as to its import. We turn to the Acts of the Apostles, the opening chapters of Baptist church history, and find that the qualification for baptism was the same *after*, as that which had been required *before*, the ascension. When on the day of Pentecost, the inquiry, "men and brethren, what shall we do?" arose from the lips of the hearers of Peter, who, by the power of the Holy Ghost were convinced of sin—pierced in their hearts, in the expressive language of the record—his answer was, "*Repent*, and be *baptized* every one of you in the name of Jesus Christ, for the remission of sins. * * *Then they that gladly received the word were baptized.*"* Philip went into Samaria, carrying the glad tidings, "and when," says the history, "*they believed* Philip preaching the things concerning the kingdom of God, and the name of Jesus Christ, *they were baptized*, both men and women."† So when Paul was obedient to the commission in Corinth, "Crispus, the chief ruler of the synagogue, believed in the Lord, with all his house;

---

* Acts ii. 37, 38, 41.   † Acts viii. 12.

The Qualifications for Baptism. 141

and many of the Corinthians *hearing, believed,* and *were baptized.*"* To the Philippian jailor, who—terrified at midnight by the earthquake, which, as by the touch of the Almighty, had shaken to their foundations the massive walls of the prison, and loosed his prisoners—fell trembling at the feet of Paul and Silas, crying, "Sirs, what must I do to be saved?" they replied, "Believe on the Lord Jesus Christ and thou shalt be saved, and thy house." Then assembling the household they spake unto him the word of the Lord, and to all that were in his house. Then were they "baptized, he and all his, straightway," "and he rejoiced, believing in God with all his house."† Here is first, *instruction;* then, *faith;* afterward, *baptism: household instruction, household faith, household baptism.* The limits of my discourse forbid me to quote all the abundant proofs which appear as we turn from page to page of this part of the sacred history.

We are clearly authorized to say, that the common English version of our text gives the essential import of the commission; although objection may be made to the translation as, perhaps, not strictly accurate.

The first clause, "Go teach," or go make disciples of, "all nations," embraces as to the idea the following clauses, with the preliminary and conditioning thought of a preparation of heart wrought in men by the supernatural power of the Son of God. "All power is given unto me in heaven and in earth," he said. On this firm foundation, he builds his commission: gives us in these pregnant words a clue to a right understanding of those which follow, and a reason why he bade the apostles to tarry in the city of Jerusalem, until they were endued

---

* Acts xviii. 8. † Acts xvi. 30–34

with power from on high, saying, "behold I send the promise of my Father upon you."

Go make Christians, go attempt a superhuman task, and when, by the Holy Spirit's aid, you have made men willing to take my yoke upon them, baptize them, and instruct them in all the duties of their profession.

To bring men into the condition of discipleship is to bring them into a moral fitness for baptism and all other Christian duties. The subsequent clauses of the commission, baptizing and teaching, rise out of and expand the first; and enjoin the outward expression and completion of an inward work, wrought by the Holy Ghost. The testimony thus far examined is so uniform, without ambiguity or contradiction, that even those who contend for a change of administration are constrained to admit, with Calvin, " that persons of *adult* age, who are capable of hearing the gospel, are to be instructed, in order that they may believe before they are baptized:" or, with Edwards, that "baptism, by which the primitive converts were admitted into the church, was used as an exhibition and token of their being visibly, that is, in the judgment of Christian charity, regenerated:" or, with Dr. Bushnell, in his romance entitled Christian Nurture, that "Christianity must needs make its chief address, at the outset, to adult persons so as to meet *only* the conditions of adult minds." We submit, therefore, that the great commission, whether we consider the force of its terms, or whether we interpret it in the light of its history as given in the New Testament, prescribes regeneration as the indispensable qualification for baptism.

II. In support of this conclusion, we appeal to the teachings of the word of God respecting *the spiritual constitution of the church under the New Testament.*

Our position is this:—that, according to the design of its Divine Founder, the church of the new dispensation

The Qualifications for Baptism. 143

should be constituted of those, and those only, who have been regenerated by the Holy Spirit. This may be justly inferred from what has been discovered concerning the first converts to Christianity; but when it shall appear that our interpretation of the commission is in exact accordance with the plan of God as revealed in prophecy, and in the apostolic epistles, all doubt will be excluded. Every thorough student of Christian institutions will certainly be led back to the covenant with Abraham as a starting point in human history. "In thee," said God, to him, "shall all families of the earth be blessed."* But the institutions of the visible people of God, under the Mosaic economy, which were engrafted upon this promise as a part of its unfolding fulfillment, were but "shadows of good things to come,"† "patterns of things in the heavens,"‡ as we are expressly taught. As such they deserve our study, and will afford us much instruction touching the realities foreshadowed. It is to be observed, then, that the promise to Abraham had a double meaning: the first, spiritual, insuring a spiritual seed and a heavenly Canaan: the second, temporal, insuring a carnal seed and an earthly Canaan. This is the key which unlocks all the succeeding mysteries. Under the first dispensation, the temporal predominated, and gave shape to all its institutions. In the first place, an earthly Canaan only lay on the face of the prophecy: "I will give unto thee, and to thy seed after thee, the land wherein thou art a stranger; all the land of Canaan for an everlasting possession."§ Consequently, the hope of the great majority of the people never rose above Palestine. By this hope they were bound together into one. As a *nation* they were to inherit the promised land. It was the purpose of the Most High to make them, in their national character, his repre-

---

* Gen. xii. 3.   † Heb. x. 1.   ‡ Heb. ix. 23.   § Gen. xvii. 8.

sentative people on earth. His address to them was, hence, in these terms:—" The Lord thy God hath chosen thee to be a special people unto himself above all people that are on the face of the earth."* They were the depository of his law written on *tangible tables of stone:* to them Jehovah *visibly* revealed his glory: to them he spake in an *audible* voice. They were the visible Israel of God among men. In the second place, we notice, that, in harmony with this plan, there was no separation of the children of God by faith and the children of Abraham by natural generation; but all were recognized, in virtue of their birth in the line of promise, as entitled to all the privileges and sharers of the hopes of Israel.

We find, in the third place, as a necessary corollary in this logical sequence of facts, that the initiatory ordinance was administered without reference to spiritual qualification. Only in the case of Abraham, who was himself a believer and the type and father of believers in every age, was circumcision a seal of the righteousness of the faith which he had being yet uncircumcised, and, hence, it did not certify fitness for heaven, except in this single instance. Every child, in virtue of its birth of Jewish parents, met all the conditions of entrance into the national Israel, and was, therefore, circumcised: entitled to that side of the promise, so to speak, by which they were separated from the gentile world, and were heirs of the earthly Canaan.

Hence, in the fourth place, the institutions of national Israel corresponded to the carnal character of those for whom they were intended: they were outward in the flesh,† and, temporary, imposed till the time of reformation.‡ There was a worldly sanctuary, and a gorgeous ritual: there were sacrifices of dumb animals, and priests made after the law of a carnal commandment,§ qualified by de-

---

* Deut. vii. 6. † Rom. ii. 28. ‡ Heb. ix. 10. § Heb. vii. 16.

scent in the priestly line; there was ceremonial uncleanness and ceremonial purification; there were multiform laws with temporal sanctions. But these shadows of realities in the heavens, for a time falling upon the earth, were destined to pass away. The finger of prophecy steadily pointed to the coming of Messiah, when the types should find in him and his church their fulfillment. In the fullness of time he appeared. The key note of the new dispensation which he came to establish was struck when he said to the Samaritan woman, "The hour cometh, when ye shall neither in this mountain, nor yet at Jerusalem, worship the Father. God is a Spirit: and they that worship him must worship him in spirit and in truth."* Then Judaism and formalism fell to the earth. The spiritual import of the promise becomes now evident and paramount. It rules the future. No longer to Mount Zion in Palestine, should Israel of the Spirit come; but, pilgrims and strangers on the earth, they should seek the city of the living God, the heavenly Jerusalem. The bow of promise is now seen to stretch beyond Jordan in Judea, to span the Jordan of death, and rest in the heavenly Canaan. In conformity with this exaltation of the spiritual import of the promise over the temporal, as relating to the inheritance, the great high priesthood of Christ is lifted into its proper place. No merely human priests, having infirmity, made after the law of a carnal commandment, offer repeated sacrifices of beasts upon earthly altars; but Christ, made a priest after the power of an endless life† is entered, *not* into the holy places made with hands, which are figures of the true, but into heaven itself now to appear in the presence of God for us.

Manifestly, to become heirs to such an inheritance, to

---

* John iv. 23, 24.   † Heb. vii. 16. Heb. ix.

avail themselves of the benefits of such a priestly offering, and the sympathy of such a priest, men need other preparation than natural birth. Hear, then, what Paul says when giving to the promise a depth of meaning, which Israel of old could not have anticipated :—" The Scripture foreseeing that God would justify the heathen through faith, preached the *gospel* before unto Abraham, saying, " In thee shall all nations be blessed. * * * Know ye, therefore, that they which are of faith," which resemble him in spiritual character, without reference to natural descent—" the same are the children of Abraham."* " For ye are all the children of God by faith in Jesus Christ. And if ye be Christ's, then are ye Abraham's seed, and heirs according to the promise."† But to bring men into union with Christ is the work of the Spirit. The condition is the result of regeneration. Hence the memorable words of the Saviour to Nicodemus, " Except a man be born again, he cannot see the kingdom of God :" ‡ which are but an echo of the prophecy of Jeremiah, foretelling the manner in which, under the new dispensation, its members should be qualified for the Church of Christ. " Behold the days come," saith the Lord, " when I will make a new covenant. This is the covenant that I will make with the house of Israel after those days," saith the Lord ; " I will put my laws into their minds and write them in their heart, and I will be to them a God, and they shall be to me a people ;" adding, as a result of this, " they shall not teach every man his neighbor and every man his brother" (as was necessary in the national Israel), " saying, know ye the Lord : for they shall all know me from the least of them unto the greatest of them."§ The latter clause, so often quoted as foretelling the universal prevalence of piety in the millennial age,

---

* Gal. iii 7–9. † Gal. iii. 26–29.
‡ John iii. 3–7. § Jer. xxxi. 31–34.

The Qualifications for Baptism.

is here expressly applied as descriptive of the church of Christ in Messianic times. It is a picture, glowing with life and beauty, painted by a Divine Hand, of a household of faith. It was a foreglance of that era which drew from Isaiah's lips the exultant summons to Israel, "Awake, awake; put on thy strength, O Zion; put on thy beautiful garments, O Jerusalem, the holy city; for henceforth there shall no more come into thee the uncircumcised—the unrenewed in heart—and the unclean."* We find, therefore, members of the Apostolic churches always spoken of in terms, or addressed by titles, which assert or imply regeneration. They are always contemplated as saints. As the change wrought in them is regarded from different points of view, they are spoken of as "born of the Spirit"† "led by the Spirit;"‡ as an "habitation of God through the Spirit;"§ "as having received the Spirit of adoption;"‖ as made "alive from the dead;"¶ as "walking in newness of life;"** as "temples of the Holy Ghost;"†† as "a chosen generation; a royal priesthood;"‡‡ as "one body" animated by "one Spirit."§§

Moreover, they were commanded to exclude from their communion heretics,‖‖ and the unclean, and the disorderly;¶¶ some went out from them that it might be evident that they were not of them;*** they were afflicted by false brethren, who had crept in unawares††† in spite of their guarding scrutiny of the purity of the body of Christ.

It is clear, we think, from even this slight survey of the evidence, that it was the design of their Founder that the churches of the New Testament should be composed of persons, who, in the judgment of charity, have

---

* Isaiah lii. 1. † John iii. 6. ‡ Rom. viii 14.
§ Eph. ii. 22. ‖ Rom. viii. 15. ¶ Rom. vi. 13.
** Rom. vi. 4. †† 1 Cor. vi. 19. ‡‡ 1 Pet. ii. 9.
§§ Eph. iv. 4. ‖‖ Titus iii. 10.
¶¶ 1 Cor. v. 13. 2 Thess. iii. 6. *** 1 John ii. 19. ††† Jude 4.

been born again. Such only, therefore, are entitled to its initiatory rite, baptism.

III. We urge, in the third place, in support of our main position, the fact that *baptism was designed to declare in symbolic form the great and radical change which has been wrought in him who submits to it.*

Why does baptism hold its present conspicuous place in our teaching? Those who charge us with making too much of an outward rite, of exalting the form above the spirit, cannot have duly considered the significance of its position in the commission. They would do well to ask whether, under a proud pretence of escaping ritual bondage, they do not pass to an opposite extreme, exalt themselves above their baptized Master, and scorn, as unimportant, that which bears the sanctity of his ordaining seal. Why did he select this from all the obligations which rest upon his followers; exalt it where every eye must see it, uniting it in perpetual, though subordinate, union with the holy work of preaching his gospel, if he did not attach to its proper observance an importance which none of us may have duly considered? We believe that it holds its place immediately after the injunction to disciple the nations, because our Lord would have it immediately follow a believing reception of the truth, as exhibiting the spiritual change which conditions such reception: declaring outwardly the inward transition from death to life. The ordinances are not arbitrary forms: they are rooted in the essence of things. The divine idea takes on a divine expression, corresponding exactly to it. On this point, the Genevese reformer says: "this analogy, or similitude, is a most certain rule of sacrament; that in corporeal things we contemplate spiritual things just as if they were placed before our eyes, as it has pleased God to represent them to us by such figures." Are we not justified, then, in saying, that to modify, or change an ordinance, either as to mode, or time of administration—*in any respect that is essential to its significance*—is to utter, in action, partial, or mutilated truth, or downright untruth?—in saying that, since baptism was designed to represent the great fact of regeneration *as having already taken place* in the subject, it cannot be administered to the unregenerate without utterly nullifying its intent? It becomes, when avowedly so administered, either a meaningless mummery, or—a concrete falsehood.

We said, baptism was designed to represent the great fact of regeneration. To prove this and other symbolic teaching of this holy rite fell within the province of another, who recently addressed you. But it is important to our present purpose to say, that the first step in the work of the Spirit in the soul is to convince of sin. This, in the expressive language of Paul, is the "crucifixion of the old man"—"death to sin," which is followed by the resurrection of the new man. *Evangelical* conviction of sin can be experienced only by the regenerate soul, for it depends upon love of holiness. This love of holiness is the ground of the soul's anguish in repentance, and of its sympathy with Christ in his atoning work—a copartnership, so to speak, in his anguish on the cross. In this godly sorrow for sin, believers are said therefore to have fellowship with the sufferings of Christ, being made conformable unto his death: thus, too, they become partakers of his life: they become dead, indeed, unto sin, but alive unto God, through Jesus Christ our Lord.* Hence, says Paul, referring to the initiatory ordinance of the church, speaking of it as a thing well understood by those whom he addresses: "Know ye not, that so many of us as were baptized into Jesus Christ

---

* Rom. vi. 11.

were baptized into his death? Therefore, we are buried with him by baptism into death;" enclosed, so to speak, in the sepulchre of waters, as are the dead in the tomb—"that, like as Christ was raised up from the dead by the glory of the Father, even so we also should walk in newness of life."* If this be the significancy of baptism, we ask, with certainty that no Biblical answer can be given, with what propriety is it administered to those who have passed through no spiritual renewal, but are still dead in sin, and children of this world?

IV. Thus are we brought to the last reason, which we shall at present urge, why regeneration should always be insisted upon as a prerequisite to baptism, viz :—*that the ordinances of the gospel become spiritually profitable to those only who have a spiritual preception of their import.*

The ordinances are instruments of the Spirit, which he uses according to his will. They are not channels of grace, through which, as material conduits, heavenly blessings flow upon mankind, irrespective of any receptive faith on their part. "The wind bloweth where it listeth, and thou hearest the sound thereof, but canst not tell whence it cometh, and whither it goeth: so is every one that is born of the Spirit." He binds himself to no fixed methods: much less does he put into mortal hands the means by which he will quicken the dead in sin. He uses the word when and as he will: but the word is useless unless prevenient grace gives the believing heart.

The word preached by Moses did not profit those who heard it, not being mixed with faith in them:† so the ordinances, *act-words* simply, are of no efficacy whatever, their sanctifying design is nullified, if received in unconsciousness, as in infancy, or in a state of unbelief,

---

* Rom. vi. 3, 4. † Heb. iv. 2.

and blindness of mind, and hardness of heart. "The natural man receiveth not the things of the Spirit of God; for they are foolishness to him: neither can he know them; because they are spiritually discerned," judged, estimated * Hence, Paul exhorts those who come to the Supper of the Lord as follows: "Let a man examine himself,† and so"—having duly considered his fitness for the ordinance—"let him eat of that bread and drink of that cup; for he that eateth and drinketh unworthily, eateth and drinketh damnation to himself, not discerning the Lord's body:" that is, he perceives not its spiritual significance. But baptism is as truly one of the things of the Spirit of God as the Lord's Supper, and, as we have seen, the qualification for its reception in Apostolic days was spiritual fitness, manifested in faith and repentance. Hence, Peter teaches: "the like figure,"—referring to the salvation of Noah from the waters of the flood by the Ark which it bore upon its bosom—"the like figure whereunto even baptism, also, doth now save us, not the putting away of the filth of the flesh, but the answer of a good conscience toward God, by the resurrection of Jesus Christ from the dead."‡ Baptism is the response which a good, or purified conscience, inquiring after the will of God, returns to the demand of its sovereign upon it for submission to his authority, and, as such, saves:— but only as obedience saves, as Christ teaches: "Not every one that saith unto me, Lord, Lord, shall enter into the kingdom of heaven, but he that doeth the will of my Father, which is in heaven:" obedience as the evidence of justifying faith saves; as James says, "I will show thee my faith by my works."

It is a distinguishing characteristic of Christianity, that it invests the individual soul with unspeakable dig-

---

* 1 Cor. ii. 14. † 1 Cor. xi. 28. ‡ 1 Pet. iii. 21.

nity and worth. The will of God in his law is uttered to individuals: "Thou shalt," comes to each one of us as if there was but one subject of the command under the whole heaven. The warnings summon every one of us to give account of himself to God. He lays his hand, so to speak, upon every man, draws him forth from the mass of his fellows from whom he is so prone to take his opinions, and with whom to identify his destiny, and, placing him alone in the Divine Presence, summons him to choose for himself, under the awful sanctions of the life to come—heaven with its blessedness, and hell with its anguish—whom he will serve, God or Satan.

"Repent and be baptized *every one of you;*"* thus singly does the gospel address us: it solemnly warns us not to rely upon our descent from a pious ancestry; "and think not to say within yourselves, we have Abraham to our father;"† "*now* is the axe laid unto the root of the trees. Every tree, therefore, which bringeth not forth good fruit is hewn down and cast into the fire."‡ Repentance and faith are personal duties; no human being, who is capable of these acts, can be saved, except by their exercise for himself alone; nothing done for him by another—neither baptism, nor sponsor's vows, nor prayers—can avail any thing, if he neglects his personal duty toward God and his Christ.

In beautiful harmony with this teaching, baptism is the appointed public answer of a purified conscience to these demands of our sovereign upon us. So observed, as the happy experience of thousands proves, its effect is eminently salutary, comforting, and sanctifying to the obedient subject, as well as instructive to those who witness his voluntary consecration of himself to his Master's service.

---

*Acts ii. 38. † Matt. iii. 9. ‡ Matt. iii. 10.

The Qualifications for Baptism. 153

On review of what has been said, whether we consider baptism as it stands in the commission, interpreted by its anterior and subsequent history; or, in the light which the spiritual constitution of the New Testament church throws upon it, as the initiatory rite into its spiritual fellowship; or, as a symbol of the death and burial of the old man and the resurrection of the new; or, as deriving its sole efficacy through the faith of him who receives it —it is plainly evident, we think, that this sacred ordinance should be administered to those only who give credible evidence of repentance toward God, and faith in our Lord Jesus Christ: or to the regenerate. If this be true, what shall be said of infant baptism? It is excluded. It has no place among the institutions of Christ. It is a solecism, and an anachronism.

We have chosen to present the argument in support of this interpretation of the Holy Scriptures, as maintained by us as a denomination of Christians, without turning aside in its progress to examine the theories of men advanced to uphold a practice, of which Dr. Hackett, whose qualification to speak with authority on such a point will not be disputed by scholars, has written, "the opinion that infant baptism has any legitimate sanction from any passage in the New Testament is no longer a tenable opinion at the bar of biblical criticism."

We have adopted this course for two reasons:

1. Because there is no agreement among its advocates as to the ground upon which infant baptism holds its usurped place. This ghostly delusion of the Papacy eludes us: or, if we pierce it with the sword of the Spirit, it instantly assumes another of its Protean forms, and flies, mocking, away on its corrupting mission. The earnest Menno, groping through the labyrinths of Romish error toward the light of the gospel, found this rite in his path. "For explanation and evidence he went to his

pastor, who, finally acknowledged that it had no ground in the Scriptures. Afterwards he went to Luther, who taught that we must baptize children on their faith, because they are holy; then to Bucer, who taught that we should baptize children in order to be able to bring them up in the ways of the Lord: finally, to Bullinger, who pointed him to the covenant of circumcision." An inquirer of the present day finds still greater diversity of view, and, as he sees the confusion of conflicting theories, he will ask if truth, which is ONE, can lead to such discord in its defence. Contending on this point, our brethren of other names resemble the perplexed hosts of Midian, when the Lord set every man's sword against his fellow.

2. Our second, and chief reason for pursuing the argument thus is, that, if legitimate, it refutes all the theories at once: it establishes principles, and adduces facts, with which any hypothesis urged in support of infant baptism is utterly inconsistent.

I. Thus, first, the fallacy of the notion of baptismal regeneration has been exposed. If any further evidence were necessary to confute it we might urge the conduct of multitudes who received the rite in infancy as conclusive proof that it is not a regenerating ordinance. What is the testimony of the moral state of those communities where the practice is almost universal: the moral state of Italy, of France, of Spain? To ask the question is to answer it.

II. Our argument shows, secondly, that none are entitled to baptism in virtue of their connection with believing parents. On this point we may add that the passage from the Acts which is generally quoted as in favor of the usage is really against it. It is this: "Then Peter said unto them, Repent and be ye baptized every one of you in the name of Jesus Christ for the remission of sins, and ye shall receive the gift of the Holy Ghost. For the promise is unto you and your children: and to all that are afar off; even as many as the Lord our God shall call." Now, to whom was this addressed? Children of Abraham by natural descent: entitled to all the benefits of the promise in its spiritual import which birth in the line of promise can give. But on what conditions? Hear them as sinners inquiring, "Men and brethren, what shall we do?" Hear, also, the reply. "Repent, and be baptized every one of you;" adding as an encouragement to duty, the promise of the Holy Ghost is unto you and your children. That is, to *you* on *condition of repentance*, and to *your children on the same condition:* and not to you and your children only; but all those afar off, the Gentile nations, even to as many of the children of men as the Lord our God shall call:—Peter in these modes of expression simply declaring the universality of the provision of gospel grace, extending to all people, and available on the uniform condition of repentance.

III. But, thirdly, there are those who, while admitting the significance of baptism as a symbol of regeneration, contend, nevertheless, with Calvin, and Luther virtually, that children are fit subjects for the rite on the ground of a supernatural cleansing given to all children of Adam through the grace of Christ. "For if," says the Reformer of Geneva, "they must be left among the children of Adam, they are left in death. On the contrary, Christ commands them to be brought to him. Why? Because he is life. To give them life, therefore, he makes them partakers of himself." That this is a pure figment of the imagination, invented to sustain an error, is evident to all readers of the Bible, without argument. For, to be a partaker of Christ's life, is to be regenerate: to be born of the Spirit: the Spirit of life which is in Christ Jesus making free from the law of sin and death. But that this is not true of all infants is manifest to every observer. Alas! the Scripture is not obsolete: the whole world yet lieth in wickedness. History, experience, and observation unite their voices to declare that, although Christ died, the race is not restored to its original purity: men are not generally sanctified from the womb, but go astray as soon as they are born. Nor can it be pretended that the grace of regeneration received in infancy is subsequently lost by transgression. For this heavenly gift is never lost. Calvin taught, as do the Holy Scriptures, the perseverance of the saints. To them Paul utters the consoling persuasion of his soul: Being confident of this very thing, that he which hath begun a good work in you will perform it until the day of Jesus Christ. We do not say that there is no hope for a child dying in infancy. We leave those who have not reached an age which renders them capable of accepting or rejecting the Saviour of sinners where the Bible leaves them: in the hands of him who has taught, that *this* is the condemnation, that light is come into the world, and men loved darkness rather than light; and, that the decisions of the final day will be according to the light enjoyed by those who shall be judged. We believe he is able to regenerate the souls of infants, dying in the dawn of being, in the mysterious transition of death, as we hold that the sanctification of the believer is then completed, so that he enters heaven without spot of positive sin.

IV. One ground only for the practice remains to be considered. In order to retain this "part and pillar of popery," men, in later days, who admit that it has no warrant in the word of God, with astonishing audacity, propose to those who profess to be guided solely by that word, "to reform the doctrine of Biblical baptism." These are the words of Dr. Bunsen, as quoted by Professor Chase. In other words, it is proposed to engraft on

Protestantism the Romish theory of legislative power residing in the church. In similar terms the erratic iconoclast of Brooklyn, who, in his Quixotic attacks, is as likely to shatter the ark of God as Dagon, suggests the same thing. "If experience," he says, "shows a certain *ordinance*"—mark the language—"to be good, it is your right to adopt that, whether the Scriptures point it out or not." You need no authority for it except the testimony of experience that it is good. That is divine authority. Indeed, is this the charter of Christian liberty? to alter and amend, to nullify by our alterations and pretended amendments, the solemnly established ordinances of our King? What abomination of the Papacy cannot be defended on this ground? Let me quote from a Doctrinal Catechism of the Romish church issued under the imprimatur of the late Archbishop Hughes.

The question is asked, "why does the church make use of so many ceremonies, as the blessing and burning of wax tapers on the Festival of Purification, the distribution of ashes on Ash Wednesday, the first day of Lent, the blessing and distribution of Palm branches on the Sunday before Easter, the blessing of the bells of churches, etc., etc."

The answer is, "to give external expression to the interior sentiments of respect, devotion, and religion; secondly, to enliven and increase devotion and piety by moving and striking the senses: thirdly, to lead the simple and illiterate more easily to a knowledge of the mysteries of religion."

And what is this but to say, that these ceremonies having been found beneficial to these ends, the church is at liberty to introduce them into her worship; or to use the words of this Protestant teacher, "if *experience* shows a certain *ordinance* to be good, it is your right to adopt that, whether the Scripture points it out or not."

Thus Rome and Plymouth Rock are united by the invisible, yet strong bond of this ancient error.

Surely, our mission is not at an end, since there are none beside us to protest against an error that so blinds the minds of Christian men, whom we love as brethren and reverence as examples of piety, as to lead them to adopt such fatal teaching in its defence.

The mother of harlots has recognized our distinction in this respect, and admits, that in us alone does she find unqualified antagonism.

"Can Protestants prove to Baptists," asks the Romish Catechism from which we have quoted, "that the baptism of infants is good and useful?" "No," it is replied, "they cannot, because according to Protestant principles such baptism is useless."

Let us, then, contend for the faith once delivered to the saints, in the spirit of faithful Christian love, which will not suffer a brother in error, without an effort to reclaim him.

Some have thought the battle over. Wiser observers saw in the natural tendency of men to formalism in religion, and in the retention of infant baptism, carefully guarded in the symbols of organizations which had suffered the *practice* to fall into partial desuetude, the seeds of a certain harvest of death. "A reaction is now begun," says the writer before quoted, "and it is my fixed conviction that it will not stop till the encouragement heretofore given to Baptist opinions is quite taken away." Not quite taken away, we think. The eternal years of God are Truth's. Yet by action and reaction, by struggle and victory, does her cause go forward on the earth. Therefore we may not slight the warning of so acute an observer. The rapid growth of ritualistic churches, and the manifest tendency to ritualism in churches which professedly exclude it, keeping pace in this country with the increase of material wealth, sustain the correctness of his judgment. We are summoned, then, by every consideration of duty to God and love to men, to gird ourselves for the defence of principles, with which we believe the glory of God and the welfare of the race are identified. Let us remember that it will not be enough that we maintain our position by argument; that it will be in vain that we strengthen the outworks. We will rejoice rather that no iron bands of organization will keep our churches from crumbling to atoms when their inner life is gone. When the spirit is departed, let the grave cover the dead.

We must be endued with life from heaven, power from on high. We must have Christ, the living Christ, in the heart, on the lip, in the life. We shall then be able to fulfill our mission as we bring individual men to bow broken-hearted for sin at the throne of sovereign grace, to sue there for mercy till they find it, to rise thence in the power of a new and heavenly life, to consecrate themselves, by open profession in the waters of baptism, to Christ and his church.

"Make better men," said Zeller, the German philanthropist, "and you will have better times."

"Go ye," said the Saviour, the Inspirer of philanthropy, "teach all nations, baptizing them in the name of the Father, and of the Son and of the Holy Ghost, teaching them to observe all things whatsoever I have commanded you"—and so shall we save the world.

VII.

THE EVILS OF INFANT BAPTISM.

By A. N. ARNOLD, D.D.,
Professor of Biblical Interpretation in Hamilton Theological Seminary.

"EVERY PLANT WHICH MY HEAVENLY FATHER HATH NOT PLANTED SHALL BE ROOTED UP."—*Matthew* xv. 13.

THE occasion on which these words of our Lord were spoken was this. He had given offence to the Pharisees, by refusing to honor a custom which they regarded as sacred. In his view, it was important to make a sharp distinction between what was of Divine authority, and what was of human devising. And so, instead of making any apology for not conforming to their traditionary religious rites, he plainly declares that these rites must be abolished, because they have no divine sanction. He does more. Taking occasion from this one example, he pronounces a general sentence of condemnation and decree of extirpation upon all customs and ceremonies which falsely claim a divine origin. We are fully persuaded that the baptism of infant children, who are incapable of professing faith in Christ, belongs to this class, and comes under this decisive reprobation of the Lord. While we honor the characters and respect the feelings of our fellow Christians who believe this custom to be of divine appointment, the custom itself we can neither honor nor respect. Nor can we admit that any custom is *harmless*, which challenges for itself a sacredness to which it has no just claim.

The Evils of Infant Baptism.

It is not my purpose now, to set before you the *proof* that Infant Baptism has no warrant of Scripture: but assuming that, as one of the things that are surely believed among us, to call your attention to some of the *evils* which result from the practice. In one aspect, indeed, this may be regarded as a part of the proof that the custom is not of God: for every tree is known by its fruits; and if it clearly appear that the natural and constant effects of Infant Baptism are evil rather than good, it may safely be concluded that it is not of God's planting.

I. We charge Infant Baptism, in the first place, with a tendency to *ritualize Christianity*. Let me be pardoned for the use of an uncommon word: I could find no other which expressed my thought so briefly. A few words will make my meaning plain. Two opposite views of the nature of Christianity have been, from the earliest times, struggling for the ascendency in the Christian Church. The question which divides the two parties may be stated thus:—by what means and in what way does the Christian religion principally exert its beneficent power over the souls of men? To what part of our complex nature does it make its most direct appeal? Does it address the heart and conscience through the understanding, by the presentation of truth? or does it address the imagination and the sensibilities, by means of rites, symbols, and an imposing ceremonial? Does it appeal to us chiefly as rational, or chiefly as sensuous beings? Those who take the former view attribute great efficacy to the Bible and to preaching; those who take the latter view attribute great efficacy to sacraments and priestly offices. Now what we claim is, that the former of these views is the true one. The imagination and the sensibilities are not indeed to be altogether ignored: no, Christianity is adapted to our entire nature: but in religion, as in the conduct of life generally, these should have a subordinate place and power, in comparison with the intellect, that apprehends truth, and the conscience, that recognizes the obligations of duty. Men should be mainly influenced and governed, in religion as in every thing else, by intelligent convictions, and not by undefined sentiments. And what we allege against Infant Baptism is, that it tends to encourage the latter and false view of Christianity—to make it a religion of rites and forms, to affect men through their senses, rather than a "manifestation of the truth, commending" itself "to every man's conscience."

What are the facts in regard to this matter? In all the unreformed churches—the Papal, the Greek, and the minor oriental sects—Christianity has become completely a ritual religion. Its sanctifying and saving efficacy is believed to be connected, not with the clear presentation and intelligent acceptance of its truths, but with the administration of its sacraments. And even in the reformed churches, the ritual tendency has had, and still has, a powerful and pernicious influence. In a large part of the Lutheran and the Anglican churches, a regenerating virtue is attributed to baptism, and a sanctifying efficacy to the Eucharist, not dependent, in either case, upon the intelligent faith of those who receive these ordinances. Is this extensive and long-continued corruption of Christianity traceable in any important degree to the practice of Infant Baptism? We maintain that it is, and that the proof of this is seen, whether we take a practical, a logical, or a historical view of the matter.

Practically, the baptism of infant children is found to exist, wherever this perverted form of Christianity exists. And if this perverted form of Christianity is not found wherever Infant Baptism prevails, the exceptions are confined to those communities where the latter is not universally practised; and these exceptions are most marked in those communions in which it is more and more falling into disuse. In great Britain and the United States, the legitimate influence of the practice is not fully manifest; because it exists in the presence of an influential counteracting element, and is defended, among evangelical sects, on grounds which could never have caused its world-wide prevalence, and which are in fact expressly repudiated by nine tenths of all those who favor the practice. And yet even among those who hold the practice so loosely, and who formally deny its regenerating virtue, or sacramental efficacy, its ritualistic tendency discloses itself in the uneasiness which many parents feel at the prospect of their infant children dying without baptism. And no wonder: for,

Logically, there is an intimate connection between the practice which we are deprecating and the ritual or sacramental system as a whole. A religious rite, administered to those in respect to whom it can express no religious truth to the understanding, and excite no religious affections in the heart, if it have any virtue or efficacy at all, must of necessity have such virtue or efficacy " ex opere operato," or in accordance with the ritualistic theory of religion. Something more must be attributed to it than is consistent with purely evangelical views, or else it will soon cease to be regarded with reverence as a divine rite. Wherever it long prevails, one or both of these accompaniments will surely be found. The annals of the church afford abundant confirmation of these statements.

Historically, it is true that such has been the influence and effect of the practice against which we protest. Not that the whole sacramental system of religion can be traced to Infant Baptism as its primary cause. No; it has a far deeper origin, in our very nature—in the tendency of our sensuous humanity to magnify unduly the outward and visible form, and to make it first the indispensable means, and finally the wretched substitute, of the inward and spiritual reality. But it is historically certain, that exaggerated and unscriptural views of the efficacy of baptism first gave rise to the custom of administering it to infants,* and that this custom drew along with it, wherever it prevailed, other features of the sacramental system. Infant Communion appears to have followed closely upon Infant Baptism in the early ages, or rather to have been its inseparable accompaniment, defended on precisely the same unscriptural ground of its necessity to salvation ; and to have proceeded hand in hand with Infant Baptism, till it overspread the whole Western church, where it continued to be practiced till the twelfth century,† and the whole Eastern church, where it continues to be practiced to the present day.

It is a truth, which cannot be gainsaid, that the strong support of Infant Baptism, as it exists in the Christian world at large, is the dogma of baptismal regeneration. Wherever this dogma is rejected, Infant Baptism is theoretically weakened, and practically, in a greater or less degree, neglected and abandoned. If this belief should die out of the world, the practice that rests mainly upon it could not long survive.

And it is equally true, that the tendency of introducing into the church of Christ this one element of the ritual type of Christianity, is to draw along with it other usages of the same class, even the whole group of related rites and forms and carnal ordinances ; and so, to pervert the religion of Christ as a system of saving truth. And what gives special force to this tendency is, that it falls in with the

---

* See the evidence in proof of this statement in an article in the *Christ. Review* for January, 1861.

† See Bingham's *Antiq. of the Chr. Ch.* Bk. xii. ch. 1. sect. 1, 2, Bk. xv. ch. iv. sect. 7, Bk. xv. ch. vii. sect. 4.

besetting infirmity of our nature, to attach itself to outward signs to the neglect of the inner truth which they represent.

An examination of the creeds and confessions of even the most evangelical of the Protestant denominations that practice Infant Baptism, reveals this ritual tendency. It lurks, for instance, in one of the articles of the Westminster Assembly's Confession of Faith. "The efficacy of baptism is not tied to that moment of time when it is administered; yet, notwithstanding, by the right use of this ordinance, the grace promised is not only offered, but really exhibited and conferred by the Holy Ghost, to such (whether of age or infants) as that grace belongeth unto, according to the counsel of God's own will, in his appointed time." (Chap. xxviii. sect. vi.) That is to say, when an elect infant is baptized, the grace of God is really communicated to that infant at the time of its baptism, though it may not manifest itself in actual conversion until twenty, thirty, or fifty years after. It lies dormant, in some wonderful way, through all those years of worldliness and unbelief; but still it is there; and when at last the person is regenerated, this regeneration is not altogether a new gift of God to the soul, but rather the development of what was given long before—nothing else, in fact, but the delayed efficacy of Infant Baptism.

II. Turning our thoughts now from Christianity as a system of revealed truth to the church as the embodiment of Christianity, the visible form of the kingdom of God in this world, we charge Infant Baptism, in the second place, with a tendency to *secularize the church.* When baptism is made the "sign and seal" not of personal but of ancestral faith and piety, it does indeed "come in the place of circumcision." It loses its Christian significance, and takes on instead a Jewish meaning

It not only ceases to mark any distinction between the godly and the ungodly; it tends to obliterate and abolish, as far as possible, the line of separation between the church and the world. When the whole community is a baptized community, what is this in effect but the taking the world into the church bodily? This tendency of the extension of baptism to infant children to blot out all distinction between the church and the world has been acknowledged and deplored by those who have still defended the practice. Hear the testimony of that profound Christian philosopher, Blaise Pascal. "In the infancy of the Christian church, we see no Christians, but those who were thoroughly instructed in all matters necessary to salvation. Then, no one was admitted into the church, but after a most rigid examination; now, every one is admitted before he is capable of being examined. Formerly, it was necessary to come out from the world, in order to be received into the church; whilst in these days, we enter the church almost at the same time that we enter the world. So that dawning reason no longer perceives the broad line of distinction between these two opposing worlds, but matures and strengthens, at the same time, under the combined influence of both. The distinction is almost entirely lost; the church of the saints is all defiled with the intermingling of the wicked, and her children are they who carry into her very heart her deadliest foes." Hear now the best apology which this great and good man could find for the evil which he so well describes, and so sincerely laments. "But we must not impute to the church the evils that have followed so fatal a change; for when she saw that the delay of baptism left a large proportion of infants still under the curse of original sin, she wished to deliver them from this perdition, by hastening the succor which she can give; and this good mother sees, with bitter regret, that the benefit which she thus holds out to infants becomes the occasion of the ruin of adults."* It may be that some will object to this representation, and deny that Infant Baptism is responsible for these lamentable results, on the ground that such results do not always attend it; that some evangelical denominations who practice it make no less broad a distinction between the church and the world, and are no less strict in requiring evidence of saving faith as a qualification for full church membership, than Baptists are in requiring the same as a qualification for baptism. To the substantial truth of this last statement, we give our willing and joyful assent. There are thousands of pedobaptist churches, which bear a faithful testimony to the broad moral distinction between the church and the world, and are careful to confine their highest church privileges to those who give evidence that they have been born of God. Gladly admitting this, and gratefully praising God for it, we feel constrained, nevertheless, to renew the charge, that Infant Baptism tends to secularize the church. The question really comes to this issue;—where are the legitimate fruits of this practice most fully and fairly seen, in the evangelical pedobaptist churches of England and the United States, or in the unreformed communions, and the national Protestant churches of Europe? And this question again resolves itself into such inquiries as these;—where are the legitimate fruits of any particular practice, most likely to be found, most wisely to be sought—in the narrow enclosure of some specific manifestation of it, or in the wide field of its general prevalence? where it has existed but for a few generations, under peculiar and exceptional conditions, or where it has flourished, under every variety of conditions for many centuries? where it has been in contact with opposing and

---

* See Pascal's "Thoughts on Religion," chapter entitled, "a Comparison of Ancient and Modern Christians."

counteracting influences, or where it has had free course and unchecked development? where it has only succeeded in maintaining a precarious existence, and already begins to be marked with the signs of decay, or where it has held for ages its uninterrupted and triumphant sway? where it is practiced and defended on grounds entirely different from those which first led to its adoption, or where it still stands firmly on its ancient and original ground? To ask these questions is to answer them; and to answer them is to justify the charge which we bring against Infant Baptism. Its existence among evangelical Protestants is under exceptional conditions, and its effects under these conditions are no less exceptional. But even under these conditions of restraint and modification, the essential opposition between the evangelical truth and the traditional error is manifest in various ways. Of the Protestant sects that practice Infant Baptism, who does not know that it is maintained with most difficulty among those which are most decidedly evangelical in doctrine, and most distinguished for earnest, active piety? This antagonism must go on, until it results in the victory of one of these opposing elements over the other—until the evangelical doctrine abolishes the anti-evangelical practice, or the anti-evangelical practice corrupts the evangelical doctrine. Very likely the victory will be a divided one, some going forward to consistency by abandoning the unauthorized custom, and others going backward to consistency by renouncing the sound doctrine that clashes with the traditionary custom. Indeed just this two-fold movement is already taking place. A remarkable illustration of these warring tendencies is found in the history of Jonathan Edwards' ministry at Northampton, in Massachusetts. He saw clearly the evil of breaking down the distinction between the church and the world; but instead of applying the true cure, by receiving none but "visible saints," as he was accustomed to express himself, to baptism, he undertook to remedy the evil by receiving none but "visible saints" to the communion of the Lord's Supper. How signally he failed, and how sorely he was tried in consequence of this failure, all who will may read, in Mr. Dwight's account of his life. All the churches in the country except two, and all the ministers except three, were in decided opposition to him. In his own church he could not even get a fair hearing, or an impartial council; and at last, after the Lord's Supper had been wholly omitted for many months, he was dismissed from the pastoral office over them by a vote of more than ten to one—above two hundred voting in favor of his dismission, and less than twenty voting against it.—The tendency of this practice to confound the church with the world is seen in the difficulty which evangelical pedobaptists experience in defining the relation of baptized children to the church. They are far from being agreed among themselves whether these "children of the covenant" are full members of the church, or no members at all, or something between the two—members in their minority, or quasi members, or candidates outwardly qualified for membership. They are, however, I believe, coming to take the position, more and more generally, that baptized children are in the church; and herein they are coming to agree with all the ancient, and most of the modern defenders of Infant Baptism.

The two radical and comprehensive evils above mentioned comprise the heaviest part of our charge against Infant Baptism. It tends to corrupt Christianity, as a system of doctrine, by making it sacramental. It tends to corrupt the church, as a living embodiment of Christianity, by making it secular. But the practice brings with it, or draws after it, other evils, of more limited extent, but of no trifling importance.

III. It tends—this is our third charge against it—to prevent or darken the teachings of Scripture on the subject of baptism. The practice probably had its origin, certainly found its earliest and most efficient support, in a mistaken interpretation of our Lord's words—"except a man be born of water and of the Spirit, he cannot enter into the kingdom of God."* This is the standard text appealed to by all the ancient, and by the vast majority of the modern defenders of the practice. But this text is only one of a group of texts relating to baptism, all having this in common, that they connect it intimately with forgiveness of sin, regeneration, sanctification, and salvation. The following are the principal passages of this class: "According to his mercy He saved us, by the washing of regeneration, and renewing of the Holy Ghost."† "Christ gave himself for the church, that He might sanctify and cleanse it with the washing of water by the word."‡ "He that believeth, and is baptized, shall be saved."§ "Arise, and be baptized, and wash away thy sins, calling on the name of the Lord."‖ In the ark, "eight souls were saved by water; the like figure whereunto even baptism doth also now save us (not the putting away of the filth of the flesh, but the answer of a good conscience towards God), by the resurrection of Jesus Christ."¶ The right interpretation of these places of Scripture becomes plain, when we restore to baptism its true meaning and place, of both which it has been deprived by the practice of administering it to infants. Restore to it its true meaning, as a veritable profession of saving faith in Christ, and of conformity to his death and resurrection; restore to it its true place, at the threshold of the Christian life, not of the natural, following close upon the second birth, not upon the first;

---

* John iii. 5.   † Tit. iii. 5.   ‡ Eph. v. 26.
§ Mark xvi. 16.   ‖ Acts xxii. 16.   ¶ Pet. iii. 21.

and then the attributing to it of the efficacy which belongs to the truth represented by it, is but in accordance with the well known rule, by which properties and effects are commonly attributed to the *sign*, which belong in strict speech to the thing *signified*. And yet it is remarkable, that every one of these passages contains, in itself or in the immediate context, something to guard us against the danger of attributing saving efficacy to the sign alone. "The washing of regeneration," by which we are saved, is coupled with the "*renewing of the Holy Ghost.*" The church is not sanctified and cleansed "with the washing of water" merely, but "*by the word.*" Not every one who "is baptized shall be saved," but "he that *believeth* and is baptized." The injunction, "be baptized, and wash away thy sins," must not be divorced from its accompaniment of "*calling upon the name of the Lord.*" Baptism does not save us, apart from "*the answer of a good conscience.*" It is not "except a man be born of water," only, "he cannot see the kingdom of God," but "except a man be born of water *and of the Spirit;*" so wisely and carefully are the Scriptures guarded against abuse. There is not, in fact, in the whole New Testament, a single text which sustains that clause of the Nicene Creed which acknowledges "one baptism for the remission of sins." I pray you to mark the difference between those guarded words of God, and this unguarded word of man. "Repent and be baptized, every one of you, in the name of Jesus Christ, for the remission of sins."* That is Apostolic doctrine. "I acknowledge one baptism for the remission of sins." That is Nicene doctrine. The omission of the most important part of the Apostle's language leaves a bridgeless chasm between his doctrine and that of three centuries later. The passages above referred to, guarded, as we have

---

* Acts ii. 38.

seen, have really no more difficulty than those others in which our Lord makes an outward confession of him indispensable to salvation.* It is undeniable that he requires the confession of his name as a condition of salvation; and it is equally undeniable that the Scriptures represent baptism as being such a confession. "As many of you as have been baptized into Christ have put on Christ."†

It would be easy to show that many other passages are either perverted or obscured from the like cause. I will specify only two. The expression, "else were your children unclean, but now are they holy," in 1 Cor. vii. 14, has been made to do much service in the interest of infant baptism. The less it is examined, the better it will serve such a purpose. The use of the passage in support of Infant Baptism rests entirely upon the assumption that the children of parents, only one of whom is a believer, are to be ranked with the believing parent,—an assumption which is exactly contrary to the plain sense of the passage. The Apostle says, "the unbelieving husband is sanctified by the wife, and the unbelieving wife is sanctified by the husband, *else were your children unclean*, but now are they holy." Whatever holiness he attributes to the children, he derives from the holiness which he has previously attributed to the unconverted parent, with whom he distinctly ranks them. If this passage contains any warrant for baptizing them, it certainly contains an equal warrant for baptizing their unconverted parent, on whose sanctification their holiness depends.

A second passage, which has been commonly and strangely perverted to favor Infant Baptism, is that which records the bringing of little children to Christ for his

---

* See Matt. x. 32, 33. Luke xii. 8, 9, and especially Rom. x. 9, 10.
† Gal. iii. 27. Rom. vi. 3, 4. Col. ii. 11, 12; and Heb. x. 22, 23.

blessing.* Put what construction we may upon our Lord's words, "of such is the kingdom of heaven," this affecting and precious incident in his life stands forth as a distinct and unanswerable witness against the claim of Infant Baptism to be a part of primitive Christianity. The things said and done on that occasion could never have been said and done, if the Apostles had ever practiced the baptism of infant children. Pedobaptist Apostles would not have been likely to reprove parents for bringing their children to Christ. The Apostles were indeed in the wrong. They did not understand the tender condescension of their Master's loving heart; but they never could have made that mistake, if they had before that time administered baptism to children. We know that they had been accustomed to administer baptism to those who professed repentance and faith; but this narrative proves that the baptism of infant children was neither known nor thought of by them. And yet this was just at the close of our Lord's earthly ministry; only a few weeks, at most, before his crucifixion. And if they had not yet begun to baptize infants, they would not be likely to begin afterwards, especially when they had seen the Lord dismiss these children unbaptized, but not unblessed. If the Lord had ever designed to sanction such a practice, he could not have found or made a fitter occasion than this. It is not pretended that he did sanction it, then or afterwards; and, as he certainly had not before, the only tenable theory is, that he never did it at all. This Scripture does indeed show the propriety of dedicating our children to Christ, with prayer for his blessing upon them; but it equally shows the impropriety of using the rite of baptism for that purpose.

IV. We bring a fourth charge against Infant Baptism,

---

* Matt. xix. 13-15. Mark x. 13-16. Luke xviii. 15-17.

that it leads to perplexity of mind and confusion of ideas, not only on the subject of baptism, but in relation to Christian truth and practice in general. This is not so fully seen in the old, unreformed churches. There it forms part of a self-consistent whole. Infants are baptized, because baptism is necessary to salvation. It washes out the stain of original sin, makes them regenerate, members of the church, entitled to its privileges, and subject to its discipline. Here all is consistent, because all is but the legitimate development of one false idea. But among reformed and evangelical Christians, Infant Baptism becomes a source of perpetual embarrassment. It does not know, and cannot find, its proper and permanent place. It is continually tossed to and fro, seeking rest and finding none. Ask what is the *reason* that justifies it, and the answer seems to come from Babel. It is because children are depraved; it is because they are innocent; it is because they are declared to be holy; it is because Jesus said "of such is the kingdom of heaven;" it is because of the promises to the seed of the godly; it is because it is to be presumed that they will grow up Christians, without any sudden and violent conversion; it is because of the covenant of circumcision; it is because Christian parents are bound to dedicate their children to God; it is because infants were baptized from the beginning; it is because, though they were not baptized from the beginning, yet their baptism afterwards was but the legitimate enlargement and development of primitive Christianity; it is because the church has sanctioned the practice; it is because, though destitute of any scriptural sanction, the practice has proved itself useful, and therefore ought to be retained. These are only a part of the diverse and conflicting reasons urged in support of the practice. Ask what is the actual benefit of baptism to infants, and the reply is, that it signs and seals to them the covenant of grace; which means just this, that it is God's sure pledge to these baptized children to give them, on certain conditions, the same spiritual blessings which he will just as surely give, on precisely the same conditions, to those who are not baptized.

Confusion of moral ideas also results from the attempt to impress upon the minds of these baptized children, when they have grown up, the obligation of vows which they never had any part in making. An unsophisticated conscience refuses to recognize such an obligation.

Confusion of principles results from the necessity of borrowing from traditionary usage, or church authority, to make up for the deficiency of scriptural evidence in favor of the practice; and so the usage presents a weak point in the defences of Protestantism, inviting the attack, which it cannot successfully repel.

Confusion as to the relation between the two ordinances of baptism and the Lord's Supper results from the establishment of an unscriptural distinction between them, as to the extent of their application, and the qualifications for receiving them. The confusion begins in defining them both as "signs and seals," thus deriving the whole doctrine of the so-called sacraments from a text which does not contain the remotest allusion to either of them.* And then the confusion is worse confounded, by extending the one to all the posterity of believers, and limiting the other to believers themselves. For what word of Scripture intimates that there is any difference between the proper moral qualifications for the two? It is true that infant children cannot examine themselves, nor discern the meaning of the Lord's Supper; and it is equally true that they cannot confess their faith in Christ, nor discern the meaning of baptism.

---

* Rom. iv. 11.

Thus the whole subject groans under its burden, and cries out, with Job, "I am full of confusion." A multitude of different ideas and arguments are associated with it, many of them inconsistent with each other, and most of them inconsistent with Scripture. And so a divine ordinance, which in Scripture is presented in a definite, clear, and consistent light, is, by its perversion, enveloped in obscurity, perplexity, and contradiction.

V. I dare not withhold a fifth indictment against Infant Baptism, that it tends to encourage false hopes of salvation. How should it not, when, in all the unreformed churches its efficacy is so fully believed as to have given currency to a common saying that "a baptized person does not go to hell?" How should it not, when, among many who are called Protestants, baptism is believed to be accompanied by regenerating grace? How should it not, when, among those who belong to evangelical denominations, the prospect of a child dying without baptism so commonly excites alarm, or produces uneasiness? How should the older children of a family where the parents show such uneasiness or alarm, fail to infer that *their* baptism has rescued them from the danger of perdition, or done something, at least, to give them the advantage over others, as to the prospect of salvation? Indeed this idea seems to be involved in the very practice. Why is it practiced, it is natural to ask, if it has no favorable influence on their prospects of final salvation? It tends obviously to relieve them, in some degree, from the sense of personal responsibility, from the feeling that every thing depends upon their own repentance and faith. The matter has already, in a manner, been taken out of their own hands. Parents, or sponsors, or the church, have assumed responsibility for them. And if this can be done at the beginning of life, why not also at the end? Why not, in fine, all the way through life? In fact the unreformed churches practically do this. Consistent with their promise at the beginning, they stand ready with their appliances of sanctifying rites for every stage of life, and dismiss the departing soul at last to Paradise, with absolution and extreme unction.

VI. I must bring one more serious charge against Infant Baptism—the sixth and last. It tends to hinder individual Christians from discerning and discharging their duty. Thousands upon whom this unauthorized rite was performed in infancy, when they come to believe in Christ, and devote their lives to him, feel a strong desire to confess their faith by being baptized. Perhaps they see others doing so, who have been their companions in the sorrows of conviction of sin, and in the joys of a hope in Christ; and the ordinance received under such circumstances commends itself, as it is wont to do, alike to their judgments and their feelings, and is commended, moreover, by the serene joy which is wont to gladden the breasts of those who have received it. They cannot help asking themselves, "Is not this the right way?" And the more they inquire and search the Scriptures, the greater is their desire; the more it seems to them to be their duty, to be baptized as believers in Christ. But there is a great, immovable obstacle to their receiving believers' baptism. They have been told that they have already been baptized. Baptism ought not to be repeated. In this we are all agreed. What, then, shall they do? Shall they set at naught the rite which their revered parents, with so much piety and prayer, it may be, caused to be performed upon them? Undoubtedly this is what they ought to do, if they are convinced, in their own consciences, that Christ requires believers, and none others, to be baptized. But oh! how hard it is to do this duty! How hard it is to admit the full conviction that it *is* a duty! How the heart shrinks from the thought of treating with disrespect what is regarded as a divine rite by their dearest Christian friends—what was regarded with so tender and sacred a reverence by a mother, a father, now, perhaps, in heaven! It seems as though it could not be a duty, because it appears to be reflecting dishonor on those whom they know they are sacredly bound to honor. There is a fearful conflict between seeming duty to their parents, and seeming duty to Christ. How dare they disobey his command? How dare they take a step which will be virtually accusing their parents of having passed off upon them a counterfeit in place of the genuine Christian ordinance? And it will not be without precedent, if some of their Christian friends press this last consideration, and enforce it with the most moving appeals. Strange, indeed, is it not? that any Christian should dare to appeal to their reverence for their parents, in order to hinder them from complying with what they believe to be a command of Christ. It is assuming a fearful responsibility, and the Christian who assumes it must have forgotten what the Lord says of those who love father or mother more than him. But they *do* sometimes so forget. May God forgive them! I pretend not to know how many, or what proportion, of those whose minds are troubled with difficulties of this kind are ultimately hindered from doing what they believe to be their duty, and so carry for the rest of their days a sad and burdened, or, which is much worse, though not so painful, a seared and blinded conscience. But I *do* know that the inward struggle here described is an actual, and not an imaginary one. I *do* know that many, who are not ultimately hindered from doing their duty, suffer intensely in their tenderest affections before they come to the full decision; and, from the manifest strength of the temptation, and the known weakness of human nature, I think it is neither unreasonable nor uncharitable to believe that the number of those who are hindered, in this way, from doing their duty, is much greater than the number of those who are successful in overcoming the hindrance. Not that all such come to a clear conviction of their duty, but rather that the larger part are prevented from having such a clear conviction. They see their duty but dimly, and uncertainly, at a distance, because they dare not approach near enough to see it plainly and surely. Here, then, is a real, great, practical evil of Infant Baptism, which not only amply justifies, but imperatively demands, our most earnest protest. We believe such cases are numerous, and rapidly multiplying; and we dare not withhold our testimony against a practice which ensnares so many Christian souls in a painful and perilous temptation.

If I had reason to suppose that there was one here who was experiencing this temptation, I would try to strengthen that struggling soul with such thoughts as these. It is your plain duty, and your only safety, to do what you believe to be, on the whole, most agreeable to the word and will of Christ, at whatever sacrifice of your tenderest earthly feelings. In following this rule, you can do no dishonor to your parents. On the contrary, if they were Christians, and acted in reference to your baptism, according to what they believed to be the will of the Lord, you will dishonor them, and show yourself unworthy of their example and instructions, if you refuse to do now what you believe to be the will of the Lord in reference to the same matter. You will best honor them, whether living or dead, by acting, with your light, on the same principles on which they acted with theirs. If that sainted father or mother could speak to you now from the blessed abodes, the revered and familiar voice would not say to you, "honor every thing which

I honored, and believe every thing which I believed, if you wish to show respect to my memory." Oh no! that voice would rather say, "honor and obey Christ, the Lord, before all others, even before me : if you act otherwise, you will act contrary to my example and instructions; you will indeed dishonor me, and make me ashamed of my child." Make this dutiful resolve then at once, that the will of Christ, according to your own best understanding of it, shall be your supreme and controlling rule of action, whatever may be opposed to it. And if in your deliberate judgment you have never received any thing that ought to be regarded as Christian baptism, this is the Lord's message to you to-night—" why tarriest thou? arise and be baptized." The closing year reminds us all, that we must make haste to discharge our unfulfilled duties, lest we lose forever the opportunity of fulfilling them.*

And one of the duties which we ought not to leave unperformed is, to endeavor to correct the errors of our brethren. We are to do this, indeed, in a spirit of humility and charity, not as if we were infallible, any more than they; nor as if we had any dominion or superiority over them; but as if we had sincere and earnest convictions; as if we loved the truth, and felt bound to bear witness to it; as if we loved our differing brethren, and longed to see them partakers of every good which we enjoy. We have, as Baptists, had the privilege and honor of helping our brethren of other names to gain some valuable acquisitions of Christian liberty and Christian truth. Our testimony in times past against all persecution for religious belief, all restraint upon Christian worship, and all unhallowed alliances of church and state, has not been in vain. It is mainly through

---

* This discourse was preached on Sunday evening, December 31st, 1865.

The Evils of Infant Baptism.

the fearless testimony and the patient sufferings of Baptists, that these evils have come to be so generally seen, and so extensively abolished; and that they are now so sure to be ere long abolished universally. Nor has our persistent testimony against Infant Baptism been without effect. It has resulted in the very extensive, and continually extending renunciation or neglect of the practice, to the great advantage, as we honestly believe, of those who have so renounced or omitted it.* We are encouraged, therefore, to continue this testimony. We are not afraid nor ashamed to persist in bearing witness against what we firmly believe to be perversions of the Lord's ordinances. We know that for this we are regarded by some as disturbers of the peace of Zion, and hindrances to the union of Israel. But we have no hope of any union of Christians, and no desire for any, which

---

* The following facts, taken from official reports, are cited in proof of the growing decline of Infant Baptism, especially among the more decidedly evangelical Pedobaptists. In the Old School Presbyterian Church for the year ending May, 1863, there were 2165 adults baptized to 10,194 infants, a little more than 1 to 5. In the New School Presbyterian Church, during the same year, there were 1556 adults baptized, to 3,191 infants, about 1 to 2. In the Methodist Church North, in the year 1865, the number of adults baptized was 29,150; of infants 32,891, or 14½ to 16. In the Congregational Churches of the United States, the number of infants baptized in the year 1864 was only a very small fraction above 1½ to each church. In the following year, the number was less by 149, and the adults baptized exceeded the infants by 841. The former were only in the proportion of 7 to every 5 churches, while the latter were in the proportion of 7 to every 4 churches. In more than half the New England States, the number of adults baptized in the Congregational Churches has been for many years greater than the number of infants. In Vermont, there was, in 1859, 1 infant baptized to every 52 members; in 1860, 1 to every 80 members. Where Infant Baptism is universally practiced, the annual proportion is about 1 to every 20 members. In Connecticut, the proportion of infants baptized in 1852 was about 3 to every church; in 1862, about 2 to every church; and in 1864 there was a falling off of more than 100 from the previous year. In 82 churches, including 7421 members, there were no infants baptized during the year.

requires the suppression of individual convictions, or any restraint upon their suitable utterance. The only union which we hope for and pray for is such as can be attained by "speaking the *truth* in *love*." We look for the time, and if our wishes do not deceive us, we see it approaching, when religious controversy, or, if that term is objectionable, religious discussion, shall be an acknowledged means of grace and help to union. Nothing more is necessary to make it so, than the observance of this simple apostolic rule, " speaking the truth in love." If you will take the trouble to examine the passage * where Paul uses this expression, you will see that he uses it in just this connection. He recommends it to us, as a means of removing the errors that divide us, and attaining to unity of faith and knowledge, so as to become one compact body, under Christ the common head. To this glorious consummation, so long desired and waited for, the swift years are hastening the church of God; and whoever persuades one disciple of Christ to exchange one error which he held for one truth which he lacked, contributes his mite toward the perfect union of all disciples in the truth. "Every plant which my Heavenly Father hath not planted shall be rooted up." God is continually fulfilling this word—now tearing up these plants in the mass, by the rude violence of revolutions, to the great disfigurement of the ground for a time; and now loosening and eradicating them, one by one, with the gentle hand of Christian patience and faithfulness. Both processes are needed, and he will suffer both to go on, until every thing that poisons the air, or offends the sight, or encumbers the ground, is removed from his garden, and nothing remains but what his hand has planted there.

---

* Ephesians iv. 15.

VIII.

THE COMMUNION.

By HENRY G. WESTON, D.D.,
Pastor of Madison Avenue Baptist Church, New York.

"For I have received of the Lord that which also I delivered unto you, That the Lord Jesus, the same night in which he was betrayed, took bread: And when he had given thanks he brake it, and said, Take, eat; this is my body which is broken for you: this do in remembrance of me. After the same manner also he took the cup, when he had supped, saying, This cup is the new testament in my blood: this do ye, as oft as ye drink it, in remembrance of me. For as often as ye eat this bread, and drink this cup, ye do show the Lord's death till he come."—1 *Corinthians* xi. 23-26.

AROUND the ordinance, the institution of which is here described, gather the controversies of centuries. A history of the communion would be almost a history of the church. By a sad mockery of its true character, it has been brought into unhallowed alliance with nearly every sphere of man's activity or interest. It has been made a means of regeneration, a declaration of admission to church-membership, a qualification for office, and a sacrifice for the dead; it has been played with as a puppet, and worshiped as a God; it has been the shibboleth of parties; it has been pressed into the service of bigotry, and made a test of fellowship; hate and revenge have used it as their instrument; but these very perversities have testified to its inherently high position in the system of Christianity. O Spirit of God! guide us as we approach this Holy of Holies! direct us into the true knowledge and understanding of its divine nature, and specially fit us to lay hold of it in our hearts, that we may know that true communion with Christ which this service declares.

On the very threshold of our discussion we are met by an objection, urged ordinarily on the ground of the spirituality of the new dispensation, that in the kingdom of Jesus Christ an ordinance like this could not be meant to be perpetual, that it belongs to those carnal rites suited to an immature state of religious education, and that, if it be continued, the method of observing it must be a matter of comparative indifference to him who looks at the heart. But the words of the Scripture in our text seem to be decisive on the first point; "Ye do show the Lord's death till he come." This is the language of an apostle, who, more than any other, denounces every thing which conflicts with his sublime idea of a kingdom that is not meat and drink, but righteousness, peace, and joy in the Holy Ghost, and if he saw no inconsistency here, we may reasonably conclude there is none. It is a strange spirituality which leads us to reject, not rites of human device, but those of divine appointment, or to undervalue even the manner of celebrating an ordinance which holds such a place in Christ's esteem, that when, after his death, he commissioned a new apostle, he gave him, by special revelation, information with regard to its origin, and directions how it should be kept; "For I received from the Lord," says Paul, "that which I also delivered unto you."

The nature and design of the communion, and the methods, occasions, and incidents of its observance, can be learned alone from the New Testament. Abstract reasoning has little weight in relation to positive institutions. They derive all their authority and meaning from the will of their Founder, and, in their domain, his words, with whatever light may be thrown upon them from competent sources, must be our sole guide. The study of the New Testament, I think, will reveal the following as the chief features of this ordinance.

I. It is commemorative. "This do in remembrance of me."

Symbolic and other memorials of important occurrences have been known to all ages, and have their origin in the nature of man. These monumental witnesses are far more effective in diffusing and perpetuating the knowledge of such events than any record in words could be. When incorporated into religious customs of more or less frequent observance, they gain a hold on the common mind which nothing else can equal. The ordinance before us recalls continually the great fact of facts in our Lord's history, *that he died.* Not even the express and emphatic language of the Scripture seems to present so incontrovertibly the truth that Christ's great mission in this world was to make a sacrifice for sin, as this constant commemoration of his death, in accordance with his directions. It would be much easier for those who deny the scriptural doctrine of the atonement to pass by or explain away those portions of holy writ which express this truth in positive and dogmatic statement, and to dwell rather on those which speak of his life and teachings, than it is for them to account for this undeniable and most noteworthy fact, that the great Christian feast commemorates Christ's *death.* Other men are remembered by their followers; schools and sects and philosophies have their celebrations; but, while the admirers of the great observe festally the birthdays of their heroes or the anniversaries of their accession to places of power and influence or of their recognition by the world, where can be found an instance of men's commemorating with joy the dying hour of the one they wish to honor? And what explanation can be given of this, other than the ready

16*

and all-sufficient one, that, whereas other men accomplished what they did by their lives or their teachings, Christ wrought his great work for mankind by his death.

It is one of the features that commends this ordinance to every Christian, that it is a *positive* institution and thus offers an opportunity for presenting a test, an evidence, and an offering of love, which is specially grateful to him who gives, and to him who receives. Coming into being in closest proximity to our Saviour's passion, its birth hour touching Gethsemane and Calvary, solemnly appointed in the last moments of life when nothing can be conceived of as engaging our Lord's attention which is not of the greatest importance—this rite holds on every account a special place in the Christian's affections. It is often the want of true love to the Saviour which makes men turn from the representation of Christ's death, made by himself as he would have it remembered and set forth, to sensuous pictures and images of the crucifixion and burial and resurrection, drawn by fancy, adapted to awaken the emotions of the natural heart, but, to nourish faith or love, utterly powerless.

II. It is declarative. "Ye do show the Lord's death."

In this ordinance, we do more than remember an act or a person. The word translated "show" means to declare, to announce, and, in most passages where it occurs in the New Testament, is translated "preach." "They *preached* through Jesus the resurrection from the dead:"* "Through this man is *preached* unto you the forgiveness of sins:"† "Whom therefore ye ignorantly worship, him *declare* I unto you."‡ The em-

---
* Acts iv. 4. † Acts xiii. 38. ‡ Acts xvii. 23.

blems, also, which are spread on the table, so significant in their teachings, show that the rite is more than commemorative. In setting forth Christ's death, it declares not merely the fact that he died, but the manner and purpose of his death. And as the death of Christ was the great central point of his history, toward which every line in his life converged, so this ordinance gathers unto itself all that death includes and comprehends.

It declares an incarnated Saviour—a Saviour who had body and blood, a Saviour who became for our sakes subject to death. It shows forth the manner of his death. His body is broken before our eyes. It tells more than this —it announces the purpose of his death. He might have died for us out of love to man, as human benefactors have done, he might have died because the earth could not endure his holiness, and then his death would have been worthy of commemoration. But what means this wine, typical of his blood? Why are these two elements used? Does not the broken bread set forth sufficiently his death? Yes, if it were only his death that we commemorate, his blood, which in a being merely human, would have no significance apart from his body, has great meaning here, because he is a sacrifice for sin. It is the *blood* that maketh an atonement for the soul.* "This is my blood of the New Covenant, which is shed for many for the remission of sins."† Hence, this ordinance declares those things in us which made that death necessary; our guilt, our deserved condemnation, and our utter helplessness. How utterly has Rome, in that strange ceremony which she calls the mass, departed from Christ's institution; denying the cup to the laity, and putting a wafer on the tongue of the communicant; having no broken bread, no poured

---

* Leviticus xvii. 11.   † Matt. xxvi. 28.

wine; recognizing neither Christ's death, nor his atonement.

But it tells as much of life as of death—of what Christ works in us, as well as what he has done for us. It declares Christ to be the life of our souls—our daily bread, nourishment, and strength. It sets forth the identity of Christ with his people, their common life, the union taught in the Bible both in express terms and in many similitudes. It assures us of our possession of Christ, that he is not only given *for* us, but is given *to* us. As freely as the officiating minister breaks and gives the bread, and as truly as we receive it, so freely and truly does Christ give himself to us.

Not only does this ordinance declare what was done on Calvary, and what is doing in our souls, it announces what is to be. The Past, the Present, and the Future are closely intertwined in joyous fellowship, in every celebration of this rite. "Till he come." The gathering of the disciples to break bread looks to the future as well as the past. The thoughts of the communicants turn backward to Calvary, but they go forward also. They hear something besides the groans of a dying Saviour. They look for the glorious and triumphant Messiah; that brow which was crowned with thorns they are soon to behold bearing the diadem of regal dominion. The suffering and the conquering, Emmanuel, so closely associated in the pages of the prophets, and so separated by the Church's night-time, are brought together by faith at this table. Here the saints continually proclaim their expectation of the return of their now absent Lord. They declare their unwavering conviction that he will come: that his kingdom will not be overturned by the malice of foes or the treachery of friends: that there shall never be wanting those who will celebrate his death in this simple and touching rite, until he come again.

III. It is an act of communion. "The cup of blessing which we bless, is it not the communion of the blood of Christ? The bread which we break, is it not the communion of the body of Christ? For we being many are one bread, and one body; for we are all partakers of that one bread."*

That the ordinance is something more than merely commemorative and declaratory appears from a variety of considerations. Observe the name itself; it is the communion, κοινωνία, a word which, by its own force, and by its scriptural use, must always embrace more persons than one. The broader design of the institution is taught also in the command, "Eat, drink ye all of it." An exhibition of the elements would have served all the purposes of commemoration, and if any thing more were necessary to make the rite declaratory, it would be sufficient that an individual eat and drink in the retirement of his closet. But this would not be complying with Christ's requirements. The communion cannot be observed by a single person. It is a joint act. There must be "the many," † or the significance of the one bread and the one body is lost. It is the church's privilege when they are come together in one place. To a like conclusion are we led by a study of the circumstances which surrounded the original institution of the rite in the upper room at Jerusalem. Not all of Christ's disciples were there; some were absent, whom he loved most dearly; Mary, and Martha, and Lazarus received no summons to the sacred assembly. But around the board were gathered *all the apostles.* Christ did not, as in Gethsemane and on the Mount of Transfiguration, select from among them three special friends. It is a question deserving serious attention, why that company

---

* 1 Cor. x. 16, 17. † 1 Cor. x. 17.

consisted of the twelve, and of them only; and the answer is a reply to most of the objections which are made to the principles which govern the Baptist Churches in the administration of the rite. It is a church ordinance; it is the ordinance of that one body of which the Apostolic College was the representative; and therefore, it was with them, and with no others, Christ partook of the feast. And we no more confine Christian affection and the name of Christians to those whom we invite to the table of the Lord, than did Christ refuse his name or love to those beloved ones who stood by him at the cross, but who did not partake with him, on the preceding evening, of the symbols of his death.

But the Communion implies more than the presence and act of the church, in distinction from the act of an individual; it includes HIM of whom his people are made partakers. The Scripture gives no countenance to the figment of transubstantiation—a view which it has been well said is poverty itself compared with the evangelical —nor to the theory of consubstantiation; but we must be careful, in our eagerness to avoid the error of materializing the solemn words of Christ, "This is my body, this is my blood," not to adopt the shallow opinion that the only benefit of this rite consists in its power to affect the Christian's feelings. This hollow theory has been applied to prayer and other religious duties, but it has no attractions for the true Christian. He approaches the table of his Lord with the deepest solemnity, for he beholds his Lord's body, he hears the words of the apostle—" The cup of blessing which we bless, is it not the communion of the blood of Christ? The bread which we break, is it not the communion of the body of Christ?" He does not undertake to define, in exact words, those spiritual ideas which elude expression by clearly-marked logical lines and boundaries; for he recognizes fully the evident fact, that on the ordinance which is the most affecting symbol of the sublimest of truths—"Except ye eat the flesh of the Son of Man, and drink his blood, ye have no life in you,"* "He that eateth my flesh and drinketh my blood, dwelleth in me and I in him,"†—there must rest, in a measure, whatever obscurity belongs to that most profound and mysterious subject. When the union between Christ and his people can be exactly set forth in any form of words, so that the understanding can grasp it; when that mystical union, transcending, as it does, any other possible union — a union, as good Bishop Hall says, "not merely virtual, accidental, metaphorical, but a true, real, essential, substantial union, so that in natural union there may be more evidence, there cannot be more truth"—a union embracing the bodies, as well as the souls of the believers—when this union can be divested of all mystery, and expressed in words so as to be perfectly intelligible to the intellect, then may we explain, with equal fullness and clearness, every thing pertaining to these symbols. Until then, faith as well as knowledge, the heart as well as the mind, must interpret these words—"The communion of the body of Christ;" "the communion of the blood of Christ;" words which, by the sanctified consent of Christendom, have given to this ordinance a unique and holy character. For if no other partaking of Christ is here than may be found in prayer or meditation or other religious exercise, would it not have been called communion with Christ, rather than the communion of the body and of the blood of Christ?

And let it not be supposed that we teach by this that there is any thing in partaking at the Lord's table essential to salvation. Not at all. The salvation of the soul does not depend upon any outward ordinance. But as

---
* John vi. 53. † John vi. 56.

there is a blessing in public worship which can only be obtained by participation therein, though a believer may be holy and happy who has never seen a gathering of the saints; as there is a blessing found in the reception of baptism, and nowhere else, to the finding of which multitudes can testify, although unnumbered happy ones have gone to heaven who have never been baptized; so the communion of the body and blood of Christ, to the worthy recipient, has its own special blessing, that can be found only at the table of our dying Lord. It is a blessing which far transcends that which Rome seeks in her interpretation of the words of Christ, even if her highest conceptions and all her boasting were true. Our service is *a communion*. "The Christ of the mass is not turned toward the soul, but toward God; and the feelings of the church in the mass are to be just such as it would experience were Christ actually dying over again his sacrificial death."* With us it is a living Christ whom we come to meet. We find and recognize his death here, but it is more than death that we find—more than the results of his death even—more than the merits of his atonement; we come to the table, not so much to secure the divine redemptive virtues, or any impersonal thing, even grace itself, as to "further the celebration and intensification of direct, personal, loving fellowship between Christ and the soul."

The Communion is not merely a commemoration, telling what Christ once did—a monument of blessed service performed and love shown centuries ago in other lands, nor merely a prospect of good things to come; we are not shut up to remembrance and expectation, having only absent joys in our mind; we worship and meet a living and present Lord.

IV. In this ordinance, the New Testament worship

---

* Dorner.

culminates. The end of Christianity for man is living fellowship with God. All Christian worship announces and celebrates the reconciliation of the worshiper, with God in Christ; and this idea finds its climax in the Communion. All preceding religious rites appear here in spiritual meaning and fullness. Circumcision, which promised a peculiar people for God ; the passover, which foretold the redemption of that people; baptism, which declares the redemption accomplished and owned of God by the resurrection from the dead; the sacrifices which smoked on Mosaic altars—are all gathered and fulfilled here. The various methods of worship—individual, social, spiritual, external, etc.—kindly provided by God to meet the manifold wants of man, and to accomplish the great purposes of spiritual training, are combined in this rite in their highest forms. Here is the act of the individual, for unlike any other social service, this requires a distinct participation by every person. But it is more than an individual act, as we have previously seen—it is associated worship, and yet not a promiscuous gathering, but the worship of the church, solemnly convened for that purpose—and God, who has declared that he loves the gates of Zion more than all the dwelling places of Jacob, has given his largest promises to his assembled saints. Here is set forth Christ—Christ, the Atonement—Christ, the Life—Christ, the King. In the common preaching of the gospel, where Christ is declared, he is too often rejected by many to whom the tidings of salvation come. But in this ordinance, the public reception of Christ is coextensive with the presentation of him. In accordance with this idea, in the primitive times, none but communicants were permitted to remain during the celebration of the Eucharist. In other religious ceremonies, in baptism and the preaching of the gospel, there is no absolute necessity for any accompanying vocal prayer or praise. The service is complete without them. But the communion cannot be, without audible address to God; the mere eating and drinking do not constitute the feast. The cup and bread must be blest; the church's thanksgiving and request must come up before God. Devotion, moreover, in its highest moods, demands silence as well as speech. The soul in its soarings after Christ becomes impatient of words—they are too weak to bear the burden which it lays upon them, and the instinct of Christians always requires that there be a portion of time during the communion when every voice is hushed, that the heart, undisturbed by any intruder, in solemn silence, may syllable the emotions of love and gratitude which the tongue is powerless to express. The offering of our substance is always a component part of complete public worship, and by the same instinct, immediately after the reception of the elements, a contribution is taken for the poorer members of the church. The singing of a hymn closes a rite in which all other rites are brought together and intensified—in which the church has assembled as a body for the solemn purpose of the celebration—in which the pastor and deacons, the full New Testament complement of church officers, have officiated—in which every individual member has taken an outward and equal part—in which Christ has been set forth and accepted in solemn symbols—in which the great facts of the gospel, past, present, and future, have been declared—in which the voice of prayer and praise has been heard—in which an offering of our substance has been made, remembering both our Lord and our needy brother. It is the complete circle of Christian worship, a fitting type of that coming kingdom of the Father, in which Christ is to drink the fruit of the vine new with his disciples.

If the views of this ordinance presented in this discourse are correct, it is evident that a due regard to the high and holy place which it occupies, forbids its being employed as a preliminary or adjunct to any thing else, however important. All other things may prepare for the communion, but it may not rightfully be made a means to any thing except those great ends, all of which are to be regarded in every celebration. Superstition has carried the elements to the bedside of the dying; the influence of the same false faith has caused them to be hastily spread and partaken of in the hour of danger on shipboard, and elsewhere; the eating of the broken bread has been made a prelude to sacred and civil office, a manifestation of brotherly kindness and the union of Protestants; but, however we may respect the motives of those who thus use the sacred rite, our study of the word of God forbids our compliance with any such custom. An institution occupying the place this does in the Christian economy, must be kept for the purposes for which Christ designed it.

Thus jealously guarded and exalted, there will be no necessity for fencing it about with those hindrances and restrictions, unknown to the New Testament, with which it has often been encircled; no need of surrounding it with such fastings and discipline, that the trembling soul dares approach but seldom, and then with a fear and terror that almost destroys the true character of the ordinance. It is the great gospel feast; it is the table where Christ summons his beloved and ransomed ones and communes with them. Solemn as is the place, the celebration should be one of the devoutest joy. Here faith, and hope, and love should burst the bounds which too often confine them. Here every Christian grace should be in highest exercise. It is none other than the very gate of Heaven.

IX.

THE SYMBOLISM OF THE COMMUNION.

By REV. LEMUEL MOSS,
Professor of Systematic Theology in the University at Lewisburg, Pennsylvania.

"AND AS THEY WERE EATING, JESUS TOOK BREAD, AND BLESSED IT, AND BRAKE IT, AND GAVE IT TO THE DISCIPLES, AND SAID—TAKE, EAT; THIS IS MY BODY. AND HE TOOK THE CUP, AND GAVE THANKS, AND GAVE IT TO THEM, SAYING, DRINK YE ALL OF IT, FOR THIS IS MY BLOOD OF THE NEW TESTAMENT, WHICH IS SHED FOR MANY FOR THE REMISSION OF SINS. BUT I SAY UNTO YOU, I WILL NOT DRINK HENCEFORTH OF THIS FRUIT OF THE VINE UNTIL THAT DAY WHEN I DRINK IT NEW WITH YOU IN MY FATHER'S KINGDOM."—*Matthew* xxvi. 26-29.

FOR I HAVE RECEIVED OF THE LORD THAT WHICH ALSO I DELIVERED UNTO YOU, THAT THE LORD JESUS, THE SAME NIGHT IN WHICH HE WAS BETRAYED, TOOK BREAD; AND WHEN HE HAD GIVEN THANKS, HE BRAKE IT, AND SAID, TAKE, EAT; THIS IS MY BODY WHICH IS BROKEN FOR YOU; THIS DO IN REMEMBRANCE OF ME. AFTER THE SAME MANNER ALSO HE TOOK THE CUP, WHEN HE HAD SUPPED, SAYING, THIS CUP IS THE NEW TESTAMENT IN MY BLOOD; THIS DO YE, AS OFT AS YE DRINK IT, IN REMEMBRANCE OF ME. FOR AS OFTEN AS YE EAT THIS BREAD, AND DRINK THIS CUP, YE DO SHOW THE LORD'S DEATH TILL HE COME."—1 *Corinthians* xi. 23-26.

"THE CUP OF BLESSING WHICH WE BLESS, IS IT NOT THE COMMUNION OF THE BLOOD OF CHRIST? THE BREAD WHICH WE BREAK, IS IT NOT THE COMMUNION OF THE BODY OF CHRIST? FOR WE BEING MANY ARE ONE BREAD, AND ONE BODY; FOR WE ARE ALL PARTAKERS OF THAT ONE BREAD."—1 *Corinthians* x. 16, 17.

THESE passages of Scripture at once bring before us the theme of this discourse, to wit—THE SYMBOLICAL SIGNIFICANCE OF THE LORD'S SUPPER.

I. The Lord's Supper attests and symbolizes the life, death, and resurrection of Jesus Christ. It is, in this aspect of it, of the nature of a monument, erected to commemorate events contemporary with its institution. It is thus one of the stones in the solid historical basis upon which Christianity rests, and becomes a powerful argument for its truth and divinity. It may be confidently asked of the objector to the gospel, How could this ordinance have been established, professedly at the time of the events which it memorializes, if the events never occurred ? It is not put back in a mythological period, nor in a region of obscurity, separated from known facts by intervening chasms of ignorance and conjecture. There is a clear, white track of history, kept open and continuous by the Bible and the Church, up to and beyond the time of its establishment. The chain of evidence is complete through all these centuries, to the last link. And just as the Passover attested, beyond the possibility of cavil, the deliverance of the Jews from Egypt, so we claim that the Lord's Supper attests the life, death, and resurrection of the Saviour. The recently-discovered monuments, tablets, and inscriptions of the ancient empires of the East, are rightly regarded as of the highest historical value. They attest and celebrate contemporary transactions, and could not, when the facts were fresh in the minds of the people, greatly falsify them. In like manner and for like reasons— though stronger in this case than in those—the ordinances of Christianity authenticate the gospel. They were established openly, when the vast majority of the people were hostile, and their record has descended to us in the testimony of foes as well as of friends. Every requisite of a valid and sufficient historical argument is here met, and it cannot be successfully disputed.

When, then, we partake of the Communion, we declare our belief in the New Testament narrative of our Saviour's life. It is a Confession of our Faith, drawn up by Christ himself, and solemnly signed by us. It is the affirmation of our belief in the historical character of Christ and Christianity,—that the works, sufferings, and final victory over death of our Saviour, were veritable occurrences on this earth, at the time stated in the sacred record. "As often as ye eat this bread and drink this cup, ye do show (that is, announce or proclaim) the Lord's death till he come." And the Saviour's injunction is, "Do this in remembrance of me." It testifies for him.

II. But this symbolic ordinance exhibits also the purpose, or object, of the Saviour's life and death. It shows that this was vicarious—for us and for our sins. The marvelous words of distribution are, "Take, eat; this is my body which is broken for you;" "This is my blood of the New Testament, which is shed for many for the remission of sins." We are not to forget that the earthly *life* of Christ, no less than his death, has a vicarious, a substitutionary, relation to our justification and forgiveness—just as his glorified life is the source of spiritual life in us. The actual work of redemption began with the incarnation. Christ assumed human nature, endured its limitations and weaknesses, and finally took it to the cross, under the curse of God as our sin, that we might be redeemed from the curse of the law, and be made the righteousness of God in him. As Pascal says, "We bear with life, for the sake of him who suffered both life and death for us."* Or, as Miss Greenwell has beautifully sung it:

> "And first with Life
> Thou madest friends for us; our lives in thine
> Grow kind and gracious, Lord! When thou didst make
> Thy soul an offering for sin, thy love
> Was even unto Death; yea, far above,
> For thou didst suffer Life for us!—to take,
> More hard than to resign." †

And you will here notice, how, in this ordinance, the truth symbolized gains breadth and clearness of expres-

---

* See Miss Greenwell's Poems, page 314, note E.
† Poems, page 207.

The Symbolism of the Communion.

sion, beyond what it finds in Baptism. There the symbol sets forth facts of deepest moment in Christ's earthly history—to wit, his burial and resurrection—and it sets forth our faith in them. He that is baptized into Christ's name is avowedly baptized into a confession and participation of his burial and resurrection. But the fact and effect of his death are only *implied* in Baptism, not expressed. True, the symbol takes up and memorializes those events which render the implication obvious and necessary. Still, it is the outward and visible with which Baptism deals, only suggesting and hinting the inward and spiritual. But here the order is reversed. The Lord's Supper, in the breaking of the bread and the pouring out of the wine, and in their distribution to all the disciples, brings out and emphasizes the actual *dying* of the Lord Jesus—the surrender of the life he had assumed—and that this is for the behoof of those who share the elements. See how the significant emblems cry out to us, with repeated energy, that the body of our Lord was *broken*—that his blood was *shed*. By this ordinance, then, Christ is evidently, or visibly, set forth, crucified among us. He is declared to be the sacrificial Lamb of God, which taketh away the sin of the world. And so, all that was typified by the sacrifices of the old dispensation, and fulfilled in Christ, finds commemoration here.

I say, all that was typified by the sacrifices of the old dispensation. What a vision of smoking altars rises up at these words—a long line of bleeding, burning victims, stretching through four thousand years from Calvary back to the gates of Eden. It would seem that immediately after the Fall, even before the expulsion from Paradise, God instituted sacrifices, and from the skins of the immolated beasts made coverings for the nakedness of our first parents—thus sending them forth into the uncultured and accursed world, clothed with the prophecy and hope of a divinely-provided redemption. We know, at least, that very early in the history of the race the service of such offerings was permanently established, for it was no single or singular incident, when Abel, the keeper of sheep, brought unto the Lord of the firstlings of his flock, and of the fat thereof; and the Lord had respect unto him and to his offering.* "By faith Abel offered unto God a more excellent sacrifice than Cain, by which he obtained witness that he was righteous, God testifying of his gifts."† And the fires then kindled, never went out until they were quenched in the blood of the Lamb of God. The faith of righteous Abel, and of the successors to his promises and patience, was destined to long and severe trial. From Adam to Noah; from Noah to Abraham; from Abraham to Moses; from Moses to David; from David to John the Baptist; through the flood, and the great dispersion, and the sojourn in Egypt, and the wanderings in the wilderness, and the desolating captivity; the growing prediction of a divine and triumphant Deliverer had been nourished, as the common and crowning inheritance of the race. It sustained those earliest sons of God in their loneliness in the midst of wicked multitudes, and directed the pilgrimages of the patriarchs; it awakened desire and expectancy in every maternal heart, from the birth of Cain until the angel's salutation sounded in the ear of her who was highly favored of the Lord—blessed among women; it stirred the soul of the Psalmist, and glowed upon the lips of the prophet; it shaped the legislation of the statesman, and guided the administration of the king; and it gave life to the religious ritual and service of the people. Above all, those sacrifices which they

---

* Gen. iv. 1–5.   † Heb. xi. 4.

The Symbolism of the Communion. 201

offered year by year continually—morning and evening, on the Sabbath, at the new moon, and in the general annual gathering; especially the Day of Atonement and the Passover; although they could never make the comers thereunto perfect—added strength, clearness, and ardor to the sublime expectation of one that could.

All this comes before us as we sit down to the Supper of our Lord. The great cloud of witnesses—those who all died in faith, not having received the promises, but having seen them afar off, and were persuaded of them and embraced them, and confessed that they were strangers and pilgrims on the earth—they encompass us about, to assure us that their hopes have been fulfilled. Our simple sacramental feast is the testimony that he, to whom all these altar-flames, and streams of sacrificial blood, and columns of smoking incense pointed—the mighty Deliverer—has indeed come. "For it is not possible that the blood of bulls and of goats should take away sins." "But this man, after he had offered one sacrifice for sins forever, sat down on the right hand of God. * * * * For by one offering he hath perfected forever them that are sanctified."*

But there have been, and are, other altars and other victims than those prescribed and sanctioned in God's ancient covenant with man. Does our eucharistic ordinance bear any relation to these? All over our earth, and in every age of the race, a sense of sin, and a desire to remove the divine wrath, or propitiate the divine favor, have kindled the flames of animal and human sacrifices. Some of these fires are still burning. Now, when you have admitted the ignorance, wickedness, cruelty and wretchedness attested by these heathen sacrifices, do you not still feel them to be the most cogent witnesses for the universal presence and power of sin,

---

* Heb. ⸚. 4, 12-14.

and for the source and character of any adequate redemption? Are they not altars to the *unknown* God, whose forgiveness and blessing these sinners of the Gentiles vainly seek to secure? And does not this holy rite of our only true and universal religion commemorate him whom they ignorantly worship? Does it not say that he—*the desire of all nations*—has actually come? that now, once, in the end of the world, he hath appeared to put away sin by the sacrifice of himself? Yes; the new covenant of grace and redemption is for the world. The high contracting parties—Father, Son, and Holy Spirit—signed the solemn league on Calvary, in the blood of the eternally-ordained and effective sacrificial Lamb, and now the promise and proffer of free salvation has gone forth to every creature under heaven. The symbol of this ratification and commission is the communion of the body and blood of Christ.

And here you must notice the spirit of readiness and joyful satisfaction with which Christ made this sacrifice of himself, as shown in the institution of the Supper. He says, "With desire I have desired—*i. e.*, I have earnestly longed—to eat this Passover with you before I suffer." And then, over the bread and wine, he gave thanks and invoked the divine blessing. What does all this indicate, but the gladness of his loving heart in that he could offer such a salvation to man by the sacrifice of himself. It was love pervading his heart—divine and infinite love—eager to bestow upon its objects the highest gifts within its power. He never gave any thing nor did any thing grudgingly—not even when he made his soul an offering for sin, and had laid upon him the iniquities of us all. It was for the joy set before him, in seeing many sons brought to the glory of their Father, that he endured the Cross and despised the shame. He delighted in doing the will of God. The travail of his

The Symbolism of the Communion. 203

soul was that God and man might be joined in everlasting blessedness. He went to Calvary for us with benedictions and thanksgivings for the opportunity and power of giving eternal life to a ruined race.* The joy with which you come to the table of the Lord, as you remember from what and unto what his dying grace has saved you, is but a faint echo and image of his gladness of heart when he bestowed the grace.

III. There is, however, something still deeper and more vital in this ordinance. It symbolizes the dependence of the soul on Christ for spiritual life; and it shows that this life is solely by personal union with Christ, and by constant participation of his grace. Not only, then, do we herein set forth our historical belief in Jesus Christ; not only do we declare our belief in his vicarious sacrifice as the Lamb of God to take away the sin of the world; but we make public and solemn confession, also, that our personal salvation is secured and retained alone by living faith in him, by intimate intercourse and incessant nourishment. What could more impressively signify this than the partaking of those elements which represent the body and blood of the Lord?' "Take, eat," says the Lord himself, "this is my body;" "Take, drink—this is my blood." We want no blasphemous theory of transubstantiation, no fiction of sacramental grace, to disguise and hinder the blessing in this feast of love. It is not that our bodies are nourished by the body of Christ, but that our lives are fed from his life; not that some miraculous energy goes forth from the elements themselves, because manipulated by consecrated hands; but that there is an awful and holy communion of the believer with his Saviour, direct and personal. These elements are in the stead of his visible body, so that we may the better

---

* See Krummacher's Suffering Saviour, pp. 50, 56.

realize his promise, "Lo, I am with you always." They are the memorials of his grace; the signs of his presence; the occasion of the ineffable intercourse. They shadow forth that indissoluble union which subsists between Christ and the Christian, as the prime and essential condition of spiritual life—a oneness, as of the members in the body, as of the branches in the vine.

You have observed that John alone of the evangelists has no account of the institution of the Lord's Supper; but you have doubtless also felt that in the sixth chapter of his Gospel is such an exposition of the ordinance—its nature, its ground, and its significance—as only Christ could give. It was given shortly after his feeding the multitude from a few loaves and fishes—itself a striking symbol of the same truth, that Christ is the Bread of Life. The eager crowd gather around the Saviour, not from conviction of his divine power and authority, but because he had satisfied their earthly wants. They wished now to make him king. He exhorts them to labor, "not for the meat which perisheth, but for that meat which endureth unto everlasting life, which the Son of man shall give unto you." The figure of this exhortation recalls to the Jews the ancient miracle of their history, when man ate angel's food. "Our fathers did eat manna in the desert; as it is written, He gave them bread from heaven to eat. Then said Jesus unto them, Verily, verily, I say unto you, Moses gave you not that bread from heaven, but my Father giveth you the true bread from heaven. For the bread of God is he which cometh down from heaven, and giveth life unto the world. Then said they unto him, Lord, evermore give us this bread. And Jesus said unto them, I am the bread of life; he that cometh to me shall never hunger, and he that believeth on me shall never thirst." But the Jews "murmured at him, because he said, I am the bread which

The Symbolism of the Communion.

came down from heaven." For they were unwilling to recognize the marks of his heavenly origin, and could not see beyond the material meaning of his words. His reply is, "I am that bread of life. Your fathers did eat manna in the wilderness, and are dead. This is the bread which cometh down from heaven, that a man may eat thereof and not die. I am the living bread which came down from heaven. If any man eat of this bread he shall live forever; and the bread that I will give is my flesh, which I will give for the life of the world." When the Jews again strove with each other in their confusion over his language, saying, "How can this man give us his flesh to eat?" Jesus reiterated his wonderful statements, with a more personal application: "Verily, verily, I say unto you, Except ye eat the flesh of the Son of man, and drink his blood, ye have no life in you. Whoso eateth my flesh, and drinketh my blood, hath eternal life, and I will raise him up at the last day. For my flesh is meat indeed, and my blood is drink indeed. He that eateth my flesh, and drinketh my blood, dwelleth in me, and I in him. As the living Father hath sent me, and I live by the Father; so he that eateth me, even he shall live by me. This is that bread which came down from heaven; not as your fathers did eat manna, and are dead; he that eateth of this bread shall live forever."

I have cited these words in full, and shall weaken them by no comments, that you may have the Saviour's own statement and illustration of the dependence of our spiritual life on him, and of the richness and bounty with which that life is sustained.

And here we are again impressed with the analogy and contrast between the Lord's Supper and Baptism— the peculiar beauty and significance of each. Baptism signifies our burial and resurrection with Christ. These events can occur but once, and so Baptism is administered but once. It is that birth of the water and of the Spirit which, being once accomplished, stands good for all time, and for all eternity. But here it is the continuous living from Christ which is signified. It is not so much the dying, and rising again, the being born unto God, as the nourishing, and strengthening, and perfecting of that which has been born—that we may thereby walk in newness of life, and grow up into him in all things who is the head. Hence there is an actual partaking of the elements; hence also the Supper is frequently administered. The soul must eat, and eat constantly of Christ. Justification, regeneration, conversion, are once for all; but growth in grace, assimilation to Christ—in a word, the sanctification of body, soul, and spirit, requires continual supplies from the divine fullness, a continual feeding upon the Bread of God.* The earthly bread I eat I assimilate to myself. It nourishes for a time, but it is food that perisheth—perishes in the using—decays with the decaying body; it is *dead* bread. But this Bread of God is *living* bread. It assimilates me to itself. It, and not I, has the transforming power. And so I become like it—immortal, holy, and blessed. "Whoso eateth of this bread shall live forever." Here is the prayer of the communion—for the ordinance is a prayer—that we may become like him upon whom we feed in symbol, even as that which we eat becomes like us.

> Bread of heaven! on thee I feed,
> For thy flesh is meat indeed;
> Ever may my soul be fed
> With this True and Living Bread;
> Day by day with strength supplied
> Through the life of him who died.

---

* See Neander's *Planting and Training*, Robinson's edition, page 453.

> Vine of heaven! Thy blood supplies
> This blest cup of sacrifice;
> 'Tis thy wounds my healing give;
> To thy Cross I look and live;
> Thou, my Life, oh, let me be
> Rooted, grafted, built on thee!

Union and intercourse with God are the condition and source of all spiritual blessedness. This doctrine pervades the Scriptures like a perpetual presence. And the figures everywhere used to set forth this truth, seem to be a rehearsal of the symbols in the ordinance of the Lord's Supper. I can only allude to this thought, without expanding it. The eating of the sacrifices offered before the Lord; the solemn Passover meal, and other sacred festivals; the ordinance of the shew-bread; the miracle of the manna; the gushing rock that followed the journeying Israelites; the constant representation, in the prophets, of religious blessings by the figure of a feast, and of religious desolation by a famine; the "cup of salvation," to denote the portion and prosperity of God's people;—what are all these, but so many ways of saying that man can truly live only as he lives upon God? You at once recall that sweetest expression of this universal experience, in the twenty-third Psalm. The trusting, happy, hopeful child of God can find no more fitting symbols of his present joy and blessed prospects—" Thou preparest a table before me in the presence of mine enemies; thou anointest my head with oil; my cup runneth over."*

Even where these figures denote affliction and punishment, as in the "cup of indignation," "the wine of God's wrath," or the bitter cup which the Saviour drained, that he might fill it with life and joy for us— still the fundamental conception is retained of direct

---

* Ps. xxiii. 5.

relationship to God. It is the soul's portion, immediate and personal, from the hand of the Lord.

We may perhaps go a step further, and say that the ancient hospitality, which formed so prominent and charming a feature of Hebrew domestic life—so generously proffered and so jealously guarded—had its root and significance in this: that it was a responsive image and reflection in man of the divine bounty and grace of the Almighty Benefactor. And so, when Abraham entertained the angels unawares—even the angel Jehovah—he faintly symbolized the continual favor by which the angel Jehovah had cherished him.

Nor can we forget that the gospel salvation is in no way more richly proclaimed by the Saviour himself, than in the miracles of feeding the multitudes, the parables of the royal banquet, and the prodigal son feasting upon the fatted calf, and that ever-shining apocalyptic type of the marriage-supper of the Lamb.

With these thoughts in mind, how impressive and tender become the Saviour's plea and promise: "Behold, I stand at the door and knock; if any man hear my voice and open the door, I will come in to him, and will sup with him, and he with me."* Here is the love, the fullness of the love, of him who can find no illustration of his grace so equaling his own desire, as in that intimate personal intercourse, where he can share his favor with the favoring soul. He pleads for it as though his own blessedness must be fulfilled in blessing those who welcome him. He brings his feast with him. He is the feast himself. Surely, to turn him away is loneliness, desolation, death.

Now, all this is gathered up in our Christian ordinance of the Lord's Supper; for it all grows out of that which the ordinance pre-eminently symbolizes, the

---

* Rev. iii. 20.

sacrifice of Christ in expiation of the sins of the world. The cup in the hand of the Lord must be drunk by every soul of man. To the believer, it is the memorial of a sacrifice accepted, and so becomes the symbol of peace, communion, salvation, blessedness; because the "wine of the wrath of God in the cup of his indignation" did not pass from the Saviour in the awful garden, but was drained by him to the dregs in the sinner's stead. To the unbeliever, it is the memorial of a sacrifice rejected; the "cup of the wine of the fierceness of his wrath" who is unpropitiated and unappeased; the inevitable portion of him who hath trodden under foot the Son of God, and hath counted the blood of the covenant an unholy thing; the sacrament of endless woe. We cannot escape from some relation to the blood of Christ. If it be not upon us to cleanse us from our sin, it will be upon us to seal our perdition.

IV. This comprehensive Christian ordinance is also a pledge of obedience. For it not only symbolizes our communion with Christ, but also our solemn covenant to fulfill all the conditions of Christian discipleship. By partaking of it, therefore, we consecrate ourselves to Christ in purity and fidelity. We enter into closest intercourse with Christ, eating his flesh and drinking his blood; thereby seeking his holiness and pledging ourselves to manifest it. You remember, that no one could come to the ancient Passover or other sacrifices, except through the most scrupulous ceremonies of purification and vows of obedience. "When Moses had spoken every precept to all the people, according to the law, he took the blood of calves and of goats, with water, and scarlet wool, and hyssop, and sprinkled both the book and all the people, saying, This is the blood of the covenant which God hath enjoined you."* And so our

---

* Heb. ix. 19, 20.

Saviour says, in consecrating these memorials of his perfect sacrifice, "This cup is the new covenant in my blood." We pray and hope for a fresh sprinkling from this pure and purifying sacrifice, as we take the cup of the communion of the blood of Christ. We pray and hope for the thorough purging away of all impure and corrupting influences, as we partake of the communion of the body of Christ. "For even Christ, our Passover, is sacrificed for us; therefore, let us keep the feast, not with old leaven, neither with the leaven of malice and wickedness, but with the unleavened bread of sincerity and truth."*

And this eating is a consecration to fidelity. No act of the Christian life so proclaims entire devotion to our Lord as the participation in his Supper. We thereby acknowledge our whole reliance upon him for salvation, and undertake to live out before men the life derived from feeding upon him, at whatever cost of trial, privation, or pain. We avow ourselves ready, according to our measure, to fill up that which is behind of the afflictions of Christ in our flesh for his body's sake, which is the Church.† It is a fellowship of the sufferings of Christ; in a word, a readiness to drink the cup which he drank, and to be baptized with the baptism with which he was baptized.

It is also a consecration to zealous labor, in publishing the gospel to the world. "As often as ye eat this bread and drink this cup, ye do show, or, ye are to show, *i. e.*, publish, proclaim, preach, the Lord's death till he come." The whole of the great commission is symbolized here; the whole of the church's duty to Christ and to the race. This is not a feast for selfish and passive enjoyment. These elements are to be distributed to the world, and we are debtors to the world until the distri-

---

* 1 Cor. v. 7, 8.   † Col. i. 24.

bution is made.* When, then, we receive these memorials of our Lord's body and blood, it is a surrender of ourselves to him and his service; a pledge that we will not rest in our Christian activity, until every starving wanderer from God has been fed with the bread of life and is prepared to drink the new wine with our Saviour in the heavenly kingdom. Not until the streets, and lanes, and highways, and hedges have all been explored, and the poor, and maimed, and halt, and blind, all gathered into the marriage feast; not until the gospel is preached to every creature, can our communion vow and covenant of blood be fulfilled.

V. Again: As has been already intimated, in this communion with Christ by the Lord's Supper, there is also symbolized the communion of Christians through him with each other. I shall not here discuss the question, whether the Lord's Supper should be called distinctively a *Christian* or a *church* ordinance; *i. e.*, whether it indicates the organic and visibly associated relation of church fellowship, or the broader spiritual relation of Christian fellowship. It does both. It is an ordinance of the Christian church, to symbolize the unity of its members as members of the body of Christ, and the derivation of their life from him. The New Testament assumes, that all disciples of Christ will profess themselves such, and that they will do this by becoming openly united with other Christians, *i. e.*, by coming within the visible church through its appointed ordinances. Still further; the New Testament does not recognize schism or sectarianism in the church of Christ, *i. e.*, it makes no provision for differing or antagonistic denominations. "There is one body and one spirit,

---

* There is no allusion here to the *terms* of communion. It is only meant that the Lord's Supper, as observed by the church, symbolizes its duty to preach the gospel to every creature.

even as ye are called in one hope of your calling. One Lord, one faith, one baptism, one God and Father of all, who is above all, and through all, and in you all."* "For as the body is one and hath many members, and all the members of that one body, being many, are one body, so also is Christ. For by one spirit are we all baptized into one body, whether we be Jews or Gentiles, whether we be bond or free, and have been all made to drink into one spirit."† Or, as it is in that wondrous intercessory prayer of Christ, the pledge and pattern of his present incessant pleading for us: "Neither pray I for these alone, but for them also which shall believe on me through their word; that they all may be one, as thou, Father, art in me, and I in thee, that they also may be one in us. And the glory which thou gavest me I have given them, in order that they may be one, even as we are one; I in them, and thou in me, that they may be made perfect in one."‡ Now this unity is nowhere more vividly or significantly set forth, than in celebrating the Supper of our Lord—at the first celebration of which this prayer was offered. "For we being many are one bread and one body; for we are all partakers of that one bread." All the analogies of nature and of human relationship are put under contribution in the Scriptures to signalize and illustrate the oneness of Christians with Christ, and through him their oneness with each other. The church organization is designed to express visibly this all-encompassing unity, and the divinely prescribed ordinances are the distinctive outward marks of the true church—the manifest body of Christ. In the communion, these analogies find their highest and most striking exhibition. It is the union of the brethren of one household at their father's

---

* Eph. iv. 4–6. † 1 Cor. xii. 12, 13. ‡ John xvii. 20–23.

table; the confession of sinners to a common Saviour; the fellowship of saints in a common hope; the knitting together of the members of one body, as fed by the same heavenly food and inspired by the same divine life; the covenanted followers of one Redeemer and King, pledging their obedience to his every command, and their devotion to his cause until the world shall be subject to his authority; the heirs of one inheritance, rejoicing in the foretaste and assurance of coming glory. What, then, is more appropriate, or beautiful, or obligatory, than Christian unity—unity in Christ!

And yet, under the circumstances that now actually surround us, we may not invite all who profess and call themselves Christians to join with us in this solemn feast. In fact, we may not invite any one, for it is not our table, but the Lord's. He has prescribed the order of the church and of its ordinances. We may not modify his prescription. We must forbid the approach of all who do not comply with it. For while it is not given unto us to alter the legislation of Christ, it is required of us, that we contend earnestly for the faith delivered once for all to the saints. The ordinances of the Christian church are a constituent part of Christianity. To change them, is to change the doctrines of the gospel, implying a presumption and temerity no whit less dangerous here than in any other article of divine truth. We sit in judgment upon no man's convictions and motives by our practice in this matter; we arrogate no jurisdiction over his conscience; we do not disallow his claim to an experience of the grace of God. We simply leave these questions to him and to his own Master. We will go with him to the utmost limit of devotion and duty that does not violate the clear command of the Head of the church. If we agree not in the interpretation of such command and requirement, we must separate, for neither he nor we dare think more of outward uniformity among ourselves than of obedience to Christ. "To obey is better than sacrifice, and to hearken than the fat of rams."* There is no uncharitableness in this, for charity will not sanction any failure of fidelity to the Saviour and to the truth. It can hide a multitude of sins, but it cannot prompt them; and every failure in obedience to a known command of Christ is sin. We only ask what we readily concede to all, freedom to follow our convictions of duty, and to keep our consciences pure and true for him who is our Lord. No man could respect us, nor could we respect ourselves, should we do otherwise or insist on less. There is undoubtedly a great responsibility laid upon us in this thing. If we are not correct and honest in our views of church order and ordinances, then are we schismatics in the body of Christ; if we are honest and correct, then are we worse than schismatics, if we do not maintain our trust.

But let not this controversy hide from you the precious fact, so clearly symbolized in our Christian passover, that the people of God are one—delivered from the same bondage, divinely attended through the same pilgrimage, and heirs of the same conquest and inheritance. Our communion with Christ and with each other, inspires us to labor for the conversion of the world and the unity of the church; these emblems of the one sacrifice for sin becoming a prophecy of that time, when the outward unity shall be as complete as the inward spirit—when there shall be one fold and one Shepherd, one family and one feast.

VI. What can I say more! Is not this simple Christian ordinance seen to be full of significance, gathering

---

* 1 Sam. xv. 22.

up in itself all the doctrines, duties, and motives of the gospel? Nothing can surpass its beauty, impressiveness, and eloquence. It is the confession of our faith, the sign of our oneness with Christ, the vow and oath of our devotion and fidelity to him, the token of our fellowship with the Christian brotherhood, the pledge of our activity for the salvation of the world. Surely we cannot suffer this chief religious rite to be a mere appendage to another service, a subordinate matter, to be observed simply because it is prescribed. We need time, while the emblems are before us, to draw some of their mighty lessons and fix them in our hearts, to receive somewhat of the grace of which they are the means and occasion, to feel the refreshment and quickening of the holy communion they symbolize.

But, to give you my closing thought, there is more in this ordinance than we have yet disclosed. It has relation not only to the past and present, but also to the future. It is at once the symbol of faith and of hope. It is a memorial; it is also a prophecy. Even this Supper of our Lord, with all its glories, is only a shadow of good things to come—of a glory that excelleth. As the old Passover commemorated the deliverance from Egypt, and pointed to what Christ should accomplish in time, so this new Passover commemorates our deliverance from sin and points forward to what Christ shall accomplish in eternity, when to principalities and powers shall be made known by means of the church the manifold wisdom of God. For he who said, "Do this in remembrance of me;" in remembrance, that is, of what I have done, what I am doing, what I shall yet do in my coming and glory; added also this marvelous word, "I will drink no more of the fruit of the vine until I drink it new with you in the kingdom of God." Here are the fruits of that new creation, when, under the new heavens and the new earth, it shall attain to the liberty for which it is groaning with the children of God. Then shall be fulfilled the reconciliation of the universe by the cross of Christ;—the tree of life no longer have a flaming sword. We cannot know all that this divine promise enfolds, until we find ourselves at the marriage Supper of the Lamb. If even now, our hearts burn within us while he opens to us the Scriptures, and oftentimes he makes himself known unto us in the breaking of bread, what shall it be when we become like him and see him as he is and share his glory? when we drink the wine new *with him* in his Father's kingdom? But we know this, that in our communion now, we look forward as well as backward; we enter into a fellowship of glory, as well as of suffering; we call before us the new Jerusalem, not less than the old; it is the Passover of Canaan as well as of Egypt and the wilderness; we sit together as in heavenly places in Christ Jesus, and have an earnest of that day when the vail of invisibility shall be rent asunder, and all shall be fulfilled in the kingdom of God.

"They shall hunger no more, neither thirst any more; neither shall the sun light on them, nor any heat. For the Lamb which is in the midst of the throne shall feed them, and shall lead them unto living fountains of waters; and God shall wipe away all tears from their eyes." *

---

* Rev. vii. 16, 17.

X.

QUALIFICATIONS FOR THE COMMUNION.

By JOHN W. SARLES, D.D.,
Pastor of Central Baptist Church, Brooklyn, N. Y.

"Then Jesus said unto them, Verily, verily, I say unto you, Except ye eat the flesh of the Son of man, and drink his blood, ye have no life in you."—*John* vi. 53.

"Go ye, therefore, and teach all nations, baptizing them in the name of the Father, and of the Son, and of the Holy Ghost; teaching them to observe all things whatsoever I have commanded you: and, lo, I am with you always, even unto the end of the world. Amen."—*Matthew* xxviii. 19, 20.

"For I have received of the Lord, that which also I delivered unto you, That the Lord Jesus, the same night in which he was betrayed, took bread: and when he had given thanks, he brake it, and said, Take, eat: this is my body, which is broken for you: this do in remembrance of me. After the same manner also, he took the cup, when he had supped, saying, This cup is the new testament in my blood: this do ye, as oft as ye drink it, in remembrance of me. For as often as ye eat this bread, and drink this cup, ye do shew the Lord's death till he come."—1 *Corinthians* xi. 23-26.

The Lord's Supper, then, is appointed the perpetual memorial of "the Lord's death."

That central truth of all revelation, foundation of all hope, living medium of all life, the atonement, is the burden of its ministry.

"Till he come." No narrower limit bounds its mission. Beginning on the night of his betrayal, and stretching on to the hour of his second coming, it quite spans the opened dispensation.

"As often." Then, during all that period, frequently. Immediately connected with all that is vital to godliness among men, demanding unremitting and frequent observance, it is intensely practical, and *ought* to be understood.

Living only because Jesus died, and breathing only with

> "Love
> Higher than the heights above,
> Deeper than the depths beneath,
> Free and faithful, strong as death,"

its study should be grateful; and the heart where most love dwells must understand it best. Fully to understand and possess the qualifications for its observance cannot widely differ from fully understanding the mystery of redemption, and freely participating in its largest benefits.

As this series of sermons was designed to be denominational, I shall give special prominence to those particulars in which Baptists may differ from others.

I. That qualification for the Communion, which is first, and underlies evermore all besides, is faith in our Lord Jesus Christ.

With no reference to the supper did Christ say, "Except ye eat the flesh of the Son of man, and drink his blood, ye have no life in you." Communion at the Lord's table, was subsequently added, to explain and enforce that language.

In those words, Christ is tasking language and figures to the utmost, to make intelligible and appreciable what is meant by *believing with the heart unto righteousness.* Through successive verses, 52 to 57, he presses the truth that, in order to share the benefits of his mediation, it is not enough that he has come into the world, that he shall live and die for sinners, and ascend to his Father's right hand a Prince and a Saviour; it is not enough merely to accredit this, and defend and discourse ever so correctly and religiously upon it; there must be, beyond that, a conscious, cordial, grateful acceptance of him in the offices he came to fill, and in the work he came to perform; there must be this taking him to do and be for us individually; there must be this appropriation of him to ourselves, as when at a table a man not only sees and handles the bread, but takes and eats it, does and must make the appropriation of it to his bodily necessities by eating it.

The supper alone can present, more boldly and more fully explained, that great cardinal doctrine of the Bible, "The just shall live by faith." It is an actual physical exhibition of what is here only described. In one, you hear a description; in the other, you both hear the description and see faithfully and exactly acted out each successive particular. Of the bread, he says, "This is *my body;*" of the wine, "This is *my blood.*" Having made the bread and the wine the symbols of his body and blood in the work of human redemption, he says, "Take, *eat.*" Each one, in the act of eating, then appears in the act of appropriating Christ to himself, Christ in the merit of both his obedience and his death.

In God's completed revelation to man, this is the crowning representation of that faith by which men are justified and sanctified.

From the foregoing, it will be seen that participation in the Communion without faith in Christ is, of necessity, a delusion or a mockery. No subjection to catechetical instruction; no observance of rites, human or divine; no judgment of men or acts of churches; no standing; no office; no service; and no depths of sincerity; can supply the lack of a believing heart in the Communion.

How pointedly this is taught will be seen from such passages as the following:

Mark xvi. 16; John iii. 14–16, 18, 36; vi. 29, 47; viii 24; Acts viii. 37; xiii. 38, 39; xvi. 31; Romans iii. 28, x. 4; Hebrews xi. 6.

The past existence of faith, moreover, does not meet

the truth. In the observance of the supper, its very form insists upon the immediate and present exercise of faith, *walking in Christ as* he *was received.* A life of faith upon the Son of God—nothing short of that will meet the first Scriptural Qualification for the Communion.

Nor is a living faith the full measure of qualification. The Scriptures promptly bring forward a second—it is:

II. Personal submission to the ordinance commonly called baptism.

This is taught:

1. By the symbolical representations of the supper.
2. By express command.
3. By inspired example absolutely uniform.

1. Symbolically.

In connection with the *primary* design of the supper, it has a form significant, additional to participation in the atonement.

Partaking of bread and wine in any possible way, is not the Communion. It is a *supper* that Christ appointed, the later Greek δειπνον, the principal meal, and after the heat of the day. It is a family gathered, an evening banquet, a kingdom in possession.

Symbolically the supper alone would be unaccountably abrupt. It brings forward results without antecedents; a family without an origin; a feast without preparation, and guests without invitation; a kingdom without a history; a sudden consummation without a beginning. The supper alone has no knowledge of us till after we have entered the family; does not recognize us till seated at the banqueting-table. From that point it looks forward to the heavenly state when the whole redeemed family will sit down together in the everlasting kingdom appointed to them; but makes no attempt to reach back over our history. It knows nothing of even our introduction to its circles.

If there were no *other* Christian rite, we might infer that no one rite could be instituted which should cover the past, present, and future of our relations. But see! there *is* a *sister* rite; one and no more. That rite is, in its *form*, introductory and *avowedly* initiatory—a rite in the observance of which, Christ is said to be "*put on ;*"—a rite in which our past relations, both our sin and our death to it by the death of him who was delivered for our offences, and our appearance again, risen with him who was raised for our justification, one and forever inseparable from him, in which all this is told by its *form ;*—a rite evermore singing, "To him who loves us and washed us from our sins in his own blood, and made us a kingdom, priests to God and his Father, to him be the glory and the dominion forever and ever. Amen." That other sister rite is *baptism*. "Buried with him in baptism, wherein also ye are risen with him."

With this brought to view all is explained. These sister rites joining hands, cover the past and the future of the redeemed; and the elder is baptism.

It is designed to precede, not to follow the supper. As a symbolical ordinance submission to it is indispensable to the other; without it, there cannot be qualification for the other. There may be qualification scripturally to eat the flesh of the Son of Man and drink his blood, without baptism; but not for the Communion. One may also scripturally eat the flesh of the Son of Man and drink his blood without appearing at the Lord's table; nay, he must, before he ever appears at the table; but as a symbolical ordinance, baptism has no place, if not before the supper. Coming in after the supper it is too tardy, it comes uncalled, it is superseded. Its subsequent appearance fails to supply history, where it is needed, and can only serve to make jargon by disjointing history and reversing its order.

2. Express command.

"All power was given to me in heaven and on earth. Go, therefore, and disciple all the nations, immersing them in the name of the Father, and of the Son, and of the Holy Spirit; teaching them to observe all things, whatever I commanded you."

This is our Lord's final charge till "he comes amidst the clouds." It is laid upon his apostles, standing before him to represent the whole church on earth, including every disciple of every age, the world over. Whatever is here enjoined, falls, first and directly, upon the churches of Christ; and then, by implication, upon every one who has ears to hear. It contains three specifications in the following order:

1. They shall go into all the world, seeking to make all men Christ's disciples, by preaching the gospel to them.

2. They shall baptize all who become disciples.

3. They shall instruct all baptized disciples to practice, hold unaltered, and pass down inviolate, all things whatsover Christ has commanded.

If the *order* here given is inspired, there is no more room for the supper before baptism, in the *command*, than there is place for it before baptism as a *symbol*. Whether infinite wisdom and love have less to do with the order than with the subject matter, will be made to appear in looking at some possible changes in the order of carrying it out.

First. Reverse the order entire; make that first which is here last.

We shall then go into all the world, first teaching them to observe all things whatsoever Christ has commanded. Teaching whom? All among the nations whom we *can* teach. Teaching them what? Whatever commands of Christ do not relate to discipleship, and that unconverted people can be taught to observe.

Qualifications for the Communion. 223

In this reversed order, faith in Christ does not yet appear. Next, baptize those so taught, in the name of the Trinity; and, now, seek their conversion by preaching the gospel to them.

We shall then have men, women, and children schooled in formalism, and baptized into hypocrisy preparatory to discipleship. We shall compass sea and land to make proselytes to Christ, and shall succeed in turning out self-sufficient, conceited, haughty, hardened religionists, trained to mockery, practiced in deceit and self-deception, ten times more the children of Satan than before.

In the Jewish nation, there had been an extended trial of this order of teaching religious observances, with the most lamentable results. There was no class of men so personally hopeless, and requiring, both for their own sake and that of others, such unsparing severity at the hands of the great teacher, as that class.

It will make some difference, then, whether our Lord's great charge is carried out in one order or another. The change we have named would much more than neutralize its design.

Let us attempt a change less radical.

Second. The specification that stands second, let it be put first. Simply transpose the first and second. Baptize first, then disciple, then teach.

Already it has been tried. Let history bring forward the results. On the map, you will see the outlines of a vast empire, stretching across all the northern parts of Europe and Asia, and compassing nearly half the globe. That is Russia, with its sixty or seventy millions of inhabitants. Those living masses of immortals, as well as those of Greece and contiguous States and large islands, are mainly without God; and almost no missionary effort is put forth for them by any Christian people. What is it that has rendered the condition and prospects of these even worse than that of the heathen? Why! that is *itself* called a Christian land—the Bible has been in their possession for long centuries; churches are scattered far and near, having some of the most magnificent structures in the world, with various orders of officiating ministers, all sustained at governmental expense. Missionary effort among such a people! They accept it as an insult. Scarcely a man is in the realm who has not been three times baptized, and who is not in full fellowship with the churches.

What is it that, in those lands, has rendered truth powerless, paralyzed every Christian effort, and made these the pitiable victims of delusion they are? Is it Popery? No! Tens of millions of them loathe and detest it. Not Popery, but this:—*Baptism before discipleship.* For see: they begin with baptism, that rite which is initiatory; baptism, then, must change the heart, or induct the world into the churches, sweeping away all distinction between the churches and the world. But as baptism does not change the heart, it has done the other thing; and you see these fruits. Ah! yes, and much more than this twice told. Baptism *before* discipleship! that is what the Catholic church avows—that is what the Lutheran churches intend—that is so-called *Pedobaptism.*

Many nations have been sprinkled with clean water. They have also been taught much of revealed truth, and been schooled in many religious observances. Discipleship has not followed; the possibility of it has been put further from these than from others. See Austria, Spain, Portugal, France, Italy, Mexico, South America, and Germany. All of it traceable to that change—baptism *before* discipleship. It has churched the unsanctified world by nations, but only to corrupt or stifle and strangle the truth. It has produced monster forms of godliness, but with no other power than to silence or menace, and pursue with malignant hatred, all spiritual religion; for all of which, it claims the sanction of Christ. It has not only fatally subverted all truth in its march, but it has poisoned the fountains of life.

Whether any thing else than Baptist testimony and influence have prevented a worldly membership from following Pedobaptism, with results similarly disastrous to the cause of truth and the souls of men, in England, Scotland, and America, judge you.

There is possible yet another change in the order of carrying out that last injunction.

Third. Begin, as commanded, with discipleship; then transpose the second and third, so as to allow training in the observance of all things (except baptism) to come in before baptism. We shall then go into all the world, faithfully seeking to make all men Christ's disciples by preaching the gospel to them. We shall persistently insist upon discipleship before baptism; we shall refuse to take a step in advance without it; but when men truly believe, we will say, Who can forbid the Communion that these should not partake, who have received the Holy Spirit as well as we? Waiving their baptism, we will invite them at once to the Lord's table as *disciples*, take them into membership, and proceed to teach them.

This too has been tried, and some of its results are before us.

It may seem very harmless to make changes in the order, after once discipleship has been secured; and a very loving thing to pass from discipleship at once to the table. Not so has it proven. Under the beguiling thought that, by this change, baptism was only transposed, good men have easily yielded; but that apparent change of place has proven to be a daring *erasure*.

See:—The unbaptized disciple, in an Open-communion Baptist church, if he persists in absenting himself from the table, or in neglecting other duties recognized by the church, forfeits his standing, and is put away. But never did you hear it that if, at the expiration of five or fifteen or fifty years, one who had been admitted to such a church unbaptized did not see it to be his duty to submit to that rite, he should be put away. The thought even is unknown. No; he may persist ever so long in neglecting baptism; his standing is not forfeited; his relations are not disturbed; his position was never fairer; his influence increasingly weighty. There is no remonstrance, no labor, no reproof; nay, he passes on into the position of office-bearer and pillar. He may live in the neglect of it till the day of his death, and the church of which he is a member takes no notice of it.

What does this mean? It means that Open-communion Baptist churches, *in their official capacity, have consented to drop* from the commission the ordinance of baptism. If, in individual instances, baptism comes up afterward, it comes up from individual convictions, and not from any church action; it comes up, outside of the acknowledged jurisdiction of the churches, and after, as churches, they have agreed upon its sacrifice. They have drawn up and signed the stipulation, that baptism shall be observed or not, at the option of each applicant for admission. If he says "no," they bow assent; if he says "yes," they acquiesce; but will be no judge of such matters. They leave the ordinance to stand without a witness. Yes, it is that; as *churches* they have consented, they have *agreed* to drop it from the commission. Deliberately they take away its place, as if under promise to give it a better, and then *desert* it. In their practice, as churches, in which capacity alone it is that they are immediately charged with whatever the commission contains, in that *charged* capacity they have betrayed the ordinance of baptism.

What a humiliating spectacle is presented! Century

after century withstanding the Pedobaptist brother to his face, because he was to be blamed in the matter of *changing* an ordinance, and still having a separate existence to remonstrate against that wrong; and finally discovering that the controversy may be settled by an *abandonment* of the ordinance in dispute. The living child shall be divided! and as the other is not the mother, the proffer is not unacceptable. Where the Pedobaptist dared to *change* an ordinance, the Open-communion Baptist has dared to *strike it out*.

The spectacle is not only humiliating as before men, but fearful as in the sight of God. As a *command*, the estrangement from it is complete. From such lips, of course, it can come no longer as a command. They do not know it as such: how *can* they utter it? So held, the ordinance will cease to be administered under individual convictions. Will the fire of God's Spirit descend to burn that command into the souls of men from their lips? God not often so works. By utter neglect it will die. Another must take their crown.

We say this—mourning over a development of human weakness, such as has often attached to the greatest and best of men—to give another instance of the perversion of judgment that follows every attempt to change, in the slightest degree even, the order of Christ's great charge. Results are accumulating such as these:—The subject of baptism, in the pulpit or in the church, the apple of discord; the pastor, unconsciously drawn aside from it, and bribed by the mixed character of the church itself; the ordinance taught or practiced, unwelcome, and finally distasteful; its administration transferred from the Lord's Day to a day of the week, to be witnessed by the little group, not the multitude; Baptist ministers pastors over Pedobaptist churches; and Baptist churches of a century's standing transformed to Pedobaptist churches.

The venerable and excellent Pengilly is now the pastor of a Pedobaptist church. The fearless and faithful Mr. Spurgeon, apparently seeing the peril of the churches, modifies the system—admitting none to membership who are not Baptists, but leaves the table open to all. That modification means that the organization itself and the property shall not share a common fate with the principle involved. Thus much already, and more in promise. "Every kingdom divided against itself is brought to desolation."

All this, from attempting the least disturbing change possible in the order of the commission. Can further proof be needed that the subject-matter of that charge, and the order in which it is given, must stand or fall together? To carry out its specifications is *possible in one order only*, and that order the one given. The particulars enjoined are so related to each other, that change of *order*, as certainly as change of matter, vitiates the whole. Why should the inspiration of the order ever have been a question? Where was it learned that the substance, but not the order, of any part of the word is inspired? Then, any argument may be broken, each sentence torn asunder, every verse displaced. Last of all, may explicit *orders* from the ascending Conqueror be tampered with. If Christ does not determine in what order that commission shall be carried out, who shall determine it? And if his determination is not expressed in the commission itself, where shall it be expressed? But, if it is expressed here, let it never again be asked where there is direct authority, or the force of a command, for requiring us to see that disciples are baptized before sitting with them at the table. Rather, where is the line or the hint in the living oracles that seems to *permit* it? On his avowed disciples this farewell charge falls and rests. An attempt to shift this responsibility is in the

Qualifications for the Communion. 229

immediate direction of anarchy against government in the kingdom of Christ.

Yes, here it is—express *authority*—the churches *required* by Christ to give the undivided weight of their influence to secure the baptism of every disciple; required to be as unyielding in it, as in insisting upon discipleship before baptism, and undeviating in both.

3. Inspired example absolutely uniform.

The time *when* the apostles were baptized is not on record. Instead of a direct statement specifying the time or the fact of their baptism, we have the following:

First. Strong presumptive evidence that the apostles, who alone participated in the supper on the night of its institution, had all been John's disciples.

It was early in his ministry that Christ made choice of these men. From among whom? From among those just called in by his own ministry, or from among those whom John had been sent expressly to prepare for him?

Following immediately upon John's ministry, the choice of men for office, highest in the kingdom, next to Christ, would be sure to affect John's standing and work in the public estimation. Would our Lord so far appear to be a competitor with John for honor as to reserve for his own ministry the calling in and preparing of even *one* for that office? Why should thus much of honor be withheld from the one to whom it would naturally belong, if he had done well the work for which he was so signally raised up and sent? To no other would such an act have been so painful as to the one whom John delighted to herald. How tenderly he guarded whatever might affect John's reputation, you will remember. Rather than allow disparaging comparison, he withdrew entirely from the vicinity of John's labors. He coveted opportunity to honor that faithful servant. Hear the extraordinary language he uses of him: "What went ye out to see? A prophet? Yea, I say unto you, and more than a prophet. For this is he of whom it is written, Behold, I send my messenger before thy face, which shall prepare thy way before thee. Verily, I say unto you, Among them that are born of women, there hath not risen a greater than John the Baptist."

In the choice of apostles, the opportunity had come for putting upon John and his work the most signal honor. There were also special reasons for such an expression. That noble man was now in prison, and his scattered disciples, without a leader, were all to be gathered to Christ. The choice of every apostle from among the tried disciples and fast friends of John was the act whereby to win over the whole body of his adherents, and publicly vindicate the martyr.

Probably Andrew is given as a specimen for all.* The instance of Matthew is no exception.† Many publicans were baptized by John, and were not under charge to leave their callings, but only to exact no more than was just.

But we have more than presumptive evidence; we have,

Second. Implied testimony.

It is in the Acts i. 21, 22. In proposing to fill the place of Judas, the special condition of a choice was, that the call and discipleship of the man to be chosen should reach back entirely through Christ's ministry to John's baptism. That was acceptable to all. But it could not have been acceptable had there been one among them who had been called in later than under John's ministry. Had that been true, there could have been no reason for making the condition, "beginning with the baptism of John."

If, then, the apostles had been John's disciples, they were among the unnamed multitudes whose baptism by

---

* John i. 35-40.   † Matt. ix. 9.

Qualifications for the Communion. 231

him is recorded. On no other terms could they have been his disciples.

Besides, the argument for their baptism is not dependent upon evidence that they had been baptized by John. There is a much shorter method, and beyond the power of evasion. They certainly were *Christ's* disciples. Very well. Their Master was himself baptized. Like his harbinger, also, he baptized all who received his doctrine. More than this, his own disciples were the administrators in each instance, and were subsequently sent out under charge to baptize all who became disciples.

Is it conceivable that notwithstanding, they themselves had never submitted to the ordinance! Wherein, then, were they disciples? They could not be his avowed and accepted disciples, as they certainly were, and reject his baptism; the thing is impossible, because contradictory. The evidence of the baptism of the apostles is circumstantial, but none the less convincing. If there was a hint that any one of them was not baptized, that passage would be hopelessly inexplicable. No unbaptized person partook of the supper on the night of its institution.

The subsequent acts of the apostles can be regarded in no other light, than an inspired commentary upon the commission. Only about forty days later, it was given; and ten days later still, by the endowing of the Holy Spirit, they commenced their work under it.

An attempt to trace the inspired history of the immediate triumphs of the gospel, in the *multiplication* of believers, will serve to show whether there is evidence that any person unbaptized participated in the communion, during the times of the apostles.

A record of their first acts, in doing what Christ enjoined in that last charge, is found in Acts ii. 14–47 The Spirit came in his promised fullness. Peter, with characteristic promptitude, arises and preaches the gospel to the assembled multitude. Conviction seizes on the hearts of thousands, and the cry is heard, "Men and brethren what shall we do?" Hear the answer: "Then Peter said unto them, repent and be baptized, every one of you." What followed? "Then they that gladly received his word, were baptized; and the same day there were added unto them about three thousand souls."

Were any added without baptism? The preacher had said, "Repent and be baptized, *every one of you;*" and it is recorded, "They that gladly received his word *were* baptized." The number of these baptized persons, it was, that had swollen to three thousand. All were added to the church, but not one without baptism.

And next what? "And they continued *steadfastly* in the apostles' doctrine and fellowship, and in breaking of bread, and in prayers." In living deeds, could there be a more perfect transcript of the letter of the commission? The apostle preached the good news to as many as he could reach; he baptized as many as were discipled; these, and no others, he took to the table. This was the first official act under the commission; its keynote was struck; the record is full, and was for all time. With noon-day clearness, each of its specifications, and each in their divinely appointed order, stands out.

If this coincidence was without design, some other order of procedure will be likely to spring upon us, in following the narrative.

To show the steady triumphs of grace, but without any attempt at detail, the closing verse in the chapter reads, "And the Lord added to the church daily, such as should be saved."

The next record of enlargement by conversion, is in Acts iv. 4. " Howbeit many of them which heard the word believed; and the number of the men was about five thousand." Not only baptism is not named but no

Qualifications for the Communion.

conviction, no question, no answer, no avowal of discipleship, no addition to the church, no fellowship with the apostles, no prayer, no supper. For *instruction*, it was not needed. All *that* was covered before, and there was no call for repetition, unless something *different* was introduced. And now, *other* facts crowd in for notice.

In the act of preaching, the apostles were assaulted, and laid under arrest by the public authorities. While they are thus dragged off to prison, the Holy Spirit is pleased to note, for future instruction and encouragement, what the Lord was doing in the hearts of the hearers. Instead of a detailed account as before, this is written: "And the multitude of them that believed, were of one heart and of one soul." There were no differences in their belief or practice. But there would have been differences if one was baptized and another was not. Such difference was then unknown.

Beside this, there are eighteen other passages where no particulars about the repentance, or the faith, or the preaching, connected with the persons spoken of, are given, except to point them out as the trophies of grace. They are as follows: v. 14; vi. 7; ix. 31, 35, 42; xi. 21, 24; xii. 24; xiii. 12, 43, 48; xiv. 1; xvi. 5; xvii. 4, 12, 34; xix. 17-20; xxviii. 24.

If from that silence about baptism, one were tempted to infer that it was not in those instances administered, he would need to be reminded, that by the same species of reasoning, another might infer that multitudes of believers never made a public profession of religion, were added to no church, lived without prayer, had no fellowship with the apostles, and never participated in the supper. In speaking of the accession of believers, the supper is not so much as once named, after the day of Pentecost. Silence may not be interpreted to mean something different from what is declared.

Turn again to the history of additions, while I group the remaining instances where baptism is particularized.

Read viii. 5-16. This relates to the preaching of Philip, in the city of Samaria. Here is the first instance, under the commission, of preaching the gospel outside of what was strictly the Jewish nation. Here, particularity was again called for, to show that no change of circumstance could change the course of these divinely instructed men. On the point in dispute, it is full and explicit. Read verses 12-16.

In the 26-39 verses of the same chapter, a peculiar case presents itself, and still more emphatically the order of the commission is enforced. See especially verses 36-39.

In the next chapter, a man is brought before us, in whose conversion the ordinary preaching of the gospel was superseded. None the less rigidly discipleship was insisted upon, and baptism upon the evidence of it. This man, though called in at that late day, "born out of due season," this man was to become the chief of the apostles. Twice we are informed of his baptism. Compare ix. 18, with xxii. 12-16. As soon as Ananias is informed of the conversion of Saul, he approaches him with his charge, "And now why tarriest thou? arise, and be baptized." How impressively the procedure and the form of address in this instance, shows that baptism was uniformly *required* of every one making claim to discipleship. Could there be a reason for approaching Saul thus, that would not equally apply in every other instance of conversion? Why hold Saul to this rite, and leave it optional with another? Read that record, and if you can, believe Paul capable of pursuing a different course toward any discipled by his ministry.

In the next chapter, the first convert from among the Gentiles, under apostolic preaching, is brought in, and again is rehearsed the fact and the order of baptism; x. 47, 49.

Qualifications for the Communion.

Under Paul's labors, occurs the record of four instances of discipleship and baptism, with the same undeviating exactness in the order; xvi. 14, 15, 30–33; xviii. 8; xix. 1–5.

As if anticipating the time, when, in this matter, men would seek to separate what Christ has joined together, not a single instance of baptism is named, where the context does not show that it took place immediately after avowed discipleship.

The evidence that no unbaptized person partook of the supper, during the times of the apostles, is overwhelming.

With such an accumulation of testimony on this single point; every case where particulars are attempted, uniformity absolute; not the shadow of an intimation that there was any other practice; all of it, in the exact order of the commission, and in symbol demanded, can there be room for a rational doubt that baptism is a divinely appointed prerequisite to the communion? Not for an instant, may it be supposed, that the course of the apostles would be different from what it was, should they now re-appear. With authority, they would re-assert and re-establish the ordinances as at the first. This record of their acts stands here to-day, in the place of living apostles.

III. The third and remaining scriptural qualification for the communion, is a life governed, so far as men have the means of judging, by Christ's revealed will.

We enter now the province of church discipline, provided for also in that last charge.

The churches having given the whole weight of their influence, first to disciple men, and then to baptize the men discipled; and having thus brought them into visible, or church relationship, they are now to watch over each other, lending the same weight of influence in teaching and tutoring them to the faithful, unaltered observance and perpetuation of all things commanded by Christ.

In the exercise of this watch-care, a limit is reached when the communion must be denied. That limit is described thus: "Now we command you, brethren, in the name of our Lord Jesus Christ, that ye withdraw yourselves from every brother that walketh disorderly, and not after the tradition which he received of us."

The phrase, "walketh disorderly," is borrowed from military life, and means out of line, or a failure to keep the ranks. In a disciple, it means conduct or a course of life before men, not accordant with what Christ has taught. The rule, generally stated, is withdrawal from any one who persists in any course of conduct seen to be inaccordant with the will of Christ. The fact, that you may still believe him to be a brother, may not shield him; "from every *brother*." Christian affection is not allowed to enter a plea for him; "we *command* you, in the *name* of *our Lord Jesus Christ*." The leaven of insubordination will leaven the whole lump; cast it out. From that root of bitterness, many will be defiled; pluck it up. That departure allowed, will increase unto more ungodliness; withdraw from him, though a brother beloved, but count him not an enemy.

And this withdrawing, if it does not deny the brother a place at the table, what does it deny? How *withdraw* from him, and still sit with him at the Lord's table?

Of this general rule I will make one application as a specimen. It shall be the discipline of a baptized brother, in a Pedobaptist church, or sitting at the table in such a church.

Those with whom he thus walks, in visible fellowship, do not keep the ranks. "So many of us as were baptized into Jesus Christ," were "*buried* with him by baptism." *Not buried with him by baptism* were these. He is under imperative orders to withdraw from them. Refusing to do so, he becomes a partaker with them in the disorder. To prevent the contagion from spreading, nay, to avoid complicity in it, we must withdraw from him. He gives countenance and the weight of his example to human tradition, a doctrine of men, a ceremony not from heaven, an observance which holds *competition* with Christ's own appointed ordinance of baptism, and which, so far as it prevails, crowds out Christ's appointment. Say not that he keeps the ordinance of baptism. He parts with it, in the act of sitting down to the communion with the unbaptized. He recedes from the position which he took in his baptism. The light set up in his own example, he quenches. He walks not by the light which God gave *him*, but by his brother's darkness. Say not that it is his *purpose* to observe that ordinance.

The word rendered "observe," means not only personal submission to it, but to guard, and keep from violation, and to pass on unchanged, that ordinance, or whatever else Christ has enjoined. That same Greek word occurs in the sentence, "And sitting down they *watched* him there." The centurion, with a company of soldiers, was stationed there to guard the crucified, against any attempt to wrest him from the authorities. Paul uses the same word when he says, "I have *kept* the faith."

The churches, *in training* the membership to *keep* all things commanded by Christ, must withdraw from every such brother. He who gave the order knew that in no less summary way, could demoralization be arrested. The church that refuses, becomes itself a party to disorder and disorganization, that has no limit but the complete subversion of the faith.

A marked example, on a large scale, is now before us.

The strict Baptist churches of England freely admit to the communion baptized believers in the open churches. They do this under the plea that these have submitted themselves to the rite. After that, need we be told, that year after year, some of the churches that were strict, become Open-communion, and that, in many instances, the settlement of an Open-communion pastor is all that is needed to make the change? Of course, it must be thus. In the practice they allow, they virtually yield all. They have surrendered Maryland Heights "to hold Harper's Ferry at all hazards!" In admitting Open-communion Baptists to the table, they do one of two things—they convict themselves of wrong in not themselves opening the table to the unbaptized; or, by giving fellowship to those who are doing that thing, they make themselves a party to the wrong. When Baptists and Pedobaptists unite, as in the Open-communion churches, the body that is formed thus, of course is not Baptist; it is simply Pedobaptism unchanged. If it were a bar of gold, with one end dipped, and the other sprinkled, no difference could be made by refusing the sprinkled end and taking the other. When Pedobaptism can extend a baptized or a sprinkled hand, it is vain to refuse the one while we take the other. It is not left discretionary with our strict brethren what to do; they are under orders from the Lord Jesus Christ to withdraw from every Open-communion brother. Obedience to that order is all that can save, from entire subversion, Baptist principles in England.

See how the great commission, by itself, covers the whole ground. That combination of words is not less marvelous and instinct with divinity, in its order and completeness, than in its thoughts. See how grand its conception, and how majestically it moves forward to realize it. It contemplates first the salvation of the soul. But its design has not been reached, in any instance, where it has secured only the salvation of the soul. Next, it demands the baptism of the saved. Nor is its design then reached. It holds the baptized to the stated and frequent observance of the supper, and but little is yet secured.

As compared with its whole design, all that is quite incidental. What it contemplates, is not reached when any number of men, living at the same time, are made true disciples, are baptized, and meet monthly or weekly to observe the supper. All that might soon leave Christ without a witness on earth, and unnumbered generations to live and die in heathenism. Unless these shall go further, and besides personally accepting Christ as a Saviour, and submitting to baptism and the supper, unless they shall as faithfully carry out the third specification entire, all efforts to extend the gospel will presently die out; baptism cease to be administered for lack of converts; tutoring and training become a thing unknown; and every trace of that first generation disappear, as writing upon the sand, over which the sea wave breaks. The commission is framed to *secure* to each successive generation of men, every advantage of the first, augmented by the living testimony of every convert that is made. It makes it the duty of every generation of Christians to teach and school both to the personal observance of all things, and to the subsequent training of others to perpetuate unaltered *all* things *whatsoever* Christ has commanded, so as to keep bringing forward upon the stage, in swelling numbers, men and women, apostolic in faith and practice, and Christlike in fidelity to God, and self-sacrifice for men. To neglect the third particular in this charge, is to make the two preceding impossible in the next generation.

The generation of Christians that is on the stage,

themselves baptized, send out that generation inspired and impelled by the Holy Spirit and his word, both to hold inviolate, in their own practice, all things whatsoever Christ has commanded, and also to make and baptize disciples everywhere, and everywhere to teach and school all the disciples, made and baptized, to do the same, to hold *fast* the faithful word, to be as incapable of *deviation* as of open apostasy; then for every generation following we have what is better than apostolic succession; we have Christian men and women, and Christian churches, apostolic in spirit, in faith, in practice, in infallibility, and more than apostolic in power, by as much as their number and gifts keep swelling, and their opportunities multiplying.

To reach *that* result every word in the commission is divinely chosen and set. Each thought prepares the way for the following. One requisition follows another, in a given order, and all stand compact and invincible. Change a word, or its plan, and it is like an army demoralized.

Conclusion. Faith in Christ, baptism for a badge of discipleship, and a life accredited for loyalty to the King in Zion, are the scriptural qualifications for the communion. Each in its place is equally indispensable to God's design.

Probably few will demur, except in the matter of baptism. On that point, equally with the others, pause a thousand times before you vary a shadow from either the act described by baptism, or the plan assigned for it. Learn at length that you are not to plan the campaign, but to study and execute orders. "It is as high as heaven; what canst thou do? deeper than hell; what canst thou know? The measure thereof is longer than the earth, and broader than the sea." On *that* point it was, that variations, too apparently trivial to be

Qualifications for the Communion.

noticed by Martin Luther, required but three centuries to subvert the Reformation. In the little tiny seed for the garden, God has provided for the stalk, the stem, the leaves, and the flower, as also for all the different colors, each stroke, and line, and spot, and the place for each. If, now, by some chemical analysis, we could separate, without injury, all the minute particles of a flower seed, and should then attempt a combination of them different from the original, we should not know what bright colors we might be striking out from the matured flower which God contemplated; nay, we should not know whether we might not be striking the flower itself from the stem, or preparing for some monster deformity. So, in his word, God has provided for the grandest possible development of thought and character, and all that he covets in connection with human redemption; but to secure *all* of that, to secure it at all, his word must be received without addition, diminution, modification or change. In changing, or suppressing, or withholding any part of it, we know not what we do. We know not what part of perfected redemption is supplied by this line or that; we know not what mighty interests are linked with this ordinance or the other; and we know not what systems of religious oppression and wrong may not, in embryo, lie in any change that may be effected by a human touch. "Be still, and know that I am God."

If one who knows nothing whatever of the human system should attempt to use the scalpel about the region of the heart, he would be likely to strike some vital part causing instantaneous death. What interests then must be periled by any human attempts to change what God has chosen, or separate what he has joined together, in this volume, every line of which underlies the sweet mystery of redeeming love, and infinitely transcends the reach of all but the Author of this book. If there is any part of it that, by deliberate agreement, might be set aside or changed with impunity, it would require a revelation from the Author to know what part that is; and, therefore, the fearful sentence that hangs over him who, presuming to usurp the prerogatives of God, shall dare to make a solitary change in the book itself: "If any man shall add unto these things, God shall add unto him the plagues that are written in this book; and if any man shall take away from the words of the book of this prophecy, God shall take away his part out of the book of life, and out of the holy city, and from the things which are written in this book." Next to the sin of changing the Bible, is the sin of falsifying its teachings; and, therefore, Christ says, "Whosoever shall break one of these *least* commandments, and shall teach men so, he shall be called the least in the kingdom of heaven."

I hope I have not spoken the truth otherwise than in love. Any other spirit would be foreign to every thought of the Communion. "By this we know that we love the children of God, when we love God and keep his commandments."

XI.

THE RELATION BETWEEN BAPTISM AND THE COMMUNION.

By THOMAS D. ANDERSON, D.D.,
Pastor of First Baptist Church, New York.

"THEN THEY THAT GLADLY RECEIVED HIS WORD WERE BAPTIZED; AND THE SAME DAY THERE WERE ADDED UNTO THEM ABOUT THREE THOUSAND SOULS. AND THEY CONTINUED STEADFASTLY IN THE APOSTLES' DOCTRINE AND FELLOWSHIP, AND IN BREAKING OF BREAD AND IN PRAYERS."—*Acts* ii. 41, 42.

RELIGIOUS error exhausts not its power for evil in substituting falsehood for truth. Its mischievous influence is not limited by the extent of its direct sway or the number of its perverts. It compels the adherents of the right to conquer by argument their positions. It drives the valiant supporters of the inspired record into a controversial maintenance of their views. It renders necessary the faithful to *withstand* in the evil day. The attitude it enforces is one of combat. The clash of arms resounds, not only along the extended line of outposts where the conflict is waged with the enemy, but the sword must be drawn within the very camp of our friends. Error demands a base surrender of allegiance to truth. A manly spirit has no alternative; he must enter the contest, bearing his most precious convictions with him to be triumphantly vindicated, not for himself alone, but for them also whom he has vanquished. Valuable as may be the result, necessary as may have been the conflict, still we must hold at best this contention among brethren as far from unmixed good. While we rejoice in the rescue of every Bible principle from the thraldom of doubt, and of each scriptural ordinance from the corruption of tradition, still we can but regret that many of the sweetest themes of Christian contemplation and purest acts of Christian devotion must be deferred until human formularies have been examined, opinions received, opposing arguments weighed and the perplexed reason has feebly assented to what the heart, Spirit-taught, was impatient to confess.

It is well that the doctrines of the incarnation and the atonement have been defended; and that, freed from the perversions of philosophy, falsely so called, they are settled firmly on their inspired foundation. Yet who does not regret withdrawing the rapt attention of the soul from their absorbing contemplation to search for arguments, to parry the thrusts of error, or to hamper the emotion with nicely balanced logical expressions, lest the truth should suffer from some offending word? At the entrance of a new life, the soul, glowing with its first love and hasting to confess Christ before men, regards as an impertinence, the controversy which human differences have raised over the simple command to be baptized. Nor does it conduce to the serene joy of a participation in the memorial supper to be agitated by the conflicting claims of qualifications for a seat at the table of the Lord. But whatever of evil arises from the discussion of themes like these cannot be charged on the defenders of the truth. Cost what it may, God has enjoined the duty to "contend for the faith which was once delivered unto the saints." We contend, not because contention is enjoyed, but that we may maintain, in their divine simplicity and fullness, the doctrines and ordinances of Christ. The wisdom that is *peaceable* must be first *pure*.

The relation between Baptism and Communion, we

are happy to know, has been admitted theoretically, in all ages and by all denominations of Christians. The ground-principles are not in controversy. With a singular unanimity, Christendom has held and taught the dependence of the one ordinance on the other; Baptism conferring the right to the Communion; Communion scripturally possible only to the baptized. So uniform has been the testimony of the various confessions of faith submitted by the different Christian Churches, that were this testimony logically maintained, and faithfully reduced to practice, Baptists and all other denominations would stand on the same platform in respect to the relation of the ordinances, and our discussion have been unnecessary. Although our opponents have sought strenuously to force us into a hostile attitude to the convictions we hold in common with nearly all other professing Christians, we generally have remained faithful. We have not become Schismatics as to this one common bond of opinion. The strange spectacle therefore, has been presented, of effort put forth, (not always in the friendliest spirit,) in the *name* of UNION to make us as a denomination to divide from the body of Christ on the almost only point where there is concurrent belief; while on the other hand, *apparently* in DISUNION, this body of the faithful is made to stand contending for its common inheritance in the almost only uncontroverted position of Christendom. We cannot desert this ground, and however our testimony may not be desired by our Pedobaptist brethren on this point, because of its effect on their unscriptural observance of the ordinances, we nevertheless must carry out practically the universally admitted view, and limit the communion to the baptized.

"Having," dear brethren "a good conscience; that, whereas they speak evil of you, as of evil-doers, they may be ashamed that falsely accuse your good conversation in Christ," we commend to your consideration the views you have so persistently held as supported by the word of God.

I. In the first place, let us view the relation between Baptism and Communion as *organic*.

By this, we mean that the relation is neither incidental nor fanciful. The ordinances are not grouped together by some arbitrary generalization of the mind, nor are they united by some chance tie, which, if severed, would still leave them unaffected in their normal condition. We hold that they are related as constituent parts of a perfect whole. Inasmuch as we believe Christianity to be no amendatory scheme to supplement deficiencies in the original plan, or a reparation of losses unfortunately sustained, but the primal thought and aim of God, toward which creation tended, so we believe the outward embodiment of that thought of God to be a *unity*. As the historic event of providence is the carefully prepared vestment of Jehovah's purpose, as Jesus is the express image of his person, so the Church in its instituted order is not a contingent development of Christianity, fashioned according to the demands of different countries and diverse ages, but a divine organism, ordained by God and made ready for the Spirit of the new creation as was the moulded dust of Adam for the soul of the old.

According to Ephesians iii. 10, it is Jehovah's intent " that now unto the principalities and powers in heavenly places might be known by the Church, the manifold wisdom of God." It cannot be supposed that the expression of God's manifold wisdom should be an indefinite and unordained combination of non-essential and irrelevant particulars. But admit the other alternative, that the Church, as a visible embodiment of the spiritual verities of redemption, was planned and matured by "Him who worketh all things after the counsel of his own will," then must we also admit the organic relation between the several parts of the one perfect whole. If in our *spiritual oneness* with Christ we dare not mutilate the provisions of grace, by asserting our union with him, although we have never been born again; or, professing our regeneration, then turn the grace of God into lasciviousness by a life conformed unto the world; so, in our outward visible fellowship with the Saviour, should we refuse to impair its design by sundering the appointed relation between the ordinances; by which a carefully adjusted organism is changed into a mere mixture of conventional ceremonies.

In the inspired plan of a Christian church, there are the prescribed qualification of membership, the initial rite, the doctrines to be believed, the duties to be practiced, the law for its preservation and extension, the designation of its officers, and the memorial ordinance, which, by its significance, sets forth the distinctive peculiarity of the body over every other association. It is impossible to conceive of an organization more perfect. Nothing is wanting. There is nothing superfluous. A careful study of the Acts, which contains the record of the founding of the church, under the immediate and miraculous influence of the Holy Spirit, will convince the unprejudiced that, before the death of the apostles, who were promised to be guided into all truth by the Comforter, the church completely organized stood forth before the world. Human interference can only mar its symmetry and change its simple expression of truths into a channel for the transmission of errors respecting the work of Christ.

Omit the initial ordinance of Baptism, and there

exists no body that has a right to the ordinance of the Communion, for then is there none "baptized into Jesus Christ." This phrase is used, Romans vi. 3, as the expression of a union to Christ, through death unto sin and a resurrection to newness of life. Hence, to such only who through the symbol of Baptism profess their oneness of life with the Lord, is the correlated symbol of the Communion—expressive of supporting that life on his broken body and shed blood—scripturally possible. Again, administer Baptism as enjoined in the New Testament, and the person thus *formally* made one with Christ not only *may* sustain *formally* his new life on the emblems of the Lord's body and blood, but, if he *refuse* he *denies* the Lord that bought him.

If now, Baptism be scripturally administered to the unconscious babe, on the confession of another, on the same ground must that babe communicate. If it be sin not to compel the infant into a testimony of its being born again, it is equally sin not to force it into an outward exhibition of maintaining its baptized life on the flesh and blood of the Son of God. Should it be objected that the very nature of commemoration is such as to render it necessary that the subject should of his own volition approach the table, we admit the statement; but as we have Baptism and the Communion as parts of a complete external embodiment of our relations to Christ, the denial to the candidate of the one until he voluntarily presents himself, demands the withholding of the other until a like conscious application is made for it. The connection between the ordinances, as parts of a perfectly organized outward profession, is an *essential* connection. Administering the one while we deprive of the other, is rending the seamless robe of Jesus; and, while we supply the lost part with a fabric of human device, we dishonor the perfect righteousness of the Crucified by the indignity offered to his vesture.

II. In the second place, let us view the relation between Baptism and Communion as *symbolic*.

As these ordinances are used by Inspiration as symbols, the relation between them must be in accordance with such usage. Since they are found united in the embodiment of the gospel as set forth in a church, we must so interpret their relation as not to make it false to the great truths signified. I do not intend to trace the symbolism of the ordinances. That has been entrusted, in this course of sermons, to another. I refer to it only to bring out *sequence*, or *order of succession*, as a characteristic of the relationship between the two great Christian rites.

Before phonetic characters were used in writing, images of objects, with signs representing different conditions, were employed to record the history of events. In this picture-writing, each form became a symbol, and it was essential to a correct reading, to note carefully two things:—1. *The peculiar form of the image:* 2. *Its relative position to other images.* For illustration; if the victory of the Egyptians in battle over the Jews, were represented hieroglyphically, you would discover figures signifying men, then certain modifications distinguishing them as Egyptians and Jews, also signs indicating that they were engaged in battle. If this were all, the representation would leave you in doubt which were the conquerors, or indeed whether there was a victory. On closer inspection, however, you find that the forms representing Jews, are either prostrate, or fleeing before the victorious ranks of the Egyptians. We can hesitate no longer—the cartoon asserts the victory of the Egyptians over the Jews. The correct reading demands not simply the study of the symbols, but absolutely requires the exact interpretation of their *relative* position. In the instance above, by simply altering the relation of the symbols, you reverse the record, and read the victory of the Jews over the Egyptians.

This necessary relation of the objects holds true, not merely in picture-writing, but wherever truth is taught by symbols. It could not be indifferent whether the mercy-seat was above or below the shekinah, whether the altar of sacrifice was in front of or within the sanctuary of the temple, or whether sins were confessed on the head of the victim before or after its sacrifice. Whenever symbols are incorporated into a unified service, no more important is the *emblem* than is its *relative position* in the piece of symbolism of which it makes a part.

In the order of the visible church, to observe the rites of Baptism and Communion, irrespective of their serial relation, would lead not only to *defective*, but to *erroneous* impressions. Not less important is it that they are observed in their given order of succession, than that they are observed at all. Baptism first, and Communion afterward. By the former symbol we have typified regeneration, the new birth. The candidate, in the name of Jesus, buried within the water as in a grave, submits to the justice of the retribution of death for sin; but hiding himself in the mighty Christ, who has power to suffer the penalty, yet survive the infliction, he becomes, through the Spirit, a "partaker of the divine nature," and thus rises with his Lord from the liquid tomb to newness of life. Then, and not till then, follows appropriately the other symbol. In the Lord's Supper are spread before the regenerated man the means of sustenance for his spiritual life. As the communicant partakes of the bread and wine, significant of the Lord's broken body and shed blood, he gives evidence of an appetite that is not satisfied with meaner food, of a strength that is derived only from a divine source, and of a life that must be ever nourished on the flesh and blood of the Son of God. We have now the new life and its divine subsistence. The symbolic relation demands that the initial rite of Baptism be followed by the observance of the Supper; else we have a life created and left to perish without its proper aliments. It equally insists on the Communion being always preceded by Baptism, or divine food is presented to sustain an unchanged carnal nature. Either of which must bring the ordinances of Christ's appointment into contempt, and change what he designed to be the symbols of redemption into mere ritual ceremonies, imposed and interpreted by man. Let us not, brethren, elect of God, in setting up our banners, plant our ensign with its symbols reversed, significant only of mutiny and desertion, but throughout all our ranks let us unfurl our standards with their heavenly device in order, telling our confidence of victory in our allegiance to the Captain of our salvation.

III. In the third place, let us now turn to the *doctrinal* view of the relation between the two New Testament ordinances.

When we consider the authority that sustains this view, and its far-reaching import, perhaps there is no aspect in which our subject assumes a greater consequence. From the fact that Jesus instituted these rites, and commanded their observance by all his disciples, it follows that they are invested with a doctrinal as well as practical bearing. Indeed, in a strict analysis, it is impossible to separate doctrine and practice in the instructions of the gospel. Under every performance of the new creature, there must be the intelligent comprehension and design which constitutes its doctrine, or the service is unmeaning mummery. On the other hand, whatever is professed as doctrine must be incorporated into the life, or the profession is as hollow as "sounding brass or a tinkling cymbal." Therefore, to celebrate these ordinances is to declare the doctrine of *obedience to the simple, positive command of Christ.* They lie side by side, the doctrine being strengthened by its repetition in the two rites, and obedience tested by a double requisition. There cannot possibly be an argument against observing the one, that exists not with equal force for the omission of the other. The doctrine requires an unquestioning submission to the laws of Christ, solely because he has commanded them. It is nullified as much by making a selection between two acts, which he has enjoined by the same authority, and declining to submit to one, as though the refusal extended to both. Indeed, it is more dangerous to the doctrine of obedience, (not to pronounce the spirit more culpable,) to admit the authority of positive institutions, while a part is subjected to the judgment or caprice of the worshipper, than to reject the whole as unnecessary. Can a regard for sound doctrine suffer the severance of two positive ordinances, parts of an integral profession of gospel truth, and allow a person, while neglecting one, to extenuate his violation of authority by an imperfect compliance with the other? Must not such a course necessarily demoralize the spirit? Indeed, while one command is apparently honored, would not its disjointed observance but ill conceal the fatal attack made on the principle of Christian obedience?

Again, wrapped up in these ordinances lies the doctrine of *the disciple's confession of Christ.* Is it, or is it not, a principle of the gospel, that what is wrought inwardly by the Spirit, shall be by the person outwardly expressed? If it be, is that law fully met by an oral declaration? Not until human language can adequately utter the divine significance of the plan of salvation. Nor is it enough that the life should bring forth the fruits of holiness. These but express, when most abundant, the effects of the gracious change. Both are but imperfect manifestations of the actual condition of the renewed soul. Christ, therefore, has supplemented the words of the lips, and the conduct of life, with a perfect confession, that fully represents the unseen spiritual state. That confession is found in the two positive ordinances he has enjoined on his disciples. These, committed to the voluntary observance of every Christian, become, when thus complied with, his own perfect confession before the world of a state of heart that otherwise would have no adequate exponent. In this view, how intimate is the relation of these rites. As the external rendering of the sublime verities of faith, Baptism and Communion gather around them all the sanction of divinely-drawn articles of confession, united in an inviolable relation, that forever excludes the right to alter, transpose, or omit. To accept this confession is our privilege; to decline it may be our choice; but to modify it, is not merely refusing, it is offering insult to our Lord. For, in claiming the right to amend, we assert the superiority of human wisdom over divine in moulding the form that images the glories of the new creation. Nor can this confession be made, except by the ordinances in their instituted relation; where the one unrepeated act of regeneration is illustrated by the one unrepeated Baptism; while the oft-recurring Communion beautifully confesses the soul's continual living on the Crucified. The Christian has no scriptural right to represent only his individual interest in Christ by the use of one of the signs belonging to the visible kingdom of God. Having declared himself by Baptism to be dead to sin, and risen to newness of life, he should seek an outward fellowship with the baptized; and in waiting attitude around the table, where the hallowed emblems are a perpetual prophecy of Jesus' second coming, exultingly should he confess that "the greatness of the kingdom under the whole heaven shall be given to the people of the saints of the Most High."

Once more, there is a most intimate doctrinal relation between Baptism and the Communion as they are employed to illustrate *the vicarious work of Christ*. Of the many passages in God's word sustaining this view, I shall allude only to two—one in Romans vi. 3: "Know ye not, that as many of us as were baptized into Jesus Christ, were baptized into *his* death?" Another in John vi. 56, 57: "He that eateth my flesh, and drinketh my blood, dwelleth in me, and I in him. As the living Father hath sent me, and I live by the Father; so he that eateth me, even he shall live by *me*." These passages have one marked feature in common—whatever advantage is figuratively represented in them, it is entirely founded on another's work. We are not baptized merely into death, but into *Christ's* death; and our life is not our own, but by *Christ* we live. We do not improve our nature, but we lose it; in the expiatory death of Christ, it is condemned, and dies in the penalty visited on our substitute. We share, in rising with Christ, a new nature; and as it had its source in him, so is it fed on him. Thus, both the perfect righteousness whereon the believer stands accepted before God, and his own personal holiness, we are taught in these passages, alike come from Jesus. The relation, then, of these ordinances in this aspect, is that which exists between the two grand gospel doctrines of Justification and Sanctification. How fearful should we be of disturbing the inspired harmony between the divinely appointed illustrations of such fundamental truths in the system of redemption. It was probably by just such interference, more than by any other one cause, that the glorious doctrine of justification by faith was vailed for so many ages, and consequently a holy life was driven from the nominal church.

Deny to either one of the ordinances a conscious appropriation by the candidate of the vicarious merit of Christ, and you necessarily invalidate the significance of the other. Join to the work of the Saviour the belief of a parent or sponsor as the ground for baptism, and a traditional faith will come to celebrate the virtue of *inherited* piety around the table where only Jesus should be remembered; while by degrees the visible church will be composed of those born of blood, of the will of the flesh, of the will of man, but not of God. Or, inconsistently refuse to the baptized a seat at the supper until some qualification is gained that is not expressed by the initial rite; and baptism, which, coupled with belief, the Holy Spirit has made in the commission the published condition of salvation, is degraded into an unmeaning ceremony, while the mighty truth of justifying righteousness has, in the perfect system of divine hieroglyphics, no corresponding emblem. If in words we would not dare sunder the connection of the doctrines of grace as they lie revealed on the inspired page, let us beware how we act the violence we would shrink from speaking, by a perversion of the equally inspired Font and Table.

Another doctrine, *The spirituality of the gospel*, is illustrated by an allusion to the ordinances in the tenth chapter of the First Epistle to the Corinthians. This reference is peculiar in many respects. We will quote the first four verses: "Moreover, brethren, I would not that ye should be ignorant, how that all our fathers were under the cloud, and all passed through the sea; and were all baptized unto Moses in the cloud and in the sea; and did all eat the same spiritual meat; and did all drink the same spiritual drink; for they drank of that spiritual Rock that followed them; and that Rock was Christ." This should satisfy any person who reverences the Bible, that the ordinances of the New Testament were shadowed forth ages before, when the Jewish nation was chosen as a type of the spiritual Israel. But the point to which I especially call your attention in the above Scripture is very striking; namely: That to the rebellious Hebrew there was no inherent efficacy in his typical baptism and typical communion. He, indeed, in common with others, was baptized unto Moses in the cloud and sea. He, with others, partook of the spiritual, that is, supernatural meat and drink; but, nevertheless, he entered not into the promised land—"For with many, God was not well pleased; for they were overthrown in the wilderness." It is said immediately after, "Now these are our examples," or figures. The Apostle pressed spiritual holiness on those who might otherwise suppose that there was a ritual efficacy, an *opus operatum*, in the ordinances themselves. When so peculiarly coupled together by the Holy Spirit to show their utter futility, without inward spiritual grace, I ask by what authority have Baptism and Communion been violently rent asunder? Why is the one rendered of ritualistic efficacy, so that the babe is hurried to the font lest he should die in his sins being unbaptized; and then, being fitted for heaven, is denied the other, because without some further change he is unprepared for the imperfect earthly Communion of the pious with their Lord? Strange confusion, to avoid some of the legitimate consequences of a perversion of Christ's symbols! More consistent have been the vast majority of Christendom, including all national churches, who, knowing that the two gospel rites must have the same effective value, have ritualized both and always have given the Communion to the baptized, and simply because baptized. This consistency in error, however, has turned the symbols of Christianity into an effete Judaism, not even holding forth emblem types of future realities; but cowering among the empty shadows of the past. Hence there is one aspect in which the gross inconsistency of ritualizing Baptism, while the Communion is held in all its spirituality, becomes hopeful, namely; that of transition, when to eyes gradually opening to the light, the orderly relation of objects is unperceived.

Finally, The doctrine of the *oneness of Christ's disciples*, as illustrated by Baptism and the Lord's Supper, bears most significantly on the relation existing between the two. While very far from admitting the design of the Lord's Supper to be *directly* to exhibit Christian fellowship, we do believe that it is impossible rightly to celebrate the Communion without setting forth *indirectly* the oneness of communicants. As no provision is made in the Scripture for the perversion of a truth, we see how beautifully, by the ordinances, by one as well as by the other, is the doctrine of the oneness of the disciples of Jesus expressed, being baptized into one Lord and all partaking of one bread. The fellowship of Christians is the result, not the aim, of the observance. I am baptized into Christ, and my brother is baptized into Christ; *therefore*, I and my brother are one. We were not baptized to show that we are one, but our oneness appears from our being baptized. If it be necessary, moreover, emblematically to sustain this life in Jesus by eating and drinking the emblems of the one body and blood, then, not to show our union do we communicate, but from the necessary Communion flows the evidence of our fellowship. Keep, then, the symbols as the Saviour delivered them to us, and he is responsible for their expressing Christian unity. But let the original design be corrupted, and, depend on it, the God of truth will exact of no honest man the expression of a union that does not exist. Least of all, will he require from him, for the sake of union, or any thing else, a forced observance of one of his ordinances intended to pervert forevermore the observance of the other. No! brethren, no outward union over a suppressed command of Christ!

This question never would have arisen; the church never would have been divided in its symbolic confession, if the relation between these ordinances as expressive of gospel truth had been preserved inviolate. On those, then, who sever this connection; on those who force these rites to speak a different language from their inspired utterance; on those who will not, by one Baptism, in one Faith, profess their allegiance to one Lord, rests the fearful responsibility of giving to the church more than one Communion. Sunder the triune motto of the church, "One Lord, one Faith, one Baptism;" divide the one personal object of the church's reverence; multiply the faiths professed; enter into fellowships through different initial rites; and in vain is the cry raised for organic union. The remedy cannot be found in any external badge of fellowship, but exists in restoring to the disciples of one Lord the one divinely appointed mode of entrance into the profession and enjoyment of their common faith. We feel ourselves as Baptists justified from the blame imputed to us, of causing divisions among the followers of him who prayed "That they all may be one." Convict us of altering, omitting, or transposing these symbols, thus disturbing the relation originally established between them; and we not only will be recreant to our principles, but by them will stand condemned before God and man, if we haste not from any false position to restore to its primal integrity on the authority of Scripture either the form or order we have broken. But, if we have kept the ordinances as they were delivered, those same principles and our profession of them hold us bound, even against the pain of separation from the loved in Christ of other denominations, to maintain the relation between Baptism and Communion to be so essential, so orderly, so inviolable, that Baptism shall mean a full qualification for the enjoyment of the Communion, and that the Communion is only possible to the baptized. Still will we continue to pray, " O, Saviour! in the obedience to thy own commands, make thy disciples one, as thou and the Father are one."

The application of the views just discussed, affords suggestions of practical value to the *minister*. He is the scripturally appointed administrator of the ordinances. He holds in his hands the divinely fashioned moulds, into which, from time to time, he casts the material used in the building of the visible temple of God. Let him be careful, not only as to the quality of what he builds upon the foundation of the apostles and prophets, but also that all may be "fitly framed together." In plain words not only should the minister seek the evidence of faith in Christ, but he should baptize none but those who acknowledge their obligation to celebrate the Communion, which only can be the Communion when, like the former ordinance, its form and subjects are according to the pattern of the word of God.

To the *candidate* for these ordinances, the above views teach a lesson not always learned. Sometimes, while one would not dare himself to approach the Lord's Table until he has been baptized on a confession of his faith in Christ, he hesitates not to encourage in others a violation of this order which, in his own case, he would feel to be sin. Now, if the Spirit has enlightened him on a point of such importance, how can he vail his testimony? Would he inculcate that the Holy Ghost has been at pains to teach him a truth of no value? Or that he has so little love for others, that what he has freely received he refuses freely to give? If it be sin for him to communicate before Baptism, it is sin for him to encourage or invite others to commune before they have been baptized. If he decided what is Baptism, it must be, in his opinion, the same for them and him. If their baptism was not baptism for him, it could not be for them. To him they are either baptized or unbaptized. If the former, then his profession is false. If the latter, then he encourages in others what he acknowledges in himself to be sin. By the relation existing between the ordinances, it is plain that the whole question of free or restricted Communion is a question pertaining entirely to Baptism. Oneness of Communion where there are different Baptisms is maintained as essential to Christian fellowship, only to throw Baptism into disrepute, where scriptural positions cannot be invalidated.

On the *church* rests the sacred obligation to preserve inviolate the relation of the symbols of confession "till we all come, in the unity of the faith and the knowledge of the Son of God, unto a perfect man, unto the measure of the stature of the fullness of Christ."

XII.

CHURCH POLITY.

By GEORGE W. SAMSON, D.D.,
President of Columbian College, D. C.

"LET THE ELDERS THAT RULE WELL, BE COUNTED WORTHY OF DOUBLE HONOR; ESPECIALLY THEY WHO LABOR IN WORD AND DOCTRINE."—1 *Timothy* v. 17.

THERE is, from the very nature of the case, a "rule," a government, or form of polity, in the church of Christ; and three fundamental principles enter into legitimate church polity. Without any explanation, as if they already understood its principle, without any exception, as if all churches were conformed to its practice, Paul takes for granted that a class having official rank as "rulers" are found in every church; that the necessity for such an order, even among Christians, is recognized in the very nature of man; that the character of this rule is only moral, implied by the very name "elder," or experienced counselor; and that its vital, practical power is doubly honored in those "who labor in word and doctrine." The subject of church polity, then, is revealed for Christian inquiry; and it is as much more important than domestic, or civil polity, as Christ's kingdom is more important than the State, and as God's household is more dear than the human family.

This is not an isolated reference by inspired men to this department of revealed Christian truth. Christ constantly alludes to his family, made up of those that do the will of his "Father:" to his kingdom, formed of those who "follow him in all things;" and to the church, which, as his own organized and authorized association, acting in his name, has committed to it "the keys of heaven and hell." The history of the Acts of the Apostles and the Epistles of Paul and James, of Peter and John, are studded with examples and precepts, illustrating the nature and the benefit of the plan of church polity which Christ has appointed. No commissioned herald of him whose requirement is, "Teaching them to observe all things whatsoever I have commanded you," no successor of the early Christian pastors, to whom inspired Paul wrote, "The things that thou hast heard of me among many witnesses, the same commit thou unto faithful men, who shall be able to teach others also," no ordained minister of Jesus Christ, called "rightly to divide the word of truth," can be excused if he neglect to study and to unfold Christ's inspired word as to this relation which the members of his church must hold toward each other.

From among numerous inspired teachings as to church polity, the words above quoted have been selected as specially instructive, because in every great crisis of the history of Christ's church, this single declaration of Paul to Timothy has been found so full of instruction. Thus, when evangelical Jerome and others, in the days of Constantine, were resisting the worldly influence which sought to crowd itself into the Christian church because it was now the State religion, again, when, in the age of Charlemagne and Alfred, faithful and true missionaries were leavening central and northern Europe, our ancestral home, with a pure gospel, yet again, when the spirit of the Reformation was leading men, in different countries of Europe, leaving the Roman church, necessarily to adopt new forms of organization—at every such practical era, no single expression of the inspired apostle has been deemed more full and explicit, and none has been so often quoted as comprehensive and authoritative. The theme of Paul, with its points of important illustration, is CHURCH POLITY; its *necessity*, as indicated by man's social relations on earth; its *nature*, as revealed in the inspired words of the New Testament; its *fruits*, as illustrated in the progress of Christ's truth and grace among mankind.

The first of the points for special consideration may be thus stated:

FIRST. *The necessity, from the nature of men, in their social relations, for a positive and authoritative system of polity in the Christian church; as it is suggested to the common judgment of mankind.*

In all our religious reasoning, it should be remembered, that the common judgment of men is that to which revelation itself is addressed. The first announcement of the Old Testament: "In the beginning, God created the heavens and the earth," takes for granted that men already believe in the existence of God; for, if they did not, how could a revelation from him be made to them? When John began to preach, "Repent, for the kingdom of heaven is at hand," his hearers must have already known the meaning of the words he employed. The fact that Christ "reasoned," and Paul "persuaded" men, hints that the common judgment of mankind is always appealed to by the gospel. In writing now on the subject of order in the church as an associated body, it is to these convictions of common judgment that Paul specially appeals, when he urges, "Doth not *nature* teach?" "If any man seem to be contentious, we have no such *custom*, neither the churches of God."* In every land and age, there have been suggestions of man's common nature which have been the rule of domestic and social

---

* 1 Cor. xi. 14, 16.

relations; and the law of civil society has been immemorial customs, like the common law of England, adopted from the first in American courts. When Paul wrote, the Greek and Roman people had been made familiar, by their writers on religion, morals, government and law, with these words, "nature," and "custom," which the apostle is divinely directed to employ in unfolding the principles of order and polity that should govern Christian assemblies.

The well-known models of the family and of civil government are those by which Paul illustrates that order. In alluding to these relations, Paul uses, as appropriate in the Christian church, the words of Aristotle, the commonly received Greek authority. In the family, organized in part for the protection of the dependent, but more for the cultivation of virtue in the superior, servants and children, as helpless and inexperienced, are to "obey" their superiors; while the wife, who is the head of the family in the husband's almost constant absence, is, as second in authority, to show "official deference" in the husband's presence. The forms of *civil* government, as the same writer shows, have been, the *patriarchal*, or an extended family rule; the *monarchial*, often usurped and generally hereditary, excellent if the monarch be worthy, but liable to unjust despotism; *democracy*, the rule of the majority, the most oppressive of all governments, when, as in Athens, without restriction of constitution or law, the excited crowd, led by unscrupulous partisans, voted that Socrates, untried, should drink the hemlock; and *oligarchy*, or the rule of a few who possess landed property or hereditary rank, always, as in Sparta and in feudal Western Europe, destructive of the interest of the mass of the people, and of little profit even to the lordly few. To these he adds *aristocracy*, the rule of the best men; or of those who, in the opinion of that portion of the community whose intelligence from education, whose interest as property holders, and whose position of influence, as heads of families, are most gifted with the wisdom requisite to the construction of civil government, and with the means necessary for its support. This was the form of civil polity studiously attempted, and in a measure realized, in the Roman Republic; and it was virtually professed in the Roman Empire, which, when Paul was writing, held dominion over the world.

When, now, Jesus in his teaching, and Paul and other New Testament writers recognize in the common nature of mankind the necessity of family and of civil relations, and, in referring to their legitimate obligations, use the very words of a writer so just in his views, and when, at the same time, they quote these as models for the organization of the church of Christ, they manifestly recognize the necessity for order and rule in the church as in the family and State. As then the family and the State are organized for a special end, and each has its official head as a means to an end, so must it be in Christ's church. Neither the nature of its mission, nor the spiritual character of its members, exempts Christ's body from this necessity.

With the points calling thus for special observation in the study of the New Testament as to church polity before the mind, two facts in the past history and present condition of American churches seem to call for special sincerity and earnestness in every Christian's consideration of church polity. The very names Roman Catholic, English Episcopal, German Reformed, Scotch Presbyterian, and New England Congregational, relate directly to the old nationalities and forms of civil government, under which these several churches originated, and whose secular spirit may now be keeping alive their special form. So far as its logical consistency and practical tendency is concerned, it is worthy of special thought, that the principle on which these distinctive names of churches and their peculiar polity are maintained, is directly in opposition to that of American civil polity; in which "the children of this world" may be "wiser than the children of light." While, in civil association, the varied people of this new and vast land are one, it may be that ancient differing, and therefore, clashing and inconsistent principles of church polity, should seek a similar harmony, by a new study, in the light of modern times, of Christ's revealed truth. Yet again, our country has just passed through a crisis, which has compelled men united with churches, however varied in form, to resort to one common, and that the simplest form of religious service, of clerical rank, and of organized Christian effort. One tenth of the active men of the different States have been away from their homes, spending months and years in the camp. There, bell and candles, books and surplice, printed formulas of church order and rehearsed creeds, carefully prepared manuscript sermons and well-appointed orchestras, were left behind, and were found practically inefficient. There, bishops and elders were reduced to the rank of simple Christian teachers and counselors, with no position or influence but the moral power they could secure among their comrades. Many spoke and wrote in favor of a more artificial organization, and of more authoritative official rank; but the spirit of our institutions as a nation seemed always to stand in the way of a different polity. Perhaps it was a voice from God's providence to thousands of the more thoughtful, the sincerely devout and earnestly useful of Christ's people, bearing different names before, but, now, in their practical efforts at Christian organization, one in theory and practice. Perhaps it was meant to be a Divine call to review this whole subject again, to look back at the origin and end of the church of Christ, to think of its work, and see how men have sought to perform it; and thus to reach a form of church order, whose theory and practice shall not in great emergencies be found to conflict. It may be that a careful review of the words of inspiration, and a survey then of their manifest interpretation, as eminently Christian leaders have realized their meaning while applying them, may guide to that system, true in itself, and true because taught by the inspired record. Certainly, no other means of reaching truth seems to be open to us.

We approach then, the second proposed point of examination, guided by the second suggestion of Paul's words to Timothy.

SECOND. *The nature and extent of official authority sanctioned by Christ in his church; as indicated by the inspired words used to designate its office, and by the apostolical example recorded to illustrate the meaning of those words.*

Words, in themselves having an established meaning in one application, may have a modified signification, when used to represent kindred connections in widely distinct relations. It is necessary, therefore, first, to observe what words relating in general to official position in the church, are used in the New Testament; and then, perhaps, it is even more important to remark what terms, used to set forth *civil authority, are not* employed to represent *ecclesiastical* authority. After this careful scrutiny of direct Scripture teaching, the indirect teaching of examples, having the force of precedents, in the inspired history of the early church, should also be carefully scanned.

The words used by the New Testament writers to express authority in the family or state, and the submission that is becoming in these relations, are mainly the following. The term *archon*, used by the Athenians to designate their chief executive, is applied to both Roman civil magistrates * and Jewish ecclesiastical authorities, as members of the Sanhedrim and rulers of synagogues.† The fact that it is *not* used to represent the authority of officers of the Christian churches, seems to hint that neither Roman nor Grecian civil governments, nor even the Jewish synagogue, were in this respect models of the Christian church. The word *hēgemon*, or leader, applied by the Greeks and Romans either to civil or military chiefs, generally rendered in English, *governor*, is applied to civil rulers; as to Pilate, to Felix, and to the Roman governors at large.‡ It is instructive to observe that this term is never applied to a leader in the Christian church. The verb corresponding, having the idea of moral as well as compulsory leading, is applied to the gentle sway of Joseph in Egypt, to the moral influence of Christians in private life, and to the spiritual control of Christian pastors over the people of their charge.§ The word most used to express authority in domestic government over servants and children, is *proistēmi*.‖ The word is applied to the two classes of officers in the Christian church, the bishops and deacons; and is the word specially chosen to set forth the authority of what are called rulers in the church.¶ The moral element, in the authority expressed by this word, is seen in its use twice by Paul, to represent that self-control

---

* Matt. xx. 25. Rom. xiii. 3. 1 Cor. ii. 16.
† Matt. ix. 18. John iii. 1; vii. 26. Acts iii. 17. Luke viii. 41.
‡ Matt. x. 18; xxvii. 2, etc. Acts xxiii. 24, etc. 1 Pet. ii. 14.
§ Acts vii. 10. Phil. ii. 3. 1 Thess. v. 13. Heb. xiii. 7, 17, 24.
‖ 1st Tim. iii. 4, 5, 12.
¶ Rom. xii. 8. 1 Thess. v. 12. 1 Tim. v. 17.

which enables a Christian to "maintain" the habit of "good works."*

The expressive title almost always employed by the New Testament writers, to designate the office of rulers in the Christian church, is *presbeus* and its derivatives. It is the word used by the early Greek poets, as Hesiod, to characterize the patriarchal head of the earliest and simplest form of civil government, copied after that of the family. In the later writers, as the sages Plato and Aristotle, the historians from Herodotus to Thucydides, and the orators Æschines and Demosthenes, it is applied to *ambassadors;* whose office is not only aside from, but contrasted with forcible authority. As the name of a civil office, this term corresponds to "alderman" or *elder-man;* a member of the advisory branch, or council, of modern city governments. It certainly is significant that a word of such moral import is so generally chosen by the spirit of inspiration to set forth the office of the Christian minister.

A second word of the same nature is *episcopos;*† a title applied at first to an inspector of treaties and laws, afterward of public works; and, yet later, to men sent out as prefects to conquered and tributary cities and states, to examine their laws prior to their subjection to Grecian sway, empowered to decide how far they were adapted to the new civil relation of the conquered or subject people. This title applied to the chief officer of the Christian church,‡ purely moral as it was even in its civil applications, must have been designedly

---

* Tit. iii. 8, 14.

† 2 Cor. v. 20. Luke xv. 25. 1 Tim. v. 1. John viii. 9. Acts xxiv. 1. Acts xi. 30; xiv. 23, etc. 1 Tim. v. 17, 19. Tit. i. 5. James v. 14. 1 Pet. v. 1. 2 John i. compare Philem ix.

‡ Acts xx. 28. Phil. i. 1. 1 Tim. iii. 2. Tit. i. 7. 1 Pet. ii. 25; verb, 1 Pet. v. 2. Heb. xii. 15.

selected by the Divine Spirit. Directly associated with this is the noun *poimēn*, shepherd, and its derived verb, a word used by Homer, to denote the simple mild sway of early patriarchal rulers, and by Xenophon to picture Socrates' ideal of the relation a civil ruler ought always to hold to his people. The noun and verb are both applied by the inspired penman* to Jesus, as the "good shepherd;" while the verb is also used by Christ and his Apostles, to designate the Christian pastor's office.

Turning again to a class of counterpart words, designating the submission on the part of the ruled to those placed over them, in domestic, civil, and ecclesiastical relations, three terms are found to be most important and significant. The word *hypakouō*, to obey, indicative of absolute submission, is used by Paul, as it is by Aristotle, to indicate the obedience due to the superior in two of the domestic relations, that of children and servants; but is never applied to the first domestic relation, except under the Old Testament dispensation, as illustrated in Sarah's subjection to Abraham.† This word is employed to represent the submission, absolute, though not unreasoning, which Christians should yield to Christ, and also to apostles in their character of inspired men only;‡ but it is never employed to indicate submission to rulers in the church. The word *hypotasso*, to range under, used by Aristotle to indicate the voluntary and assumed official deference rendered among equals, as by a wife to her husband, by a subordinate in military service or in civil life, to a chief of his own choosing, is employed always by Paul and Peter, not only to indicate the wife's relation and the citizen's

---

* John x. 1-10. Eph. iv. 1. Heb. xiii. 20. 1 Pet. ii. 25. John xxi. 16. Matt. ii. 6. Rev. ii. 27.

† Eph. vi. 1, 5, etc. 1 Pet. iii. 6.

‡ Acts vi. 7. Rom. vi. 17. 1 Pet. i. 2. Phil. ii. 12. 2 Thes. iii. 14.

duty to civil government,* but, also, the deference due from members of a Christian church to those having official authority among them.† A third word, *peith-archeō*, implying the rule of *persuasion*, is also employed to indicate submission to Divine authority, to civil rulers, and also to those holding office in the church.‡

It is worthy of special notice, in surveying the words thus considered, that Paul, mingling chiefly with Greeks rather than Jews, and using words familiar to the common people, manifestly intended to direct their minds to a likeness between legitimate civil government and that appropriate in the Christian church; while he is also inspired to indicate, in the most expressive manner, that the two are most unlike in the power which their officers may employ. Every word designating the arbitrary authority that belongs to civil government, authorized to employ physical force, is studiously omitted in representing the power of church officers; a fact deserving careful consideration by those who would suggest that the form of ecclesiastical polity may, in different countries, be with propriety conformed to the prevailing state polity.

Again, while the church of Christ may, in some measure, have been modeled after the order of the Jewish synagogue, the authority of the chief ruler of the Jewish synagogue is as strictly denied as is that of the Athenian *archon*, in the Christian church; since this office of the Jewish ecclesiastical and the Grecian civil *archon* is, by omission, denied a place in the assembly of Christ's people. It is perhaps more conformed to the entire teaching of the New Testament, just considered and to be yet observed, to suppose that "na-

---

* Eph. v. 22. Col. iii. 18. Tit. ii. 5. 1 Pet. iii. 1, 5. Rom. xiii. 1, 5. 1 Pet. ii. 13.
† 1 Cor. xiv. 32, 34; xvi. 16. Eph. v. 21. 1 Pet. v. 5.
‡ Acts v. 29. Tit. iii. 1. Heb. xiii. 17. James iii. 3.

ture" and "common custom" as to organizations, domestic, civil, or social, familiar to Greeks and Jews as they are to all nations, substantially the same in authority though varied in application, were adopted in the Christian churches, planted in different lands, just so far as the character and mission of Christ's spiritual body admitted the *moral* sway necessary to be allowed in the presiding head of all associations of men.

We are prepared now briefly to allude to the history of New Testament examples, often dwelt upon at large by writers on church organization; that we may see how these examples illustrate and develop the hints already received from the words designating ecclesiastical authority.

Christ twice alludes to his "church,"* and often to the authority and duties of its officers. His requirement, that an offending brother first be remonstrated with alone, then by two or three, then before the whole "church," when, if still unyielding, he be regarded as a "heathen man," certainly intimates these three principles: First, that moral conduct, indicated by positive acts, is the proper subject of church discipline, and, as such, moral means are to be used for the offender's recovery; second, that the whole church is the authoritative body to whom final appeal is to be made, though chosen men are to act for the church in efforts to convince and persuade the wrong-doer; third, that the authority, even of the church, extends no further than to exclude the unworthy member from their number. Again, when Christ declares, "On this rock will I build my church," and announces that he gives to Peter and the other apostles the keys of heaven and of hell, as emblems of absolute authority in his church,

---

* Matt. xviii. 17; xvi. 18.

Church Polity. 273

a power never repeated afterward as belonging to Christian pastors, it is manifest that this absolute authority relates only to their *writings*, rather than to themselves; to their writings, only when they were *inspired*; and to their inspired writings, not as *their own*, but as God's word. Their relative rank, common to all Christian ministers, aside from the peculiar authority they possessed at hours when under the influence of inspiration, is clearly taught by Christ. When "they disputed which should be the greatest," Christ, alluding to the different grades of official dignity existing among civil rulers, expressly declared, "It shall not be so among you;"* while to Peter, the leader of all, he described their office as that only of the shepherd tending and feeding his flock; three times repeating it, though in varied language, "Feed my lambs;" "Tend my sheep;" "Feed my sheep."†

Passing from the life and teachings of Christ to the Acts and Epistles of his Apostles, numerous precedents and precepts of significant import are to be traced. When an apostle to fill Judas' place is to be selected, the whole company, men and women, are appealed to in common, in reference to the election.‡ Two classes of officers, one to attend to the secular, the other to the spiritual ministrations of the church, are seen to have early arisen. For, as among the twelve one had been chosen by Jesus to carry the bag, so, in the church at Jerusalem, persons whose appointment is not mentioned, it arose so naturally, were occupied in distributing to the needy; when, because of complaints of neglect, seven men were formally elected to superintend this work.§ In the church afterward, the office of deacon is mentioned with,‖ though

---

* Luke xxii. 25, 26.   † John xxi. 15-17.
‡ Acts i. 15-23.   § John xii. 6; xiii. 29, 30.   Acts vi. 1-4.
‖ Phil. i. 1.   1 Tim. iii. 1 and 8.

subordinate to,* that of bishop; an office which, among the Greeks proper, though not among the Jews and Grecian proselytes at Jerusalem, required female aids;† whose appointment and office Paul unfolds in writing to Timothy.‡ When Barnabas and Saul are sent forth as the first foreign missionaries, the whole church at Antioch co-operate in their election; while their "prophets" and "teachers" ordain them to the work by prayer and the laying on of hands.§ When the question, how far Old Testament requirements were binding on Grecian Christians, was to be authoritatively settled, and Paul and Barnabas went from Antioch to Jerusalem to consult the apostles and brethren on this subject, Paul says that they "communicated, first, privately to them that were of reputation" their message; that then the "apostles and elders came together to consider of this matter;" but when the decision was made and read, "then pleased it the apostles, and elders, and the whole church," to send letters expressive of their conviction. The restricted field of the legitimate action of the council is seen in the fact that only the moral bearings of a just interpretation of Old Testament teachings on religious conduct came before them for discussion. The ultimate authority of decision as residing in the church again is seen in the fact that after Peter, Barnabas, and Saul had stated facts which had occurred, and James had given his opinion, drawn from a comparison of events with the teachings of Moses and the prophets, the address of the Council to the churches begins, "The apostles, elders, and *brethren* send greeting unto the *brethren* which are of the Gentiles in Antioch, and Syria, and Cilicia." The purely

---

* Included Tit. i. 5, in the general term "elders," but not specially mentioned as in v. 7, the bishop.
† Rom. xvi. 1, compare Acts vi. 1–6.   ‡ 1 Tim. v. 3–16.
§ Acts xiii. 1–3.

moral, or advisory character of the decree, yet again, is manifest throughout the letter, declaring their decision in such expressions as these: "It *seemed good* unto us, being assembled with *one accord;*" "it *seemed good* to the *Holy Ghost* and to us to lay upon you no *greater burthen* than these *necessary* things;" and, in conclusion, "from which, *if* ye keep yourselves, *ye shall do well.*"*

Turning from the Acts of the Apostles to their Epistles, we note the following instructive items. To the Romans, Paul pictures the church as a body made up of many members, with varied gifts, ranking the prophet, minister, exhorter, giver, and ruler all on the same level; instead of addressing a bishop or pope as the vicar of Christ, he writes, "to all that are in Rome, beloved of God, called to be saints;" and, in conclusion, he sends salutations to no less than twenty-seven individuals named, several of whom are females, some of whom have households and churches in their houses, to whom the salutation is also addressed.† It would seem as if wisdom incomprehensible to man guided the inspired penman so to embalm for all time the memory of what the primitive church of Rome was, that its deep teaching should escape the ken of degenerate leaders in that church; so completely, indeed, that those corrupt successors to the responsible care of the inspired epistles have given them unadulterated to the Christian world, never suspecting the condemnation they gave to their own perversions.

In his exhortations to the Corinthian church, we see the genuine character of the early Christian church in its excesses. Even Paul, Apollos, and Peter had no controlling authority; for the church was divided between them, each following his favorite. In their assemblies for worship, every one had a psalm, an address, or

---

* Acts xv. 1-29. Gal. ii. 1, 2. † Rom. i. 7; xii. 4-8; xvi. 3-15.

a prayer; even women praying and prophesying, sometimes uncovered: while to correct these extremes of independence, Paul urges, that "nature" and "custom" should restrain women from public ministrations, that "God is not the author of confusion, and that all in the church are alike honorable and to be honored as members of the body; yet God has assigned, as for the hand and foot, the eye and the ear, each his own place in the body, "first, apostles; secondarily, prophets; thirdly, teachers; after that, miracles; then gifts of healing, *helps in government,* diversities of tongues," in which enumeration not only *government,* but "*helps* in government," are recognized as having legitimate place.*

In later epistles the offices of the church and its authority as a body are frequently urged. The Galatians† are taught, "If any be overtaken in a fault, *ye that are spiritual* restore such a one in the spirit of meekness," indicating the character for special spirituality, that should belong to rulers in the church. The Ephesians‡ are reminded that as among pure angels there are "principalities and powers in the heavenly places," so God has set in the church apostles, prophets, evangelists, pastors, and teachers, for the edifying and uniting compactly of the body of Christ. To Timothy and Titus§ he describes the virtues, all moral, which should belong to a bishop and deacon. He pictures the rule of the church so perfectly like that of a family, that only a successful father can be expected to prove a successful pastor; he declares that he expects that the authority and influence of the ruler in the church will reside, as it ought, chiefly in those who "labor in the word and doctrine," and he limits its personal power over a member guilty of wilful insubordination, error, or vice, to the duty

---

* 1 Cor. i. 12; ix. 3; xi. 3–16; xii. 12–28.   † Gal. vi. 1.
‡ Eph. iii. 10; iv. 4–12.   § 1 Tim. iii. 1–13; v. 17–19. Tit. i. 5–9.

of withdrawal from such a member, while, as we have seen, the church's authority extends no further than to exclusion from their number.*

Most impressive and affecting of all is the language of that apostle, specially impulsive and forward, ever accustomed to be seen as a leader, and made by some the special vicar of Christ. His estimate of his own official character, as a model for all others holding position in the church, thus wells up as a sweet stream from a purified fount. "The elders among you I exhort, who am also an elder; Feed the flock of God which is among you, taking the oversight thereof not by constraint, but willingly, not for filthy lucre, but of a ready mind, neither as being lords over God's heritage, but as examples to the flock. And when the Chief Shepherd shall appear, ye shall receive a crown of glory that fadeth not away."†

While throughout the Acts of the Apostles germs of association among Christian churches appear, in the epistles these indications are so manifest that they must be regarded a rule of duty. Members are commended, by letters both of the apostles and of churches, as Phebe by Paul, and Paul by the Corinthian church.‡ Co-operating efforts for the poor disciples in distant regions are made; Paul himself acting as a general agent, while pastors and messengers, approved by letters from their churches, combine in these wide-spread efforts.§ Organized associations sustain missionary heralds; Paul and Barnabas, being first sent out from Antioch, but sustained, as also the other apostles were, by regular stipends, and occasional gifts sent to them; Paul thus being enabled to live in his own hired house at distant Rome.‖ Through

---
* 1 Tim. vi. 5. 1 Cor. v. 5. † 1 Pet. v. 1–5.
‡ Rom. xvi. 1. 2 Cor. iii. 1. § Acts xi. 28, 30. 1 Cor. xvi. 1–12.
‖ Acts xiii. 3; xv. 3; xxi. 5. 1 Cor. ix. 4–7. 2 Cor. xi. 8, 9. Phil. iv. 10–18.

kindred associations, the epistles of Paul, written to individual churches, are multiplied, like the other Scriptures, by the pen; and are sent to distant churches and regions, until they become so numerous that they are in the hands of even the unlearned.*

All these testimonies seem to confirm the principle, that the official heads in the Christian church are the selection of its membership, having only advisory authority as agents of the church; while the church has no other province than that of watch-care over the spiritual life of its members, and the securing of co-operation in Christian effort for others. It seems equally apparent, that associations of churches are made up of representatives selected by individual churches; that their authority is simply advisory; and that it relates only to such subjects as belong to the Christian advancement of those already believers, and union for the extending of the gospel to those that either have not heard or have not believed the word.

There is yet a third point of consideration, at the same time confirmatory of the principles thus developed, and illustrative of their essential truth by their practical power and excellence.

THIRD. *The beneficial fruits of adherence to the gospel standard of church polity; as exemplified in the Scripture interpretation, and the adopted policy of evangelical Christian leaders in different ages.*

There were certain statements of Christ, whose meaning, John says, his disciples did not apprehend till he had arisen from the dead.† So, doubtless, there are statements of his apostles as to church polity, and even inspired words of far-reaching meaning as to domestic and civil government, which no human mind can comprehend

---

* Col. iv. 16. 2 Pet. iii. 15, 16.   † John ii. 22, etc.

till the progress of Christian civilization unfolds their import. It certainly must be instructive to every sincere inquirer after Christ's revealed plan of church polity, to find that in many a successive era of the history of the church, the wisest and best, the most thoughtful and useful men, have sat down to personal study of the words of Christ and of Paul, relating to the offices and the government of his church, and, aided by the light of Providence, amid the troubles of the church in their day, have arrived at substantially the same conclusions, as to its necessary establishment, and the nature of its legitimate, happy, and useful organization.

The source from which we are to draw the history of the church, after we leave the inspired history of the Acts and the Epistles of the apostles, is the writings of Christian men succeeding each other from generation to generation; first, the contemporaries and disciples, or pupils, of the apostles, such as Clement, to whom Paul alludes; Polycarp and Ignatius, disciples of John; then Irenæus and others of the second generation; Tertullian, Justin, and others of the third; and so onward in an unbroken chain. The relation to the inspired writers of all these uninspired, yet intelligent and sincere Christian men, is illustrated by two classes of native preachers now observed in the mission fields of Southern Asia. The most intelligent and thoroughly cultured Hindoo, Burman, or Chinese, when converted to Christ, is as clear in judgment and as accurate in his testimony as the trained American missionary, when speaking of matters appealing to the eyesight in observation, to the understanding in history, or to religious consciousness in spiritual experience. But, if such a man attempts to unfold the meaning of the statements of Christ or of Paul, he unconsciously mixes up with revealed truth his former heathen notions and reasonings. Hence, an instructed Christian, sitting in a convention of native Christians, can readily pick out the young men trained for years under the missionary's teaching, from among the men of maturer years and education that have not had that training; the one presenting only truth, the other mixing up with the truth errors, whose principles can be traced to their former superstitions. Just so, it was easy for Christians of the age after the apostles to select the inspired writings of Paul from ordinary letters that he wrote when uninspired; and still more easy was it to discriminate between the writings of apostles and of their immediate successors. The latter are extremely valuable as to matters of fact, in Christian history occurring in their day; though in matters of doctrine specially marked by Grecian and Roman errors in philosophy and faults in morals, the failure to discriminate between which has led to the error of the Tractarians in the late controversies in the English Episcopal church.

Turning to these writers, Ignatius, receiving his Christian instruction under John, evidently replying to some perversion of official authority, such as Paul and Peter anticipate would arise, exclaims, "What indeed is the eldership, but a sacred constituted body, fellow-counsellors and judges with the presiding pastor;"* an expression which indicates the purely moral nature of the office of both the pastor and his appointed advisers. Again, Irenæus, living about a century after the apostles, writing as *episcopos*, or presiding pastor, at Lyons in France, to Victor, who held the same office at Rome, and contending for the simplicity and independence of their official authority, enumerates all who have held his office since Peter at Rome, and states that as

---

* "Τί δὲ πρεσβυτέριον αλλ' ἡ συστημα ἱερὸν, συμβουλοι καὶ συνεδρευταί τοῦ ἐπισκόπου."

episcopoi, or presiding pastors, they were *presbyteroi*, or elders.

When, at length, the natural ambition for official superiority, which Christ rebuked among his apostles, and which Ignatius and Irenæus saw in the church even during the dark days of the age of persecution, could throw off its cloak in the age of Constantine, Jerome argued at length what his predecessors had occasion to allude to; urging, "The elder is the same as the bishop or presiding pastor.* * * * Should any one think that it is not the sentiment of the Scriptures, but our opinion, that the bishop and the presbyter are one, this the name of age that of office, let him read again the words of the apostle to the Philippians, 'Paul and Timothy, servants of Jesus Christ to all the sanctified in Christ who are at Philippi, with the bishops and deacons, grace to you and peace,' etc. Philippi was a single city of Macedonia; and certainly in a single city there could not be several such as are now regarded bishops. But since, at that time, the same men were bishops as were called elders, therefore, he spoke indiscriminately of bishops as of elders." Proceeding to argue from the Scriptures, as evangelical Christian men always have, this clear-thinking and sincere-hearted writer, living only two centuries after John, cites again Paul's indiscriminate use of the titles elders and bishops, in his address recorded in Acts 20th; then the humble acknowledgment of Peter, the head of the Roman church, that he was but an elder. Turning finally† to the history of the church, then so brief, he adds this important statement, "At Alexandria, from the evangelist Mark down to the bishops Heraclas and Dionysius,

---

* "Idem est presbyter, qui et episcopus."
† Hieron. Annot, Epist. ad Titum; et Epist. ad Evagrium.

the elders always gave the name of bishop to one whom they elected from themselves, and placed in a higher rank; in the same way as an army may create a general, or as deacons may elect from their own number one whom they know to be laborious, and may call him archdeacon."

About two hundred years later, or in the sixth century, when, under Justinian, the great church builder, danger from aspiring men was still greater, the devoted Chrysostom brings out repeatedly, the added fact, that the elders in the early church were nothing else than the pastors and deacons associated; his words being, "The elders anciently were called bishops and deacons of Christ; and bishops, elders." Yet three hundred years still later, in the ninth century, when, under Charlemagne of France, truly pious men, like Alcuinus, were seeking to spread true Christianity among the people of central Europe conquered by his army, an effort in which the emperor, often with wisdom and always with zeal, co-operated, so wide spread and long prevalent was the simple evangelical view of the office of the Christian bishop, that it became for centuries the avowed doctrine of leaders in the Roman church. Thus Bernaldus, a zealous advocate of the arbitrary assumption, A. D. 1088, of Gregory, contends that as bishops, according to Jerome's authoritative proof, which he quotes, had originally no higher authority than elder, therefore, the Roman Pontiff is truly supreme over bishops as over elders; a turning of the tables upon their own heads, from which the lordly bishops of the time found it difficult to extricate themselves. In the first canon of the council held at Beneventum, under Pope Urban II., A. D. 1091, occurs this admission: "We declare as sacred orders, those of the deacon and elder. Indeed, the primitive church is said to have had these only." Even in the Council of Trent, convoked in the sixteenth century to meet the spreading fire of the Reformation, policy compelled this declaration found in the preamble of one of its decrees: "Whereas the *preaching of the gospel*, which is the *special office of bishops*, is as essential to every Christian community as the *reading of the word*, therefore, this sacred synod has determined and decreed," etc.

The discussion of every point of Christian doctrine and practice which arose during the early spread of the Reformation, called out a reconsideration of all that Christ and his apostles had taught, and of all that the history of the church afforded, illustrative of church polity. In that discussion, the main effort was to discriminate between elders and bishops; the discussion turning mainly on the statement of Paul, 1 Thess. v. 12; 1 Tim. iii. 2; and especially in our text, 1 Tim. v. 17. These discussions were revived in the great Methodist movement under Wesley and Whitefield; the adherents to the Episcopal and the Independent forms of church organization being of opposite views. These discussions, continued to this day, have tended more and more to an acknowledgment of the manifestly simple system shining on the very face of the New Testament statements.

A remarkable instance of the power of the truth in its simplicity to appeal to and compel a mind of deep thoughtfulness and sincerity, is seen in the "Essays on the Kingdom of Christ," published about A. D., 1840, by Archbishop Whately, of the English Episcopal Church, and republished in New York, by Rev. Prof. Thomas H. Skinner, D.D., A. D., 1842. The volume consists of two essays; the first on "Christ's account of his own Person, and of the nature of his Kingdom;" the second on "The Constitution, Powers, and Ministry of the

Christian Church." Designed, as the treatise was, to bring out evangelical and scriptural truth to oppose the tendency of the party in the English church who would return to the views of the Church of Rome, all thought of disguise was forgotten, if conceived; or rather, the whole soul of the truly pious prelate was absorbed in the feeling of personal and official responsibility to defend Christ's simple truth. He finds the model of the Christian church in simple, voluntary associations for literary and other purposes; more familiar to the mass of the early Christians who were Gentiles, than was the Jewish synagogue. He thinks the *omissions* of the Scriptures as to details of church polity were directed by the Divine Spirit, "*on purpose* that other churches in other ages and regions might not be led to consider themselves bound to adhere to several formularies, customs, and rules that were of local and temporary appointment." As to the separation of civil and ecclesiastical rule, he says: "Magistrates would cease to act on Christian principles, who should employ coercive power in the cause of Christianity." Of the primitive organization of Christian churches, he unhesitatingly says: "The plan pursued by the apostles seems to have been to establish a great number of small, distinct, and independent communities, each governed by its own single bishop." "A church has a right to admit or refuse to admit members. This right it possesses as a *society*; as a *Christian society* it has a right to decide who shall or shall not exercise certain functions, and under what circumstances." "In a *voluntary* community the *ultimate* penalty must be expulsion." "A church and a diocese seem to have been, for a considerable time, coextensive and identical. And each church or diocese, and consequently, each bishop or superintendent, though connected with the rest by ties of faith, hope, and charity, seems to have been perfectly independent, as far as regards any power of control; occasionally conferring with the brethren in other churches, but owing no submission to any central, common authority, except the apostles themselves." Certainly, the idea of a Christian church, as presented in the former part of our present consideration, could hardly have been more fully stated. When great emergencies in the history of Christ's kingdom arise, how the true watchmen see eye to eye!

The important practical conclusions to be borne away from our whole survey of the subject of church polity, as principles of personal Christian conduct, may be thus summed up.

First. The necessity of human nature makes a form of organization, rules of order, and official rank in the Christian church, essential to its success. It is not simply among men, a depraved race, but among pure angels, that grades of intelligence and subordination prevail. In every branch of the Christian church, even the least formal sect of Friends, there are appointed weekly assemblies of separate congregations, and yearly meetings of associated congregations; and in these, there are recognized leaders and presiding officers, established rules of order, and prescribed limits as to subjects considered.

Second. The source of authoritative teaching as to church polity, at all times, when circumstances have made the issue one of practical importance, has been the word and example of inspired men, interpreted in the light of present providences. Every church begins with a simple union of equals; as numbers and popularity increase, and worldly ambition draws men into it, efforts to introduce worldly distinctions among men, plans of organizations and topics for conventional action are made; but in times of danger from corruption and of return to spiritual consecration, there is a return to the word and example of Christ, interpreted and applied by the circumstances which impress the inspired truth. The advancing spirit of the whole body of professed believers in Christ has been strikingly illustrated in the published writings of the Protestant leaders of Italy, who contend for a return to the primitive church of Rome as pictured in Paul's epistle; in the evangelical scholarship of Germany, combating the tendencies of rationalism; in the spiritual party in the Church of England, resisting the leaning toward the doctrines of the Roman church; and even in the remarkable letters of the Archbishop of Paris, in 1852, opposing the new dogma of the Immaculate Conception of Mary. The simple truth of Christ will always, in trying times, win the homage and allegiance of good men.

Third. The *nature* of church organization is clear to Christian men, when Christ's mission is the end at which they are aiming. A church is an association, voluntary so far as any human authority is concerned, though obligatory on all believers in Christ, because of his command; it is made up of believers in Christ depending on his sacrifice for justification and on his spirit for sanctification; it is united to observe his ordinances, to maintain his worship and to coöperate in extending his kingdom; it has, as its directing leaders, one class devoted to the spiritual interests and another to the temporal necessities of the body; and it has power to receive, discipline, or exclude members, according as their views, spirit, and conduct seem conformed to Christ's doctrine and precepts, and to select men, who seem best fitted for it, as their spiritual and temporal leaders. In the association of Christians for benevolent and spiritual objects, the principle of a voluntary society, made up of individuals, who pay a fixed sum, or of church representation, may control the membership; and in either case, the action of the body should be limited to the objects stated in their constitution or to those appropriate for church action.

Fourth. The duty of adhering to the New Testament standard of church polity is *virtually* maintained by all good men, when, in an emergency which tests an established church, such men invariably go back to that standard to resist perversions. Dr. Wayland says of civil society, that no nation has a right to organize a government on any other than just principles; or such as would exclude any right-minded conscientious man. This principle, certainly, tacitly recognized by all good men in church polity when emergencies arise, should enter into every church at its origin, since thus trying emergencies would be anticipated. Archbishop Whateley, earnestly resisting unjust authority seeking to get control of the English Episcopal Church, says, "to vindicate the institutions of our own or of some other church on the ground, that they are not in themselves superstitious or ungodly, that they are not at variance with gospel principles or with any divine injunction that was designed to be of universal obligation, is intelligible and reasonable. But to vindicate them on the ground of the exact conformity, which it is notorious they do not possess, to the most ancient models, and even to go beyond this, and condemn all Christians whose institutions and ordinances are not 'one and utterly like' our own, on the ground of their departure from the apostolical precedents, which no church has exactly adhered to, does seem, to use no harsher expression, not a little inconsistent and unreasonable." To adhere, then, to the gospel standard, is certainly the only way to oneness in church organization, and seems also to be the only legitimate Christian rule.

Fifth. The special seasons, when both theoretical and practical attention is called to forms of church polity should be well improved; that this oneness of church polity and conformity in it to Christ's rule may be secured. After the American Revolution, alike in Episcopal Virginia and South Carolina and in Puritan Massachusetts, the ministers of which former church adhered to the royalist and of the latter to the popular parties, confidence was shaken in the Established Church order; especially in its resort to the civil power for its maintenance. Whole sections of Virginia, and numerous communities in Carolina and Massachusetts, embraced the principles of adherence to scriptural precedent as to church polity maintained by the Baptist denomination; and an influence was begun which made this denomination, from being the least, to become the most numerous in the United States. The agitations now rending the Established Churches of Italy, Germany, France and England, and the experience of Christian coöperation in our own country during the years of war just passed in which true Christians of all these nations and of varied denominations have been united, have stirred the pens and have awakened the voices of many of the best men of Europe and of America, who pray and plead for Christian union. They seem to be the call of Divine Providence demanding a new and most earnest consideration of Christ's method of Church Polity.

XIII.

CHURCH WORSHIP

By SAMUEL L. CALDWELL, D.D.,
Pastor of First Baptist Church, Providence, R. I.

"FOR WE ARE THE CIRCUMCISION, WHICH WORSHIP GOD IN THE SPIRIT, AND REJOICE IN CHRIST JESUS, AND HAVE NO CONFIDENCE IN THE FLESH."—*Philippians* iii. 3.

"YE ALSO, AS LIVELY STONES, ARE BUILT UP A SPIRITUAL HOUSE, A HOLY PRIESTHOOD, TO OFFER UP SPIRITUAL SACRIFICES, ACCEPTABLE TO GOD, BY JESUS CHRIST."—1 *Peter* ii. 5.

WORSHIP is the natural offspring of religion, of all religions. Gross or spiritual, they take form and body, they find instruments and expression, a ministry and a ritual, each after its kind. It is a necessity of the religious and of the social nature alike. Religion takes hold of society, and brings men together in the fellowship of worship of a common place, time and service of devotion. There has been no living, perpetuated religion in the world without an outward *cultus;* without some altar, or sacrament, or pulpit—a visible ministry and service. Worship has been a universal custom, as common as government, as natural as dress. Whatever has ceased among men, this never has. The dead races, the distant times, have left little beside the relics of their worship. Into its structures, the wealth and the genius, as well as the reverence and the faith of mankind have gone. The wondrous stones of Philæ and Pæstum, the spires of Strasburg and Salisbury, no less than Jacob's rude pillar in Bethel, or Moses' tent of skins in the desert, the transient or the enduring houses, where men bow to one God or many gods, tell that worship is in man, a necessary part of his nature and his life; that wherever there is a religion there will be a worship corresponding.

And so Christianity being a religion for society no less than for the private soul, falls into the same line, and organizes worship after a law of its own. Having first organized a church, it makes this its primary and proper office. In its spirituality it does not disallow, it has not superseded this constant fact of human nature, but takes it up, spiritualizes it, and converts it to its own spirit and use. Sabbath and temple and priesthood it accepts, to renew them to itself and its service. It does not consist in worship, but it depends upon it, puts itself into it, does not live without it. It is a doctrine and a spiritual life, it is a faith of the soul; but so also, it is a church and a worship; and these all go together and affect each other. Especially does worship grow out of the church, and become its natural function. They are indispensable and ancillary to each other. One of them never goes alone. They are both organic growths of the same spirit of life, simple or artificial, spiritual or formal, scriptural or traditional together. The church exists for many purposes, but for none before this. It is a depository of truth; it is a home and school for religious nurture and education; a society and fellowship of the faithful; a light to lighten the gentiles; a corporate agency, a missionary institute, to preach the gospel and turn men to God; but so, also, is this its calling and function, to perform, to keep and maintain the worship of God. It exists for this end, that there may be a body charged with this obligation, fulfilling this sacred office for society. If worship is not left to chance, and the spontaneous offering of individual souls; if, instead of being the fleeting breath of the hour, it is to be an institution and social custom; if it is to have order and permanence, it must have an organized body, a church, something to sustain, to offer it. And if there is a church, a Divine institution, a spiritual society, a body of Christ, it has little use or power, or even reason to exist, without a worship. Seeing they are so inseparable, seeing, too, I follow in a course of sermons which have been developing the true idea of the church, it is most natural to take up my assigned topic of worship in this relation, and look at it first as a function of the church, as one of the great ends and uses of its organization, as the duty and office with which it is specially charged.

Worship belongs to the church as a part of its priestly character and work: "Ye also, as lively stones are built up a spiritual house, a holy priesthood, to offer up spiritual sacrifices, acceptable unto God by Jesus Christ." In Judaism an hereditary priesthood performed all religious offices for the people. When Christ came, the Mediator and High Priest of a better covenant, the priesthood ceased, or rather passed over in spirit to the whole body of Christians, and became the function of all the church of God. Through and under him, as their Chief Priest, passed into the heavens, they here on earth come into a character, place, relation in things pertaining to God, not merely individual, but representative; ordained and anointed of the Spirit to draw nigh to God, and for others as well as for themselves to make their requests known unto him.

They are qualified and separated to this very thing by their personal religious experience. They have found, they know, the way to God. He is in the dark, remote, uncertain, hidden, till he is found in Christ. He does not come near into the field of human knowledge and trust, till he reveals himself in Christ Jesus. But he whose faith is there has open communication, and access by one Spirit unto the Father. He no longer gropes in the dark, feeling after God, if haply he may find him. God is no longer cold, distant, dead under the laws, impersonal beyond the stars. The vail falls; doubt and distrust disappear with all our sin, at the vision of Jesus' face, at the touch of his blood, and we can speak to God, asking what we will, and know that he heareth us always.

In virtue of their regeneration, also, they have an anointing to this very office. They are made priests unto God, because they have passed from death unto life. Their own personal experiences of want and sin and grace, the prayers, confessions, praises they bring for themselves, prepare them also to stand for others; even as it is the argument of the Epistle to the Hebrews for Christ's priesthood, that he had passed through all human experiences, and knew how to pity the tempted, and plead for the suffering and the guilty. All experience acquired, all the light and power of religion in them, all God's discipline upon them, all Christ's tuition in them, that they have been taught by conscious need, by Divine grace to pray, makes them an instructed and qualified priesthood, is a power in them to this very thing. Even as Christ has ascended into the heavenly places, worshiping in the presence of the Father, a Priest forever, not after the law of a carnal commandment, but after the power of an endless life, so they in their place and under him, stand for others before God; every Christian parent a priest for his household, offering their daily praise, and speaking for little children, who, perhaps, not yet have words to tell their thanks or wants; every Christian citizen a priest for his country—her blessings, her troubles, her evils, all her great hopes and burdens, are on his heart, and he must go into the secret place of the Eternal to plead her case, to hold up to merciful Heaven the tremendous issues of her struggling hour; every Christian church a holy priesthood, keeping its Sabbaths, lifting its hands to heaven in behalf of multitudes who feel or acknowledge no such obligation; the Church of Christ, anointed priest of this sinning, suffering world, appointed to speak in its behalf to God, to give the thanks which it withholds, to implore for it a mercy it never asks, to utter the inarticulate cry of all the wretched nations for light, to keep alive in it God's constant praise. For all things dear and true; for all men; for the church; for your children; for the poor; for tears wanting a heavenly comfort to dry them; for souls fighting a hard battle anywhere; for the shoulders which hold up the State; for the tongues which teach in church and school; for those who have lost their faith; for the prodigals who are burning up their hearts; for purer manners, nobler thoughts, equal laws; for the Spirit out of heaven, which brings life and bloom and harvest to Christ's vineyard; for all blessings which the world will not pray for, and yet which must come in answer to prayer, are Christians ordained to make supplication.

And so for praise, even more than for prayer, that God's mercies may not, unacknowledged, fall upon a world which makes no return. The receivers are often silent. They forget God their Maker. They bend no knee. They sit at a thankless table. They keep no holy days, and from them comes no worship. But shall there be none *for* them? Shall God have no honor except for such blessings as fall upon the grateful, and not also find those who are ready to remember and praise in behalf of the unthankful and the forgetful?

The generous heart of Paul found inspiration to worship in what God had done for his brethren. "I thank my God upon every remembrance of you, always in every prayer of mine for you all, making request with joy, for your fellowship in the Gospel, from the first day until now." It is the spirit of Christian love to feel gratitude for all God lets fall into the world, however remote from ourselves. All we see of God's goodness falling anywhere, in day or night, in the beautiful fields, in happy life, in all that makes men better, in every quiet example of goodness, of meekness under trials, of faithfulness under great responsibilities, in every triumph of religion—all that any creature receives of blessing from God, is an occasion for somebody's praise. And he has his priests, whose privilege it is and whose office, to take up the neglected duty, and thank him for what he has done even for the unthankful and the evil. Nicholas Ferrar, in the seventeenth century provided, in his house at Little Gidding, for a perpetual service through every hour of the day and night so that whatever might happen, at all hours, in the day and in the dark, the voice of praise might be always ascending; that though everywhere else in the broad earth, there might come times when no praise should be heard, there might be one spot, where it should never cease. And so has God provided that there shall be one place and one people from which amidst the silence of the thankless, his unforgetful praise shall always rise. To the Church he has delegated this duty, that, as his priests, they may gather up and carry to his altar the sacrifices which the world withholds. For prayer, for praise alike, for man, for God, for God's honor, for man's sin even, does the body of Christians stand between earth and heaven, does every church stand in a community, holding this priestly and vicarious office. Great and noble, and divine it is. The high priest went into the tabernacle in gorgeous robes. But we go into the holy place of God clothed upon with human wants,

Church Worship.

bearing in there for our garment the sins and sorrows and wants and blessings, the thanks and prayers of our humanity waiting at the door. We go in representative of the nations that perish, of a race waiting for Christ's salvation, of children, and neighbors, and our brethren in the faith, and all the household of God. And so, in the very constitution of the Church, as a body of regenerate people, has God provided for his perpetual worship. All tongues may be silent, but they will show forth his praises. Whoever forgets God, here is a church organized and charged with this as its first function, a priesthood called, as was Aaron, to keep always burning the fire upon God's altars.

Worship belongs to the Church as the bond of its fellowship and the organ of its spiritual development and increase. This *is* its fellowship—a fellowship in worship. When the Church comes together in one place it is for this. Nothing is so near a spiritual union, nothing is so productive of it, as that which unites men in the same prayers and praises. Nothing requires them to be of one mind, no creed or establishment can make them one, like coming before the same God, in one service of devotion. Nothing, more than this, promotes the sympathies as well as the religious experiences which are the common bond of unity in the Church. But it is not love only, and the sympathetic sentiments, but all religious life which is nourished by worship. It is the appointed minister to all spiritual edification. It is the grand public ordinance for instruction and for all religious culture and quickening. It touches the spiritual life of the Church on all sides, to purify and strengthen. It not only operates upon it in the way of impression, as external stimulus, but especially in social worship, in which many have part, all religious feeling and thought goes into active exercise.* There are more private methods of spiritual culture, and nothing goes before a personal and inward religion. Its secret life is nourished in the soul's solitary and individual communion with God. But leave all piety to this separate, private, solitary growth, silence preaching, close the churches, let Christians forsake the assembling of themselves together, dry up the streams which take their rise under the altars of God, and where is the Church, or even religion itself? It would exist, it would live, it would make its own sabbath and sanctuaries. In some breasts, in some strong, self-sustaining souls, it might grow and make its power felt. God's invisible grace would find many channels into the life of Christians. But it is through the "means of grace," as by distinction we call all services of the Church; through prayers and hymns and sermons, through a day of rest, a house of God, the communion of saints, the influences, conscious and unconscious, of public worship, that this secret life of piety is fed. There much of it was born. There carelessness was touched and doubt convinced. There the world lost its hold for a day, and so by the grace of God forever. Thither, like a sparrow to its nest, the heart, weary and hungry, flies, and shut out from the courts of the Lord is in a desert land. Thither, as the soul to its closet, must the Church go to recruit her power, for comfort, for learning, for all spiritual benefit.

And the power it has within the Church is the power it has abroad. Worship is a part of that larger function to which Christ has ordained it, of evangelizing the

---

* The relation of the Prayer-meeting to the life of the Church is close and vital. It supplements its more public service. It diversifies its ministries of edification. It opens a branch of the subject too large for present consideration, but of great practical importance.

world. Through such public service it comes in contact—brings Christianity into contact—with the souls and the life of men. There may be instruction by other methods, and without any worship of the Church. There is the great domestic ordinance of household teaching and religion, "the church that is in the house." There is a great influence and power of religion, leavening human life, which comes not by observation and through outward ordinances. Christianity is a spiritual power, possessing and using many things, invisibly invading the heart of society through example, through books, through a thousand direct and indirect channels, and by mysterious movements of the Spirit of God, which bloweth where it listeth. But it does not seem to be the Divine intention, it does not seem to be even common wisdom, to trust it to work its mighty spiritual results by itself, without some special and public instruments. Religion, in one sense, only wants a soul; it is faith, fear, love, and hope in that. It lives not in wood, though cedar be carved into a temple; nor in stone, though groined into the aisles of St. Peter's; nor in a worship, though it be venerable with the hoar of centuries; but in the affections of a human soul—and there alone. But how does it get into men's souls, and keep there? Knowledge is a thing of the mind. But society does not trust to its going in there by itself, through some mysterious contagion in the air. There is the school, and the university, the press, the library, the lecture. These are not knowledge, but the means and creators of it, without which ignorance would be the eternal doom of society. So the house of God, with Sundays, and prayers, and sermons, and hymns, is needful for religion—not for instruction only, but to awaken man, naturally so asleep to spiritual ideas and relations, to beget in his pre-occupied heart the consciousness of divine obligation, of guilt, of an immortal existence, to touch it to a penitent and nobler life. Without it, religion might live in scattered bosoms, a sporadic, and, at best, languid existence, but not at all as a social power, impressing itself upon numbers and masses of men, extensive, pervading, abiding in social life. Where there is no house of God, there is no God; none acknowledged, regarded, obeyed; as little of God's fear as of his worship; and therefore, as much of human selfishness and passion, ignorance, and superstition, and violence, as there is little of God's praise and God's truth. The house of God, with its worship, is necessary to religion, therefore, in both ways, and in all ways, to its social existence and power, as it is to its more secret and spiritual life. The Church of God holds this as a great trust for society, as it does for Christ himself, and is ordained to the sublimest office known to human civilization—to order and maintain among men the worship of a living God. For the sake of Christianity, and of society, purified only by its sanative energies; for the sake of souls going all wrong and wretched till they come to God in Christ; for the sake of that kingdom of light and redemption which comes shining through the windows of churches, and heralded by the pulpits which publish salvation; for the sake of him whose blood sprinkles her altars, whose love inflames her praise, whose salvation is her message to all people—is the Church to stand in this great office of worship, the constituted priesthood, "to offer up spiritual sacrifices, acceptable to God, by Jesus Christ."

Having now this office laid upon the Church, how shall it be discharged? What is the nature and style of that worship which the Christian Church is to offer? What shape does Christianity give to this institution, ancient, constant, universal, as man's faith in a living God? I seem to open the question which divides Christendom, which has been waiting and contending through all the generations for its answer. Whatever minor differences remain, in one point, and that primary and essential, the whole question is settled, and settled forever. It must be in the spirit. Worship, which is not spiritual, is void; which is not in the right spirit, is offensive. The spirit—not the form—the spirit, which builds itself into architecture, splendid or lowly; which goes into the service, simple or grand; which uses ancient words, or the fresh utterances of the hour; which worships in chapel, or cathedral, in a Baptist prayer-meeting, or a Roman ritual—it is the spirit alone which is accepted or rejected. That our Lord settled so summarily at Jacob's well, that for Chrstians no question remains. In a breath, in one sublime sentence, he undermines the whole controversy, lifts our relation to God, all worship, up above Moriah and Gerizim, out of time and place, into the spiritual and everlasting. God is a spirit. That one idea, how it goes through the earth, discrowning hill-tops of their sanctity, sanctifying all places rather to him; unclothing religion of its thousand forms; transferring it from the golden altar of the temple to the bosom of a bowed publican; the Jew, the Samaritan, the high-priest in his shining cloth, the poor widow with her slender gift; the well, where a sinful woman smiles to a new vision of God, the mountain, which trembles before the unfolding law—all distinction abolished, all place, all time, all persons, one to him who is a Spirit. From the nature of God to the nature of worship, short, straight, inevitable, the inference goes. They must be alike. God is a Spirit; and they that worship him must worship him in spirit and in truth.

Standing fast, then, upon the spirituality of worship

as its vital law, unless worship remains a wordless thought, an unuttered feeling, private, and only invisibly reaching after God—if it is to be public, associate, a custom—it must take form. Spirituality does not exclude form, and expression. If it does, there is nothing left but to relapse each soul into its own silent, private communion, and let no sign of outward worship be seen in all the world. But does the doctrine of Christ drive, of necessity, to any such ultra-spiritual conclusion—forbid all convocations of Christians, abolish the Lord's Day, send each man home to the solitude of his own prayers? May not a time, a place, a manner, be subordinate, and yet be needful even, and required, and produced by the true spirit of devotion? May not the spiritual and the external go together, and the one into the other, as thought and language, as soul and body? Indeed, do they not interact; and may not the feeling be repressed or transmitted, choked or stimulated, encumbered or assisted, by the means employed? Worship may be in the spirit, and yet may build its house, and gather its congregation, and sing its hymns, and bow the knee, and so become outward and visible. This, indeed, it must do, that it may serve its purpose. It is to be not only expressive, but also *im*pressive. It is first for God, the offering of the heart to him; but it is also his ordinance for us, and for a purer and higher life in us. It is for the individual, but not for him alone. It is not even for so many individuals. It is for a congregation. The church is not a private oratory. The individual cannot be a law to himself, as if he were the only one—standing when others sit; sitting when others stand; coming, going, singing, praying, after his own caprice, and not according to the order of a common, consenting service. Then worship is dissolved, and confusion comes. It is the Tower of Babel, not the

House of God, and God is made the author of confusion, and not of peace, as in all churches of the saints. Worship must have an order, a manner, a time, a place, some form or other, in order that it may be social, and not private. But still, the place, the posture, the act, is not the worship. That must be spiritual, and of the soul.

And, therefore, that it may be spiritual, it must be simple. If spirituality does not exclude some form and outward observances, it puts discouragement, and practically prohibition upon all artificial, ceremonious, ritual worship. It disallows the very principle on which that has always been practiced, namely, that religion, religious feeling, is to be promoted by impressions made on the senses, the imagination by any thing but the action of truth upon the moral nature. It favors and requires simplicity in all rites of worship. It may be asked what is the criterion of simplicity? When do forms become excessive and hurtful? Where is the limit? Is there a line, beyond which spirituality is imperiled; within which it is preserved?

It is safe to say that they exceed, when they attract the mind to the form and divert it from the truth; when they are not natural and spontaneous suggestions and helps of feeling, but sought out and contrived for effect, elaborate, artificial, antiquated, remote from the real and present feeling of the worshipers; when they are fixed, traditional, inelastic; when millinery and gilding and show take the place of the Word which is a fire and a hammer; when they tempt the mind to stop, to rest in them, instead of taking it up to God. There is a line which practically divides ceremonious, ritual, liturgical, formal worship, from that which is free, spontaneous, simple, spiritual; broadly, the Catholic from the Protestant; more closely, the priestly from the congregational, the ceremonial from the puritan, the liturgical from the extemporaneous. And we set our faces against forms and toward freedom, simplicity, spirituality. "For we are the circumcision which worship God in the spirit, and rejoice in Christ Jesus, and have no confidence in the flesh."

In the first place, the gospel prescribes no form. That everybody allows. There is no sign of any order, or ceremonial, or dress, or written and repeated prayer, of uniformity, or establishment of worship—nothing but freedom and simplicity. There are two simple sacraments. There are signs of a Lord's Day of joyful praise. But no liturgy, no order. Indeed of the prayers of our Lord and of the apostles—none are repeated; but each one sprung out of the occasion. They were not repetitions of previous prayers, nor were they designed to be repeated. What is called the Lord's Prayer is given in different forms of phraseology; the context indicates that it was a prayer to be offered in secret; it is expressly given as a specimen of that simple spirituality which is opposed to vain repetitions and heartless formalities; and there is no sign that it was in public use, in the age of the Apostles, or of their successors. And as Christ and his Apostles established no form, so the New Testament gives no right to anybody to do this, to *fix* worship and stereotype it, to prescribe prayers any more than sermons, to lay upon the people of God an unvarying, canonical order. Its whole spirit is against the assumption of a right to fasten upon the Church forms of dress, of action, of prayer, which, however antiquated or outgrown, or unsuitable to new times, and the variable conditions of men and of society, cannot be altered. Indeed, if any form could have been devised which would, on the whole, have been so perfectly adapted to human nature as universally and always to promote pure, spiritual worship, our Lord and his Apostles would not have been likely to leave it unwritten and unknown. The omission is clearly intentional, that the Church might be free.* Moreover, if the clergy are competent for any thing, for their office, to preach, why not to pray? If they can be left to teach the people of God, why not to lead their devotions, free to adapt sermon, and prayer, and reading of Scripture to the occasion?

The liturgies of the Church, the written prayers of her fathers and saints, are a rich and blessed legacy, a fund of spiritual impulse and instruction. They can be used freely, wisely, as all other productions of good men. The clergy need to draw from them. But when they are enforced upon the church, and men are obliged to pray after fixed forms, and by a rubric, then there is an assumption of power, an invasion of Christian liberty somewhere, which belongs to none under Christ himself. Neither are they all so scriptural, pure, and edifying. They come from darker ages, and are mixed with much which an enlightened spirit must discriminate or refuse. They were adopted because so many of the clergy were unfit to perform religious worship without a book. The English liturgy, which is one of the best, is an expurgated edition of the Romish missals and breviaries, accommodated to the controversies and half-reformed prejudices of the times of Henry VIII. To use it, to use all liturgies in a wise Christian liberty, is one thing; but to be obliged

---

* "These omissions present a complete moral demonstration that the apostles and their followers must have been supernaturally withheld from recording a great part of the institutions and regulations which must, in point of fact, have proceeded from them—withheld on purpose that other churches, in other ages and regions, might not be led to consider themselves bound to adhere to certain formularies, customs, and rules, that were of local and temporary appointment; but might be left to their own discretion in matters in which it seemed best to Divine wisdom that they should be so left."—*Whately, Kingdom of Christ*, d. 29, Am. Ed.

to use it, and every syllable of it with slavish repetition, is quite different and not reasonable at all.

The tendencies and dangers and effects of ritual worship are not to be disregarded. The tendency, under the simplest form, is to stop in it, and make that worship; to rest and be satisfied with the outward observance, with keeping a day sacred, and going to a place, and even saying words of worship, without gathering and girding up the mind to think, to embrace the truth, to wrestle with the Invisible and Eternal. And this tendency, so natural, so strong, the less spiritual, the more carnal the mind, is of course and inevitably aggravated as forms are multiplied, as they are more elaborate, attractive, impressive. It is a tendency not only to vitiate the purity and sincerity of worship, but to make the religious character of a people superficial and shallow. This is the *tendency*, not always the result. When religion is a matter of costume and etiquette and ceremonial, it loses dignity and manliness, as it will be likely to lose its nobler and holier qualities. This is history. The Roman Church has carried out to the last and worst results this tendency, and shown, for the warning of all who love the substance rather than the form, to whom religion is not a social appearance, but the life and power of God in the soul, that spirituality is kept only by simplicity, that when the mind of a people is tickled by parades and not fed with truth, and so much of its worship is trivial and gaudy, instead of being an exercise of thought, then it lacks vigor and manly tone, as well as the highest spiritual force. And all ritualism travels the same road, though it may not go so far, and is liable to corrupt simplicity, and enfeeble religious earnestness, and have the same effect that attention to surfaces and shows instead of realities has in every thing else.

Church Worship.

Simple, unritual, spiritual worship belongs to an advanced stage of thought and character, to the intellectual and spiritual manhood of the race. Pictures and pageants are for children; men put away childish things. As general education prevails, society drops, in courts, in assemblies, in social life, the elaborate ceremonials, the stately etiquette, the outward and gaudy show of earlier and less intelligent times, when such things had their significance and use. The pageants of chivalry disappear with a more mature civilization. And why keep them in the Church after they are dropped elsewhere?

It is claimed, that taking men as they are, human nature as it is, a simple, naked, austere worship, will not affect them; that as it was with the Jews, so always on account of the hardness of men's hearts, to accommodate the low, unspiritual nature, there must be a ritual of outward pomp, such as will captivate the senses and the imagination; that with the mass of men, with their inert minds, art is necessary, something besides simple truth, prayers made for them, symbols to impress them, outward helps and incentives. But is the race to be kept in childish ways forever? To make the young bird fly, throw it into the air, let it use its wings and help itself. A religion of forms, invented to attract men by display, because simple truth has not enough power, will keep them in intellectual infancy, and suppress when it ought to stimulate. The form will hide the truth rather than reveal it. Like the pagan's idol, it will take the place of God.

A simple, free, unritual worship belongs to American society, and is most congruous with our republican spirit, with the liberty which is the animating breath of our institutions, with the habits and life of a people brought up as we have been. We have cast away the old clothes of darker ages, and of the life of prescription across the sea. Society here takes a new form and a freer life.

"Here the free spirit of mankind at length casts its last fetters off."

Why need it retain the rituals congruous to monarchical institutions, which were born of the union and subjection of the church and the state, and put religion into moulds cast for it in times less enlightened, and among people driven and led by rulers, by kings, and bishops, instead of allowing it the freedom and simplicity of our popular institutions, which is the spirit of the gospel itself? The people abroad grow weary of it, and groan being burdened. They sigh for this free air, where religion is not a prescription, but the belief of the voluntary and enfranchised soul. Shall we now turn back, and desire the yoke of bondage? Rather let our religion be like our government, our education, our popular life. Let it be free to cast itself into its own shapes; let its worship be simple, unpretending, fresh with the breath of the present hour, unhampered by tradition, unencumbered with formalities.

To the Church, then, is intrusted this sublime and holy function of worship; and to it also, is committed the unspeakable responsibility of making it worthy, consonant with the gospel, acceptable to God, effective for its divine ends, of keeping it uncorrupt, free, spiritual.

To us, my brethren, according to the light we have, it is given in our day to stand for its liberty, simplicity, and spirituality. Men will, as always, run after a gaudy and taking style of religious manifestation. Causes are at work in our society to draw certain classes of mind after a worship more imposing and ceremonious than that we have received of our fathers, and learned of Christ. Let us hold fast the profession of our faith without wavering. "We are the circumcision, which worship God in the spirit and rejoice in Christ Jesus, and have no confidence in the flesh."

Be not alarmed or discouraged at temporary recessions towards formalism; as if time were turned back towards its immature and childish beginnings; as if mankind were not prepared for higher spiritual attainments, and must be kept under a Judaic discipline. Be not ashamed of the simple, plain way in which we worship God, nor think it best to win men by even doubtful measures, or a more dramatic and taking style of Sunday service. Better that men stay away than come to receive stones for bread, or fall under influences false and corrupting to their faith. Do not be afraid that the people will run away from you, and therefore try gilded baits to lure them. Truth has a long run and will win in the end, only hold it fast. It will work itself clear, and show at last that it needs no adventitious adorning, nothing purer, more beautiful, mightier than itself. It will justify itself and you, only be faithful and patient, and hold it in love. Having begun in the spirit, it is not for us to be made perfect by the flesh. After we have known God, or rather are known of God, why turn back to weak and beggarly elements whose use is gone, whose use is bondage?

The style of worship in all the unliturgical churches might be much improved. That is sure. The same thought is not given to the prayers as to the sermon, and therefore, the worship becomes secondary, an unwritten liturgy by repetition. The singing is apt to be too fine and artistic by contrast, while the rest of the service is careless, low, not tuned to the loftiest strain. The congregation is left passive, and the poor preacher has the hard task of playing upon them by his single hand to draw out their emotion, without the accessories of pictured walls, and dim religious lights, and the sensuous appliances of ritualism. It seems as if the Scriptures were more intelligibly read by one man to the congregation, than for the whole congregation to be repeating them together, some in whisper and mumble, some high, some low; now the minister, a verse which is heard, now the congregation, a verse which is not heard. But yet if the congregation could have some part more positive than hearing, it would seem to be of advantage. Giving the service of song to them is right in theory, and ought to be made impressive in practice. There is room for improvement in all the externals of our worship. But it is a purer, larger, warmer religious spirit and life which after all is the greatest improvement, making itself felt as a cleaner, brisker, milder atmosphere does, the nobler feeling making for itself a nobler form, rather illuminating, consecrating, vivifying any form. Without that, the simplest form, the holiest rite, is dead, being alone. It is the letter which killeth, the spirit giveth life. Whether is greater the gold, or the temple that sanctifieth the gold? the day, the house, the music, the posture, the congregation, or the reverence, the faith, the aspiration, the communion with God, which makes here or there, any place the house of God, the gate of heaven?

XIV.

BAPTIST CHURCH HISTORY.

By REV. R. J. W. BUCKLAND,
Pastor of Calvary Baptist Church, New York.

"CALL TO REMEMBRANCE THE FORMER DAYS."—*Hebrews* x. 32.

THE events of the past do not become history by being simply recorded. Characters that have filled their day with excitement, are only men of straw, their garbs of greatness, but stuffed stage gear; the scenes of their lives, but painted stage scenery; their toils and sufferings, only an idle show; unless they take hold on men's hearts in all time, and teach us how to live and die, to be heroic, to be Christian now. When this is done, the narrative of the past becomes history. It has a philosophy. It has an immortal life in it. It has power upon the hearts of men, that cannot die.

Even the word of God, if it were merely a record of past events, would be powerless; but it proves itself to be the inspiration of the Almighty—a living, a divine book—by its undying hold on men's lives, ruling and saving them. Church history ought to stand next to the divine word in this living control of the human heart; but instead, it is acknowledged to be far below mere secular history, in interest and power. And the reason is plain. The true key of church history has not been found, and hence its living power has not been experienced.

It has been written as the dry annals of the dead past. It has been written in behalf of a worldly hierarchy. It has been written on the theory that the prevalent is of necessity the true; and on the principle of development, which leaves the faith once delivered to the saints far behind, as an embryo state. But it has not been written as the history of a life and faith and church completely set forth in the New Testament, whose spirit takes living hold on men of every age, surrounding them with its cloud of witnesses and moving them with the power of an endless life. Indeed it could not be so written, because that life has not been rightly discerned in the church—because its constitution has been violated; its order perverted; its faith destroyed; and its two witnesses cast out as dead, and trampled under foot of men.

The splendors of a hierarchy, or the grandeur of a national establishment, or the poison of a traditional dead faith and worldly philosophy, have had controlling influence over the minds of European historians, and have moulded their labors according to such false ideas of the historic plan. They have built one upon another, and not upon the only foundation which was laid by Christ. They have tested their building, stage after stage, by these models, and not by the open word and pattern which Christ gave; and so, despite their great talents, and wonderful labors, they have neither shown us the church of Christ, nor traced its history.

A better hope is kindled in our land and day, because we are far removed from the enslaving trammels of these false principles; because God's two witnessing Testaments have arisen to new life; and because his church, coming nearer to her promised land, can better look back over all her journey through the wilderness. Already a new influence is felt both by the European scholar who comes to our shores, and by him who has been nurtured in the air of civil and religious liberty. The time seems to have come when the history of God's church can be written in the light of God's word.

With that word open before us as our guide, our pattern, and our law, in this great realm of study, two questions only will occupy us in the present discourse;—Have Baptists a history? and if so, What, in its briefest outline, is that history?

I. HAVE BAPTISTS A HISTORY?

Prejudice and passion have always answered No. Historians, whose names and works fill a large space in the eyes of the world, have concealed their distinctive principles, when to name them would give them praise; and have held them up to the gaze of men, when dishonor and shame could be attached to them. They have thrust them aside into the purlieu of heresies and sects; ascribed their origin to fanatics; traced their lineage by commotions and uproars. They make them the offspring of darkness and the pit; their growth, the mushroom of the night; their principles, the dreams of wild enthusiasts; their forefathers, unlettered visionaries and madmen. Thus they have been "made as the filth of the world, the offscouring of all things unto this day." There is hardly a conceivable crime against God or man which has not at some period been affixed to them. Holding those fundamental truths which, like their Divine Leader, are holy, harmless, and undefiled, they have been accused of all uncleanness and lasciviousness. Worshiping the Lord in the beauty of holiness, they, like him, have been branded with blasphemy. Exemplifying the meekness of unresisting piety, and uncomplaining suffering, and going forth on missions of peace and love, bearing the pure light of civil and religious liberty through the dark night of the past, they have been characterized as arrogant and lawless; the subverters of all government; the destroyers of public peace; the foes of human society; the very apostles of unbridled anarchy, lust, and crime.

From the time when Christ walked the earth, down to the present, there has not been a period in which they have not suffered persecution. From the age of John the Baptist to the massacre in Jamaica, bigoted religionists and governments have not ceased first to slaughter, and then to slander them. The mightiest powers on earth have expended their strength to crush them; but, prostrated beneath the heel of tyrants, they have been a spectacle worthy of angels and men. The haughtiest hierarchy the world has known, commanding the resources of subservient kings, has endeavored to uproot them from the face of the earth; but they have lived and multiplied under its anathemas. Its whirlwinds of hate have only scattered them as the seed of the kingdom; and they have sprung up far and wide anew, to exhaust its malice and power. Calvinists, Lutherans, and Papists, have alike abhorred them, burned them, cursed them. All three have left their mutual contentions, and leagued together to destroy them.*

Through a great part of history, their existence, principles and numbers, are known to us only by the testimony of their foes. Every writing of their own has been assiduously destroyed. It was the aim of

---

* Mosheim's Ch. Hist. part ii. ch. 4, § 8.

their adversaries to utterly blot out their name from under heaven. Their record has been literally on high.

Can such a people have a history? The materials of it, through the papal night, must be drawn from the writings of their enemies against them. Fragment by fragment, it is culled from the controversies of doctors, the decrees of councils, the anathemas of Popes, the records of the Inquisition, the death sentence of civil tribunals. It is read by the light of the fagots that consumed them.

And so a place in history is given them by such witnesses, but by no means A HISTORY.

Others would not give them even a place. While embittered enemies perpetuate their name and their faith, others, following the milder principle of Fleury,* who would pass in silence and bury in oblivion that which mars the smooth career of the Romish Church, lest the statement of false opinions should contribute to perpetuate them, have quietly ignored them; and as Charles the Fifth buried Baptists alive in the Netherlands, so have these tried to bury Baptist history alive. But it rises again, and confronts them at history's judgment seat, the bar of impartial posterity.

Rome, with all her bitterness, proves in this less unkind, and with all her bigotry, more honest than many modern writers, who claim to be loving, impartial, and evangelical. Her writers state the tenets of our forefathers while they condemn them; but many Protestant historians make such partial and perverted statements as conceal our distinctive principles: or, if the Baptist Church is admitted into their family of churches, it is regarded as the base-born child of shame.

Such obloquies have too long had their influence on

---

*Fleury, Premier Discours, ₰ 5.

the Christian world. We fear they are having influence on writers of our own, and even leading them to concede that Baptists have no place in the great history of the church, except only in modern times.

Such concessions can never be allowed. We cannot accept a place in the catalogue of sects, or broken schismatical fragments of God's church; nor can we give up our part in the glorious past, and settle down contented among the denominations that have arisen in modern times.

We claim not only a place in history, but *A History*, A History of the Church of God.

Holding to the faith once delivered to the saints, to the word of God and the law of Christ as our sheet anchor, we claim that when the History of the Church shall be written in the light of God's word, it will be, in the noblest and truest sense, our history. There has been great error, in tracing the lineage of our faith simply as a sect or division, running parallel with general church history, through all ages. While much truth has thus been reached, this method falls short of reaching the whole truth. We are by no means to apply the secular idea of historic descent to the church of God. It is perpetuated not in a natural lineage. It descends, not from father to son through human generation, but from faithful soul to faithful, by a divine affiliation. And this, too, in such a way that each draws his life, not from those who have gone before him, but each in a higher, truer sense, directly from Christ alone. In a sense, all God's children are truly autochthonous. None are their fathers on earth, they are all brethren. And so the links of their history are not human but Divine. Their perpetuation from age to age has been of grace and of God. The golden line that runs through all the ages is the one Lord, one Faith, one Baptism. That which gives them unity and identity is not parentage, or race, or place, connecting them with the faithful before them; but the Faith once delivered to the saints.

Have Baptists then a history?

I answer—if the Faith once delivered to the saints has a perpetuity and a history, so that the gates of hell, however they have seemed to prevail, yet have not prevailed against it—then Baptists, who make that Faith their law, have a history.

If a people holding from age to age these fundamental doctrines—that the Bible is the supreme law of Christians; that personal faith in Christ gives salvation; that baptism in water is the covenant of a believer with his Saviour; while infant baptism, and all other commandments of men, are not to rule Christ's followers; if such a people are Baptists, then Baptists have a history.

If the principle of Vincentius—*quod semper, quod ubique, quod ab omnibus*—is correct, and that doctrine which has been held always, everywhere, and by all, is vindicated as truth in history, then are the principles of Baptists the great principles of history. For all acknowledge that this maxim is not to be taken of the whole body of belief, but of that which is fundamental; not of the prevalent, but of the underlying, the unchanging, and unchangeable.* And a personal faith in the Lord Jesus gives salvation—all ages of church history being the judges. The baptism of a believer in water is obedience to Christ's law; the gathering of baptized believers together in church relations, to be ruled by the word of God, and to maintain Christ's ordinances, is his command—all ages of church history being the judges.

---

* Stanley, Eastern Church, p. 69.

A people holding such principles, so far from being unhistorical, must be recognized as resting on the fundamental principles of historic truth.

Oftentimes they have been a remnant, but so was God's Israel of old. Oftentimes they have been left alone in the earth, while the dominant and the prevalent faith of the world was all against them, but so were God's churches in the days of Elijah.

Oftentimes they have been a hidden people; but so was God's church when driven in prophetic vision into the wilderness. And so they have a history, the word of God being judge.

It is the history of the Church of God, in the light of those great principles which were made essential to it in the New Testament, its charter and constitution.

It is the history of the church as Jesus Christ organized and completed it, and gave it, by his Holy Spirit, an undying vitality, and an incorruptible character, to leaven and change all ages, but not to be changed by them. It is the history of the New Testament faith, and life, and law, and power; and of those who maintained these; embracing the perversion of these, and the consequences of such perversion; the perpetuation of these, and the Divine might which perpetuated them; the triumph of these, and of the people who triumphed through them.

II. WHAT IN ITS BRIEFEST OUTLINE IS BAPTIST CHURCH HISTORY?

The New Testament law gives us the constitution of the church complete and perfect, and the New Testament prophecies give us the outline of its entire career. From that divine foundation we cannot turn aside. If we should, we must accept the authority of a traditional faith, and a worldly development; and we should find ourselves resting on the grand principle of the papal church, while all its errors would follow in logical order; or, rebelling against papal authority without the word of God to guide us, we must yield to the spirit of a worldly philosophy, and be led into the waste of scepticism, rationalism, and moral death.

Between these two issues choice must be made. Adopting God's word for our law, we have the Baptist Church and its history. Adopting the authority of human tradition, we have the Church of Rome and its history, with its inevitable reaction from absolutism into rationalism.

No other alternative is left us.

To God's word then we turn, and learn the founding and organizing of that body of Christ, whose history through the ages is to be the fullness of him who filleth all in all. The New Testament gives us the church complete. The stone cut out of the mountain without hands, needs no modern workman's tool to add an after-finish of higher beauty. The New Covenant, written in the hearts of a people who are each personally taught of God, and have each a living faith, and who, from the least of them to the greatest, all know the Lord, has been once divinely sealed, and no man need amend or improve it. Surely it is enough to make this our model, and live and walk and act in Christ's church, as he himself lived and taught with his apostles. If not, who will show us a more excellent way?

1. *The first or formative period of Church History is that of the Apostolic Church.*

In this, Christ is the central figure, its head and life and light. In his advent, the fullness of time was come, and the kingdom of heaven set up. By him, the nucleus of the church was gathered and fed and taught. Its laws and ordinances were given it by himself. By his atoning blood, he cemented its structure, and fixed its foundations deep on the everlasting love and purpose of God.

The spiritual power which should be its means of growth was imparted to it by him; and all its order and symmetry were unfolded by inspired apostles, guided by the Holy Spirit, so that when the labors of the apostles were ended, Christ's church was complete in every essential requirement for all time. Then he sealed up its divine charter, never to be added to nor taken from, and sent it forth upon its earthly mission. And no age nor exigency has shown the need of a new feature in its constitution, or shape, or spirit, which the church had not when the volume of inspiration closed. Thus the history of the Apostolic Church is, in no true sense, rudimentary or incomplete, and after ages have added literally nothing to the church, except that, by its own inherent living, power, and growth, it spreads more and more widely to fill the world.

This apostolic period shows us, in the life and labors of Christ and his apostles, the source and organic development of the church: in their teachings and writings, its inner life, and the development of its doctrine; while lastly, in their prophecies, we have given to us the errors and corruptions which should assail it, and an outline of those mighty events which were to mark its progress through time, and a glimpse of the glories to which it should at last arrive.

Was the Apostolic Church Baptist?

I reply that as regards modern names, sects, and divisions, there were none. Christ's seamless mantle had not yet been rent in twain. But the reality of a perfect Baptist church was there; and ever since have our churches made it their pattern, and their first obligation is to conform to this God-given ensample.

* * * * * * *

Every church planted by the apostles was such, and the Christian world knew none beside.

As we leave this glorious period, and look forward over the lapse of time, we see three remaining periods of history delineated in the New Testament prophecy. The Church of God—the woman clothed with the sun—flees into the wilderness to escape from her great enemy.* For twelve hundred and sixty prophetic days,† she remains hidden in the wilderness and persecuted; and for the same length of time, God's two witnesses,‡ the sacred Scriptures, either prophesy in sackcloth, or lie slain in the streets of the Mystic Babylon, while Antichrist triumphs. At last the two witnessing Testaments rise filled with the spirit and power of God, and are exalted to the highest dominion and glory;§ and the church comes up out of the wilderness; while the kingdoms of this world are given to the Son of Man. Thus prophecy shows us, as the second period, the church driven into the wilderness; as the third, the church hidden in the wilderness; and as the fourth, the church coming up out of the wilderness.

2. The second period, or that following the Apostolic, is one of trial and suffering, and also of corruption and decay. Its thorough understanding is of unspeakable importance.

The Christian faith had been widely spread; churches of believers gathered in the chief cities of the Roman empire, and above all in Rome itself, before the imperial power was turned against the rising superstition. As early as A. D. 45 or 50, there is good proof that Chris-

---

* Rev. xii. 6-14.   † Rev. xii. 14.   ‡ Rev. xi. 3-8.   § Rev. xi. 11.

tianity reached the shores of Britain.* There it flourished longer in purity than elsewhere. Each church was an independent Cor,† or congregation; its authority lay, not in the pastor, but in the body;‡ a holy membership was sought; no trace of infant baptism can be found, but the streams of England were consecrated by the burial in them of believers in the likeness of the Saviour's death. These characteristics of the British churches were not wholly lost until they were driven in the western mountains by the Saxons.

In the Roman empire generally, persecution soon began. Then, as related by Pliny and Justin Martyr, Christians met together on the Lord's Day at dawn, in secluded places, for worship, praise, and prayer,§ covenanting with each other to live in meekness and holiness, and gathering around the Lord's table in a brotherhood of love. Those who came to join with them were taken after prayer and fasting to a place where there was water, and baptized.‖ Each church regulated its own affairs as an independent body; each chose its own bishop, or pastor, and deacons. Its members were all believers, giving evidence of a holy life.

The young and unconverted were taught as catechumens, waiting for evidence of faith before putting on Christ in baptism. All the Christian world was Baptist, one wide brotherhood of believers. As early as the death of John, the beloved disciple, Christianity had spread from the cities to the villages, from the villages to the hamlets and farm-houses of the country. Heathen tem-

---

* Gildas refers to Tiberius Claudius of Stillingfleet, Orig. Brit. and the Triads.
† Nennius, edit. by Giles, Pref. p. 24, note.
‡ Bede Eccles. Hist. Bk. ii., ch. 2.
§ Justin Mar. Apol. ‖ C Plinius Trajano, Ep. xcvi.

ples were deserted, and multitudes of all classes turned to Christ.*

Two things especially awakened persecution; the clamors of heathen priests whose sacrifices were deserted, and the uncompromising faithfulness of believers. Had Christians temporized, had they recognized the heathen worship, while holding their own, there would have been no persecutions. Their firmness caused their faith to be styled a depraved superstition and inflexible obstinacy. "This brought," said Julian, "the execration of the world upon them, and aroused the hatred of the priests and populace." If any evil occurred, in city or country, by land or sea, it was ascribed to them; if flood or fire, famine, plague, or earthquake came, the blame was laid on them, and the people clamored for their blood.† They met death with inconceivable courage and joy; they went in triumph to the wild beasts and the fires. When they might escape by silence, they avowed themselves Christians; when their numbers would have overawed persecutors, they refused to resist, but died, like Christ, praying for their enemies.

Persecution promoted piety and spread the faith. But when, afterward, it ceased, or men avoided it, evils came in—degeneracy and decay.

Let us trace this dark history of decay.

The New Testament prophecies flow in one grand channel, and their burden is the fortune of God's church. They dwell upon corruptions and apostacies. False prophets must arise; love wax cold; offence, hatred, and betrayal come. Wolves were to invade the fold; antichrists to come; and the mystery of iniquity to rise in the church. False teachers, covetous, boasters, lords over God's heritage, were to bring in dam-

---

* Plin. Epis. 96. † Tertullian, Apology.

nable heresies, hypocrisy, formality, envy, and strife. Fables and traditions were to usurp the place of God's word; celibacy and fastings to be enjoined; until the church should lose her spirituality and incur the frown of God. The woman, through the fear of persecution, flees into the wilderness, a waste moral desert, a state of drought and decay of spirituality—the same wilderness in which, afterward, the harlot Rome is seen to arise with apostate glories. Here is where the stream of Baptist history is first checked, and much of its life and power lost, flowing down into the stagnant morass of papacy. All the evils of the Romish apostacy, all the errors of the Christian world, came first by repeated corruptions of the faith of Baptist churches. Men turned aside from it, and step by step went into apostacy; men added to it, and so built up a worldly hierarchy. All this was done by forsaking the faith and order of God's church, as the New Testament teaches it, and as Baptists hold it. The steps of that progress are many and plain, and began even in the days of the apostles. Persecution checked them; but when it was removed, the evils abounded. To trace them, or even to indicate them all, would exceed the limits of this discourse.

Among them must be named the chief. And first—not in time, but in influence—was the baptism of babes. The steps of its rise were these: as baptism was the profession of a new life, it came to be regarded as imparting a new life itself, and was held to be a saving ordinance. Hence, many believed that their children would perish unless they were baptized, and sought it for them. This drew forth the rebuke of Tertullian. But, in an after age, the doctrine of original sin was so held as to doom babes to eternal death; and Augustine, pressing this theory, demanded that all infants must be baptized, else they would burn with the devil in eternal fire.* Such was the logical ground for the practice. But, were the churches in his day pedobaptist? Let facts answer. Not a writer of that day, whose name has come down to us, was baptized in infancy. Augustine, Paulinus, Jerome, Ambrose, Martin, Severus, Gregory, all were baptized in mature years on profession of faith. Besides, the order of Catechumens, embracing the unbaptized youth, still existed in full force. Infant baptism existed, but was not prevalent, and Augustine would make it so. Here begins that departure from a living faith, which has blighted God's church ever since.

Previous to this, Christian life decayed. Men temporized with their persecutors, while others protested against it; and thus a division arose; the Donatists demanded a faithful, spiritual church membership, and would not commune with the time-serving and worldly party, which was most numerous. In reply it was argued that the Catholic Church was one outward body, into which all must come or be lost. From this arose the germs of the papacy, and the supremacy of Rome. When argument failed, force was used, and the civil power was employed to compel the pure-minded to conform to a worldly church. Augustine demanded that those who would not, should be persecuted, banished and slain.† Thus were planted the germs of the papal tyranny and the Inquisition. At the same time, the haughtiness of human authority was asserted over the faith of Christians. Humble piety was despised. Aristotle's philosophy was more valued than Christ's teaching. Mighty doctors lorded it over God's heritage, not caring for the flock, and prostituted their powers in

---

* Augustine, Op. Imp. iii. 199; Wiggers, August. and Pelag., p. 74.

† Wiggers, August. and Pelag., p. 34, note. Esist. ad Vincen pium Epist. ad Bonifac. 185.

bitter debate, and advocacy of fasts, vigils, asceticism, and superstition.* With the influence of great names, came in the dominion of bishops, and the civil authority was used for building and ruling the church. The pagan population was turned to Christianity by engrafting heathen ceremonies upon Christian ordinances, and the church made one vast compromise with heathenism.

Thus, by steps like these, did God's church, with all her external grandeur, go into the wilderness, and the eye of the historian sees little but a waste of spiritual decay and death. Where then was the line of Baptist history? Not in any one pure church. Here was the wreck of Baptist churches everywhere. But had not God foretold that it should be so? The history of the Baptist faith embraces that of an apostacy, and of the rise of Antichrist. A pure faith is to be discerned only in its vestiges and scattered fragments. Under the gilded rubbish an holy people are yet to be found. In Africa, the barbarian invasion swept away the power of a worldly church, but humble Christian bodies abounded and flourished. In the Alps and Pyrenees, humble, faithful churches abounded.† Sweeping across central Europe, went a tide which left Christ's lowly followers to live in peace. Baptism was still the burial of a believer in water in likeness of Christ's death. Though sprinkling had arisen, it never prevailed. Congregations of believers, rejecting infant baptism, and worldly authority, still met as of old, drawing their faith and life from Christ's word and Spirit. But they were scattered fragments of the wreck, mostly hidden from the eye of man.

---

* Hieron, Epist. Cont. Vigilantium Gillies' Vigilantius.
† Peyrat, Hist. de Vigilance, ch. vi. Allix, Chs. of Piedmont, passim.

3. The third period is that of the Church in the wilderness, hidden from the face of the Serpent:—the remnant of God's seed.

Rome throws out the taunting challenge; "where was your church before Luther?" She was where God said she would be—where his chosen ones were in the days of Elijah. Now, as then, God had reserved to himself a seed, a remnant,* a lineage of faith. The light had not utterly gone out, nor the gates of hell wholly prevailed, though to human judgment it might seem so. But so it seemed in his day, to Elijah; so it seemed in the Babylonian captivity; so it seemed to the disciples, when their Lord was crucified.

The northern invasion sweeping over the Roman Empire caused a long age of confusion and change; but there were those widely scattered in the East and the West, who held to the faith and word of Christ, practicing his ordinances and rejecting the commandments of men; and after ages were destined to bring them to light. The rise of the Paulicians shows a biblical faith in the East.† In the West, the Welsh were driven into their mountains, there to preserve for ages a distinct faith.

The followers of Vigilantius and Jovinian thronged the valleys of the Pyrenees and Alps;‡ and while such men as Paulinus and Claude of Turin spoke aloud there were thousands to whom and for whom they spoke.§ Thousands were driven by persecution from the valleys of Italy into France, who rejected the teachings of Rome and the baptism of infants, and held the word of God to be their only guide.‖

---

* Rev. xii. 17.   † Neander's Ch. Hist. vol. iii. pp. 245, 247, et. seq.
‡ Gilly's Vigilantius, p. 480 et seq.
§ Biblioth Patr. Paris, 1624, vol. iv. pp. 197, 538.
‖ Jones' Ch. Hist. vol. i. p. 430.

It was in sympathy with these Christians that Berengarius wrote and taught. If he was not himself free from the trammels of Rome, those who by thousands held his sentiments were so: and all Normandy was aroused to spiritual life, and filled with Christians holding evangelical doctrines.* They penetrated Germany, and went in the train of William the Conqueror to England, where they found a voice in Piers Plowman, Chaucer and Wickliffe. The same doctrines had utterance in Arnold of Brescia.†

The people holding the same faith appeared at Cologne in 1140,‡ and it was there discovered that they existed in great numbers through Germany, Flanders, France, Savoy, and Lombardy, claiming a distinct history back to the pure days of the church,§ and a dissemination in all countries. Their lives were conceded by their enemies to be honest and pure, and their faith Christian. They made the Bible their only guide, denied infant baptism, and practiced that of believers upon profession of faith in Christ, and maintained congregational church government. Manichean sentiments have been ascribed to them, for such were widely disseminated, but it can be plainly shown that their doctrines were directly antagonistic to those tenets.

It was among this people that Peter de Bruys arose,‖ who preached a long time, converting thousands, and teaching immersion in water upon a profession of faith; rejecting infant baptism and holding the Bible to be the

---

* Allix, Chs. of Piedmont, p. 102-110. Jones' Ch. Hist. vol. i. p. 474. Neander, vol. iii. p. 600.

† Biblioth Max. Patr. Lugdu. vol. xviii. p. 437. p. 441. Allix, Albigenses, p. 133.

‡ Neander, vol. iv. p. 149, et seq.

§ Allix, Piedmont, ch. xvi. Epist. Evervini. Jones' Ch. Hist. vol. i. pp. 479-486.

‖ Neander, vol. iv. p. 595.

law of Christ's church. Following Peter came Henry of Tholouse,* his disciple, preaching the same Baptist faith. Baptist churches were multiplying everywhere under his labors in the south of France, until Rome seemed to have lost her hold upon that region.† Perhaps there were as many evangelical Baptist Christians then in that country as in the same extent of territory in our land to-day. It was in this same lineage of faith that Waldo‡ arose about 1160. He caused the Bible to be translated into the language of the people, and went forth to scatter it and proclaim its truths. Persecuted and hunted, he passed with many of his followers into Picardy, thence through Flanders and Germany to Bohemia, where he died, after disseminating God's truth over a great part of Europe. At the same time, spreading along the Alpine valleys, through Lombardy and the Tyrol, the Waldenses reached Bulgaria and Hungary. Here their colonies rested, and their numbers increased to eighty thousand in Bohemia alone. They rejected infant baptism,§ immersed believers, and made God's word their sole authority.‖ Their confessions from the earliest times make the ordinances to belong to believers only, reject all which does not agree with the word of God, and place baptism after a profession of faith and a change of life.¶ Their great treatise against Antichrist, says: "Antichrist teaches to baptize children into the faith, and attributes to this the work of regeneration; thus confounding the work of the Holy Spirit with the external rite of baptism; and on this,

---

* Neander, vol. iv. p. 598.
† Bernard, Epist. 241. Serm. lxv., in Cant. Orchard's Bapt. Hist. p. 188.
‡ Neander, vol. iv. p. 606.
§ Treatise on Antichrist. Also Grassern Waldensian Chronicle, p. 87.
‖ Allix, Piedmont, p. 206. Neander, vol. iv. p. 611.
¶ Morland, Chs. of Piedmont p. 30, *et. al.* Sleidan, book xvi. Jones Church History, vol. ii. p. 52.

grounds all his Christianity."* This treatise is claimed to have been written by that eminent Baptist, Peter de Bruys, and the testimony of impartial scholars is, that these Albigenses and Waldenses, who can never be distinguished from each other, resembled most closely the Baptists of a later day.† As to their numbers, it may be said that central Europe was full of them. They could travel through Germany and Lombardy, and find a lodging each night with their own brethren.‡

Such was the hidden Baptist church. Such, after the woman fled into the wilderness, was the remnant of her seed that remained, which kept the commandments of God, and had the testimony of Jesus, against whom the dragon made war.

Such is our lineage. Errors unquestionably there were, diversities and mistakes, but these pertain to every age and every opinion held by man. Yet it is impossible to see the remarkable unity of faith, in different lands and times, without acknowledging that it must have come from one source—the Bible. The great struggle of God's people was toward the New Testament faith as Baptists hold it. Baptist principles moved the hearts of all these Christians, and were held, more or less purely, by thousands, who lived and died in them and for them.

4. We come now to the fourth period, when God's church was to come up out of the wilderness: when the two witnessing Testaments were to be exalted to universal honor and power. It comprises a period of the

---

* Leger Waldenses Gesch. p. 189.

† Ypei and Dermont quoted in Orchard, Hist. of Bap. Introd. p. 17. Mosheim, Ch. Hist. Part ii. ch. iii. § 1. Limborch, Hist. of Inquisition, vol. i. ch. viii.

‡ Perrin's Hist. des Vaudois, bk. ii. ch. xi. Jones, vol. ii. p. 157–163.

birth throes of a new awakening to spiritual life, with bitter agony and long travail; and a period of liberty and gospel triumph which is still widening with the power of the Bible over all the earth.

It is, from Luther's time to the present, one great struggle toward the principles of Baptists, and an increasing acknowledgment and adoption of them as the soul and life of evangelical religion.

Let us survey the field. No controversy had arisen or was yet to arise about immersion. And with reason. Immersion was regarded as the natural and proper administration of Baptism. The Church of Rome, while approving sprinkling, still always taught immersion. It was never denied, nor did it attract attention when practiced by heretics. Thomas Aquinas had set it forth in his Summa as the normal rite. The Gregorian decretals, the canon law of the church, did the same. The reformers in their confessions did the same. Hence we need look for no controversy upon this now distinctive practice, in the ages before the Reformation, nor to any extent during its progress.

We have seen that Germany was leavened with Waldensian Baptist sentiments up to the days of Luther.* Bohemia held thousands of Picards—cave dwellers, who, according to Theobald, were Anabaptists,† and whose confession of faith, held long before Luther's day, was Baptist.‡ Wickcliffe taught the same opinions, and many of the Lollards held Baptist principles.

Luther's first power was in appealing to the word of God alone: his own grand doctrine, Justification by faith alone: these had been held by thousands before

---

* Of Luther's Epist. ad Waldenses.' De Bussierre, Introd. p. 22.
† E. M. Plarii, Epideigma, p. 30. Sliedan lib. iii. p. 68.
‡ Schomanni Testamentum.

him. When he asserted, in his treatise on Liberty, that "a Christian man is lord of all things, and in subjection to none," he spoke the truth which humble Baptists had rejoiced in for ages; and thousands of hearts instantly responded at once. Those who had longed for the utterance of such truth in high places, hailed his appearing and flocked to him at Wittemburg. Among these were men from Zwickau,* who had proclaimed the same truths more clearly, upon the basis of God's word, and who longed to have them united in by all. But the impetuous monk could not tolerate those who would go further than himself, and they were unsuccessful with Luther, yet found men of equal learning with him, who adopted their doctrines.† They left Wittemburg, some to seek in Bohemia those Picards who were prepared for the faith, and others to proclaim it in the valleys of Switzerland and the Tyrol, the haunt of Waldenses for ages past. Thousands were gathered into churches in Silesia and Bohemia by Nicholas Storck, Hutter, and Gabriel Scherding;‡ great numbers, under Stubner and others in the Alpine regions. Grebel, Mantz and Hubmeyer arose in Switzerland.§ Grebel was baptized by those who held these principles before him, and in turn baptized many converts himself in the waters of the Rhine. These were by no means ignorant men. Equal to Luther and Zuingle in power and learning, acquainted with the Scriptures in their original tongues, skilled in theology, and honored in the

---

* De Bussierre, Hist. del'Anabaptisme, Introd. p. 10. E. M. Plariis Epideigma, p. 9.

† De Bussierre, Hist. Anabap., Introd. ? 2.

‡ Meshovius, Hist. Anabap. p. 23. Plarius, p. 27. De Bussierre, Introd. p. 26.

§ Meshovius, p. 27.

schools of theology,* they were at least the peers of those who would call them mystics and ecstatics.

The first thing which brought upon them the opprobrium of their enemies was the famous Peasant War—a movement which lacked only success to make it praised, but in which the soundest principles of justice were marred by a wild enthusiasm which came from another source. Munzer, its leader, was never an Anabaptist. He did not agree with them at first in Zwickau,† taught infant baptism long afterwards,‡ and the employment of force in God's cause. These were the sentiments of Luther,§ but contrary to those of the Anabaptists. Later, when his purposes demanded it, Munzer sought to identify himself more closely with Anabaptism, in order to reach the masses of the peasants, who in great numbers held‖ or favored it. But he was never baptized or baptized others.¶ That which was called Anabaptist doctrine in him was simple Millenarianism.** The peaceful Anabaptists held this, and sought it by peaceful means; he held it and sought it by force. Many Anabaptists were led away by his error, followed him, and after his disastrous end, scattered the same doctrine of force; but it was a fundamental departure from the peaceable principles long held by the Anabaptists. Still it was enough to draw down condemnation on them all.

Unable to conquer them by the word of God or by ar-

---

* Meshovius, pp. 27, 46. † De Bussierre, p. 18.
‡ Gebser, Comment. de Primordiis Anabapt. p. 9.
‖ De Bussierre, La Guerre de Paysans, vol. i. p. 305.
§ Lindanus Tabulæ Haereseon.
¶ Bullinger adv. Anabap. p. 2. Gebser Comment. p. 9, note. De Bussierre, Guerre des Paysans, vol. ii. p. 311. Floremund Raemund, lib. ii. ch. i. p. 89.
** De Bussierre, Hist. Anabap. Introd. Sleidan, lib. v. Varillas, Hist. des Revolutions, lib. vi.

gument, the Zurich magistrates employed force. They were imprisoned and tortured to extort confessions and recantations; and when they would not yield, were drowned under the famous sentence—*qui iterum mergit, mergatur*—who plunges again, let him be plunged.*

Then the Baptists met in retired places at midnight, or before the break of day, to worship and baptize. They were called "bathing men and bathing women."† They were charged with "the fanatical delusion of thinking to form a church free from sin," because they received none but believers. While Luther had hanging over his head the brief of Pope Adrian, demanding his death, he dissuaded from persecuting them; but when he was secure in the protection of the German princes, he advocated their destruction by force.‡ The Reformation which he led, was one resting on human authority and arms. Men might leave the Church of Rome, but they must enter that of Luther. There was no liberty in his plan. It was the gospel enforced by the police and the sword.§ The Anabaptists asked for liberty to worship God, and notwithstanding their slaughter by thousands, they held fast to the authority of the word of God alone to rule the soul.

Great numbers of them, in Bohemia and Moravia, following their doctrine of non-resistance, left home and lands to go into banishment for conscience' sake.¶ Poland and the regions about were filled with Baptist sentiments, and dotted with Baptist churches, whose confessions of faith declare immersion to be the only bap-

---

* Meshovius, Hist. Anabap. p. 35.
† Faber adv. Catabapt. Raynald's Baronius, A.D. 1527, § 75.
‡ De Bussierre, Guerre des Paysans, vol. i. p. 305.
§ De Bussierre, Hist. Anabap. Introd. p. 8. Motley, Dutch Republic, vol. i. p. 260.
¶ Plarii Epideigma, p. 27–29.

tism, and believers, holy men and women, to constitute the church of Christ.* Their lineage is perfectly distinct from that of the advocates of force.

These also had many followers; they practiced polygamy in some instances,† and at a later date were wild enthusiasts. They united the worldly principles of Luther as to civil power, with the Millenarian views, and rejection of infant baptism, of the true Baptists. They frequently practiced effusion or sprinkling.‡ These were men destitute of true faith, who set up their visions and dreams above the word of God. Connected in their origin with the peasant war, their influence culminated at length in the reign of Boccold, at Munster, in 1534. This arose from the fancies of Matthison, and drew to itself the elements of disease that abounded in the confusion of the times; but its principles were diametrically opposed to those of the true Anabaptists or the Baptists of that day. It was enough that our forefathers believed in the reign of Christ on earth, to enable their enemies to class them with those who would take his sceptre and set up a kingdom of their own in his name.

And yet the atrocities of Boccold's wild reign have been exaggerated, and were really no greater than those which marked its punishment, and Hortensius, who recorded with horror, the deeds of the Munster Uproar, lived to see, with his own eyes, tenfold greater atrocities inflicted on the Reformed by the Papists, and on the Papists by the Reformed.§

Far removed from this brief turmoil, which quickly

---

* Ludovici Wolzogenii Compendium Relig. Christ. p. 13. Schowmari Testamentum. Mosheim, vol. iv. p. 491.

† De Bussierre, Hist. Anabap. Introd. p. 16. Thuanus, Hist. lib. L., p. 765.

‡ Floremund Raemund, lib. ii. chap. iii. ₴ 5. Hortensius, Oproer der Weder-doopern, p. 20.

§ Motley, Dutch Republic, vol. ii. p. 422.

rose and died away, the peaceful Baptists flourished in secret, in Bohemia, Moravia, and Poland; and afterward, in the Low Countries, they were blessed under the pious labors of Menno, and even grew amid the persecutions of Alva, who slaughtered far more of them than of all the Reformed beside. They were the first of all in heroic devotion to support William of Orange, with their money, and sympathy, and prayers, in his darkest day; and their churches survived the desolations, and rose, with returning peace, to great numbers and strength.

Here, at length, the light of peace, and civil rights and religious liberty dawned upon them. Their leaven had long before entered England, and met the spirit of religious liberty there. English Christians, also banished for conscience' sake, taking refuge in Holland, met them there. History, as it is unfolded, will show more connection between them, and though both the English and the Dutch Baptists arose from the study of God's word, and drew their origin and order directly from it, and so were spiritually without fathers, autochthonous, we may safely hold that the Holland Baptists were their elder brethren and forerunners in the faith of Christ.

Such were the far-famed Anabaptists of the Reformation. They were no more mystics and ecstatics than many Baptists of our own land now. Some of their leaders were slow in reaching true views of baptism, as they came step by step to the truth; but it was a baptism of believers on profession of their faith in Christ. Some unquestionably adopted other scriptural views without that of immersion; but when they rested their whole order and practice on the Bible they came to it as the plain consequence.

This was the birth period of bitter agony in the awakening of God's church to come up out of the wilderness. In it we see a Baptist biblical faith, struggling for utterance and life, underlying the Reformation; and, as expressive of the living principles of the word of God, constituting its soul, and life, and spiritual power.

It was truly said, in that day, that whenever the Reformers would find arguments to conquer Rome, they used those of the Anabaptists; and when they contended with Anabaptists, they were compelled to use the arguments of Rome—the authority of the church, and the established customs and traditions of the past. They could not appeal successfully to the Bible. This inconsistency was again and again urged upon them by Romanists, and it was with truth declared that there is not, there cannot be, any middle ground between the Baptist Faith and the Faith of Rome.

The spiritual power of the Reformation lay wholly in those Scriptural principles which it held in common with us. Its elements of decay and formalism were in those principles which we reject.

In one word, the long struggle of God's church against the overlying dominion of the Papacy has been, up to the present day, a struggle of New Testament Baptist principles for life and power. These made the Reformation, these will complete it. These, in their living hold on men's hearts, have moved, and are now moving the world with the power of a divine life.

The later course of Baptist History is plain. The people who held this faith, once delivered to the saints, have multiplied, have shown it to be of God, have exemplified its excellencies in promoting human welfare, favoring civil liberty, elevating the race, and advancing the cause of Christ. Its power has been demonstrated in the heathen world, turning nations to God; and in lands burdened with a dead formal faith, recreating them with the gospel.

All evangelical Christendom is coming up to the

standard of a biblical Baptist faith, with a rapidity never known before. Errors, against which our fathers contended and died, are passing away, and God's two witnesses are arising to assume the dominion over human faith which God has decreed to them.

May the day soon come, when God's word shall rule one universal church of believing souls, holding to "One Lord, one Faith, one Baptism," and when Jesus shall see the answer to his prayer—"Father, I will that they be one!"

XV.

THE RISE AND DEVELOPMENT OF SECTARIANISM IN CHRISTENDOM.

By WILLIAM HAGUE, D.D.,
Pastor of Shawmut Avenue Baptist Church, Boston, Massachusetts.

"THERE AROSE UP CERTAIN OF THE SECT OF THE PHARISEES WHICH BELIEVED, SAYING, THAT IT WAS NEEDFUL TO CIRCUMCISE THEM AND TO COMMAND THEM TO KEEP THE LAW OF MOSES. AND THE APOSTLES AND ELDERS CAME TOGETHER FOR TO CONSIDER OF THIS MATTER."—*Acts* xv. 5-7.

It has been aptly said by a close observer of the course of history, that every tidal wave of human progress enfolds the latent seeds of some new form of evil. The hour of triumph is ever the starting point of another conflict. If the verification of this sentiment could be set forth by a pen, gifted with a degree of graphical power worthy of the subject, it would trace the footsteps of humanity along the line of its weary march by the wrecks of institutions that had once seemed full of promise, plans of social reconstruction that had been hailed, in their day, as the harbingers of a brighter future. Nevertheless, in spite of these incessant retrogressions and apparent failures, there would be disclosed the working of a mystery of hidden force urging the races forward to the realization of those divinely inspired hopes which were, of old, from the age of Moses to that of Malachi, the life of prophetic song.

The thirty years' church history which lies before us, designated "The Acts of the Apostles," shows that this same remark, which was suggested by a world-wide view of the progress of civilization, is verified by the course of events that signalizes the progress of the Messiah's Kingdom. For, at the beginning of this history, we find that, immediately after the wonders of the day of Pentecost, the little church at Jerusalem enjoyed for a time externally "a heaven upon earth," having the freedom of the City and the Temple, and the favor of all the people. They were then of one heart and one soul; of one accord in doctrine and practice, "continuing steadfastly in the fellowship, in breaking of bread, and in prayers." There were sectarian divisions in the "so-called" Jewish church, but none among the disciples of the crucified and risen Nazarene. But this moral triumph provoked the wrath of the government with a ruthless mob at their back; and the murder of Stephen, the first martyr, was the signal for a hasty flight from Jerusalem, and for that dispersion by which the gospel was borne to the Gentiles in Antioch, the capital of Syria, where a strong church was soon gathered, where the Nazarines were first called "Christians," and where arose the first SECT that marred the outward form of Christian unity. That new Christian sect is first recognized in history, in this fifteenth chapter of the Acts, as a germ of the Pharisaic sect of Judaism, transferred within the bounds of the Gentile Christian church, taking deep root, having a rapid growth, and developing its evil nature as a set antagonism to the enlarged spirit of apostolic doctrine, and to "the simplicity that is in Christ." This notable event occurred in the year 52, nearly one fifth of a century after the resurrection of our Lord. It caused great agitation at the time, and was the occasion of that General Conference at Jerusalem, whose discussions Luke has reported; a conference of Apostles, Elders, and Delegates, who meant to nip in the bud this rising sectarianism, which was left, however, with a vitality in its hidden root, that afterwards overspread the face of Christendom with a rank Judaistic and hierarchical fruitage that has always flavored of the Pharisaic soil wherein it was first nourished, and whence it was transplanted, like the tares of which Jesus spake, "while men slept," into the goodly field over which had been sown "the good seed of the kingdom" broadcast from the Divine Sower's hand.

It was the body of Gentile Christians at Antioch, under the leadership of Paul and Barnabas, who first discovered the far-reaching significance of this Christianized Judaistic sectarianism, and joined together in concerted measures to arrest its spread. But far-sighted as they were, we have an advantage over them in forming an estimate of the character of the evil which they deprecated; for the lapse of eighteen centuries has furnished it broad scope for the unfolding of its germs, and for qualifying us to judge it by its fruits. The historical records of the New Testament, extending beyond the year 65, furnish the true stand-point which we must occupy in order to read and interpret the problems of church history. If for these divinely-given records we substitute the sacred formularies of the early councils, and the sayings of the fathers "of sainted memory," as the primal sources of authority, we shall be logically forced to enthrone traditionism above the gospel; thus doing the very thing which Jesus charged as a grievous wrong upon the authorized church-leaders of his day, when he said, "Ye reject the commandments of God that ye may keep your own tradition, teaching for doctrines the commandments of men." Held in the grasp of such an error at the starting point of inquiry, there will be no fair escape from the necessity of substituting, under church-sanctions, saving sacraments for the word of truth and a priestly prelacy for a teaching ministry.

For, as we know, from an early period of the Christian

era, prelacy has ruled the Christian nations, and still wields the sceptre of a predominating power. All churches ("so called") that do not acknowledge its jurisdiction, it treats as schismatic sects. It boasts of an order of high priests descended directly from the Apostles in the line of valid ordination, endowed with authority, and qualified by special gifts for the administration of saving sacraments, with power to "bind and loose," to open and shut the gates of Christ's visible kingdom. Its claim to the honor of antiquity is no vain pretension; and, when it has been made evident that authentic history sets it forth in the process of lively growth, and even of mature development at a period very near the apostolic age, thousands of honest and inquiring minds have deemed the inference clear and irresistible that prelacy had an apostolical, and, therefore, a divine origin. As has been said by a distinguished prelatical writer: "if any thing can be proved by testimony, this proposition can be proved; that the government of the church by diocesan bishops, and its ministry of a three-fold order, was an institution of the Apostles, derived from Christ, to be transmitted as a divine legacy, from generation to generation, even unto the end of the world."

If this be so, of course, none but a prelatical church can realize the scriptural idea of catholic unity; and all churches not within its pale are but *sects*, guilty of schism, "renders of Christ's seamless robe," revolters against a rightful, supreme authority.

Nevertheless, this position of the priestly prelatist, when examined by the light of primitive Christian history, is seen, we think, to have been founded upon a mistake; and the character of this mistake is quite analogous to that which Dean Milman, attributes to the learned author of "The Decline and Fall of the Roman Empire;" a work which no gifted mind has been able to displace in spite of all its lurking scepticism. In pointing out the source of the speciousness of Gibbon's error, Dr. Milman says, "the unfair impression produced, consists in confounding together in one undistinguishable mass, the origin and apostolic propagation of Christianity with its later progress. The main question, the divine origin of the religion, is dexterously eluded or speciously conceded; his plan enables him to commence his account, in most parts, *below the apostolic times;* and it is only by the strength of the dark coloring with which he has brought out the failings and the follies of succeeding ages, that a shadow of doubt and suspicion is thrown back on the primitive period of Christianity."

This statement of the English editor of Gibbon accords with the sentiment of Guizot, the celebrated French commentator on the works; and in this connection it is instructive to note the fact, that Gibbon was educated among English Christians of the national establishment who did, themselves, confound these different things and habitually overlook these very distinctions. His history was his great life-work; and it well illustrates the effect of this confusion on the mind of an independent thinker. He had not been led to regard the New Testament as the one simple, all-sufficient standard whereby to estimate the claims of Christianity, but rather, to look for that standard in church tradition or church history. It is the same erroneous principle of ecclesiasticism that is now adopted and defended, not only by Papists, but by prelatical Protestants of various names, who teach Christianity as a religion that was gradually formed and *developed* in ages succeeding that of the Apostles. Hence, they are not satisfied with the Scripture as a sufficient guide to faith and practice, but look to tradition and history for the standard or canon by which to settle the question—What is Christianity? This principle is well adapted to raise up other Gibbons in time to come, by throwing back dark shadows of doubt and unbelief over the divine origin of Christianity itself. All men in whom sentiment predominates over intellect, may be easily led by such a principle into the labyrinths of superstition; while men of bold, inquiring spirit will bound away from it over the trackless wastes of infidelity. Hence, the principle itself, harmless as it may seem to some, is like the error which the ancient prophet spoke of, as "the cockatrice's egg;" because, though so smooth and fair to the eye, it is capable of developing from within itself a twin-progeny of errors, each one armed with its dangerous fang and sting.

Evidently, the Christianity of the New Testament is one thing; the Christianity of traditionism or of church history is another. If we would judge the latter aright, we must find our points of view in the Scriptures themselves; for, as our Divine Master said, "Heaven and earth shall pass away, but my word shall never pass away."

In this connection of ideas it is a significant fact, never to be forgotten, that the authorized church of that day, glorying in its ancient line of an anointed priesthood, and its gorgeous ritualism of saving sacraments, rejected our Messiah, denied his teachings, and condemned him to death; while he, in his discourses to the people, called upon *them*, in the exercise of "private judgment" and the rights of conscience, to judge the church by the standard of the Scriptures and not to judge the Scriptures by the standards of the church. At the time of his long foretold advent, instead of finding a nation educated and prepared to welcome him, he found all the wisdom of the schools, and all the sanctity of the Pharisees, and all the common lore of the Scribes, made subservient to a traditionism enthroned above the word; so that when he stood forth to teach he had to begin with rous-

Rise of Sectarianism in Christendom.

ing up the popular mind to an independence of its masters, and to appeal from the decisions of their Gamaliels, and the highest church authorities of the age in such remonstrances as these: Ye do err, not knowing the Scriptures;* What is written in the law, how readest thou?† Did ye never read in the Scriptures, The stone which the builders rejected, the same is become the head of the corner?‡ Why do ye transgress the commandment of God by your tradition: Ye make the word of God of none effect.§ Search the Scriptures: they are they which testify of me."‖ But in spite of appeals like these, the spirit of the old Pharisaism in the ancient church, which was ever on the alert to balk our Master's work, lived long after his ascension; at an early period of the Christian era incorporated itself with forms of Christianity: and under this more modern phase, it has survived the fall of empires, the protests of dying Martyrs, the stormy conflicts of the Great Reformation, and even as of old, will " compass sea and land to make one proselyte." It fortifies itself within the bulwarks of a veteran traditionism, makes the written word of God to yield forced service in support of its priestly dominion, still warreth with the life and fire of its early youth, and is enthroned to-day in the high places of power throughout the Old World, while scheming with its pristine subtility fo the conquest of the New.

And yet, notwithstanding its high antiquity, its historical honors, and its vast domain, the story of its birth, the character of its genealogy, may be expressed in one short sentence: *This was the first sect of Christendom.*

In order to discern the nature of this sectarianism

---

* Matt. xxii. 29.   † Luke x. 26.   ‡ Matt. xxi. 42.
§ Matt. xv. 3; Mark. vii. 9–13.   ‖ John v. 39.

344 Rise of Sectarianism in Christendom.

more clearly, and set it forth in the light of authentic scriptural history, let us now proceed to do two things:

I. Rehearse the account of its introduction into the Christian Church.

II. Trace the development of its essential elements in the creeds of Christendom.

I. In pursuing the investigation of this subject the first fact to be noted is, that after the ascension of our Lord, the conquests of Christianity were confined, for some time, mainly to persons of Jewish origin. But when the Government of Judea, irritated by this success, smote the church in Jerusalem with the sword of persecution, the host of converts was scattered abroad, and several of them from the isle of Cyprus and from Cyrene, (now called Barca,) on the coast of Africa, fled to Antioch in Syria, then known as the Queen city of the East, vast and magnificent, containing at least half a million of inhabitants, and distinguished by the imperial gift of "Liberty for all religions." Pleasure, fashion, philosophy, idolatry, and freedom of speech were all flourishing there; and there the missionary exiles broke over the bounds by which they had hitherto been hampered, entered Heathendom, and preached the gospel to the Greeks, who, to the astonishment of all, received it with a joyous welcome. A new field "white to the harvest" was thus thrown open; a strong church was gathered; and the liberal-hearted Barnabas, a citizen of Cyprus, sought as his coadjutor, Paul of Cilicia, a man, as you know, of Hebrew blood, but of a cosmopolitan spirit, and an education that qualified him for an intercourse, as a teacher, with every rank and class of men. Under the joint-leadership of these two large-souled and faithful ministers of the word, the first Gentile church enjoyed a year or more of unparalleled prosperity in a

Rise of Sectarianism in Christendom. 345

city where the most ample religious liberty was guaranteed and shielded by the Roman government.

But then, this clear sky was slightly darkened by the rising of a little cloud, which, though it seemed at first "no bigger than a man's hand," was destined to gather into itself, by subtile affinities, many noxious elements and to overspread the face of the firmament.

This change was signalized by the arrival of several new teachers connected with the mother church, and designated by the historian, Luke, "certain men who came down from Judea." They inculcated a doctrine that was novel, startling, and annoying to the young Gentile church that had already grown strong on the aliment of a simple gospel, and the invigorating air of Christian freedom. These visitors from Judea were bound together by a common purpose; that was the modeling of the Gentile church into a conformity to the constitution of the old Jewish national church, which had already "had its day," had fulfilled its mission, and was about to be dismissed from the scene of earthly action by the hand of Providence, in accordance with the predictions that the Messiah had announced on the last week of his life, as he sat with his disciples overlooking Jerusalem on the mount of Olivet. It is evident that these teachers were men of more than ordinary influence; they spake in the tones of earnest men, with a voice of authority, calling attention to a certain *deficiency* which they pointed out in regard to the way of preaching Christianity adopted at Antioch. They insisted on the necessity of maintaining the perpetuity and dignity of that ancient constitution, which, as the author of the Epistle to the Hebrews said,* "decayeth, waxeth old, and is ready to vanish away," they set forth the doctrine,

---

* Hebrews viii. 13.

that Christianity is one with Judaism, or only an appendage to it, which they put in the form of their favorite dogma "Except ye be circumcised and keep the law, ye cannot be saved."

The real, far-reaching significance of this dogma was seen at a glance by the Gentile Christians of Antioch, especially by their missionary founders and leaders, Paul and Barnabas; and in them it aroused, at once, instinctive forebodings of its manifold progeny of evil, sufficient of itself, if accepted, to thwart and baffle the benign, reforming aims of the New Dispensation. They saw enfolded therein a PRINCIPLE which, when nourished into life, would idolize obsolete ideas, and attack decayed forms as drag-weights upon the wheels of Christian progress. The announcement of the dogma, therefore, startled them, like the sound of an enemy's trumpet, and of one accord they braced themselves for the contest, and so, you see, it is written in the second verse of this chapter, that with these men "Paul and Barnabas had no small dissension and disputation."

These words of the sacred historian are very suggestive, and they place before us these two apostolic teachers, all alive with zeal and courage, battling together against the introduction of a deadly error. Luke has not recorded their forms of argument. Paul was no doubt, the chief speaker. Would you obtain a just conception of his forms of speech, his manner, tone, and spirit, as he addressed himself to the task of meeting this emergency, rising with the occasion and vindicating the original simplicity of the New Testament church? Then, read carefully, in the light of the collated facts, the appeals recorded by his own pen six years afterward, in his letter to the Christians of Galatia, in the year of 58, when the first heresy of the early church had struck its roots over into that province. Hear him, while he shows that a cherished sympathy with the spirit of the new sect would generate all the evils of the old Judaism, wrested from its place and perverted from its original designs. "Stand fast, therefore, in the liberty wherewith Christ has made us free, and be not entangled again with the yoke of bondage. Behold I, Paul, say unto you, that if *ye* be circumcised Christ shall profit you nothing. For I testify again to every man that is circumcised that he is a debtor to do the *whole* law. Christ is become of no effect unto you, whosoever of you are justified by the law: ye are fallen from grace. For we, through the Spirit, wait for the hope of righteousness by faith. For in Jesus Christ neither circumcision awaiteth any thing, nor uncircumcision; but faith which worketh by love. Ye did run well: who did hinder you that ye should not obey the truth? This persuasion cometh not of him that calleth you. A little leaven leaveneth the whole lump. I have confidence in you, through the Lord, that ye will be none otherwise minded: but he that troubleth you shall bear his judgment, whosoever he be. I would they were even cut off which trouble you."

Evidently his soul was deeply troubled by the things that troubled them. Before he had written these pungent appeals, he had exclaimed, "O, foolish Galatians, who hath *bewitched* you, that ye should not obey the truth, before whose eyes Jesus Christ hath been evidently set forth, crucified among you." "When ye knew not God, ye did service unto them which, by nature, are no gods: but now, after that ye have known God, or rather are known of God, how turn ye again to the weak and beggarly elements, whereunto ye desire again to be in bondage? Ye observe days, and months, and times, and years. I am afraid of *you*, lest I have bestowed upon you labor in vain."

Every man who has formed any just conception of the

character of Paul will admit, of course, that appeals like these must have exerted a mighty influence at once in settling the new question that was now agitating the Gentile church. The principle involved in that question was so momentous that it was deemed necessary to decide it in the most formal and permanent manner that was possible. Therefore, as Jerusalem was the seat of the first church, as Apostles and Elders were still residing there, it was resolved to send a delegation, consisting of Paul, Barnabas, and others, in order to constitute a Conference for the purpose of pronouncing an authoritative decision as to the true doctrine of Christianity in its relation to Judaism. That Conference was held in the year 52; the occasion of its assembling was the rise of *sectarianism* among the primitive Christians; from Luke's record of it I have derived the words of my text; and these words disclose the fact that the first sect which uprose within the pale of the apostolic churches was the Pharisaic sect of Judaism, *transferred;* a root of bitterness transplanted from an exhausted vineyard to seek aliment in a fresh virgin soil.

We are accustomed, generally, to think and speak of the Pharisees only as a *Jewish* sect, and as Jesus found them, the devotees of a decayed past; but if we consider closely this fifteenth chapter of Luke's history of the early church, in its relation to subsequent history, we see the Christianized Pharisees becoming a Christian sect, confronting the Apostles themselves, seeking to recast the form of the Messiah's kingdom in the moulds of their old system, after its life and spirit had gone out of it. In this first Conference it lifted up its voice "with much disputing," as Luke's expression is,[*] in defence of a bad cause, which, as we now see, was destined widely to prevail.

---

[*] Acts. xv. 5–7

How long this Conference remained in session we are not informed; but when there came a lull in the disputings of the Pharisaic membership, the apostolic teachers spake; Peter, Paul, Barnabas, and James, the President; all of whom set forth the marvelous work of the Holy Spirit in the conversion of the Heathen, by the simple gospel, as the signal event of the age, tallying with the ancient prophecies, which they quoted, touching the advent of the Messianic Kingdom, that was to be set up, not for the glory of Judaism, but in order to bless the world with the knowledge of salvation, and to call all the kindreds of men into a new brotherhood, as worshipers of the one true God.

The practical conclusion which they reached was the utter inconsistency of an alleged obligation to observe the initiatory sacrament of Judaism with the free spirit of the New Dispensation; and, therefore, its entire abolition as a religious rite. This announcement, as the result of the Conference, was sent forth in a "letter missive," addressed to the Gentile brethren of Antioch, Syria, and Cilicia, and was hailed with a welcome by all alike who were alive to the spirit of the new era. When they heard that the initiatory sacrament of the Old Church had been designated an "intolerable yoke upon the neck of the disciples" they saw clearly that its entire abolition swept away the basis for the Pharisaic doctrine of conformity to the Jewish Constitution, and set forth the *Church of the Messiah* as sufficient of itself to meet the spiritual needs, not merely of the natural seed of Abraham, but of universal man.

II. Such, then, having been originally the doctrine and the spirit of the one body of churches over which the Apostles presided with divine authority, such the result of the first contest with the rising sect of Christian Pharisaism, it was hoped, no doubt, by the early Gentile Christians that the controversy had been settled for all time. Not so! the heresy of *conformity* still lived; its vital principle was restrained, not destroyed. We have already seen, from the quotation of Paul's own burning words, how it resisted and baffled him in Galatia, six or seven years after the apostolic declaration of doctrine in Jerusalem.

We find him still, twelve or thirteen years after the time of the Conference, battling against the same growing sect at Colosse, in Asia Minor, in the year 64; in his epistle of this date, remonstrating with the Christians of that city, saying:* "Wherefore if ye be dead with Christ from the rudiments of the world, why, as though living in the world, are ye subject to ordinances, (Touch not; taste not; handle not; which all are to perish with the using;) after the commandments and doctrines of men?" Again, he saith:† "Beware lest any man spoil you through philosophy and vain deceit, after the tradition of men, after the rudiments of the world, and not after Christ; for ye are *complete in him.* Let no man, therefore, judge you in meat, or in drink, or in respect of an holy day, or of the new moon, or of the sabbath days; which are a shadow of things to come; but the body is of Christ."

This spirit of the Pharisaic sect, demanding conformity to the obsolete Jewish Church Constitution, checked but not killed, gradually spread itself, working stealthily, and ceased not until it had tainted with its priestly Judaism the whole mass of Christendom; so that, in the end, it realized Paul's brief description of it, "a little leaven leaveneth the whole lump."

Whosoever has derived his knowledge of the Christian religion from the New Testament, whosoever has formed a clear conception of the church of the New Testament, and then has studied ecclesiastical history from the

---

* Colos. ii. 20-22. † Colos. ii. 8, 10, 16, 17.

Rise of Sectarianism in Christendom. 351

stand-point of the New Testament, in the light which the inspired word casts over the broad historical landscape, will be profoundly interested in observing the rank development of this element of error in two grand far-reaching issues.

I. It transformed the simple, spiritual, evangelical religion of the New Testament into a *Sacramental religion*, distinguished by its materialistic and ceremonial character; *a religion of saving sacraments*.

This statement, let it be observed, is not intended to describe the state of things in the Middle Ages, nor, particularly, in the times immediately preceding the establishment of Popery, as a supreme power; but it is intended to characterize the style of Christianity that was beginning to prevail at the close of the first century, even before the death of the last of the Apostles. As has been truthfully said by one of the most celebrated historical writers of our age, already quoted in another connection, Dean Milman, a man of acknowledged erudition and candor: "Paul's public expostulation had the effect of allaying the discord at Antioch; and the temperate and conciliatory measures adopted at Jerusalem, to a certain degree reunited the conflicting parties. Still, in most places where Paul established a new community, *immediately after his departure* this same spirit of Judaism seems to have rallied, and attempted to re-establish the great exclusive principle, that Christianity was no more than Judaism completed by the reception of Jesus as the Messiah." "This conflict," he adds, "may be traced most clearly in the Epistles of St. Paul, particularly in those to the remote communities in Galatia and in Rome."[*]

Even so: the great sectarian controversy began in

---

[*] Milman's History of Christianity, New York, p. 170-1.

that early day, during the life time of the Apostles themselves, and its vital fires have never been extinguished. So mighty was the prejudice against Paul's view of "the simplicity that is in Christ," that in addressing churches that have been planted by his own hands, he was obliged to vindicate his claims to authority as a delegated teacher of Christianity. And when he died the sect that opposed him triumphed and prevailed. For as early as the second century, far and widely, throughout the broad area of the Eastern and Western Churches, that is, among the Greeks and Latins, they did, "for substance of doctrine" as really insist on retaining the rite of circumcision as did those first converts of the Pharisaic sect who raised the Judaistic battle-cry in the Gentile church of Antioch. To all intents and purposes they urged its observance; for, while they acknowledged the validity of the decree published by the apostolic Conference at Jerusalem, as to the letter, they revolted from its spirit, saying that though the outward form of circumcision had been set aside, yet baptism had come in its place, a seal of the same covenant, designed to answer the very same ends!

One of the most popular and venerated writings among the Christians of the second century was a work entitled "The Shepherd of Hermas;" so called because the author, Hermas, in the second book, describing his visions, introduces his guardian angel in the character of a shepherd; and this work, (believed by many to have been written by Hermas, recognized as a friend by Paul in the fourteenth verse of the sixteenth chapter of the epistle to the Romans,) clearly proves, (or as the German historian, Dr. Hase, says,)* "contains evidence that baptism had *already* taken the place of circum-

---

* A History of the Christian Church. New York, 1855, p. 36.

Rise of Sectarianism in Christendom. 353

cision." This book announced the doctrine that the Apostles left the world and went into Hades, where they performed the rite of baptism on the pious souls of the Old Testament who had not been baptized! And this strange idea was popularly received, as well as the visionary book that taught it, a book quoted even by *Irenæus*, of the second century, as of apostolical dignity. As the first troublers of the Gentile Church at Antioch had laid it down as a Christian law, "Except ye be circumcised ye cannot be saved," the prevailing belief of the second century was expressed in a similar manner; "Except ye be baptized with water ye cannot be saved." And, as of old, the uncircumcised son of Abraham was not to be reckoned among God's chosen people, so now, at the early period of which we speak, death before baptism was regarded as the sealing of one's doom forever among the outcast heathen.

As circumcision, in the view of the ancient Pharisee, was the great "saving sacrament," so, in the second century of the Christian era, the water of baptism washed away all sin, and placed every recipient within the pale of God's well-ordered covenant. So deeply rooted and widely spread did this sentiment become, so thoroughly did it intertwine itself with men's elementary ideas of religion, that the eloquent Chrysostom, Bishop of Constantinople in the fourth century, expressed the real catholic doctrine of the age when he wrote, as he did in one of his exhortations to the candidates for baptism—"although a man should be foul with every human vice, the blackest that can be named, yet should he fall into the baptismal pool, he ascends from the divine waters purer than the beams of noon."*

Who that marks the connections and course of events

---

* Isaac Taylor's Ancient Christianity, vol. i. p. 236. London, 1841.

does not discern in this momentous change the fulfillment of Paul's prophetic warnings; seeing that the very class of teachers that the apostle had put down as a troublesome *sect*, at last prevailed in numbers and in power, until they appeared in the eyes of the world as the true apostolic, catholic Church, the visible body of Christ? Could they, by virtue of mere numbers and regular succession, become the representative Church of a New Testament Christianity? By no means. Could the originally heretical sect become thus transubstantiated? When Charlemagne, the champion of the Romish Church, sent to the Saxons his church-creed, in that brief message "Baptism or death," he expressed, in the tersest manner possible, the spirit of the transferred old Pharisaic sect, not the spirit of the true church, the "Bride of Christ."

The anciently popular idea of which I have spoken, the necessity of baptism in order to salvation, the saving efficacy of the outward rite, naturally led, in due time, to a variety of administrations, so as to suit the circumstances of the sick, the dying, and of tender infants who had never seen the light. The anointed priest, hurrying with his vial of water, at night, to the chamber of death, was authorized to say that this administration might suffice as a saving sacrament in case of extreme necessity, by "special grace;" and there bending over the couch of the dying, hailed as a ministering angel, in that attitude represented the theology of the time, the crystallized essence of the anti-Pauline sect which marred the work of the great Apostle of the Gentiles, and saddened his last days by imposing upon him the bitter task of building again that which it had destroyed.

Tallying with all this sectarian corruption was the development of the early Christian Pharisaism in its relation to the Lord's Supper, which was also administered as a "saving sacrament" for sins committed after baptism. In many places consecrated bread, soaked in wine, was placed between the lips of infants, in order to secure to them a happy destiny. For six hundred years INFANT COMMUNION was the universal practice of the prelatical churches of Christendom until the eleventh century, when the Romish or Latin church, asserting the doctrine of transubstantiation, that the substance of the Eucharist is converted into the real body and blood of Christ, the bread and wine were withheld from the lips of infants so that they might not incur the peril of rejection and defilement; while in the eastern prelatical churches of Greek origin, wherein the Latin language was not spoken and the Papal authority was not acknowledged, the custom has been continued unto this day. As far back as the fourth century, however, the sacrament of the Eucharist was invested with such an air of mysterious sacredness that the people were afraid to receive it, so that at the first Council of Toledo, in the year 438, they made this canon: "If any one does not swallow the eucharist when he has received it of the priest, let him be excommunicated as a sacrilegious person." More than two centuries afterward, in the year 675, another council at Toledo released infants from this censure on account of their ignorance and weakness. The names which our Lord gave to the simple rites of his own appointment were applied to the strange substitutes of man's device. The number of rites, too, was constantly increasing; and thus there grew up among the Christian nations a gorgeous ritualism, that threw into the shade the ancient splendors that had once charmed the eye of the Pharisaic devotee, had nourished in his heart the love of shadowy forms, and had erased from his mind all just conceptions of "the simplicity that is in Christ."

When this gloomy Ecclesiasticism had overspread the whole area of Christendom, except those recesses where lay hidden the scattered representatives of the primitive church, like the Waldenses and Piedmontese, of whom Milton speaks in his sonnet-prayer "Even them that kept thy truth so pure of old"—a "church in the wilderness"—suddenly, in the fifteenth century, Europe was electrified by the appearance of a band of heroic men sounding out a call for reformation; champions of God's word, who came forth like the prophets Elijah and Elisha, in Israel, in an age of comsummated degeneracy.

The mission of the Reformers signalized the modern era. As far as the essential doctrines of salvation, in their relation to the soul of the individual was concerned, it restored the purity of the primitive Christian age; but in regard to the reconstruction of the degenerate church, it repeated the great sectarian error of the first and second century, retaining, as it did, the old element of the Pharisaic sect in the form of a substitute for circumcision, sealing the church membership of infants under the name of Christian baptism. Since then, more than three centuries have rolled away, exhibiting just such fruitage as might have been anticipated. As, in accordance with Judaism, all children were born at once into the Church as well as the State, the same rite sealed their connection with both; and, throughout Protestant Europe, the Baptismal Register became a charter of worldly citizenship. A religious creed was made a part of state policy, established by the civil law, and enforced on all consciences. This was regarded as the perfection of order. To-day, however, in the country of Luther, there is a national church which claims to be child of the Reformation, but which has no fellowship with its spirit. It has "a name to live, but is dead." And yet, though spiritually dead, it is carnally alive, smiting by the magisterial sword, with penalties and pains, all those who consistently preach the great principle of Luther himself, the supremacy of God's word over the individual conscience; a State church which has long dispensed to the people a kind of Christianity which is "the leaven of the Pharisees," a mere religion of sacraments; and which, where it is not this, is "the leaven of the Sadducees," a merely rationalistic philosophy. What has been the practical result? It was well expressed by Lord Macaulay, when he said that for three hundred years Protestant Christianity had scarcely gained an inch of ground in Europe.

2. Besides this rank development of a sacramental religion as the antagonist of an evangelical religion, the next great result in which the doctrine of the Pharisaic party in the first century became evolved, was the *reconstruction of the Christian ministry into a conformity to the three-fold order of the Jewish priesthood.* In the New Testament we do not read of any such three-fold order as Prelates, or Diocesan Bishops, with Presbyters, or Elders, and Deacons, subordinated to them; but we do read of such a three-fold order at a very early period after the apostolic age. No man of knowledge and of candor, probably, would deny the truth of this latter statement. And this high antiquity is deemed by many a solid foundation for maintaining this order now and universally, and for asserting its claim to a divine origin. They declare with confidence that it *must have been* established by the Apostles. This conclusion, they say, is as clear to their view as a mathematical demonstration. Not so: to us the reverse is clear; for, admitting that they quote and interpret correctly the earliest testimonies upon which they depend, the great question still remains, upon what foundation was this constitution of the church placed by its first advocates? On the authority of the Scriptures, the recorded word of Christ?

By no means. It was grounded upon this principle, that the priestly constitution of the Jewish church was designed to be, throughout all ages, a pattern for the Christian; and on *this ground* conformity was demanded. There is but one writer of the first century who is claimed as the advocate of this three-fold order; this is Clement of Rome, or Clemens Romanus, who is regarded as the very man to whom Paul sent the friendly salutation recorded in the last chapter of his Epistle to the Romans. A few lines from an Epistle of Clement, addressed to the Corinthians, are cited as the proof of this position.

Now, let it be remembered, that there are hosts of learned and candid men who say that the prelatists misapprehend and misinterpret these quoted lines. The interpretation remains an open question. But what is worthy of special note in this connection is this fact; if the interpretation of the Prelatists be correct, it only affirms the Pharisaic doctrine, that the constitution of the Christian church ought to be conformed to the priestly constitution of Judaism. This prelatical interpretation of Clement's words is thus stated by a learned and devout defender of Prelacy: "Clement reasons that from the subordination in the temple, first of the High Priests, then of the ordinary priests, then of the Levites, and, last of all, of the people, there is to be inferred a necessity of a like subordination in the Christian church."

Again "from the set time and place of offering the Levitical sacrifices, which it was penal in any to transgress, is to be urged a like duty of observing the set times and places of ecclesiastical assemblies, and other things."* Clement of Rome, be it remembered, is the most ancient of the Christian Fathers, appealed to by both Catholic and Protestant prelatists; the first ques-

---

* See Clement ad Cor. i. 18.

Rise of Sectarianism in Christendom. 359

tion is, do these interpret his meaning aright? Admit that they do so, what then? What shall we say of Clement's church doctrine *thus rendered*, with the whole range of Paul's Epistles before our eyes? Simply this; that Clement had joined the *Anti-Pauline party* of the day. If these were really the ideas of Clement, then it is clear that he belonged to the Pharisaic sect that stealthily gained its foothold within the bounds of the Christian church, in spite of all that had been done to "head it off" by the Apostolic Conference at Jerusalem. That is the only logical conclusion that the case admits. We cannot be followers of Paul, and at the same time receive teachings and reasonings that are the direct antithesis of what he made it his lifework to inculcate.

Yes, friends and hearers, the questionings of the parties in controversy are reduced to this one: shall we take side with Paul or with his sectarian antagonists? The testimonies of Paul we have already cited. Does he argue from the set times and places of Jewish observances the necessity of like appointments in the Christian Church? Just hear him again in his appeal to the consciences of his brethren in Galatia.* "But now, after that ye have known God, how turn ye again to the weak and beggarly elements whereunto ye desire again to be in bondage? Ye observe days, and months, and times, and years. I am afraid lest I have bestowed upon you labor in vain." "I would they were even cut off who trouble you." "A little leaven leaveneth the whole lump." Evidently, either Paul misunderstood Christianity, or else the men who taught such doctrines as the prelatists insist upon attributing to Clement, corrupted the streams of Christian truth at the fountainhead, and are identified with that Pharisaic sect that

---

* Galatians iv. 9–11; v. 12.

were of the Anti-Pauline spirit, and marred the beautiful simplicity of Gentile Christianity.

Accountable as we are to our one Lord and Master who died for us, rose again, and is enthroned as Head over all things to the church, shall we allow such teachers, though invested with *patristic* honors, to become our Rabbies and legislators, to mould our opinions by ecclesiastical authority, and wield over us the sceptre of canonical dominion?

By no means. "One is your Master, even Christ." They may laud highly a Christian priesthood, a threefold order and subordination in the Christian ministry; but the inspired word recognizes nothing of this sort except as a doctrine antagonistical to the primitive truth. I admit its antiquity; but the more deeply I penetrate into its nature and history, the more clearly I perceive that it is sacramental, priestly Judaism; that its first advocates were striving to vitalize an economy destined "to vanish away;" that it is the very thing, in principle and aim, against which Paul constantly protests; that their claims on its behalf bears on its front the mark of its sectarian origin in that party of Pharisaic Christians whose tenets the Apostolic Conference condemned: and that it is a part of that grand *apostasy* from the primal truth of which the voice of inspiration said to the Thessalonian church, "it doth already work;"* of which it was predicted that it would exalt itself and bear sway in God's temple before the advent of that day wherein he "will consume it with the breath of his mouth, destroy it by the brightness of his coming," and restore the purity of the Pentecostal day.

And now, in view of this subject, as seen in the light of sacred Scripture and history, let us learn to guard

---

* 2 Thess. ii. 1-8.

ourselves against the illusions of a very common error in regard to the proper method of settling those questions of great "pith and moment" pertaining to Christianity and the church, which every devoutly inquiring mind must meet, at least once in a lifetime. Every one who has been born and educated in a Christian country, starts forth upon his life-course in the midst of conflicting religious opinions, and of church establishments that exhibit a great variety of observances, which they commend to our acceptance as being invested with divine sanctions and obligatory upon the conscience. At the very outset, the inquirer after truth is met by Christian ministries, designated Catholic or Protestant, as the case may be, and is charged to beware of the peril of attempting to read and interpret the Scripture for himself, in the exercise of "private judgment." He is bidden at once to hear and submit to the church as God's appointed witness and interpreter. He is told, perhaps, of what his sponsors in baptism did for him; then he is called upon to receive the rite of confirmation; he is urged to observe with reverence a number of festivals and fasts; to avoid meat and be content with fish and eggs on Fridays, as well as to abstain from his ordinary aliments during the forty days of Lent. Thus he is bidden by authorized and validly ordained teachers to advance step by step to the mastery and practice of a minute and gorgeous ritualism. If he venture to ask in regard to any one of these observances upon what authority it is grounded, seeing that he cannot find any allusion to it in the New Testament, he is told, that its existence may be traced by the light of authentic history so far beyond the beginning of Popery, so very near the apostolic age, that it *must* have been of apostolic origin. He is not prepared, perhaps, with any reply, not having had, as Paul expressed it, "his senses exercised to discern between good and evil." He deems the argument conclusive. He *crosses the line* that separates the church of the New Testament from that of a degenerate age, and bows himself to the yoke of traditionism, which, though at first it may sit lightly on his neck, becomes, in the end, a yoke of galling bondage, rasping his sensibilities, dwarfing his manhood, and transforming him under church sanctions into a ceremonial devotee.

When that line is once crossed there is no telling at what point the inquirer will stop for that repose his spirit craves. For, as he touches the ordinances of Romanism, one by one, and traces the history of each, he finds that the same argument of antiquity avails on its behalf to substantiate its claim. Auricular confession, priestly absolution, invocation of saints, homage paid to sacred relics, worship of the Virgin Mary, the degradation of marriage as unsaintly, the efficacy of fastings and penances, and ascetic abstinences from those things which, as Paul said, "God had created to be received with thanksgiving," and a vast aggregate of human devices which the Protestant Reformation swept away as intolerable burdens imposed by a half-paganized Judaism under the name of Christian law, all find their vindication in the established usages that long preceded the inauguration of the Papal power. Of each of these it has been affirmed again and again, from age to age, with the majority in Christendom concurring, its early prevalence proves that it *must* have had an apostolic origin.

Friendly inquirer, seeking truth, of unsettled mind as to what light to follow, yet parleying with the priestly representative of church authority as your soul's guide— beware! Your next step may *cross that line* into a devious path on an inclined plane, along which descent you will move at a rapid pace, impelled by the gravitating power of an irresistible moral law. Beware! Hold fast to Christ's word as the only sure lamp of your feet. Bow down before no authoritative interpretation of that word except the recorded testimony of those Apostles whom he himself ordained to "sit on twelve thrones, judging the twelve tribes of Israel." If from the depths of antiquity the voice of some Saint, as a witness of the truth, challenge your reverent submission, challenge him back with the appeal, Who art thou? To which party didst thou belong, the Pauline or the Anti-Pauline? And if any man, be he called saint or angel, "preach any other gospel" unto you than that which Paul preached, let his teaching be to you as Paul commands, "Anathema," that is set aside under the ban and interdict of utter rejection. Remember the great Apostle's solemn adjuration, "I certify you, brethren, that the gospel preached of me, is not after man; for I neither received it of man, neither was I taught it, but by the revelation of Jesus Christ." Remember, too, the words of the Apostle and High Priest of our profession, Christ Jesus: "I am the good Shepherd, my sheep hear my voice; they know not the voice of strangers; I know them and they follow me; and I give unto them eternal life; and none shall pluck them out of my hands."

> Behold the sure foundation stone
> Which God in Zion lays;
> For men to build their hopes upon,
> And his eternal praise.

It is worthy of everlasting trust: this is solid rock "and all is sea besides."

XVI.

MISSION OF BAPTISTS.

By J. B. JETER, D.D.,
Of Richmond, Virginia.

"Now I praise you, brethren, that ye * * * keep the ordinances, as I delivered them to you."—1 *Cor.* xi. 2.

The Apostle had censured the members of the Corinthian church for their connivance at idolatrous practices. The eating of things offered as sacrifices to idols, though it might in itself be lawful, was, under the circumstances, inexpedient and unbecoming. Paul, with a thorough knowledge of human nature, aiming to conciliate those whom he would reform, mingled commendation with reproof. He praised the Corinthian Christians for their steadfast adherence to the "ordinances," which he had delivered to them.

The term "ordinances," or "traditions," as it is in the margin, signifies the doctrine of the Apostles, relating to either faith or practice, and communicated either by the tongue or the pen. "Therefore, brethren," says the Apostle, in his second letter to the Thessalonians (ii. 15), "stand fast, and hold the traditions which ye have been taught, whether by word or our epistle." The precise thing which Paul exhorteth the Thessalonians to do, he commended the Corinthians for having done—that is, for holding firmly the "traditions," or "ordinances," which they had been taught by inspired, and consequently infallible, men.

In popular phraseology "the ordinances" denote baptism and the Lord's supper, or the positive institutions of Christianity. The apostolic ordinances, though not limited to these institutions, certainly included them. Baptism and the Lord's supper were among the ordinances delivered by Paul to the "Church of God, which" was "at Corinth," and for the preservation of which their praise has been perpetuated. In this discourse I shall use the word "ordinances" in its popular, and not in its scriptural sense, or rather not in its full scriptural sense.

The ordinances—Baptism and the Lord's supper—are of divine origin. They were established by the Lord Jesus, not arbitrarily, oppressively, or inconsiderately; but wisely, kindly, and authoritatively. The Apostles received the ordinances from Christ. Baptism was given to John, the forerunner of Christ, directly from heaven; and it was ratified by the example of Christ, and by him solemnly committed in trust to his Apostles. "All power," said the risen Jesus, "is given unto me in heaven and in earth. Go ye, therefore, teach all nations, baptizing them in the name of the Father, and of the Son, and of the Holy Ghost." Paul was not with the "eleven disciples" when they received this commission; but what was intrusted to them orally by the Lord, was committed to him by the inspiration of the Spirit. "But I certify you, brethren," said the Apostle, "that the gospel," and this gospel included Baptism and the Lord's supper, "which was preached of me is not after man. For I neither received it of man, neither was I taught it, but by the revelation of Jesus Christ."*

---

* Galatians i. 11, 12.

Paul informs us explicitly, in the context of the passage under consideration, that the Lord's supper was committed to him by the ascended Saviour. "For I have," said the apostle, in speaking of this ordinance, "received of the Lord Jesus that which also I delivered unto you."

Paul, by the divine blessing on his ministrations, having succeeded in founding a large and prosperous church in the city of Corinth, committed to them, by the Spirit of inspiration, the ordinances which he had received of the Lord Jesus. In number, form, substance, and order, as the servant had received them from the Master, they were delivered, as a sacred deposit to the church; and their duty it was, with all docility, to understand and embrace them, and with all fidelity and perseverance, to hold and maintain them; and they were praised by their infallible instructor for their faithfulness to the momentous trust.

The apostolic ordinances were, in their very nature, liable to be perverted. Nothing is too plain, too important, or too sacred to be corrupted by the folly or pride of men. "Unto them that are defiled and unbelieving is nothing pure." The liability of the "ordinances" to be perverted, and the guilt of changing them, are clearly implied in the commendation divinely bestowed on the Corinthian church for maintaining them inviolate. The Mosaic institution, originating, not with Moses, but in the wisdom and goodness of Jehovah, was, through the perversity of the Scribes and Pharisees, converted into Judaism—a monstrous system of bigotry, intolerance, and hypocrisy. It was, in the nature of things, as probable that the gospel should be corrupted as it was that the law should be. The perversion of the gospel was foretold by the Spirit of prophecy. "For the time will come," said the Apostle, "when they will not endure sound doctrine; but after their own lusts shall they heap to themselves teachers, having itching ears; and they shall turn away their ears from the truth, and shall be turned unto fables."* This prediction has been fulfilled. Every fact, doctrine, and precept of the gospel has been denied by the perverseness or vitiated by the ingenuity of men. None can doubt the corruption of the ordinances, baptism, and the Lord's supper, in their forms, substance, order, and design. Some have rejected them altogether, as incompatible with the spirituality of the new dispensation; some have viewed them as unimportant rites, to be observed or rejected, according to the convenience or caprice of men; others have ascribed to them an efficacy due only to the blood of Christ and the influence of the Holy Spirit; and comparatively few have maintained them in their divine authority, their scriptural import, their relative value and sanctifying efficacy. They have been the great battlefields of theologians, in every age, from the apostolic down to the present; and they will probably continue so to be until the mists of error shall be scattered by the beams of the millennial glory.

In the providence of God, the Baptists have been raised up. If he feeds the fowls of the air, notices the falling of a sparrow, counts the hairs on the heads of his people, and clothes with beauty the lily of the valley, he certainly is not regardless of the growth and influence of a religious denomination, who, with their adherents, must be numbered by millions. Whether their origin and progress are to be traced to the folly and fickleness of men, or to the truth, grace, and overruling care of God, they are, doubtless, destined to perform an important part in the concerns of the world. Their rise, ad-

---

* 2 Tim. iv. 3, 4.

vancement and struggles; their persecutions, sufferings and perils; their numbers, resources, and prospects; it is not my purpose to trace. These have been considered, more or less minutely, by others, in the series of sermons, in which this occupies an humble place.

Agreeing with other denominations in all the principles of evangelical Christianity, Baptists have peculiar views of the ordinances—baptism and the Lord's supper. They maintain that only immersion is baptism; that only believers are proper subjects of the ordinance; that baptism is a prerequisite of church membership; that the Lord's supper is a symbolic feast, never to be observed except by a church in its corporate capacity, and for no purpose, except to promote the spiritual life of the communicants and the glory of its Divine Author. Some of these articles of faith are held by Baptists in common with a few other Christian denominations; but taken together, and in their various relations, they are embraced only by Baptists. These views, in all times and in all countries, have constituted them a peculiar people—a people in direct antagonism to all other classes of professing Christians, whether Roman Catholics or Protestants. I shall, in this discourse, take it for granted that Baptist principles are scriptural. They have been discussed by others, in this series of sermons, better qualified than I am, to prove their divine authority.

For what purpose, then, has God, in his far-reaching and inscrutable providence, raised up and, through so many ages, preserved the Baptist denomination? They have, in the divine economy, a momentous mission to fulfill. This mission, supposing their principles to be true, is perfectly clear. *They are God's witnesses to bear testimony against the corruption of his ordinances, and to restore them as they were delivered to the churches by the apostles.*

To the discussion of this high and sacred mission we consecrate the time remaining for this service, and invite you, hearers, to grant us your candid attention while we present some points worthy of your profound consideration.

I. It is an Important Mission.

There is in all communities a prevailing disposition to make light of the distinctive principles and practices of Baptists. "Are they not among the non-essentials of religion?" "What good can there be in immersion?" "Can water wash away sin?" "Is not a drop as good as an ocean?" "What harm can the sprinkling of an infant do?" "If infants are not fit for church membership, who are?" "Are not all who are qualified for heaven fitted for communion at the Lord's table?" "How can those who refuse to commune together on earth, hope to commune together in heaven?" We frequently hear these and similar questions propounded with the design of disparaging Baptist sentiments. Even Baptists themselves, generally supposed to be unduly zealous in the propagation of their peculiar tenets, are but half awake to their importance. It might be a sufficient vindication of our cause, to affirm that, on all these points, we follow the teaching and example of Christ and his Apostles, as these are recorded in the Holy Scriptures. What they ordained, and preached, and practiced, must be worthy of supreme regard and the most careful observance, and cannot be neglected, perverted, or changed without marring the harmony of the divine plan, and injuring the souls of men. As in the natural, so in the spiritual kingdom, every deviation from the divine law is fraught with mischief. Can a man take fire into his bosom and not be burned? Can he disobey God and prosper?

But there is something more to be said on this subject.

The perversion of the ordinances has been the chief source of the corruption and reproach of Christianity. For proof of this position let us examine the moral influence of infant baptism. To the superficial observer nothing seems more harmless than the sprinkling of a few drops of water on the forehead of a child, as a religious ceremony; but it appears far from harmless to those who carefully consider its tendency. By an immense majority of all who practice the rite, infants are believed to be "regenerated, made members of the mystical body of Christ, and inheritors of the kingdom of heaven," in their baptism; and this doctrine is held, not in a vague and figurative sense, but as a plain, vital, soul-saving reality. It is directly taught, or darkly hinted, that infants dying unbaptized are lost, or, at least, are left to the uncovenanted, and, therefore, uncertain mercies of God. Baptized children are instructed to believe that their spiritual condition is incomparably better than that of other children. These regenerated little ones, so soon as they attain to consciousness, find themselves members of the church, and, in virtue of this connection, invested with peculiar religious advantages. In spite of their pride, selfishness, anger, falsehoods, and waywardness they grow up in the church. For no vice or ungodliness are they excluded from it. Usually, at about the age of fourteen years, as a matter of course, and in virtue of their baptismal regeneration, they are catechised, confirmed, and admitted into full communion with the church. Thus by infant baptism, and its kindred, unscriptural rite of confirmation, all the profane, the licentious, and the sceptical in the community are initiated into the church, and become permanent members of it. From most communions they are afterward excluded, not for any impiety, but only for resistance to ecclesiastical authority. This blending of the church and the world laid the foundation for national hierarchies. The church no longer "called out" from the world—as in apostolic times, and as the term imports—and antagonistic to it, but imbued with its spirit, and governed by its policy was made subsidiary to human governments. For the sake of tithes, and perquisites, and rich endowments, she allied herself to the state, and gave her sanction to tyranny and oppression. The chaste spouse of Christ became "the mother of harlots and abominations of the earth." The incongruous and monstrous union of church and state gave birth to spiritual domination, laws of uniformity, religious intolerance, and relentless persecution. To this source we must trace the Inquisition, with its appalling corruptions, its refined cruelties, and its fearful mischiefs. It was this that kindled the fires of the *auto da fe*, and deprived the world of many of the noblest specimens of piety, wisdom, and moral heroism with which it has ever been adorned.

It would be easy to show that the corruption of the Lord's supper has been an equally fruitful source of mischief, and a source of the most degrading superstition and the most revolting idolatry.

We would do no injustice to any class of men, especially any sect of Christians. All who practice infant baptism, do not run to the extreme which has been pointed out. Many are held in check by the countervailing influence of their piety and the truth which they embrace. They sow the seeds of evil which are fortunately prevented from germinating. Baptized infants are theoretically recognized as church members; but practically, in many communions, they are treated as if they were not. They are not disciplined, nor permitted to commune at the Lord's table; but are, in all respects, dealt with as if they were beyond the pale of the church.

Nor are the monstrous absurdities of transubstantiation, and its kindred evils, to be charged on Protestant Pedobaptists; though some of them have grievously perverted the Lord's supper.

To all these evils Baptist principles are directly and immutably hostile. A converted, baptized church membership is utterly irreconcilable with a national hierarchy. Other churches may be perpetuated by hereditary membership; but a Baptist church can be preserved only by piety, constant activity, and frequent accessions by a voluntary profession of faith and submission to baptism. Freedom of conscience underlies the Baptist system. If none are required, or even permitted, to enter the church, except such as make a voluntary profession of faith in Christ, furnish evidence of their conversion, and are baptized in the name of the Lord Jesus, then, persecution for conscience' sake is impossible. A church, according to Baptist principles, is a perfectly voluntary association, to which none can be properly admitted without piety and baptism, in which none can be retained without their free consent, and by which no penalty can be inflicted beyond exclusion from its privileges. By these principles Baptists have been invariably led to claim and to grant the fullest liberty of soul. In the maintenance of these principles, they are called, in the name of their Lord Redeemer, to bear testimony against Pedobaptism, and all its affiliated evils, by their example and their ministry, with their tongues and with their pens. The importance of their mission is proportionate to the number, the magnitude and the power of the evils which it is their duty to oppose. When we cast our eyes over Catholic and Protestant Europe, and see how pervading, and deep, and ruinous are the mischiefs which have sprung from the perversion of the Christian ordinances, our mission rises, in our estimation, to sublime moment. It is impossible to overstate its importance. We may well exclaim, "Who is sufficient for these things?"

II. It is an unpopular mission.

To testify against error is, always and everywhere, an ungrateful task. Never was a ministry more gentle, and kind, and winning than that of Jesus; and yet he said, "The world hateth me, because I testify of it, that the works thereof are evil." The testimony is odious in proportion to the prevalence and popularity of the error which it assails, and the strength of the prejudices against the truth by which it is proposed to supplant that error. Both these considerations lend their influence to increase the unpopularity of the Baptist mission.

Pedobaptism, apart from any question of its truth and importance, is a popular system. To say nothing of its sacred associations, infant aspersion is a pleasing ceremony. It appeals for its support to parental love; the tenderest, strongest, and most enduring affection of the heart. What parent, not lost to humanity and godliness, can withhold from his child so beautiful, so fitting and so common a ceremony? Pedobaptism, too, is firmly intrenched in our popular literature. It is incorporated in our works of fiction, artfully inculcated in our school books, and illustrated and commended by beautiful paintings and engravings, suspended in the parlors of the rich, and in public halls. Then, too, it is enforced by the example of the good and the great, the refined and the learned, and admitted by the worldly and the refined to be a significant and impressive rite. To all these attractions must be added its supposed mysterious influence; an influence not well defined nor well understood; a regenerating influence, say most; a sealing influence, say others; an influence which, if it does not ensure religious benefits to its favored recipients, does, at least, in some way, increase the probability of their salvation. And, to conclude, it is assumed that the interesting, even if not divinely sactioned rite, can do no harm. It is not surprising, then, that infant baptism should be prevalent, admired, and strongly defended.

On the other hand, the principles which it is proposed to substitute for pedobaptism are unpopular. Immersion, as a Christian ordinance, is repulsive to the world. The restriction of communion at the Lord's table to church members, and the privilege of church membership to such as have been baptized on an intelligent and voluntary profession of faith, have subjected, and will continue to subject, the denomination to the charge of sectarianism, bigotry, and inconsistency. In some communities, under favorable circumstances, their principles have secured a measure of popularity; but, in general, and especially among the rich, the gay, the fashionable, and the learned, they have been distasteful.

That the current of the world sets strongly against Baptist sentiments, we have many and decisive proofs. We pass briefly over the evidence on this point furnished by the persecutions of Baptists, not only by Romanists, but by every dominant Protestant sect. Baptists are even now, in the light of the nineteenth century, watched, restrained, fined, imprisoned, outlawed—accounted "the filth and offscouring of all things"—in most of the Protestant countries of Europe. Not for their disloyalty, much less for their crimes, but simply for their principles, have they been put under the ban of governments and treated as felons.

We can furnish other, if less revolting, not less convincing, testimony in support of our position. The ritual of the Church of England positively enjoins baptism by dipping, except in certified cases of sickness or debility; and yet in the face of this unrepealed statute, and in opposition to the strong conservative tendency of that hierarchy, sprinkling has almost universally supplanted dipping. Why this change of the rite? It is an obvious yielding, not to the force of truth, or the authority of Christ, but to the current of popular taste. The same influence has effected in the Episcopal church, in this country, a change of the ritual in favor of sprinkling. Many ministers, who admit the validity of immersion, swayed by popular sentiment, exert their energies to prevent the practice, and some, with strange inconsistency, ridicule it.

The progress of Baptist principles has been mainly among the poor of this world. The rich and the great, with a few noble exceptions, have been repelled by them. Sometimes, Baptists, becoming rich, have gone into other communions to improve their social position and to increase their respectability. The children of wealthy Baptists occasionally stray, contrary to their convictions, into pedobaptist churches, to find more congenial society. We have known persons of high worldly position, who, holding Baptist sentiments previously to their conversion, have, on professing faith in Christ, stifled their convictions, to unite with churches in which they have found, not better instruction, nor more piety and good works, but more refinement, fashion, and parade. It is certain that among the higher classes of society few have ever become Baptists, except under the constraining power of conscience; while those who have consulted their taste, convenience, or worldly advantages, have usually selected other communions. There are many Baptists in pedobaptist churches who quiet their consciences by considerations of convenience and expediency.

The causes of the unpopularity of Baptist sentiments are partly *incidental*. They have been propagated and defended chiefly by ministers—intelligent, pious, and efficient, but wanting in the learning and accomplishments which, in the eyes of the world, so highly commend a cause. Few persons have the discrimination and candor to distinguish between the advocate and his principles, or between appearances and reality. In addition to this, the Baptists have been greatly misrepresented by ignorance or prejudice, and these misrepresentations have been varied to suit the popular tastes. At one time they were censured for believing that dying infants were saved without baptism; at another, they are charged with making baptism essential to salvation. First, they were deemed unworthy to commune with the faithful; and then, they were accounted incurable bigots because they refused to commune with the unbaptized. Thousands firmly believe, and boldly assert, that the Baptists are the legitimate descendants of the "mad men of Munster;" but who these men were, or what were their principles, the accusers know not.

But there are *inherent* as well as adventitious causes of opposition to Baptist sentiments. Immersion is inconvenient, and, to the carnal mind, repulsive and humiliating; and no art in its administration can remove the offence. It has ever provoked, and it ever will provoke, the sneers and scoffs of a proud and ungodly world. The reproach brought on Baptists by their views of the communion, is too well known to need proof. Their agreement with most of their Christian brethren of other denominations in the principle, that baptism, in the gospel order, precedes communion at the Lord's table—a principle that logically leads to restricted communion—seems in no degree to abate the asperity with which Baptists are charged with bigotry and intolerance.

In the light of these facts, it is easy to perceive that the mission of Baptists must be unpopular. In its fulfillment they are called to place themselves in earnest, active opposition to the tastes, customs, prejudices, and to a considerable extent the erudition of the world; and they may reasonably expect to provoke its displeasure, if they do not incur its contempt and its fierce persecution. We must then make our calculation to have our testimony rejected, our motives impeached, our characters assailed, and we should be thankful when we escape fines, imprisonment, and flames.

III. *It is a* DIFFICULT MISSION.

To disarm prejudice, to counteract popular sentiment, to conciliate bigotry, to reduce the strongholds of error, and to disseminate offensive truth, demand consummate prudence, tact, and heroism. In this work, if in any, is needed the wisdom of the serpent, and the innocence of the dove. To this service Baptists are called; and it is a delicate, arduous task. It is not to be effected by the bitter denunciation or the indiscriminate censure of other Christian denominations. We must give them due credit for their learning, piety, and good works. We should love them in proportion as they bear the image, and commend them in so far as they follow the example, of Christ. In our efforts to convince and reform them, we must not confound rudeness with candor, nor severity with faithfulness. It is due to most of the Pedobaptist denominations in this country to admit that they are evangelical in sentiment, Christian in spirit, and fruitful in good works. We should, and we do, love them for the truth's sake. But still, it is our responsible and difficult mission to bear testimony against the errors which they mingle with the truth, and to warn them of the mischiefs which spring from these errors, and which, in other countries and in other times, have been so prevalent and fearful. We must bear this testimony, not offensively, but kindly, tenderly and faithfully, considering that the "wrath of man works not the righteousness of God." We should preach "the truth, the whole truth, and nothing but the truth;" still, truth in its just proportions and beautiful symmetry, not putting the ordinances of the gospel in the place of the atoning blood of Christ or the sanctifying influence of the Holy Spirit, nor degrading them into unmeaning and useless ceremonies. Nor must we be soon wearied in our appropriate work. Whether men will hear or refuse to hear, we must bear life-long witness to the ordinances as they were divinely given to the churches. We must put in requisition all our learning, and skill, and energy, and influence, to restore them to the churches in their apostolic simplicity and efficiency. And in this ministry, we are required to avoid whatever would tend to enfeeble our testimony and retard the progress of our principles. Our lives should be in harmony with them, evincing how highly we appreciate them, how thoroughly we are influenced by them, and how earnest we are in their diffusion. Whatever would blunt the edge of our testimony we should studiously avoid. It is in this view that the importance of restricted communion in the Lord's supper is most apparent. By the almost universal consent of Christendom, baptism precedes church membership and communion. Were Baptists to commune with Pedobaptists, they would be charged with admitting the validity of infant baptism—with gross inconsistency in so doing—and it is not easy to see how the charge could be repelled. By limiting communion in the Lord's supper to church members, and church membership to baptized believers, we maintain the consistency of our testimony, and give it full force.

Baptists have often been accused of giving undue prominence, in their ministry, to their distinctive sentiments. If this accusation has been, at some times and in some places, true, it is far from being generally true in the present day. The very reverse is the fact. Whether from a conviction of the inherent power of their principles, a lack of interest in their diffusion, or an unwillingness to wound the feelings of their brethren of other denominations, our ministers of late have rarely introduced these subjects into their sermons; or, when they have done so, have given them a full and vigorous discussion. This ought not so to be. Our profession, our sacred mission, the interests of truth and piety, and the honor of Christ, imperatively demand that we should, on all fit occasions, seek to restore the ordinances as they were delivered to the churches.

IV. IT IS AN ENCOURAGING MISSION.

If the principles for which we plead are right, they must eventually prevail. They may be hated, opposed, by the wisdom and authority of the world, limited in their influence, and checked in their progress; but they are indestructible and invincible. Neither the artifices nor power of enemies, nor the feebleness, indiscretions, and inconsistencies of friends, can prevent their final triumph. All the attributes of Jehovah are enlisted in their maintenance. He has revealed them to the world; and the wisdom from which they emanated, the holiness with which they are stamped, the benevolence which shines through them, and the authority by which they are enforced, can be vindicated only by their ultimate success. "My word," says God, "shall not return unto me void, but it shall accomplish that which I please, and it shall prosper in the thing whereto I sent it."

We take encouragement from the *past history* of our principles. They have lived and spread, from time immemorial, in spite of priests, and popes, and kings, in the face of fines, and prisons, and tortures, and fires, yielding a noble army of heroes, confessors and martyrs. And these achievements have been won, not by the advantages of wealth, and learning, and secular authority, but mostly by the toils, sacrifices, and sufferings of the poor and the illiterate, and by the inherent force of truths wholly uncongenial with depraved human nature. Principles which have made progress under such disadvantages, must be vital, vigorous, and aggressive, promising far more brilliant victories in the future than they have secured in the past.

The United States is the only civilized country in which these principles have had free course. In all other lands they have been interdicted, or restrained by discriminating taxes, or have prevailed by mere sufferance. In this land they have found a congenial soil, and have flourished steadily, and without a parallel. This success appears, not only in the increase of the Baptist denomination in numbers, learning, and resources, but in the influence which their principles have exerted in other Christian denominations. Infant baptism, in defiance of the most strenuous efforts to defend and propagate it, has been gradually decreasing, relatively to the number of communicants, in, perhaps, all Pedobaptist sects. The belief in the regenerating efficacy of infant baptism has been driven almost entirely beyond the pale of evangelical Christendom. Immersion, too, as Christian baptism, though ridiculed as superstitious and indecent, has won its way into all Pedobaptist churches, and their pastors have been constrained to lead candidates for the ordinance "down into the water," or permit them to pass into Baptist churches; and they have usually preferred the former alternative. By this means, persons embracing our sentiments, though not consistently maintaining them, are to be found, not only in every Pedobaptist denomination, but in almost every separate congregation of it.

We do not expect all the world to become Baptists in name; but we do anticipate the gradual, steady and successful diffusion of our principles among all Christian sects. If the progress of our denomination, in the future, should be in the same ratio as it has been in the last fifty years, many centuries will not have elapsed before the triumph of our principles throughout the world will be complete. But may we not reasonably hope that our denominational progress will be accelerated? If Baptists have accomplished so much in their poverty and weakness, amid reproach and persecutions, what may we not expect from them, with their schools, colleges, literature, and various organizations for the diffusion of the gospel and the advancement of the kingdom of Christ? It is not, however, on the resources and activities of the denomination that we chiefly rely for the spread of these principles; but on the changeless purposes, the unbounded resources, and the inexhaustible grace, of their Divine Author. He cannot lack means for their diffusion. He can raise up Judsons, and Onckens, and Spurgeons, in every land, to disseminate and vindicate them; and in the absence of human advocates, he can, by the gracious, potent, influence of his Spirit, so influence the hearts and minds of men, that they will discern these principles in the Bible, and cordially embrace and support them.

We will conclude our discourse with a few practical remarks:

First. If the views which have been presented are

correct, *we see the folly of attempting to succeed in our mission by courting the favor of the world.*

Pedobaptism, to a great extent, is conformed to the spirit of the world. It erects, at immense cost, its stately and beautiful houses of worship. The towers of its marble temples pierce the skies, and proclaim to admiring gazers the wealth, taste, and zeal of their builders. The internal arrangements of its churches are as splendid and luxurious as their exterior is grand and imposing. The carved pulpit, the softly cushioned pews, the crimson curtains, the tones of the solemn, high-sounding organ, the well-drilled artistic choir, performing in operatic style, combined with pleasing rites and finely polished sermons, to say nothing of elegant statuary and paintings, attract and interest the rich, the gay, the pleasure-loving, and the ambitious. Amid such displays religion becomes a matter of taste, and fashion, and pomp. To be a church-member is a mark of refinement, and the surest passport to the highest circles of society. Rising families find it expedient, in order to increase their respectability and influence, to have a pew in some church; and in its selection they are usually governed, not by a regard to truth or piety, or even convenience and cost, but by the attractions of the most splendid architecture, the most richly toned organ, the most fashionable congregation, or of worshipers, eminent for their learning, their fame or their social position. In their decision, the imperishable interests of their souls, which should wholly guide them, have little or no influence.

Many Baptists, imbibing the spirit prevailing around them, have become dissatisfied with the plainness of their meeting-houses, the simplicity of their worship, and the comparative obscurity of their congregations. These brethren, mortified at the contrast between Pedobaptist splendor and Baptist simplicity, have sought to wipe off the fancied reproach, by emulating the surrounding sects in erecting fine churches, introducing costly organs and fashionable singing, and procuring eloquent and sensational pastors. But these aspirants have been doomed to disappointment. The current of the world has continued to run in its usual channel. The rich, the fashionable and the gay, have found stronger attractions and more congenial services, elsewhere than in Baptist churches. Our distinctive principles, as we have seen, strongly repel this class of persons, and all our attempts at display have ordinarily failed to win them. We are thus taught the folly of entering on a race in which we are sure to be outstripped. It is possible, though not easy, for us to erect houses of worship as spacious, to rear steeples as lofty, to have pews as softly cushioned, music as artistic, and preaching as fascinating, as other churches; but it is not possible for us to vie with them in proselyting the higher classes of society, without an abandonment of our peculiar sentiments. Immersion, and a spiritual church-membership, will always stand as insuperable barriers to our popularity and worldly prosperity

SECONDLY. *It should not be to us a matter of surprise, mortification or discouragement, that we find our sphere of influence and usefulness chiefly among the poor and middling classes of society.*

The gospel, with its simple, touching ordinances, is designed for all mankind. It is offered to the rich as well as to the poor; but it has generally won its greatest triumphs, and borne its richest fruits, among the latter class. While the rich and the great, with rare exceptions, have spurned our distinctive principles, they have found a ready entrance and a hearty welcome among the common people. Supposing our principles to be true, this is precisely what might have been reasonably anticipated. Christ was poor—was crucified by the world. He came to establish a spiritual kingdom, whose immunities are not for the rich, but for the humble—not for the great, but for the good—not for the gay, but for the self-denying—not for the earthly, but for the heavenly. Immersion is the gate to this kingdom. How perfectly it harmonizes with the nature of the kingdom that its entrance should be narrow, not wide—difficult, not easy—repulsive to the proud and worldly, but attractive to the lowly and spiritually minded. Had Christ's kingdom been earthly, then, its gate had been higher and wider, and of beautiful architecture, and adorned with festoons. Some ceremony, fitted to impress the imagination, gratify the taste, and nourish pride, had been adopted to allure the giddy and the gay, the aspiring and the great, to share in its congenial pleasures and glories. It would, no doubt, have come with "observation." But as the kingdom is heavenly, its initiating ordinance is wisely adapted to repel the carnal and worldly, but to attract and profit the penitent and devout.

Who were brought into the kingdom in the beginning of the gospel dispensation? Christ's ministry was mainly among the poor. The common people heard him gladly. "Not many wise men after the flesh, not many mighty, not many noble," were "called."

The Apostles were chosen, not from among the Scribes and Pharisees, the philosophers and rulers, but the fishermen and mechanics. The poor of this world were divinely selected to be rich in faith, and heirs of the kingdom of heaven. In the primitive age of Christianity, all was simple, unearthly, spiritual in the churches. "But the Pharisees rejected the counsel of God against themselves, not being baptized of John."

Why then should we wonder or be troubled that the prevalence of our principles should be mainly among the lower classes of society? This fact is no proof that they are false, but rather an indication of their truth. It should not grieve or dispirit, but rather strengthen and animate us. God has opened to us a wide door of usefulness. The common people hear us, as they heard the Master, gladly. They present far the most inviting and promising field of Christian usefulness. It is *vast*. In all countries, from the necessities of our physical and social nature, the poor must constitute the mass of society. They are far more *accessible* to the ministry of the Word than the wealthy and fashionable classes. The poor may be approached any where, and under any circumstances, without ceremony and without offence, by earnest and faithful servants of Christ. They are, too, *more likely than others to be profited* by the gospel ministry. The love of the world—its riches, honors and pleasures—is the mightiest barrier to the progress of piety. "How hardly shall they that have riches enter into the kingdom of heaven!" In all ages, the great body of sincere, self-denying and consistent Christians, has been found among the lower class of society. Let us, then, thank God for the sphere of labor which his providence has so clearly marked out for us, take courage, and faithfully occupy it.

LASTLY. *Let us awake to our solemn responsibility.*

God has called us to a great work; has opened to us a wide sphere of usefulness; has committed to our hands a laborious task; has laid upon us weighty obligations; and if we would fulfill our glorious mission, we must be wide-awake and active. All our energies, all our gifts, all our resources, and all our influence, are demanded in the fulfillment of our task. The world is opposed to us. Our progress must be made against a strong current, and by continual and vigorous efforts. We should heal our divisions, consolidate our ranks, and present to our opponents an unbroken front. Our operations should be concentrated or isolated, as may best promote our Redeemer's cause. Let us have no squeamishness about proselyting. It is our vocation. To proselyte sinners to Christ, and believers to the whole system of divine truth, is our solemn mission. We should seek to convert the whole world to Baptist principles, not by any sophistry, or any motives addressed to vanity or selfishness, but by a kind, honest, and earnest exhibition of God's truth. By this course, whether we are successful or unsuccessful in the diffusion of our sentiments, we shall merit and receive the praise of keeping the ordinances as they were delivered by the Apostles, and "so an entrance shall be ministered unto" us "abundantly into the everlasting kingdom of our Lord and Saviour Jesus Christ." AMEN.

XVII.

THE RELATION OF THE CHURCH AND THE BIBLE.

By E. G. ROBINSON, D.D.,
Professor in the Rochester Theological Seminary.

"As for me, this is my covenant with them, saith the Lord; My Spirit that is upon thee, and my words which I have put in thy mouth, shall not depart out of thy mouth, nor out of the mouth of thy seed, nor out of the mouth of thy seed's seed, saith the Lord, from henceforth and for ever.—*Isaiah* lix. 21.

It was by the special agency of the Holy Spirit that the truths of the Bible were communicated to men. The truths thus communicated, as well as the Spirit by whom they were conveyed, was to be the inalienable possession of the church. The Holy Spirit, dwelling in the church as its Divine Sanctifier and Guide, was to preserve and perpetuate its life to the latest generation, while the divine truths which he had intrusted to the church were never to "depart out of its mouth," but were to constitute at once the means of its own preservation and the message from God which it must deliver to the race. Confining ourselves at this hour to the office of the church as the guardian of the Bible and the herald of its teachings to man, let me invite your attention to *the relation of the Church and the Bible*.

The subject is not a trivial one. What the relation is, is a question to which it is not a matter of indifference what answer is made. It underlies the whole broad domain of modern theology. Not only does the ever renewing controversy between Romanism and Protestantism turn on it, but there can be no comprehensive discussion of any one of the great questions of Apologetics, which does not assume some sort of answer to it. Every new phase of modern Scepticism is turned toward it. The doctrine of Inspiration involves it. Church History from its very outset must build on some kind of theory of it. Dogmatic Theology, to be properly analyzed and intelligently defended in any one of its great cardinal doctrines, must distinctly recognize it.

The theme proposed is also closely connected with the theological parties and controversies of our day. The religious thinking now prevalent, may be ranged under three general divisions—the High Church, the distinctively Protestant, and the Rationalistic. Between these three parties there rages a triangular conflict. The point in dispute is to what, in religion, shall we appeal as ultimate authority? With consistent high churchmen of the Romish school, the Bible is a subordinate book—the church, by which is meant the hierarchy with the Pope at its head, is sole arbitress in religion. With inconsistent high churchmen of the Anglican schism (the most sectarian of all the sects), the church and the Bible are in a state of perpetually disturbed equilibrium. Distinctive Protestantism holds forth its traditional motto: "The Bible the religion of Protestants:" and in its use of the Bible it has often but too plainly forgotten that one clearly marked and divinely appointed office of the church, is to stand side by side with the Bible, as the visible body of the invisible Christ, as the manifest dwelling-place on earth of the saving power of the living God; and more than all, in its unceasing, and sometimes unmeaning iteration of its motto, it has but too evidently given some show of reason for Coleridge's blundering

Relation of the Church and the Bible. 389

and most unfortunate charge of bibliolatry. Rationalism, rejecting the authority of both church and Bible, asserts most positively the competency of man to sit in judgment on the authority of both. Its highest authority is human reason.

The growth of the last named party, the Rationalist, is one of the notable signs of our times. There is no disguising the fact of its rapid encroachment on the extremes of both the other parties. The number and variety of its accessions are startling, but indisputable. How much the demand both from Romanism and Protestantism for an unthinking submission to ecclesiastical authority has had to do with its progress, we need not now stop to inquire. We here have to do only with the fact of its progress. How shall it be stayed? Shall we decry reason, and deny to it any office in religion? Shall we with high churchmen insist with renewed emphasis on the prerogatives of the hierarchy, and re-demand, on the pains and penalties of a future world, an unreasoning acceptance of canons and dogmas? Or, following the traditions of the English pulpit, since the birth of English Deism, shall we denounce all use of reason in religion, as leading to heresy and imperiling the soul? Or, obeying the latest rule prescribed, shall our reason guide us in examining the evidences of a divine revelation, but its presence be scrupulously abjured, the moment we come to an examination of the truths with which revelation addresses us? But to what does revelation address itself, if not to our reason and our conscience? In the name of reason, for what was reason given us if not to be employed on the highest thoughts and the noblest ends that can engage our attention? Is it not enjoined upon us by the Most High, that we "*prove* all things, and hold fast that" only "which is good." Because we decline the invitation of Rationalism, to go behind revelation and assert *a priori* what it *must* contain if it be from God, shall we therefore stultify ourselves by assuming that faith severed from reason, that belief unthinking and unintelligent, can ever be any thing else than credulity? Nay, nay! for traditional Churchism and for traditional Protestantism, as well as for callow Rationalism, there remains but one safe and abiding resource, and that is the church and the Bible—the Bible as understood and believed in, not by Hierarchies, Councils, and Popes, but as understood and believed in, and scientifically expounded by the universal and divinely sanctified reason of the church of the living God.

And by what has just been said it will have been made evident in what sense the words Church and Bible are to be used in this discussion. The word Bible may denote the letter of the canonical Scriptures, or it may be used in the wider sense of a supernatural revelation from God. It is in the wider sense that we here use it; and it may also be said in passing, that throughout these remarks it is assumed that the Bible is a revelation from God by the Holy Spirit, who is at the same time the ever-indwelling Paraclete and Sanctifier of the church. But the word Church has many and very different senses. With these senses we have here no other concern than to say, that it is not of the church as distinctively visible or invisible that we now speak. Certainly it is not the visible organization represented and perpetuated only by its "fertile hierarchy" and ruled over by the "vicar of Christ," that is here intended. But by the church, we mean that vast body of believers, who, through all time, by whatever name distinguished, under whatever ecclesiastical constitution existing, whether blessed or accursed of popes and favored or frowned on by rulers, have adhered with fidelity to Christ alone, as at once their Saviour and their Lord.

Now between the church (as thus defined) and the Sacred Scriptures, there has existed from the beginning a relation as indissoluble as that of thought and being. In unfolding this relation, let us notice,

I. The relation of chronological precedence. The Romanist assumption is, that the church preceded the Bible. The Protestant affirmation is that the Bible preceded the church. The point is still in controversy. The latest writer on the Roman side, Archbishop Manning, has rediscussed it with notable vigor. But neither theory seems to be exclusively true. The church and the Bible were coeval in their origin.

The question may be looked at historically. We may view the church in its widest latitude of meaning ; we may grant what some have affirmed, that it antedated Moses—that its origin was with Abraham. In one view of it, it is easy to distinguish chronologically between the origin of the divine promise which Abraham believed, and the origin of that divine life in the heart of Abraham which made him at once the nucleus of the so called *Jewish Church*, and "the father of the faithful." In another view of it, the promise could be truly recognized as a revelation from God, and so become a part of the word of God, only when, through the creative Spirit, the religious life in the soul of Abraham had made him capable of recognizing and avowing it as a promise from God. It was through Abraham inspired and Abraham renewed, that so much truth as was revealed to him and believed by him, was communicated to men. The truth and his heart, like seed and the soil, were prepared for each other. In him the Bible and the church were co-existent and coeval.

Or pass we down to the origin of the New Testament

and of the Christian Church. Christ gathered his apostles about him and imparted, as rapidly as their ignorance and prejudices would admit, the principles and spirit of the new kingdom. Three years and a half the Lord of life was their unwearied teacher. And with what results? Let us see. After two years or more had elapsed, after the Sermon on the Mount had been delivered, the Transfiguration witnessed, and the coming Passion and Resurrection re-announced, we find the apostles, their minds occupied with traditional notions of a temporal kingdom of the Messiah, in earnest dispute about their individual pre-eminence in the new empire. Another year passed; the last judgment had been depicted; the mysterious glory of their master had become more distinctly visible; and now we find two of the three disciples who had been admitted to the closest intimacy with their Lord, turning the fond love of their mother to personal account, and preferring through her the request that the first two posts of honor in the new kingdom should be promised to them. And so, again, after the dread scenes of the Crucifixion and the Resurrection, even during their last interview with the risen Lord, we see in the question, "Wilt thou at this time restore again the kingdom to Israel?" how deeply their minds had been imbued with the gross notions of their times.

But granting now all that can be claimed of misconception on the part of the apostles, admitting them to have strangely misunderstood the words, the spirit, and the aim of the great Teacher, yet who will venture to affirm that he had not imparted to them the saving power of his gospel? Surely he is a bold man who dare affirm of the apostles, that had they died between the Resurrection and Pentecost, they must have died as unbelievers. But if the apostles, with all their crude no-

Relation of the Church and the Bible. 393

tions were essentially believers; if the one hundred and twenty disciples in that upper chamber were, to all intents and purposes, the true church of Christ; then the true church may exist with even very imperfect conceptions of its supreme Lord and of his truth; and more than all, the origin of the church was not preceded, in any just sense of language, by our New Testament Scriptures. And yet, on the other hand, the apostles did have some just conception of what the Lord had taught them, of what he had promised and of what he had done for them, and inseparably connected with their conceptions was their faith in him as the Messiah, and that divine life which made them indissolubly his. Confused and imperfect as were their views, they were not absolutely false. Within the facts and principles of which their association with Christ had made them possessors, lay, germinally, the whole system of truth now expanded and embodied in the New Testament.

This question of origin may also be looked at in another light. A slight clue to the right answer to it may be found in the relation of faith and regeneration in the individual believer. Some have maintained that faith must distinctly precede regeneration. A gracious renewal of the soul, it is affirmed, can be effected only by the instrumentality of divine truth; and truth, it is said, can only be effective in the soul through that apprehension of it which is denominated faith. Others, on the other hand, have maintained that faith is more an act or state of the heart than of the understanding; that the exercise of faith presupposes a renewed heart; that there can be no saving trust in a principle or a person with which or with whom we are not already in sympathy. But between these two explanations, as thus stated, we may be unwilling to choose. It is very far from evident that faith and a new heart can be thus divided in their origin. It is plain that trusting and loving must always coexist. Christ can be trusted in, only by one who has already felt him to be trustworthy; and he can be felt to be trustworthy only by one who is already heartily believing on him.

Now what is thus true in the relation of truth and a new heart in the individual believer, is true of the relation of divine truth and the whole body of believers. The divine life of the Christian and the divine power of truth were a simultaneous communication. They sprang from one and the same creative act. They dwelt together in the person of Christ. They were communicated by one and the same process from Christ to his personal disciples. The mysterious virtue, the hidden but organific principle of life that went out of him upon his disciples, transforming their hearts, and bringing them within the great brotherhood of believers, went only by the vehicle of thought. Strange as were the misconceptions of the first disciples, gross as was their misunderstanding of the words of their Lord when first they heard them, and alloyed as was their earliest regard for him, there was yet enough of truth in their conceptions and of love in their regard, to attach them unalterably to his person and his service. The justness of their conceptions and the purity of their love were always commensurate. Truth and life, the Bible and the church, were coeval and coexistent in their hearts. That life was deepened and purified, and that truth was expounded and systematized at Pentecost; the life taking to itself a body which it organized into fitness to its ends, and the truth being gathered up into an organic whole, the church and the Bible have descended along the centuries the united and indissoluble gift of God to men. And in this descent—

Relation of the Church and the Bible. 395

II. The Church and the Bible have been mutually preservative. Each has been exposed to its own peculiar perils, and each has ever found in the other its needed protection.

To the Scriptures there has been exposure to the peril of corruption of text and of canon. Heretical leaders began at a very early period to further their designs by mutilation and forgery. No merely human writings were ever subjected to such trials as the New Testament has survived. No such passions and motives ever prompted to a tampering with other authors, as have prompted to a mutilation of the writings of Matthew and Luke and Paul. No such ends as heretics had to gain ever prompted to forgery in the name of philosopher or secular historian. And yet the New Testament has come down to us with a purity of text, which, with all the paraded variations of reading, is simply a marvel of accuracy.

There was also the peril of loss. Single churches were broken up and scattered by persecution. The Christians of whole provinces were hunted down like beasts of prey. The danger was imminent that, through fear or neglect, the precious and dangerous documents in their possession should be left to perish. Some of them seem to have passed into oblivion. Where are those "many" gospels of which Luke speaks in the introduction to his? Where that first Epistle of Paul to the Corinthians to which he evidently refers in that which is the first Epistle of our canon? Indeed, it is natural to suppose that the apostles, throughout the lengthened and diversified years of their trials and labors, with the care of all the churches on their minds, may have written other epistles of which no traces have been preserved. Is not the bountiful hand of the all-giving God everywhere scattering ten thousand seeds of which his watchful Providence preserves but here and there one for reproduction? Shall we wonder, then, that out of the literature of the apostolic period the watchful providence of the same bountiful God has preserved to us no more than is contained in our canon? Shall not our wonder be, not that any gospel or epistle of the apostolic age has perished, but that just so many as, and no more than, we possess, have come down to us? Shall we not wonder that only four of those gospels, each in itself a fragment, and written by men so dissimilar in endowments and so widely removed from each other, have reached us, and yet that these four should unitedly present us a picture so many sided and so faultlessly complete; and wonder, furthermore, that of the various epistles, written by men wholly unlike in type of mind and in temperament, just so many should have been preserved to us as mutually supplement each other, and, in combination, furnish a totality of doctrine commensurate with the wants of the race?

But to whom was the work of selection and preservation committed? Certainly not to the apostles. Even tradition fails to ascribe to them this office. Nor yet was the delicate task intrusted to the unguided wisdom of any man or body of men. Doubtless the Omniscient Mind that prompted the writings, controlled their destiny; but by what agency? Was it by bishops and popes, by synods and councils? But before these had appeared on the stage the canon had already been virtually completed. They formally recognized and endorsed what had already been determined by the great brotherhood of believers. The universal church, ruled by its Divine Head, unerringly judging by a divine instinct, quietly, slowly, infallibly, perhaps almost unconsciously, selected, preserved and carefully transmitted just so much of the sacred literature intrusted to it, as the Omniscient Mind saw to be needed by it.

To the Scriptures, on the other hand, has been assigned the reciprocal task of protection to the church. Exposed to the perils of superstition and fanaticism, of corruption of morals and of clerical despotism, some authoritative guidance was indispensable to the church's existence.

One of the first products in the heart of the Christian is zeal in the service of his Master. But zeal gathers strength by expenditure. Reacting on itself it redoubles its own energy. Unenlightened, it becomes indifferent or blind to every object but the one of which it is in pursuit. Unrestrained by law, it speedily degenerates into superstition or fanaticism. As superstition, it taints all it looks upon, and breathes blight and mildew on all that is beautiful in nature and in grace. It shrivels the soul, torturing it with diseased fancies and driving it before ghostly spectres. As fanaticism, it not only screams over its idols, it rushes on society in Quixotic attempts at the removal of evils which in human societies must continue remediless. It grows impatient at the delays of an unhasting Providence; and, vehement in its imprecations on unhelping fellows, would pull down the heavens in its hot haste. The Bible only can exorcise its foul spirit.

Christianity, also, originates a new moral life in the soul; a life that, to be vigorous, must be progressive; and to be progressive, must be healthful; and, to be healthful, must be sustained by its native aliment. That aliment is revealed truth. Unnurtured by truth, its course is short and its end certain. It is not self-sustained in the human heart. It must have both inward alliance and outward support. Left to itself, attracting the humors of an unsanctified nature, it speedily appears in unseemly and cancerous blotches on the character. Following the guidance of tradition, its way is short and easy into deadly formalism, or still more deadly Jesuitism.

There is also the peril of clerical tyranny. The organization of believers into permanent societies and the setting forth of the worthiest to be leaders and administrators of affairs, is both a natural requirement and a divine provision of Christianity. But history has shown an irresistible proneness in leaders to lord it over the led, and in the people to submit to their usurpations. Of this no ecclesiastical body has furnished its exception. The rulers of the church, beginning with by-laws at first few and simple, gradually losing sight of the Bible as their only Book of Statutes, have come in due time to appeal to ecclesiastical precedents, to canons, to directories, and books of discipline as authorities from which there is no appeal. Ecclesiastical traditions have usurped the place of the "life-giving oracles" of God. The functions of the spiritual overseer have been changed into the functions of a privileged dictator. For the authority of Christ and his truth have been substituted the authority of office and ecclesiastical custom. The government that should ground itself in love and conviction of right, has been perverted into a despotism that commands but gives no reason.

And to such usurpations and perversions of authority the one safeguard is now, as it always has been, the vernacular Bible in the hands of the laity. Revealed truth individualizes its reader—seeks out and confronts the personal conscience, announcing to the soul its one Lord and Master, to whom, and to whom alone, it must stand or fall. The Bible in the hands of the laity, whether in the valleys of Piedmont, in the glens of Scotland, or on the hill-sides of New England, soon diffuses an atmosphere which no clerical despotism can long survive. The Scriptures, though reaching the people only through traditional and liturgical interpretations in favor of priestly domination, must in due time generate an independence of both thought and life, which will brook neither despotism in the clergy nor lifeless routine in religious worship. It requires no prophetic eye to foresee the future of that ecclesiastical body or nation which, putting into the hands of its children, diligently teaches them to read, that Book, the simplest and profoundest teachings alike of which, demand that every one shall reflect and decide for himself. The Bible has but just begun to reveal something of that mighty power, which it is yet to wield when, with its divine intelligence, it shall have irradiated the mind of the universal church.

Nor need we look with misgiving to the future thus opening before the church. Commotion and conflict undoubtedly await us. Even now no authority stands unchallenged, no tradition passes unquestioned. The Bible itself has been arraigned at the bar of criticism. But alas for the critics and the wisdom of man! Never, since the last apostle laid down his pen, has the grasp of the Bible on the conscience of the church and the world been firmer or more controlling than at this hour; never the moral life of the church purer or deeper; never its type of piety nobler; never its aggressions on the kingdom of darkness more decisive and rapid. And in reaching their present positions—

III. The Church and the Bible have been mutually interpretative.

The Bible has been progressively intelligible. Each portion of it, primarily addressed to the generation contemporary with its author, had yet in it a deeper meaning for the generations to come. Our Lord was misunderstood by his apostles until after the miracle of Pentecost; and after eighteen hundred years we are still poring over the meaning of both the gospels and the epistles. To unfold that meaning, and by unfolding to develop its own strength and resources, has been one most important function of the church.

The facts and words of revelation, we are never to forget, are completed; are as immutable as the unchangeable One who speaks in them. But their meaning, like their Infinite Author, is inexhaustible. No one generation can gauge it. No one formulary can exhaustively represent it. Certain formularies, we know, have been regarded by their adherents as completely embodying it. These have been appealed to as ultimate standards. Simple dogmas have been set up as final statements of doctrine; as if any divine fact or truth could be exhaustively measured by finite minds; as if any single generation of an ever advancing race could fix on a final formula; as if there could be an ultimate dogma in theology.

Let history here teach us. First came the Apostles' Creed, of the framing of which the apostles were as innocent as we are. Then, after sharp dispute and bitter controversy, came the Nicene Creed. In due time, and as the result of fiery discussion, followed the so-called Creed of Athanasius. Ecclesiastical despotism then wielded its iron sceptre through dreary centuries, in which, what the hierarchy dictated the church unquestioningly accepted. At length the Reformation dawned; Protestantism ranged itself into the two divisions of Lutheran and Reformed; and for two generations creeds multiplied faster than the generations of men.

Now, of these creeds, each had its peculiar defects and its peculiar merits. Each bears traces of the idiosyncrasies of its author and its time. Each is a measurement of the Christian intelligence and experience of its subscribers. And to the contents and form of each, all the intellectual and moral forces of the Christian centuries had contributed. Not a Christian martyr had died for his faith; not a Christian preacher had sighed and prayed and found his way into the life and liberty of the gospel; not a commentator had pondered the letter of the Holy Scriptures, but contributed each his share. Not a theological controversy had arisen, not a religious war had been waged, not a heresy had been propounded, not a new sect had been originated, not a Christian enterprise inaugurated, that did not contribute to that understanding of Scripture, and that elucidation of its truths, out of which the creeds of Christendom have sprung, and which made their construction a necessity. Each generation has entered into the labors of all that preceded it.

Archbishop Whately, in one of his "Essays on the Peculiarities of the Christian Religion," discusses the question why the New Testament contains no creed or articles of faith. Many good reasons are given for the omission. But to the weightiest reason of all there occurs no allusion. That reason was one of necessity, rather than of design. A creed was omitted because, speaking reverently, it could not be written. One could be written, only when the church, by discussion and trial and experience, had thought out, and felt out the significancy of the facts on which it had been built. A creed, or compend of doctrinal beliefs, is to the facts of the Bible to which it must refer, what a syllabus of scientific principles is to the facts of nature whose principles it embodies. But compend and syllabus alike, could be formed only after long years of investigation, reflection, experiment, and experience. From the beginning until now, the church has been perpetually revolving in her consciousness the facts of revelation, scrutinizing and praying over their significancy, and declaring her convictions in creeds and in ten thousand beneficent activities.

So, on the other hand, the Bible has been the interpreter of the church. The church is a unique institution, animated by a spirit and working by methods which are exclusively its own. Brought into being by omnipotent grace, sustained through trials which no institution of man could survive, the source and the nature of its inner life have been to the uninitiated an unceasing puzzle. Its own life is to itself a mystery, without the explanations that are furnished in the sacred Scriptures.

The great problem of Scepticism has been, as it still is, to account for the origin and continuance of the church by some other means than that of divine interposition. Innumerable solutions have been propounded; but the one explanation that outlives them all, surviving criticism and refuting it by its survival, is the book that records the divine teachings and events amid which the church took its origin. To man it is a mystery that the church could be established only in and by the death of its founder; that its members and strength could be increased only by the persecution and dispersion of its members; that its glory and power in the earth must ever be in proportion to its independence of the state, and its exclusion of all earthly reliance. He who would understand the origin and methods of the church, must look for them in the New Testament Scriptures.

So also of that inner life which animates the church; its explanation to the world is to be found in the New Testament alone. The same mind, alloyed it may be by the spirit of this world, but still in kind the same mind, is in the church that was in its Divine Founder and Lord. The zeal, the patience, the endurance, the self-sacrifice, the unshrinking devotion, the Christian heroism that has characterized the church in every age, have had their origin, not in fanaticism, not in tradition, not in memorials of the heroic, but in him of whom we read in the gospels, and who directed his apostles both in their acts and in their epistles. The church approximates in degree to the divine life of its Lord, just in proportion to the intimacy of its acquaintance with that book through which the knowledge of his will is communicated and the energy of his life is imparted. It is in the Bible alone that we find explanation of the hidden life of the ideal church.

And it is also by recurrence to the Bible alone, that the church can understand herself. Her own inward voice is intelligible to her own ear, only as interpreted according to the sacred Scriptures. Her own consciousness becomes clear or confused, in proportion to her acquaintance with the written word. The life that animates her, and the doctrines by which that life is both expounded and measured, are intelligible and defensible to herself only by recurrence to those biblical facts from which they sprung. And thus in connection with this office of mutual interpretation, emerges at this point the—

IV. Office of mutual corroboration of the contents of each other's records. The evidence which establishes the authenticity of the Scripture records does not prove the trustworthiness of their contents. Sceptics who admit the genuineness of the writings, sometimes deny the veracity or the critical sagacity of the writers. The corroboration of Scripture facts, therefore, is no slight service, and this service is rendered by the church.

Of the facts recorded in the Bible, none have been so virulently assailed, none so offensively scouted, as its miracles. The elaborate arguments once adduced to prove their non-occurrence, are now abandoned for the short and easy assumption of their *impossibility*. So violent has been this hostility to a belief in them, that they have been regarded by some as even an incumbrance to Christianity. But they are an integral part of it. The gospel and its miracles cannot be dissociated. Christianity, if a supernatural revelation, is itself a miracle, and supernatural phenomena were its natural accompaniments.

In the defense of miracles it is idle to parley—impossible to distinguish between the probable and the improbable. All stand or fall together. But select, if you will, that which, in itself considered, is the most improbable among them—the greatest and most wonderful of their number—the last and climax of the series —the resurrection of Christ from the dead. Inasmuch as the greater always includes the less, if the fact of the resurrection can be established, the credibility of the whole series must follow. But of the fact of the resurrection, the very existence of the Christian Church is incontestable evidence. Without that fact the origin of the church is not only unaccountable, but contrary to all known relation of cause and effect.

Picture to yourselves the apostles and disciples when the sad truth first came home to them that their Master was dead and buried. They had trusted in him as the one "which should have redeemed Israel." They were sure they had seen in him the evidences of the great Messiah. All manner of diseases had been healed at his word; demons had fled at his presence; the winds and the waves had obeyed him; universal nature had recognized him as her Lord; from the heavens, legions of angels had only waited his bidding to sweep down to his aid. And yet this Lord of all had been arrested, tried, condemned, and, like any other helpless criminal, had been publicly executed. As if in an instant the whole fabric of their day-dreams had vanished. The ex-

Relation of the Church and the Bible. 405

tinction of their hopes was complete, their disappointment overwhelming. Their Master dead, and buried, they were themselves marked men. They fled in dismay, each to his own home.* On the third day it was whispered, "The Master is risen." Gliding from their homes, they stealthily assembled.† Suddenly "Jesus stood in the midst," and, "then were they glad when they saw the Lord." Slowly emboldened by the growing evidence that the Lord was "risen indeed," one hundred and twenty disciples gathered at last in open assemblage. Pentecost came, and the Christian Church was forever established. The disappointed and affrighted apostles who had fled for their lives, now challenged rulers with their bold words, "Whether it be right in the sight of God to hearken unto you more than unto God, judge ye." But for the resurrection of Christ from the dead, there had been no Christian Church, and, but for the Christian Church, it had not been possible to establish his resurrection beyond a cavil. As it is, no fact in history is so well authenticated as that "Christ died for our sins, was buried, and that he rose again on the third day according to the Scriptures."

The Scriptures, in return for this service of the church, are equally explicit in their confirmation of the contents of its records. Among their diversified records none is worthier of our attention than its Religious and Theological Literature. It is here that we may trace the course of its deepening life and its progressive apprehension of truth. Enter this literature at whatever point you choose, the indubitable signs of its origin present themselves. Follow this literature back from our day to its source, and its growth is found to have

---

* John xvi. 32.   † John xx. 19.

been organically complete. Its epochs are all known to us. Every foreign influence to which it has been exposed has been critically examined. The history of no literature was ever so thoroughly investigated; the origin of none more clearly demonstrable. No man disputes that its beginning was in the teachings of Jesus.

Select, now, any one of the great doctrines embodied in this literature; take one, if you please, against which the opposition has been most violent and uncompromising—the doctrine of the Trinity. At no period of the church does this doctrine, in some form, fail to meet you. Disputants have wrangled long over the terms that should express it, and diversified formulas have been adopted. The extraneous influence on the disputants are all easily traced; but the doctrine itself, like the life and consciousness of the church, has existed continuously from the beginning. Its origin was in the facts of the gospels. The Christians in Bithynia, at the beginning of the second century, singing hymns to Christ as God, were but the lineal continuators of that vast throng whose voice throughout the Scriptures, from Pentecost to the close of the apocalyptic visions, is heard resounding in ever swelling anthems of praise to Christ as "King of Kings and Lord of Lords." What the first Christians began and the Bithynian Christians continued, Christendom has perpetuated. Throughout the hymnology of the church, like an unbroken thread, runs the recognition of the divinity of Christ, and consequently of the trinity of the Godhead.

Starting, now, with the facts of the gospels, the rise of the doctrine of the trinity is easy and natural. Jesus on earth exercised the power to forgive sins. The forgiven heart, true to itself, instinctively worshiped the bestower of its priceless blessings. To Jesus ascended, the cry from unnumbered millions has been, "have mercy on us;" and, in answer to the petition, has been the bestowal of new hearts and new wills devoutly loyal and worshipful to the bestower. The facts of the gospel narratives, and the facts of Christian experience as well, contain in the germ the doctrine of the Trinity; and by the same process might be vindicated from the facts of the gospels every other great doctrine of the church. But inasmuch as truth vindicated is a truth made authoritative, we must here take account of another mutual office, in which—

V. The Church and the Bible have coöperated in the enforcement of each other's requirements. Both were commissioned with the same message to men, but each was to work in its own sphere, in conjunction with, and in dependence on, the supporting power of the other.

Divine truth was first revealed to men by acts and oral teaching. Of what was said and done, an authentic record by inspired men preserves to us a sufficiently extended account. That record is our Bible. But to that record it was impossible to transfer the freshness and vivacity of the original communication. Vividly as the Bible speaks to us through the eye and the imagination, it lacks the magnetic power of the living voice and person. That voice and person could be furnished to the world only in the living church. He who once tabernacled in the flesh, "heard," "seen" and "handled" of men, on withdrawing to the invisible world imparted something of the divine energy of his own person to the church—to the visible representation of his presence on earth. What he said, and did, and suffered, recorded in language, the church, re-echoing in its preaching, re-enacting in its charities, and reproducing in its graces of Christian character, has preserved and will perpetuate to the latest time as a living force in society.

What effect would have accompanied a merely *written* revelation from God to men, it is difficult now to conjecture. That some effect would have followed it seems impossible to deny. But what shall be the sustained and final effect of such a revelation, interpreted and corroborated and enforced with all the emphasis and energy of an ever-growing body of devout believers, it is impossible to over-estimate. In all her ten thousand voices of spoken words, of acted benevolence and love, of matured virtues, the church both enforces the teachings of revelation and foreshadows the coming consummation of their triumph. But in all the multitudinous agencies of the church in the enforcement of those teachings and the proclamation of their triumph, there is none so effectual as that of the breathing man and the living voice.

The value of mere preaching has possibly been over-estimated. Amid the universal laudations of the press there has doubtless sometimes been an over-glorification of the pulpit. The author and the editor, we are told, are now to rule the world. Types and not tones are hereafter to sway the minds of men. There has seemed to be no end to the rant about the "power of the press." And yet, with all the influence of the "secular press," which at present surpasses that of the "religious," there comes never a political campaign in which partizan leaders are willing to trust their cause to the pen alone. In the last appeals to the people the tripod is abandoned for the stump. It is the seen and living speaker, rather than the invisible and impersonal writer, whose thoughts reach and finally control the hidden springs of action. And what is here true in politics, is equally true in religion. It is by hearing, rather than by reading—by the living tongue rather than by the inanimate pen—that men are reclaimed to the service of God. The press has its place in the progress of the kingdom of righteousness, but that place is not to be found in supplanting the pulpit. The earth may be made to tremble beneath the thunder of its printing presses, and Bibles be scattered in its highways and by-ways, and its surface be whitened with tracts, and yet the world move on undisturbed in its course, unless the truth, welling out of the heart of living believers—the personal church—is proclaimed "in demonstration of the spirit and of power." The written truth of the Bible, to be effective with men, must also become the spoken truth of the church.

But we have said that the message intrusted to the Scriptures for men, has also been committed to the church. The former is a "light to the path of man," if he will follow it; the latter is a "light of the world," which "cannot be hid." Believers, by their very character as disciples of Christ, occupy, in relation to the rest of mankind, an isolated and contrasted position. They are not only the reprovers of vice and patrons of virtue, they are the heralds of salvation to men. Organized, notwithstanding sectarian subdivisions, into one body by the spontaneous action of the law of faith that rules in them, their presence in society is, in one aspect, a standing rebuke of all who are not within the circle of their brotherhood, while in another it is a persuasive invitation to all to enter.

And to a delivery of their two-fold message to men, believers are prompted by an irresistible impulse. To have become a disciple of Christ, is to have been laid under the necessity of proclaiming him to others. The law of love that binds to him, is as inexorable as any one of the ten commandments. The consciousness of his presence and power in the soul is so immediate, that every true believer proclaims him as by a spontaneity of nature. The sense of the justness of his requirements and the divine beauty, and love of his promises, so pervades his true people that they set him forth to others with something of the emphasis and assurance of a self-contained authority. To that authority the world is ever flinging back its querulous challenge. And to that challenge there remains for us but the one and unchanging reply: our authority is the Bible—the revelation from God.

In its use of the Bible for the enforcement of its teachings, two methods present themselves to the church. In the one, the Bible is appealed to as an objective, extrinsic document, the divine origin and transmission of which to our day is to be duly authenticated; a document, the warranty of which to be regarded as the standard of appeal, is impliedly dependent on the evidence, historical or other, which can be adduced in its support. But unfortunately the authority of the Scriptures is by too many disputed in our day. The ever-recurring question is, *has* God spoken this which the church quotes in enforcement of its message? And shall the pulpit busy itself with its never-ceasing answer of the "evidences?" Where then were the preaching of the gospel? Is there not a "more excellent way?" May we not rather assume that God has spoken in his holy word, and trust more than some have done, in the power of the truth to witness for itself in the heart? Surely, if the church, giving itself in earnest to the study of its sacred deposit—the Scriptures—and imbuing mind and heart with their spirit and truths, would address itself to the world with the assurance of intelligent conviction, the world would listen as to a voice that spoke with divine authority.

The Bible has been too much regarded as a mere history of the past. It is rather an unchangeable mirror of the soul of the race. It is more a revelation of things uncreated and eternal, than of things created and changeable. Truth has not been fitted to the soul, but the soul to truth. Man was created; truth has been revealed. Let the church speak the truth as it is in Jesus, and the world will confess that never man spake as does the church. There is a power in that truth which no criticism can sap, no science withstand, no power in the universe overthrow. With the enforcement of this truth, the church and the Bible have been jointly intrusted. And in the fulfillment of their high commission they will be found to be—

VI. Justificatory of each other's aims. The Bible is both retrospective and anticipatory—legal and evangelical—preceptive and prophetic. Its records begin with the origin of all things, and end with their final restitution. Towards that restitution it brings to bear all its double enginery of precept and penalty, of prophecy and promise. It opens before the race a stupendous destiny. To the realization of that destiny, every page of it, historical and prophetic, statutory and lyrical, doctrinal and hortatory alike, looks steadily forward. In its visions of the future, universal nature has been laid under tribute for imagery. Are its visions the dreams of enthusiasts? Are its aims chimerical and its promises delusive? Let the church answer. The past and the present must foretell the church's future. Itself, under God, is what the Bible has made it.

The career of the church thus far has not been faultless. None of its individual members have been immaculate. Its spirit has not always been pure, nor its piety always exalted. Bad men have corrupted its life, and designing ones betrayed it into depraving alliances. But after every abatement that can justly be made for crudity of results, for lack of achievement, and for perverted force, who can state the number, or measure the greatness of the blessings it has conferred on the world? Let the low level from which the nations of Christendom have been raised, remind us of the greatness of the power that has raised them. Let Christian civilization, confronting every other that history has known, recount to us the ten thousand offices performed by Christianity, every one of which has been in fulfillment of some Scriptural injunction. And, most of all, let the church remind us of the sorrows she has assuaged, the serene peace she has imparted, the moral victories she has won, the heroic and saintly virtues she has cultivated, each beneficent office having been but a fulfillment of some Scriptural promise. But if such have been the triumphs of the church in the past, amid obstacles that have steadily diminished* in numbers and force, with what rapidity may she not advance hereafter; and, aided by the multiplied agencies now at her command, to what glory of achievement may she not attain in the future? Do not the aims of the Bible find amplest justification in the deeds of the church?

The church, also, as well as the Bible, has its well defined aims. These, comprehensively stated, are the realization of the ideal ends for which man was created; they constitute, in theological language, the salvation of men. They also include the incidental benefits that accompany salvation. The gospel sends its power into every avenue of life, reaching, restraining, and re-directing, where it does not completely control the vital forces of society. It proposes also the subjugation of the whole world to the reign of Christ. It contemplates nothing less than a complete reorganization of society, the rehabilitation of the race, the construction of a new heaven and a new earth. In furtherance of its ends it appropriates, without reserve, the endowments, the acquisitions, the life even, of every one of its members.

Relation of the Church and the Bible. 413

Addressing the world and its united forces of evil with the voice of authority but of love, and sending its messages and its messengers into every corner of the habitable globe, it summons every human being to a reception of the blessings it has to bestow. Such are the aims of the church.

But to eyes that see only the present, these aims seem preposterous. This discrepancy between present achievement and ultimate purpose seems almost immeasurable. The instruments of the church, the agencies at her command, are ridiculed as hopelessly inadequate, as the relics of an effete superstition, which will readily be believed in only by incurable fanatics. The true kingdom of heaven for man, we are assured, is the dominion of natural law; the truly divine powers that give direction to human society and determine its destiny are its own inherent forces, statical and dynamical; and the "good tidings of great joy," for which the race have long waited, are now announced in the "Gospel of Science." And to minds that see only what may be read on the surface of history, these are plausible words; the unearthly aims and instruments and promises of the church seem shadowy and unreal. But let us to the "law and the testimony;" if these speak not according to the voice of the church, it is because the hearer has no ear to hear and there remains no dawn for his darkness.

According to the Scriptures, there never was a time when the resources of the church were such as human wisdom could approve. Surely, it was not from the motley and half heathenish crowd which Moses led up out of Egypt, that unaided man would look for thoughts that should shake the world, or anticipate that the Son of God himself should spring. What Invisible Mind was that which, in spite of the social forces that extinguished the glory of Tyre and Babylon and Nineveh, preserved Jerusalem and the Jewish Church till Shiloh came, and still preserves them, the lifeless but imperishable monuments of itself. Who was he that, building his church on the basis of an open confession of himself, could fulfill, as he has done, the promise that against his church the Gates of Hell should not prevail? And what resistless Power was that, which, taking to itself the little band of once disheartened and affrighted apostles, to whom there pertained none of the adventitious aids of nobility, of high alliance, of wealth, or of philosophy and learning, could mould them into a body, whose light is now irradiating the world, and making known, even to the hierarchy of heaven, the manifold wisdom of God. And where, save in the Bible, does the church learn of that Triune Being, who, having planted his church and preserved it through all the dreary past, still invigorates and expands it into fulfillment of all its glorious destiny. The church, with the Bible in her hands, knows full well the source of her present success, of her future triumphs, and of the final consummation of her hopes.

Thus the church and the Bible, coeval in their origin, have coöperated in the fulfillment of their united and indissoluble offices to man. In the light of the sketch now given of their coöperation, we may understand something,

1. Of the nature and value of Christian experience. Experience is the heart's testing of what is objectively presented to it. The apostles tested or experienced the meaning and efficiency of the facts of the life of Christ, and out of the fullness of their experience, and under guidance of the Spirit, they built up the church and wrote their epistles. Successive generations of believers, taught by the apostles, have relived the apostolic expe-

rience. Out of their Christian consciousness they have reproduced the apostolic doctrine. Their experiences, though endlessly varied by personal idiosyncracies, have been essentially one and the same; and so long as they follow the Bible alone, they will continue to have " One Lord, one faith, one baptism, one God and Father of all."

Now such being the nature of Christian experience, its indissoluble connection with Christian faith and its importance in Christianity become readily apparent. All genuine faith must ground itself in the heart's experience. No one ever truly believes in what he has not felt out and tested in his heart of hearts. A man's real creed is, and always must be, the measure of his experience. The doctrines that mould him are those that grasp his conscience; and to grasp his conscience, they must find his conscience in its hiding-place, and the finding it in its hiding-place is his Christian experience. Does a man doubt the doctrine of the Atonement or of the Trinity? it is because his experience has not taught them to him. They can be learned by him alone on whom Christ has put forth that divine power which renews the heart, and by renewing the heart, enlightens the understanding. All true knowing of the doctrines of Christianity is conditioned on a hearty doing of the will that underlies and is implied in them. And, associated with Christian experience, there come before us in the light of our discussion,

2. The true office and authority of the creeds of the church. If a creed is a measure of the experience of those who have really adopted it, then it may be appealed to in determining the kind and degree of their experience. But to appeal to it in testimony of the genuineness of their experience, is to pervert its office. If experience be the heart's response to the authoritative

teachings of Scripture, then its validity can be tested by the creed only as the creed can be proved to be an echo of the Scriptures. Only by keeping in mind this distinction between the use of the creed and the abuse of it, can we shield it at once from abuse by invective and abuse by misuse.

There are certain men who never wax so eloquent as when declaiming against creeds. The thought of a well-defined doctrinal formula throws them into oratorical spasms. But do these declaimers ever remember what a creed really is, and at what cost of anxious thought, of painful inquiry, of spiritual struggle, of protracted controversy, of final sacrifice of all that the world holds dear, the contents of the creeds were worked out by those who subscribed them? The symbol that embodies the inmost beliefs of a man, to which, with *credo* on his lips, he signs his name, and if need be, stands ready to seal his subsciption with his blood, is not to be tossed aside at the beck of the flippant talker. A creed is something for a devout man to look upon with feelings of respect, if not of reverence. Avaunt then to those theological vagabonds, those semi-agrarians in religion, who having squandered their own beliefs and convictions, are impatient that other people should so tenaciously hold to theirs.

But creeds have been abused by misuse of them. They have been perverted into crucial tests of orthodoxy. There is hardly an ecclesiastical body in Christendom that has been organized around an authoritative creed, that has not, in testing the orthodoxy of its clergy, thrust that creed into the place of the Bible—that has not trenched on the divinely established relation between the church and the Bible. In the Presbyterian Church an appeal to the standards is final. If its ministers speak not according to the letter of the confessions and the catechisms, they are condemnable and condemned. In the Methodist Episcopal Church, the question of orthodoxy is speedily settled by recurrence to the Book of Discipline. The Protestant Episcopal Church has gone still further. Originally organized around a Calvinistic creed—the thirty-nine articles—its Romish liturgy and its high church canons have come to be more authoritative than even its articles. Requiring of its clergy, as a condition to ordination, the acceptance of its articles, which nine tenths of them contradict in their preaching, it will yet wink at any error sooner than at a repudiation of its prayer-book or a violation of its canons.

The tendency of all ecclesiastical organizations that assume to themselves the title of Church, is to disturb the legitimate relation of the church to the sacred Scriptures, and to exalt the creed, the work of men, at the expense of the New Testament, the work of God. The letter of a creed may determine a man's fitness to belong to his sect, it cannot properly be made a test of his orthodoxy. Such use is an abuse of it.

And to this misuse or abuse is undoubtedly to be traced much of that waning reverence for creeds and all mere church authority, over which some are disposed to lament. But it is idle to go about with lengthened faces deploring the loss of what can no longer be retained. Yea, rather let God be thanked that the new wine is bursting asunder the old bottles of tradition, and that religion, from being a mere unthinking acceptance of the language of man, however venerable from age or sacred from association, is becoming an earnest and scrutinizing trust in the authoritative word of God.

3. In contrast with the sects just named, the Baptists have always persisted in a maintenance of the true use of creeds, and of the true relation of church prerogative to Scripture authority. They have no one au-

thoritative creed to whose wording all must bow, no ecclesiastical judicatories, no canons, no directory, no book of discipline, and yet not a sect in Christendom is more completely one in its faith, more uniform in its ecclesiastical usages, or more prompt and rigid and efficient in its discipline. Presbyterians may hesitate and waver amid the divergencies of "Old School and New School," and before the perplexities of the question of "infant church membership;" Methodists may pause and wrangle over the question of "lay representation;" and Episcopalians may falter and stammer over their "baptismal regeneration;" but Baptists, in their convocations, have no questions of polity or of faith which they fear to confront and frankly to dispose of. Their churches, brooking no assumption of authority by association or by convention, hold themselves amenable to Christ alone; their ministers, acknowledging the right of no association, or convention, or any other ecclesiastical body to introduce them into the Christian ministry, or to eject them from it, recognize themselves as responsible to the churches alone of which they are members; and each church, maintaining its independency, and aided by such counsel as, in courtesy to other churches, it may choose to ask from them, judges of the worthiness of its own members and ministers. By all true Baptists the voice of the church universal is attentively heeded, but in every discussion, whether of doctrine or of practice, their final appeal is to the Bible, and to the Bible alone. The church, while honored by her Lord in all her ten thousand offices of teaching his truth, has not been commissioned to legislate, but to learn in lowliness from his divine statutes. And hence we learn finally,

4. What kind of deference is to be paid in the interpretation of these statutes to the voice of the church universal. The voice of single sections of the church,

however imposing from age or numbers, may misguide us. These have foisted many errors on the Scriptures and perseveringly maintained them. The history of their errors is easily traced. They are not the affirmations of the church universal. But on all the great doctrines of Christianity, on which the very existence of the church is dependent, a recognition of which the church has regarded as essential to salvation, the germ of which was planted in the personal teachings of our Lord himself, and the organic growth of which has been uninterrupted from the beginning, the voice of the church has an authority which is not to be lightly set aside. It is the voice of a united testimony, coming down to us without interruption from the lips of the Lord himself. Let then the minor differences which now hedge in the compounds of the sects, be tested as best they may by Scripture, and by such testimony of the church as she can authentically pronounce. But for all that is fundamental in Christianity, for all that distinguishes the church from the world, the believer from the unbeliever, the voice of the church of God and of his Holy Scriptures have ever been and must ever remain harmonious and one.

XVIII.

THE CHURCH IN ITS RELATIONS TO THE STATE.

By WILLIAM R. WILLLIAMS, D.D.,
Late Pastor of Amity Street Baptist Church, New York.

"AND HE SAID UNTO THEM: RENDER THEREFORE UNTO CÆSAR THE THINGS WHICH BE CÆSAR'S, AND UNTO GOD THE THINGS WHICH BE GOD'S."—*Luke* xx. 25.

"AND KINGS SHALL BE THY NURSING FATHERS, AND THEIR QUEENS THY NURSING MOTHERS."—*Isaiah* xlix. 23.

SOME have doubted whether wit, in the ordinary sense of that term, ever marked our Lord's human utterances. If the word be used to describe the levity which studies mainly the incongruous and ludicrous, and which aims to enkindle merriment at any cost of truth and of feeling—then from it our Lord refrained, as from all the "idle words," which he, condemning them in others, certainly never used in his own intercourse with men. But if by that much-perverted name, wit, be meant the sudden flashes of thought, apt and felicitous, which bring out some connection before unsuspected, parry quickly a thrust, reveal suddenly an undetected flaw, and overwhelm helplessly an arrogant assailant—then, the Saviour's colloquies with the crafty and malignant Pharisees, more than once, displayed wit of the highest order, like the diamond in brightness, and falchion-like in keenness. The chief priests in the temple, the house of Christ's own Father, in allusion to the tables of the moneychangers which had just been overthrown; and whilst behind the insolent questioners pressed, perchance, more than one of their discontented retainers, with back or with cheek yet tingling from the sting of the Saviour's scourge—the priests questioned him, as they stood in the courts just summarily cleansed from traffic and left clear for worship, "By what authority dost thou these things?" It was as if they would put the inquiry, only as a just preliminary before yielding their own acquiescence and loyal adhesion, could their question be but fully answered. But the intimation was also very distinct, that, without any ostensible right, he had intruded, rudely and sacrilegiously, as a reformer, where he had at best but a dubious position as an humble and ordinary worshiper. Our Lord thrust aside the proud interrogatory with a preliminary question of his own: "Whence was the baptism of John?" And he promised them that soon as they had answered him this, he would respond to their inquiry, and produce the authority for which they asked. This was, on his part, no digression from the theme in hand, and no evasion of the query urged upon himself. John had, as the Lord's forerunner and herald, attested, at the baptismal scenes on the Jordan, which had so roused the entire nation, the divine mission and nature of the stranger whom these proud priests would fain warn off and daunt into silence. The Father himself had in the same hour, and over those same waters, proclaimed the sonship of this well-beloved One, in whose dealings and whose utterances, he, the Eternal Father, their ancestral God, had perfect sympathy. Now the people, agitated and perplexed listeners during this conference, all honored John the Baptist as a true prophet. If these mitred rulers of the nation were ready to accredit, as the people did, John, the herald and escort of Jesus, they could not well discredit the Prince thus ushered in by his precursor prophet, and to whom the Father himself had, on the banks of the Jordan, and in the very course of the ordinance, given so illustrious and distinct a voucher. No usurper, and rightfully no stranger, he had now come, in that Father's name, and bearing that Father's seal, to the Father's own house, to see that the servitors of that house kept it fit for its holy uses—and to claim from the dishonest husbandmen the stipulated fruits of the Father's vineyard, so long misappropriated. Should they impeach the Baptist, they dreaded the popular indignation. Should they admit the Baptist, his Master's feet were heard, close and loud, behind him. They were perplexed, entangled, and maddened; but they were also stunned and silenced. They had had the preliminary evidence; and could neither dispute it, nor yet would they obey it. What right had they to be demanding additional proof, when they were thus neglecting and wasting what had gone before? In the alphabet of the new dispensation opening upon them, John had repeated before them the A; and they stubbornly, stolidly, declined to pronounce it after him—without venturing, however, to call in question John's commission from Heaven to set before them the lesson which they thus neglected. Why should Christ be summoned so peremptorily to pronounce, at their pleasure, the B, when they so obstinately refused the instruction which preceded it, and which made it intelligible? If they would not deign to articulate the first letter, why put captious questions about the second? And that scene on the brink of Jordan actually involved the whole substance of the query now urged by these men. By what authority, forsooth? By the authority of their Maker and Judge, the Lawgiver on Sinai, and the Designer, as he was the Glory, of the very temple they were affecting to guard. Around this Galilean peasant lingered yet the fluttering wings of that Dove which descended on the baptismal waters—the halo of that heavenly resplendence, and the echo of that divine recognition. The flaming brightness of the old shekinah—seen by priest on the mercy-seat—beheld by prophet when pausing on the temple threshold—now had virtually reappeared, in the holiness, wisdom and majesty of him, "speaking as never man spoke," and doing works "never before seen in Israel." These all gave him fullest "AUTHORITY" to rout from the temple and its precincts every dove-cote, every stall, and every table; to displace, had he chosen to do it, every doctor in their august Sanhedrim, from Gamaliel and from Nicodemus down; and to disfrock and extrude every priest and attendant, from Annas and Caiaphas down to the lowermost of the Levites that scoured a basin, or plied a besom, or slew the lamb of that morning's sacrifice on that sacred pavement. His Father, well pleased with him at the Jordan, was equally pleased with him in all his present sayings and doings, amid that throng of the residents of Jerusalem. The Infallibility of Sinai was stamped on all that scene of the cleansing of the Temple. Such swift force was there in that brief, apt question, so timely and so pregnant, so keen and yet so simple—quiet as the daybreak, but sudden as the thunder-clap, and dazzling as the lightning's flash.

And here, in the history furnishing our text from Luke, was a similar encounter with the same Pharisees, reinforced by the Herodians—the one class especial sticklers for Hebrew dignity, privilege, and sacredness; and the other watchful guardians of the Greek culture, and of the prerogatives of Rome, by whose patronage their master Herod held his throne. Habitually antagonists the one class to the other, but now confed-

erated by their common enmity to Christ, they come, as
they suppose, well able to transfix our Lord on the one
prong or the other of an inevitable dilemma by asking
him (after some glib flattery of his independence and
frankness, intended to throw him off his guard), if the
payment of tribute to the idolatrous and alien Gentile
were at all lawful from them, the children of Israel,
God's favored people—and from himself especially, the
Son of David, as some called him, and come, if such,
to sit as rightful and sole heir on his father David's
throne. If he replies that it is not lawful, seize him, ye
Herodians, for treason, as against Cæsar! If he replies
that it is allowed, brand him, ye Pharisees, for treason
against the dignities, and the hereditary, imprescriptible
rights of the Hebrew race! For the Pharisees themselves, in secret, taught the thorough unlawfulness of
all such tribute, and begrudged in their hearts Cæsar
every penny of his taxes. And would not the Son of
David, by such assent to Gentile tribute, renounce his
own regal lineage? Christ, in all serene majesty, called
for the coin in common use—that did the day's market-
ing, and paid the day's wages. One is promptly produced, with perchance an ill-concealed smile at the
Galilean simplicity which made such a request. "Whose
is," he asked, "the head on this money, and what the
legend on the coin around the head?" The features were
Cæsar's; and the superscription acknowledged Cæsar's
supremacy, as master of the mint, and the mart, and
the camp, and the throne, for this people. If they had
been ready to exult over the rustic simplicity of the
Nazarene in asking for the penny, they were invited
now, in turn, to ponder and comprehend their own vast
simplicity in overlooking the inevitable sequence from
their using habitually this same coinage. If they, week
by week and year after year, acknowledged Cæsar's

rights of conquest, his persuasive legions, and his persistent tax-gatherers, by taking his coin for their bargains and purchases; if they had paid, perchance, the scribe who transcribed their last copy of the law, and the masons who built their last synagogue, in some of this very coin—then must they, in common equity, "render" honestly back to their imperial master, what, in professed loyalty, they had accepted from him. It was too late, having taken the badges and livery, and wages of service, to begin caviling at the lawfulness of the service itself. And they should, with equal fidelity, give to the Jehovah, the God of their devout fathers, that hearty and spiritual homage which he demanded. They, the Pharisees, notoriously taught that God cared not for the wanderings of the heart, if only the outer act of outbreaking transgression were refrained from. In this they sinned against the first principle of the divine law, which required them to love the Lord their God with all their heart and all their soul. They begrudged God his first claim, much as they begrudged Tiberius and his publicans the coin which they were in taxes paying to the hated Roman. Thus, in the very colloquy where these subtle foes had thought themselves sure to gore the Great Teacher with at least one prong of their forked dilemma, they found themselves quietly transfixed on both prongs of the Lord's calm and bright reply. Restive in heart under Cæsar's yoke, but more fiercely restive against the spiritual yoke of their Maker and God—revolters against the earthly, and more atrociously against the heavenly sovereign; but hiding the one rebellion under the mask of patriotism, and the other under the shows of formalism and hypocrisy—they came, the gentle casuists, to ensnare the Redeemer with a question about duty which grievously burdened these patriotic and pious men. True patriotism, and genuine piety, would have recognized in the national subjugation the fruit and the memorial of the national sin. And so taught, they would have accepted the advice of Jeremiah, given in an earlier captivity, that to the Chaldeans, and which bade the people, chastened and contrite, to seek the peace and good of their Gentile conquerors. Had their conscience the tenderness which they claimed for it, it would have yielded to the pleadings of the Spirit of God. Then would they, with Zacharias, and Simeon, and Anna, worshipers in that very temple of that very Messiah, have hailed the advent of the Teacher they were now striving to entangle. At Bethlehem, with the shepherds, they would have adored his infancy; at Bethabara, they would with John the Baptist have witnessed to the Lamb of God moving onward to his redeeming work, and the Son of God, the brightness, as the Father proclaimed him, of that Father's own glory. But instead, they were now contriving his entanglement, and were soon to be plotting his murder. When some of these very men voted, soon after, in the Sanhedrim, at the suggestion of Caiaphas, that this prophet should perish, they felt yet rankling in their inmost souls, we doubt not, the barbed reply that thus brought out their foiled plot, exposed their duplicity, and made both more inexcusable and more inveterate their obdurate impiety. They owed Christ henceforth a new and deadly grudge—on Cæsar's account, whose name they had failed to use as a snare; on God's account, whose law they had been detected in using as a mask; and most of all, on their own account, so quietly repulsed, so publicly and effectively shamed.

But this reply, so apt and keen, brought out also, my brethren, the great truth—so significant for our times, and for all times—of the just relations between Cæsar and God—between the claims of Human Government upon us, man's rule over his fellows, and the claims of Divine Government upon us also, in the Maker's rule over and judgment of his creatures and pensioners, who remain eternally his subjects. On the one hand is the state, God's ordinance for temporal quiet, justice, and prosperity. On the other hand towers the church—God's better, more spiritual, and more enduring ordinance—with spiritual ends as its chief aim, and eyeing eternity as its ultimate goal and the field of its legitimate range. Uplifting together our hearts to the Father of lights for the aid of his own Spirit, let us review the teachings of Revelation and Providence on this momentous theme. We may observe:

I. The evils of the *confused intermixture* of the Church and the State;

II. Their *distinct offices;*

III. Their *mutual interaction;* but also

IV. Their *true freedom and proper independence,* as leading to the *highest prosperity of each.*

I. By the Church we understand, in the teachings of Scripture, any and every congregation of true believers, regenerate men, accepting the truth of God and the headship and sacrifice of Christ, born again of, imploring the aid of, and led by the influences of the Spirit, Author of all truth; and who meet together in one place for the worship of God, for the celebration of the ordinances, and for the diffusion of Christ's gospel throughout their race. This is the Visible Church—a single, local congregation. The Invisible Church is the great congregation as it shall meet in heaven, composed of all believing and regenerate souls, from every dispensation, every century, and every land. The earthly and Visible Church may have imperfection, error, formalism, and even hypocrisy intermingled in its membership. The Invisible Church is purged from all such adherent dross. Many Christians, besides recognizing these two, speak also of an earthly visible church swollen beyond all dimensions of a single local congregation, and taking in all the believers in any evangelical denomination, as living at any one given time, either in any one country, or yet, more comprehensively, in all the countries of the entire earth. We cannot accept this mode of speech as having scriptural precedent or warrant. We find no instance in the Bible of such use of the word, the church. The New Testament speaks not of the church in Asia, collectively, including in the one singular phrase all its disciples dispersed through the several cities of Asia Minor. But it names, repeatedly, the churches of Asia; and this plural designation is used at a time when those churches were united in doctrine, discipline, and intercommunion, as churches never since were; and when, in consequence, if ever suitable, such singular appellation for them all, as the church of Asia, would have been intrinsically most suitable. But the apostles shunned employing this generalization. And so, the churches—not the church—of Macedonia; the churches—not the church—of Galatia; the churches—not the church—of Judæa; the churches—not the church—of Syria; the churches—not the church—of the Gentiles; are the ever-recurrent phrases of inspiration. This plural phrase would appear strangely significant. To us it seems the protest of the Great Head and Lawgiver of the church against the modern assumption, that all the worshiping bodies of any one entire denomination may, in propriety, be clustered together and called, in the singular form of the phrase, a church. Thus, many speak—grouping together all the congregations in one land that are of similar denominational views—of the Baptist Church in America, or the Episcopal Church in Britain, or the

Presbyterian Church of Scotland, or the Lutheran Church of Germany, or the Reformed Church of Holland or of France. Failing to find scriptural pattern or authority for such expansion and aggregate use of the singular term church in regard to earthly assemblies, we cannot adopt its use, or accept the inferences and consequences which those who do use it unconsciously derive from it.

For the assumption leads rapidly to the theoretical error, and the great practical peril consequent on that error, of imagining a vast collective corporation, overspreading a land, and with whom the state may deal, as having the same geographical boundaries as itself. The image, thus national in its ramifications, and legislation and power, becomes the incitement toward an alliance or a fusion of the political and ecclesiastical power, stretching their tent-cords over the same portion of earth's surface. The two corporate powers enlisting often each the same persons, in the one body, as citizens, and in the other as communicants or worshipers; the theory grasps readily the entire nation, as forming but one real body, under the twofold aspect of church and state; and the statesman and the churchman so theorizing, must naturally wish to provide for their final and indivisible alliance. That alliance becomes to the state often, in days of revived religious zeal annoying and onerous, and even revolutionary. Be the zeal of the religionist the ambition of a Becket or a Hildebrand, a Wolsey or a Torquemada; or, be it the flaming love of souls that burned in a Whitfield or a Wesley or a Bunyan; or, be it the heroic attachment to the truth of a Wickliffe, a Luther or a Calvin; a fervid state of the church is, more or less, uneasiness to the worldly ruler who must deal with it. To the church, on the other hand, such alliance becomes an influence to secularize, to pervert, and to cripple, whilst nominally subsidizing, arming, and patronizing her. Persecution becomes an almost inevitable sequent. Statecraft and Priestcraft, each an evil when alone, become more evil by their mutual aid and emulation, and plague together, the country, which, in common, they drain of its resources, and in common they circumscribe and fetter in its development. Revenue and power and rank tempt evil men into the high places of the church. Simon Maguses are more easily fostered than Simon Peters. And if God withdraw his hand of restraint, the Christian church sees rising within her nominal bounds, men like Dunstan and Wolsey and Richelieu and Mazarin and Dubois, trampling on truth and right, and aiming at power, won by the worst means and used for the basest ends.

Our own favored land has, for long years, enjoyed the distinction and blessedness of seeing the Christian church left alike unendowed and unfettered of the state; and yet largely influential, widely enterprising, and richly prospered. And our own churches, as a denomination, may well thank God for the memory of Roger Williams, and for the testimony by him borne to Soul Liberty, so faithfully and effectively amid general incredulity and obloquy. He called heroically for the removal of all political restraints and all political supports from the Christian church. His doctrine, resisted and decried, as in his own time it was, even by most pious men, like Baxter and Rutherford, and Herbert Palmer, as baleful and atheistic, was not the original discovery, the slow excogitation of that bold spirit, although God honored him to become so ardently and manfully its champion. That dogma belonged to our own churches in England, Holland and Germany, long before he was attached to our membership, and is found in the confessions and arguments of English Baptists, before Williams became their disciple and adherent. Yet recognized, as is now, the rightfulness of separating church from state, on our own side of the Atlantic, and our northern section of the continent, how slow and grudging has been the acknowledgment and welcome of the doctrine, north of the St. Lawrence and south of the Isthmus of Darien, in this western hemisphere. Still more slow has been its admission among the Christians of the old world. Even a thinker, so clear and so bold as Arnold of Rugby, found it hard to conceive of a Christian church apart from the body of the nation. Then to wield and harmonize the religious activities of that nation, there must be adopted the vaguest and laxest type of Christian doctrine, and the loosest and most secular type of Christian practice, consistent with any retention of the Christian name. This becomes the normal ideal of a Christian church that shall grasp, tax, and sway the entire nation. And so led on, Arnold, though not himself Socinian, would have his national church take in Socinian teachers. Thus would he confiscate Christ's own golden crown of Godhead to beat it into the thin and flexible goldleaf bands of a most perilous and unwarranted brotherhood. It becomes the interest of many, some on the devouter, and some on the more secular side, to drive the bargain of mutual alliance and co-operation to its last terms. The pulpit, in an endowed church and a monarchical government, should reflect the will of the Cabinet, and be the mouth-piece of the Court. In the wars of the League in France, it trumpeted sedition and revolt; in the days of the later Stuarts of England, it sought to graft passive obedience in the interest of despotism, on the Gospel of Paul and Paul's Master. The state in its turn, is to rear and repair the sanctuary, grant the tithe and the glebe, and appoint or approve the chief dignitaries of the church. Or, if the superior church power lodge on a foreign shore, then, solemn concordats must determine anxiously, when, and how far, statesmen will sanction the territorial enactments of churchmen. Intrigue, often in the hands of infidel politicians, and the backstair influence of the most profligate courtiers, and even of royal harlots, dictate the filling of those ecclesiastical posts, which, according to the theory and demand of the New Testament, need watchmen, called and endowed of the Holy Ghost. It is, in result, as if Herodias, having won the Baptist's head, was asked graciously to extend and perpetuate her power over the people of God, by becoming the step-mother of the new evangel, filling up, with her serene wisdom, each vacancy in the apostolical college, as a James might be beheaded or a Peter crucified. Pillories, dungeons, racks, scaffolds, and inquisitions have been invoked to establish the cause of him, who declared his own kingdom not one of this world. And the Lord said this at the bar of the Roman, where, had he chosen it, he might have converted a Pilate into a Sergius Paulus; and when he might, in the illimitable resources of his wisdom and power, have transmuted Pilate's imperial master, the hoary Tiberius, into an anticipated Constantine, or a re-appearing Hezekiah, commissioned to rear the secular interests of the church, speedily and potently, on a wide basis, and to a lofty elevation. That our Great Head did not so build up his Zion on Cæsar's patronage, was evidence irrefragable that he saw a better, surer, and more effective way, than that mode of advancing religion by worldly endowment, wealth, and control, which many thinkers regard as the way not only best, surest, and most effective, but as the only remaining and feasible way. Our gospel, unendowed not only, but persecuted and proscribed, marched from the foot of the Saviour's cross, through ghastly catacombs, and over the blood and ashes of its own thick-fallen martyrs to the evangelization of Cæsar's empire, and the conversion of remote and outlying barbarians, whom Cæsar's legions had failed to subdue.

But has not God, by his own servant Isaiah, foretold to the Zion of the latter days, that kings should become to her as her nursing fathers, and their queens as her nursing mothers? The language has been heedlessly misapplied, as if it intended to foster and sanction the state endowments which have often invited a Demas to nurse his "love of this present evil world" in church precincts, and which have installed a Diotrephes to display his "love of pre-eminence" among the followers of that Crucified Master, who would have his chiefest disciples the servants of all their brethren. The sovereigns, who have, like Henry VIII., or Louis XIV., most assiduously affected to patronize religion, have read this prediction of Isaiah, as if it virtually constituted them the cruel step-fathers, who might strangle the infant heir at choice, dictate the will and testament anew, and divide the heritage, at their own liking. But what is the actual imagery? It was the custom of the East that the sons of a regal line were often entrusted, afar from their father's capital and residence, to some of his chosen nobles for education and nurture. He, the inferior, trained thus those who were his monarch's children, and one of whom, if surviving the parent, and outranking his brothers, might become king one day over himself, the nursing father, and over his own children, the foster-brothers and the foster-sisters of that royal nursling. The nursing fathers and nursing mothers were thus, and ever remained, the inferiors of the royal progeny whom they, for the time, fostered and trained. The nobles of Jezreel were in this relation, in Jehu's time, towards no less than seventy of Ahab's sons. Now Isaiah's prophecy represents kings and queens—all earthly potentates—as occupying this inferior position toward the cause of God. Religion, daughter of the skies, is in this world afar from the celestial home and court of her Divine Parent. But in her stay here she renounces not her ancestry, her original home, and her ultimate destiny. The crowned rulers of earth, who were wont themselves to have nursing fathers, inferior in dignity and in prospects to themselves, become now, by God's appointment, the inferior foster-parents of God's Zion on this earth. They watched, in her feeble and infant beginning, the seed of an older and more illustrious line than that of Guelphs, Bourbons, or Hapsburghs; and they were called to recognize, in that infantile development, rights and prerogatives of divine bestowment. It was this maligned and martyred faith that was predestined to rule the planet, enfranchising yet all its captives, and righting one day all its wrongs. Dependency, on the part of royalty, not domination was the attitude, which in the divine scheme was to be assumed by the secular power toward the cause of God. Not, indeed, the dependence of subserviency to the churches as secular corporations, but dependence on the truth there taught, on the conscience there educated, on the kingdom of God there inaugurated, and thence radiating out upon the race enfranchisement and civilization, enlightenment, and true sanctification.

Some, in our day, have seen the evil of religious persecution, and yet have been unwilling to relinquish all national establishments, lest national ungodliness should be the result. They would have the state, by a strange impartiality, widen its establishment, varying its motley creeds and rituals according to the likings of its subjects. But they could furnish no test by which statesmen might be held to select and to establish only the true religion. Britain has thus subsidized Episcopacy in England, and Presbyterianism in Scotland; and has by more than one of her statesmen threatened to add to the staff of her ecclesiastical pensioners, by endowing Romanism in Ireland. By some of her Indian placemen she has contributed to the festivals of Juggernaut, foul and bloody as they are; and she has cashiered Protestant soldiers for refusing, in Malta, to share in the processions that gave to the Mass idolatrous honor. Catholic France pays salaries to the Romish priest, the Protestant pastor, and the Jewish rabbi. Now a faith thus elastic, indiscriminate, and all-devouring, cannot honor God, or rightly develop conscience. Parity of reasoning would require it to extend salaries and subsidies to the impurities and defilements of Mahommedanism and Mormonism, should votaries of either delusion, in sufficient numbers, colonize its soil; and would even demand its patronage for the human sacrifices of Hindooism, and the cannibal feasts of New Zealand. The God of the Bible cannot be propitiated by being thus made to occupy a divided throne with Belial and Mammon, and Moloch, as rivals or co-assessors. Christ, the Light and the coming Judge of the world, denounces as utter impossibility such blended, divided reign. Pantheism would be its natural result and final crown; and the father of lies might well hail as his victory a scheme to make all his impostures one amalgam with the truth of God, and thus writing ultimately all truths as lies, and sanctioning all lies as virtual truth.

II. The Church and the State, have, we proceed to remark, *distinct offices*. The one, born of earth, and living mainly for the earth, eyes mainly, if not exclusively, earthly good. It seeks worldly order, comfort, peace, and prosperity. Its chief reliance for defence and perpetuation is on material force. It guards its laws with the sanctions of fine, imprisonment, and death. Stripes and bonds, and pecuniary forfeitures and confiscations are its legitimate instruments. It can levy the army and equip the navy, and wage the war, if its interests and the infringement of its rights require such guards and avengers. The other eyes chiefly, though not exclusively, man's spiritual good. The soul is its chief care. It may not resort to secular punishments for its extension, and the restraint and correction of its offending membership. Its ban is spiritual disfranchisement. It sends into the world of the irreligious and the unregenerate its recreant and unfaithful disciples, as no longer worthy of its ordinances and fraternity. Its legislation is divine in origin; and became final and complete when the canon of revelation was filled out, and upon the departure of the last inspired Apostles. Earthly states may amend, and accumulate statute upon statute; but her law-book came out of her Redeemer's hand, and no more admits of human supplements than did Sinai, where God spoke, accept of the human echoes, that came reverberating back upon it from the tribes who rehearsed the law on Ebal and Gerizim, as if these acclamations of man appended to or detracted from the original edicts of Jehovah. Its life is not hereditary, the right of a clan or race; nor is it territorial, absorbing all the dwellers of any continent, or land, or homestead even. The Spirit of God, acting by moral suasion, and secret, divine energy, on man's conscience, hopes, affections, and fears, is its great controlling power and its pervasive and diffusive life. Both church and state should seek truth. But the truth of the state is secular justice, which in many of its details must be a matter of human arrangement. The church of God takes truth also as its great standard; but it is truth as contained in revelation, not to be enlarged by canons of man; and the justice to which it directs the aspirations of all its genuine membership is inward, spiritual piety, righteousness before God, as won by a divine atonement, accepted by a regenerate heart, and witnessing itself in practical righteousness before man, by a penitent, holy, and beneficent life. In the state, the condition of revolt is an exception, an anomaly unknown to the mass of the community; and pardon is a boon that few need, and of which none boasts. In the church, each true believer acknowledges as his original condition a guilty revolt against the heavenly Father; and all base their hopes of acceptance with that Father on a pardon sealed with the blood of a compassionate and Divine Ransomer. Descended from heaven, the church finds its true outward and homeward look to be one opening into the eternal world, and the hope of admission to that Paradise from whence its Founder stooped, and whither he re-ascended. The Jerusalem from above is, thus, the mother of all God's true Israel.

But it is an error in drawing the bounds of the distinct offices of church and state, to pencil the line too broadly, as is often done, by saying that religion relates solely to the immaterial, to the spiritual and to the invisible; and that political science and government concern, just as exclusively, only that which is tangible, material, terrene, and transitory. Neither of these assertions can be held to be exact and true. On the broad scale of national activities, and in the narrower field of the neighborhood and its jostlings, the political must take hold on the moral; and the material must need often to bring aid from the immaterial and invisible world. The greatest of political convulsions, in our times and those of our fathers, the first French Revolution, was more a war of ideas than of material interests, though these last were fearfully involved. The great coming war, with which Canning menaced Europe, was to be, according to his augury, a war of ideas, which of all kinds of war is the most lavish in its outlays, the most gigantic in its efforts, and the most dire in its broad, deep furrows of carnage. So the bickerings of a secluded hamlet take hold, in like manner, on something intangible and ethereal. The twelve men of a jury, summoned to adjudicate the ownership of a half acre, or to pronounce on an alleged assault by one tenant upon another, have indeed, at first sight, but material objects before them. And yet the right of property in the turf, and the right of defence for the assailed against his unjust assailant, both rest at last on spiritual, immaterial principles. The justice to be administered must be fetched from conscience, and law, and the sense of right, all great, impalpable, but ineradicable principles. The law secular then, shaping and weighing material interests, must have its immaterial root. The name and sway of God are invoked to get true testimony on the subject of litigation; and invoked again by the juror, to pledge on his part true deliverance as upon that testimony. Over every acre of soil, and every form of varied social activity, over all the material products that agriculture and manufactures heap up, and that commerce wafts and exchanges—over workshops, and banks, and village gardens, and forest clearings, broods inseparably and eternally, the great idea of duty, derivable, if traced to its roots, from a controlling Providence, and the will of the one original Creator, the inevitable Judge, as he is the sleepless Guardian of the wide universe which he has formed. The secular cannot forego—may not exclude—the spiritual. Every chip that falls from the carpenter's chisel, every grain of iron rasped by the blacksmith's file, ranges itself within the purview of ownership and right, of law and of duty.

So, too, on the other hand, it is a shallow and unworthy view of religion, that would so etherealize and spiritualize it, as to dissever it from all interference with a man's secular trade, his political activities, or his very amusements. In the days when God shall be most widely feared, and man most largely blessed, prophecy assures us, that the Lord's name shall be on the very bells of the horses; and the very pots of Jerusalem, on all its hearthstones, are to be like the bowls on God's consecrated altar. Plough, and keel, and anvil, and plane, and augur, the child's go-cart, and the grandsire's rocking-chair, are to move under the ken of the Judge above, under the shadow of the Elder Brother's redeeming cross, and in the beaming splendors of the Redeemer's riven tomb. And thus, the immaterial, the infinite, and the eternal, take hold on the things of sense and time—the every-day assiduities of common life—the worry and the repose of the home, the nursery, the kitchen, the quarter-deck, the shop, and the highway. Man, formed of soul and body, born to die but not finding annihilation in death, touches by the necessity of his nature on two worlds, in the one of which the state may have the preponderance as the governing power, but in the other of which religion as inevitably dominates.

III. Whilst we have seen, then, how the nations have groaned under the confused intermixture of the church and the state, and that the offices of the two are mainly distinct, it remains yet manifest, and this is our third topic, that *the two provinces of the church and the state*, the spiritual and the material, the eternal and the temporal, must, because of man's compounded and conglomerate nature, not only at times *impinge;* but they often *overlap and interlace* each other, and even, at times, *interpenetrate the one the other*. Both need truth, both must consider justice: but the one mainly truth, *of secular authority*, and justice as seen on *its civil side;* the other truth as *divinely stated*, and justice as *imparted by grace* and *required in the last judgment*. The one cannot care wisely for the body, without taking some thought for the soul that animates the body. The other cannot adequately consecrate and educate that soul, without making that body a temple of the Holy Ghost, and without reminding each disciple that, whether he eat or drink, or whatever he do, he must do it to the glory of that God who has bought him with the costliest and yet the freest of all redemptions, so that, body, soul, and spirit, he is become the Lord's.

No State can, in the present age, live without morality. Even the old Pagan Greek in his history of heathen Rome, rapacious as she was, found the secret of her prosperity in her high sense, as compared with other nations, of law and justice and religion, as they regarded it. And morality, to find living and permanent roots, must resort to Christianity, and in it recognize the ripest and truest morality of all the earth. Hence the state—in caring for the education of the young, which to be symmetrical or sound, or enduring, must be based in morality—is compelled in a land of Christian light to recognize and to use the morality of Christ's gospel. Even Diderot, the head of the French Encyclopedists, so bitter and audacious a blasphemer, was found once by a friend, as he was teaching his daughter out of the New Testament. Seeing his friend's look of amazement: "Where," said he, "could I find a purer morality?" Sinai and the Mount of Beatitudes must color evermore our secular education, and cannot be dislodged or replaced by any utilitarian code of modern days. So, in our courts of justice, the ministers of law find the insufficiency of earthly statutes and penalties to reach the inmost depths of conscience, and to stir up the sense of profound responsibility in the witness who bears testimony before them. They go, therefore, out of the range of human tribunes and judiciaries, and endeavor to bind the offerer of testimony by a sense of his accountability, to a more dread tribunal, that of the All-knowing Judge who reads hearts. Every affidavit recognizes the Infinite. Roger Williams, in his overstrained theory for the separation of religion from the state, held the oath to be an act of worship, and worship to belong rightfully only to the regenerate; and that, therefore, the magistrate might not tender the oath except to a converted man, since an irreligious man was not authorized to present worship. Wise and good as he was, he there erred. All men, regenerate or unregenerate, should be urged to pray. And so the unconverted may, like his Christian neighbor, well be summoned to remember God's presence and rule, when he approaches to give deliberate testimony. Society needs for its tribunals this appeal to the Omniscient Judge. And so the office-holder, from president or senator down to private soldier and exciseman, needs to be held to fidelity by an oath taken, as in that august though invisible presence. So, too, in the retirement and security of our households, the marriage which is the bond and basis of the family, is not Jewish, Mahommedan, or Mormon, as to the number of wives, or the facility of divorce. But it is Christian. The home, the very fountain of the order, virtue and freedom of the state, in large measure,—the home, we say,—is built thus on a Christian platform and principles. And so, too, the day of the Lord, the Christian Sabbath, is regarded in the process and the sessions of our courts. The judge deserts then the bench, the writ is no longer servable. So does the state interfere for the prevention, on the part of those not Christian, of any outdoor acts which should mar the privileges and the peace of the Christian in his observance of the day. So again, the state cannot overlook the rule of a Divine Providence in the affairs of the world; and calls, therefore, in days of national fasting and thanksgiving, the entire people to acknowledge, in their several modes of worship, the Sovereign Ruler, who smites and heals, and is alike the Inflicter and Remover of national judgments and calamities. Christianity is then, literally and truly, though Jefferson ventured to dispute it, a part of the common law of the nation. For no empire and no republic can build household, or freedom, or law, or order, or prosperity, or union, but on the basis of morality. And with the perfect morality of the gospel blazing before us, how can any state with us, escape indebtedness for its fundamental morals to the gospel of Christ Jesus? It is and must be a Christian morality.

On the other hand, also, the Christian church, taught of God's word and Spirit to recognize his hand in the affairs of this lower world, and to believe that "the powers which be are ordained of God," must admit and respect the rights of the state, in its own legitimate province, of civil governance, of making statutes, enforcing contracts, restraining crimes, levying taxes, and waging war. Should there be a collision at any time, between the laws of God and those of the state, she holds, indeed, the law of God paramount to all and every contravening authority. It would undeify God to claim less than absolute supremacy for his law. She honors the earthly law which thus collides disastrously with the divine law, by bearing meekly the penalty of that mistaken law, and seeking, constitutionally, the amendment and repeal of that law. But she may not at man's bidding disobey a plain enactment of Heaven more than she could, on the plain of Dura, bow down to

Nebuchadnezzar's golden image, or in Daniel's chamber restrain all prayer because the decree of Darius inhibited it. With the apostle she must ever hold that we are bound to obey God rather than man. And this recognition of the divine law, as the higher law, is implied in every oath administered: and the propriety of such preference is recognized, not only in all Christian ethics, but in the old Greek drama and in the old Roman philosophy. Thus, obeying the higher law, and braving the lower law, our Keach mounted, in the disgraceful reign of the Stuarts, in all manfulness the pillory; and our Bunyan lay twelve years, an innocent captive in the dungeon. In the like heroic temper, Richard Baxter, the meek and holy, bore the brutal calumnies and insults of the wretched George, Lord Jeffries; and Harrison, the regicide, as contemporaries styled him, the brave and pure patriot, as posterity hails him, moved with dauntless steadfastness to the scaffold, which sought to degrade him and his fellow sufferers, but which they consecrated and glorified as the high stage of an unstinted and saintly patriotism. The church thus guards law by obedience, where it can; by disobedience where it must; and by both processes, purifies the earthly fountains of legislation.

So, too, the church cherishes liberty, and is herself the best nurse and guardian of the principles that make liberty possible, and that render it resolved, consistent, and eternal. She recognizes, too, the right of the State not only to regulate property at large, but also her especial right to hinder, by the law of mortmain, the accumulation of too large a portion of the soil or of personal property, in the dead, clenched hand of ecclesiastical corporations—a clutch that, once made, is never surrendered. She holds such restraint of mortmain to be a law of spiritual prudence for the interests of religion no less than of government. She can, in our Christian republic, rejoice in the abrogation of the entail and the primogeniture, which in other lands make Wealth petulant and heartless, and render Poverty forlorn not only, but desperate. Loyalty she sanctifies. Duty she elevates and maintains. Industry she saves from greed; and Prosperity she warns against egotism and brutalism. The guardian of order, the witness of truth, the bringer of peace, and the pattern of benevolence;— hers is an especial mission to the world's forgotten ones, to the outcasts who cower in the hedges or loiter along the highways—to the afflicted, the poor, the oppressed, the stranger and the barbarian. And her errand of philanthropy, overleaping all the narrow bounds of earthly states, and throwing down the barriers of alien dialects, is not to cease till her Christ and her Lord come again to a reunited race.

In these and in other ways, the church does much work for the material and secular benefit of the community, which no political society can do effectively for itself. And whilst the Christian pulpit must lose influence and dignity, if mingling habitually and needlessly in the daily political strife; yet, on the other hand, it must, as the prophetic witness of the New Testament dispensation be called, in great national emergencies, to denounce sin in the nation, the collective sovereign of the republic, as fearlessly as did Nathan, a prophet of the old dispensation, denounce sin in David, the individual sovereign of a monarchy. Against the pulpit so witnessing for righteousness, mere politicians will charge a departure from the legitimate office of the ministry. But these critics forget that its very errand from Heaven is to preach repentance—personal repentance as the only escape from individual perdition—national repentance as God's appointed and only way for escaping national judgments and national overthrow. And how such criticism is to be heeded, the Holy Ghost taught, centuries since, when it presented Amos, the prophet of old, rebuked by a politic priest for venturing to reprove sin in Bethel, the king's chapel, and the king's court. The prophet herdsman of Tekoa faltered not. Bethel was in his commission, precisely for this reason, that it was the king's chapel and the king's court. In a republican government, as is ours, the nation is bodily its own king and kaiser. And if national trespasses become grievous, and national perils grow grave, every sanctuary in such a land becomes a "king's chapel," into which the modern Amoses may—aye, must, carry their unwelcome testimony. And its intense unpalatableness to some may only prove its thorough needfulness.

IV. Our last remarks were to be on the *true freedom* and *proper independence* of the church and the state, as leading to the *highest prosperity* of each. This freedom, on either hand, requires the jealous and perpetual remembrance of their distinctness of office. That same freedom requires also, as we believe, a preservation of the New Testament use of the term church for a single local congregation. There, as we think, the Bible leaves the visible church: and congregationalism recognizes it as there left. This very individuality, so to speak, of each local assembly, and the narrowness of the immediate territory, give greater enterprise, and leave room for more unembarrassed action. And as bribery at the hustings becomes impossible with a numerous popular constituency, so corruption of the Christian church, on the part of the state, becomes difficult when instead of one great national church, accessible in a few leaders, the land is filled with numerous clusters of churches, each entire in its own freedom and power, independent all, and yet all influential: and far as one truth rules, and one Spirit of God sways them all, this, their independence not forbidding unison of feeling, and unity of religious testimony. And, as in the human frame the life is in the blood, and the health and vitality of that blood is traceable to the minute, red globules that pervade it, each globule in itself orbed and perfect; so the welfare religiously of the land depends on the normal working and spiritual healthfulness of individual congregations, each a red globule in the veins of the nation's moral life. Let men know themselves but men, who may have personal access through the Mediator Jesus to a personal God—men, at the highest but men, when, like Nebuchadnezzar on the throne—men, when at the lowest, altogether men,—though like Jeremiah in the miry pit, or toiling in the slave gang and the cotton field. And the gospel thus bringing rich and poor, ruler and bondsman, to one level of moral accountability and guiltiness before God, and one plane of hopefulness, ransom, and brotherhood by Christ, teaches equality as no socialist could innocently realize it, as no scheming political leveler ever comprehended it. The gospel, universally diffused and obeyed, would bring the autocrat from his isolation and absolutism to become with Alfred or St. Louis, the father of his people: and must ultimately lift the serf of Russian steppes, and Cuban sugar-fields, to the rank, and the restraints of a freedman and a brother in Christ Jesus. And no nation can become generally and vitally free but by such influences as the gospel and the Spirit of God only can minister. Man needs, even for his highest earthly development, an intellect pervaded by the truth—a conscience made tender, calm, firm and wise by the Scripture and the Holy Ghost, and a humanity and fraternity which the Nazarene only imparts, as he himself, in the highest degree exemplified them. Whom the Son thus makes free, he is free indeed. And godliness, in its aim at the life to come, has thus "the promise also of the life that now is."

Earthly potentates, feeling the need of the morals and the sanction of Christianity, are slow to recognize her native and proper independence, and would burden and hamper her with the livery, wages and restrictions of secular governments. God accepts and blesses the friendship of earthly rulers to his own cause and word, in proportion as such rulers accept the inferior position of nursing fathers to a celestial progeny, not of their lineage, and still less their liege subject and servitor. The Zion of God, as to her birth and her lot, is a king's daughter, and a Redeemer's bride. And though, in the days of Christ's personal humiliation, he would receive no earthly crown or sceptre, the time is coming, when the people of the saints of the Most High God shall have dominion, when their principles shall have elevated and reconciled all earth's down trodden and jarring races ; and then shall come the voice proclaiming, that the kingdoms of this world are become the kingdoms of our Lord, and of his Christ.

How the church may interpenetrate the state, and yet retain its own spiritual distinctness, may be in part made intelligible, if we consider how the family bond, recognized of the state, may yet transcend the limits, and escape in many respects the jurisdiction of the state. We can readily imagine—we may some of us have known a single household—not, it may be, a score in numbers, who yet have become dispersed through several lands, to remote climes, and under very diverse forms of political government. Yet the family bond, stretched over such intervals and chasms, may remain unbroken. The child of parents who are now living by the Shannon or the Danube, under British monarchy or

Austrian imperialism, may be on our shores an American citizen. And the American freeman may, in turn, have a son of his a missionary witness for Christ at the Burman court of farther Asia, or in a Caffre Kraal of Southern Africa. One humble, and not numerous, household may thus interpenetrate with its family unity and life the most various grades of civilization or barbarism—the most diverse forms of absolutism or democracy, or clanship. Idle would it be for the European sovereign of the grandsire to claim the American citizen the son, and the Burman missionary the grandson, as all by family ties his proper liege subjects. It would be interference without warrant, for any African chief or Asiatic despot, where one section of the household were domiciled, should he claim, that he could dissever at his will their conjugal and paternal and filial relations. The nation and the family are, and should remain, distinct. So does the church of Christ, the household of faith, claim to retain its ineffaceable distinctness alike from the family, and from the nation. And yet, everywhere, and to the men of every hue and tongue, that church may have its quick and hearty sympathies, for the barbarian whose rudeness it does not share, the despots whose mode of rule it does not sanction, and the freemen whose privileges and home comforts it, for the time perchance, foregoes, though it can never forget them. The religion we believe and avouch, though a child of the skies, may become, for certain seasons, the nursling and foster child of any earthly form of political power. But her own internal law is from God; her life is hid with his Christ. And free, as the truth makes free, and as the Son of God makes free, no earthly wrongs can irremediably crush her; no barriers of earthly oppression or hellish malice can, ultimately or even long, check her onward course. The word of God is not bound. That word she consults, proclaims, reflects and inherits. Of that word she shares the curbless career, and must partake eternally of its predestined, inevitable, and universal triumphs.

To some the individual congregation may suggest only images of weakness and omens of failure. But let us remember God's mode of working and his warrant of success. When Nehemiah gratefully recounted before God the Lord's past benefits to the Jewish people, he enumerated among them this: "Moreover thou didst divide them into corners."* It is a difficult phrase, and variously construed. But some interpret it as an allusion to the territorial isolation with which God blessed his chosen people, and such as Balaam recognized in them: "Lo, the people shall dwell alone, and shall not be reckoned among the nations"; and such as Moses also exulted over in his dying benediction: "Israel then shall dwell in safety alone." The shutting them into corners recalls, in this light, the image of a small but heroic band, who are planted in the angles of a rocky defile, whose inaccessible, precipitous walls shut them in on either hand, and deprive their assailants of all hope of smiting them on either flank. They are men who guard a Thermopylæ, where a handful can bar the pathway of outnumbering myriads of enemies. So Jehovah, their fathers' God, in selecting the home of his elect tribes put them in the hills and valleys stretching from the foot of Lebanon to the desert and to the sea, with no large harbor of their occupancy, opening upon the blue Mediterranean. By that very seclusion he provided best for their integrity and national simplicity, to remain uncorrupted by entangling alliances and unendangered by aggressive neighbors. So has God shut

---

* Nehem. ix. 22.

up as "into corners," his own church of the ransomed and the regenerate. By their congregational individualism, not national, not hereditary—no traditional, transmitted clanship;—by their spirituality, making grace and the Holy Ghost the first terms of their continued accretions, and their perpetuated vitality, are they enclosed and hemmed in. Walled are they, on one side, by the narrow limits of the local congregation, too small a body to be separately enlisted by so large a power as the nation; and on the other, by the nature of their inner invisible life, a God-given and God-guarded power, which it was not for human governments to begin or for human governments to intercept and extinguish. Formalists and persecutors, in Pagan and in later times, have sneered at the Christian gatherings, met in corners and obscure nooks—"CONVENTICLES," tiny assemblages, as the taunting word describes them, as if bodies so feeble and isolated had and could have no power. But when their fewness and human fragility threw them back, in simplest faith, on their Divine Helper—when their conscious incompetence to evangelize the masses by their own talents and resources backed up these hunted, harried, contemned conventicles against the "ROCK OF AGES"—then came in truth, the Almighty, to the rescue. The village Dothan was girdled with the glittering Mahanaim of God's encamped hosts. "Divided into corners!" you said? Even so. Flung back, thereby, on the arm of the Omnipotent and the bosom of Jesus—they found the Jehovah-Jireh, adequate to and pledged for the impending struggle. Even so; for through the hiss of their enemies' scorn came, clear and sweet, the voice which said: "Fear not, little flock, it is your Father's good pleasure to give you the kingdom." Not so many scores of years ago, there sat in Christian Britain, on the door-steps of a prison, a Christian wife, whose husband was incarcerated within for his share in such conventicles. She nursed at her breast her little babe. That child, of pigmy frame, and thus early steeped in tears, was Isaac Watts, whose hymns have followed the English language all around the globe. The leader of another conventicle, great in genius and in the grace of God, was immured for full one third of the years of his manhood in a dungeon narrower and murkier than the conventicles he haunted. He wrote in that dark, close nook, the Pilgrim's Progress. And long as the Pilgrim of the one is read in so many a dialect, and the Hymns of the other go wafted around the globe, who shall say that the men, driven into corners, had no power with God, and have no honor on high?

In its pristine and scriptural simplicity the local church can scarcely seem a desirable ally, or a serviceable retainer to the nation, a vast territorial and hereditary aggregate. But they dwell, like Israel of old, in safety, because, in this respect at least like Israel when Balaam and when Moses surveyed them, they "dwell alone." Born not of the will of man, or of the will of the flesh, but of the word and Spirit of the Most High, they seek their pedigree, not in the herald's college, but in the Lamb's book of life. They authenticate their new credentials by the oracles of Holy Writ. Sovereigns and Congresses may cherish the religion; but they cannot rightfully elevate themselves above it to revise it, or recast its institutions, or supplement its principles by their own philosophies or policies. Its first Founder is pledged to remain its untiring Pilot—the Immortal, the Infallible, the Immutable, and the Omnipotent Christ. To his truth and his flock, all earthly patronage, be it that of a Constantine or an Alfred, an Edward the Sixth or a Gustavus Adolphus, is but that of a nursing father. Such foster-parent may be noble—may be kingly—but the charge is more noble and more kingly than is the guardian; and has been ennobled by an earlier patent, and crowned for a loftier empire. Cherishing the deposit of revelation that is in the keeping of God's church, earthly favorers of Zion find in the virtues, and graces, and prayers of God's people an abundant overpayment of all their beneficence. And the earnest study of Scripture, and the hearty love of Zion, will soon show, that, to the mutual benefit of the church and the state, it is needed that there should be a perfect and stable independence. With fields of influence that not only touch, but interlace and overlap, there adheres to the very nature of the two a distinctness. Distinct they must remain, as the soil is distinct from the dew that saturates and fattens it—as the earth is distinct from the fragrance of the roses that have scented it, and have sprung from it, and yet are of an organization and a nature apart from its own. The nation changes. Its monuments crumble; its Tyres lose commerce; and its Babylons gather desolation. The race and its language run out. But the church of God is indestructible as its Author, its life hid with Christ in God, its citizenship on high, and its record in the book which the judgment day shall open, and to which all the universe shall listen.

We love our country, and rejoice, my brethren, with a lofty gratitude for the wonders which God has wrought for the state on our shores, reared by such mercies, and guarded by such recent and wondrous deliverances. But we do well to remember that we need, as the sojourners who are soon to quit earth, "a better country, that is, a heavenly." And of our admission to that land, the evidences are to be found in our spiritual meetness. Each true church is a recruiting outer station for the great Invisible Church there, whose walls are salvation, and whose gates are praise, of which the Lamb shall, one day, be the Temple and the unsetting Light. Am I Christ's? Do I, as his liegeman, recognize cordially and habitually the great truth of Christ's uttering, that he would have all her people render to man and to God, to earth and to heaven, to Cæsar and to Jehovah, their appropriate debt of service? He would require piety to God to be adorned with all virtues toward man; and would base all earthly duties on heavenly principles. It is but this reasonable service that I render to Christ the whole heart, the solemn vow, the habitual homage, and the dedicated life which he demands, and which he fully deserves. "To God the things which be God's." And Christ, as being my God no less than my Brother, would have me bear his own *image*, and legibly display the *superscription* that stamps me not my own, but my Lord's. All true godliness is of the mintage of the Redeemer. Thus, loyal to the earthly country, and loyal with a yet more blessed consecration to the heavenly country, and to its King, my Lord and Redeemer, shall I best, with David, serve my generation by the will of God—and pass, when this briefer and lower service expires, to the endless fellowship and worship of the church of the first-born, all washed in one blood, arrayed in one righteousness, radiant with one glory, and named—the whole family in heaven and on earth—with the one name of this Elder Brother. In the dread day, when the winnowing fan of Judgment shall part the formal from the real, the chaff from the kernel—shall sunder not only the bonds of country, but the closer ties of earthly kindred and home, and of all ecclesiastical fellowship merely exterior and ostensible—when, of the children who kneeled at the side of one mother, sat in the same pew, and ate bread at the same table—that winnowing shall take one and leave the other—happy shall he be who shall then and there be owned of Christ as one who truly was owning and avouching Christ here. Such shall pass into their Lord's kingdom and glory, reigning as kings and priests with Christ forever, when the empires and monuments of earth shall have gone into the cinders of the last conflagration, molten and evanished forever.

Other Solid Ground Titles

In addition to the book in your hand, Solid Ground is honored to offer other uncovered treasure, many for the first time in more than a century:

ANNALS OF THE AMERICAN BAPTIST PULPIT by *William B. Sprague*
JESUS OF NAZARETH by *John A.. Broadus*
THE CHILD AT HOME by John S.C. Abbott
THE KING'S HIGHWAY: *The 10 Commandments for the Young* by Richard Newton
THE LIFE OF JESUS CHRIST FOR THE YOUNG by Richard Newton
LET THE CANNON BLAZE AWAY by Joseph P. Thompson
THE STILL HOUR: *Communion with God in Prayer* by Austin Phelps
COLLECTED WORKS of James Henley Thornwell (4 vols.)
CALVINISM IN HISTORY by *Nathaniel S. McFetridge*
OPENING SCRIPTURE: *Hermeneutical Manual* by *Patrick Fairbairn*
THE ASSURANCE OF FAITH by *Louis Berkhof*
THE PASTOR IN THE SICK ROOM by *John D. Wells*
THE BUNYAN OF BROOKLYN: *Life & Sermons of I.S. Spencer*
THE NATIONAL PREACHER: *Sermons from 2nd Great Awakening*
FIRST THINGS: *First Lessons God Taught Mankind* Gardiner Spring
BIBLICAL & THEOLOGICAL STUDIES by *1912 Faculty of Princeton*
THE POWER OF GOD UNTO SALVATION by *B.B. Warfield*
THE LORD OF GLORY by *B.B. Warfield*
A GENTLEMAN & A SCHOLAR: *Memoir of J.P. Boyce* by *J. Broadus*
SERMONS TO THE NATURAL MAN by *W.G.T. Shedd*
SERMONS TO THE SPIRITUAL MAN by *W.G.T. Shedd*
HOMILETICS AND PASTORAL THEOLOGY by *W.G.T. Shedd*
A PASTOR'S SKETCHES 1 & 2 by *Ichabod S. Spencer*
THE PREACHER AND HIS MODELS by *James Stalker*
IMAGO CHRISTI by *James Stalker*
A HISTORY OF PREACHING by *Edwin C. Dargan*
LECTURES ON THE HISTORY OF PREACHING by *J. A. Broadus*
THE SCOTTISH PULPIT by *William Taylor*
THE SHORTER CATECHISM ILLUSTRATED by *John Whitecross*
THE CHURCH MEMBER'S GUIDE by *John Angell James*
THE SUNDAY SCHOOL TEACHER'S GUIDE by *John A. James*
CHRIST IN SONG: *Hymns of Immanuel from All Ages* by *Philip Schaff*
COME YE APART: *Daily Words from the Four Gospels* by *J.R. Miller*
DEVOTIONAL LIFE OF THE S.S. TEACHER by *J.R. Miller*

Call us Toll Free at 1-877-666-9469
Send us an e-mail at sgcb@charter.net

www.ingramcontent.com/pod-product-compliance
Lightning Source LLC
Chambersburg PA
CBHW030813190426
43197CB00035B/133